WRIGLEY FIELD YEAR BY YEAR

WRIGLEY FIELD YEAR BY YEAR

A CENTURY AT THE FRIENDLY CONFINES

Updated Edition

Sam Pathy

FOREWORD BY
John Thorn

SPORTS PUBLISHING

Visit our website at www.sportspubbooks.com.

10 9 8 7 6 5 4 3 2 1

Library of Congress Cataloging-in-Publication Data is available on file.

Cover design by Tom Lau
Cover photos credit: Associated Press

ISBN: 978-1-61321-877-8
Ebook ISBN: 978-1-61321-885-3

Printed in China

To my mom and to the memory of my aunt Alice
Thanks for taking us to Wrigley Field!

ACKNOWLEDGMENTS

I would like to thank the staffs at the following libraries: the University of Illinois at Urbana-Champaign, the University of Illinois at Chicago, the Chicago Public Library, the Chicago History Museum, the National Baseball Hall of Fame Library, Cooperstown, N.Y., the Ohio State University, and the Columbus Metropolitan Library. I am indebted to Bob Bluthardt and Kevin Butler for reviewing the manuscript. I am grateful to Mary Brace for patiently showing me her father's significant collection of Wrigley Field photos and to John Rogers at Argenta Images for making them available. Thanks to Ray Medeiros who graciously allowed me to share his ballpark photos, Jim Schneider for the use of his vintage postcards, Charles Bober for the use of his 100th anniversary photos, Brian Bernardoni for his knowledge and his time, and the members of the Society for American Baseball Research (SABR), especially Rick Huhn, for inspiration and guidance. A special thanks to my agent, Rita Rosenkranz. And the most heartfelt thanks to my wife, Kerry, whose unending love and support made the completion of this book possible.

CONTENTS

FOREWORD BY JOHN THORN   xi

INTRODUCTION   xiii

PROLOGUE   xvii

CHAPTER 1
First Inning—1914-1926—Youthful Exuberance   1

CHAPTER 2
Second Inning—1927-1939—League Leader   45

CHAPTER 3
Third Inning—1940-1949—Standing Still   99

CHAPTER 4
Fourth Inning—1950-1959—Middle Age   139

CHAPTER 5
Fifth Inning—1960-1972—Falling Behind   163

CHAPTER 6
Sixth Inning—1973-1984—New Appreciation   205

CHAPTER 7

Seventh Inning—1985-1998—Love Affair   241

CHAPTER 8

Eighth Inning—1999-2010—Glorious Uncertainty   283

CHAPTER 9

Ninth Inning—2011-2016—Secure Future   321

POSTLUDE   345

CONCLUSION   347

APPENDIX   351

ENDNOTES   359

BIBLIOGRAPHY   371

ABOUT THE AUTHOR   379

FOREWORD

I could tell you about Wrigley Field's modest beginnings, its architectural niceties and oddities, its hosted feats, its improbable survival as a relic of a team—the Chicago Whales—and a major league that vanished after the 1915 season. But the author, Sam Pathy, does a splendid job of that, aided by wonderful photographs. He tells you everything you ever wanted to know about the Cubs' cozy old home—and a good deal more that you could not have known you wanted to know, and soon will be happy you do.

Unlike Comiskey Park, Weeghman Park, as it was originally named for the man who paid for its construction, was no "palace of the fans." It was instead an Erector Set of a ballpark, thrown up in six weeks or so and costing only a quarter of a million dollars. It was never intended to have lasted this long.

But Wrigley Field's continued existence is a principal element of its charm, just as baseball's past is an enduring feature of its present. To describe Wrigley as a vibrant anachronism is to describe the game itself. Larry Ritter, author of the classic *Glory of Their Times*, liked to remind his friends that "The best part of baseball today is its yesterdays." This cannot be said of any other sport, and cannot be said more fervently of any other National League park.

To survey the landscape of baseball and Wrigley's part in it, consider that only Boston's Fenway Park is older (by two years) and that the next oldest ball yard is Dodger Stadium—younger by nearly half a century. Your dad took you to a game here. And his dad took him, maybe sat in this section over here, sharing a bag of peanuts. And moms and daughters have come to Wrigley, too, through five generations. Ordinary people, they live on as ghosts, along-side departed Cub greats Three Finger Brown and Rogers Hornsby and Phil Cavaretta and Ron Santo. Opponents Honus Wagner and Christy Mathewson played here, and so did Hank Greenberg and Babe Ruth, who may or may not have called his shot in Game 3 of the 1932 World Series.

This is where the All American Girls Professional Baseball League was formed, in 1943. This is where the Chicago Bears of Red Grange, Sid Luckman, and pro football's first black quarterback, the aptly named Willie Thrower, long cavorted. Wrigley Field is the lone remaining ballpark where Jackie Robinson played.

This is where Gabby Hartnett hit his homer in the gloamin', where Ernie Banks won two MVP awards with crummy clubs, where Kerry Wood struck out 20, where Sammy Sosa thrilled a nation. This is Wrigley Field, a shrine of baseball, a Chicago landmark, a national treasure, a museum of a million memories.

Happy Birthday, Wrigley Field! This book does you proud.

John Thorn

INTRODUCTION

"[Wrigley Field] is the most wonderful place on earth."
—*Joe Mock's Ballpark Guide*

Many baseball fans agree with Joe Mock's statement. I was lucky enough to see my first ballgame there as a mere eight-year-old. It was July 24, 1969; Ken Holtzman beat Don Sutton and the Dodgers, 5-3.

Beginning in 1971 and lasting four glorious summers, my mom and my aunt Alice took me to Ladies Day games at Wrigley Field. The mothers got in free and my cousin Gordon and I sat in the grandstands for $1 each.

These early Wrigley Field visits were all-day affairs. We were at the park when it opened at 10:30 A.M. to claim our favorite spot, the first row of grandstand seats behind home plate. While my mom and my aunt caught up on family news, Gordon and I roamed the park for two hours: watching batting practice, scoring autographs, and salivating at the myriad of options at the souvenir stands (I still have my "Cub Power" button and Ron Santo mini-bat).

After noon, we devoured half-frozen ham sandwiches and Kool-Aid my mom trucked from home. We'd eat to the strains of Frank Pellico at the ballpark organ. Next we'd fill in our scorecards, courtesy of public address man Pat Pieper. He introduced the lineups in his familiar style—"Attention! Attention please! Have your pencils and scorecards ready, and I will give you the correct lineups for today's ballgame."

With hours of fun already behind us, it was game time. We cheered our heroes: Williams, Kessinger, and Jenkins. We'd join in the ebullient kids' chant of "We want a hit!" when the Cubs were at bat. Afterwards we'd make our way home, exhausted but joyous. These were the best days of my childhood.

But this starry-eyed ten-year-old had no notion that three previous generations of kids spent their childhoods at Wrigley Field. The park was sixty years old and the recognizable buildings over the outfield walls even older. The bleachers, the ivy, and the pennant-topped scoreboard—the most beloved attractions in the park—were already thirty-five-year traditions. I also didn't know that Wrigley Field installed the first ballpark organ in 1941 and that Pat Pieper, now in his mid-eighties, spent nearly all of his working life at the corner of Clark and Addison. The present day charms of Wrigley Field were mine. But the history and traditions were owned by those well before me.

Just as important, I didn't realize that this treasured place was lucky to be around at all. In 1914, Wrigley Field was first called Weeghman Park and housed the Chicago team in the upstart Federal League. When that league folded two years later, five of its eight ballparks disappeared. Weeghman Park survived and housed the National League's Cubs. It expanded twice in the 1920s to stay viable with the times. The upstart park, later called Wrigley Field, witnessed two world wars sandwiched around the Depression.

Beginning in the 1950s, Wrigley Field's peers, the major league ballparks of the Classic era, began disappearing. Modern multipurpose stadiums supplanted most of them. By the time my Ladies Day excursions began in 1971, only four of the thirteen Classic ballparks remained. Shrines longer-serving than Wrigley Field—Forbes Field in Pittsburgh, Crosley Field in Cincinnati, and Philadelphia's Shibe Park—were abandoned. Luckily, Wrigley Field survived these tumultuous times.

There would be more threats. In the 1980s, Cubs management fought with neighbors over lights and the team threatened to move to the suburbs. Another ballpark building boom that commenced ten years later—the Neoclassic ballpark era—threatened to leave Wrigley Field behind.

But the former outlaw ballpark survived again and thrived. Two youthful generations after mine reveled in the charm and timelessness of Chicago's North Side ballpark. Hopefully, young Cubs fans will enjoy it for decades to come.

This book is a culmination of my lifelong love affair with Wrigley Field. I've spent the last twenty-six years and thousands of hours researching its unique past. This result chronicles the year-by-year history of the park. It traces its evolution from a sturdy, Federal League stadium to its status as America's favorite ballpark. It paints a small picture of what it was like to attend a game every season. It also brings to light the fragile existence of ballparks; we are lucky to still have the ivy, the hand-operated scoreboard, and the surrounding neighborhood to enjoy each summer.

The book divides Wrigley Field's more than a hundred years into nine innings. Each inning represents a distinct era in the ballpark's history. The innings play out like a ballgame. There are good innings, when Wrigley Field thrives. There are innings when the park falls behind. By the ninth inning, the ballpark is on the cusp of major renovations to ensure its viability for generations to come. When these come to fruition, the game is over; the ballpark and its millions of fans win.

For all years, information is presented in the following categories:

Statistical:

- The Chi-Feds/Cubs record, their home record, and their league standing
- The season home attendance; average attendance per game; its average (in percentage) compared to other National League teams. For example, a 100 percent average means Wrigley Field attendance equaled the average of the rest of the league. Over 100 percent means the Cubs outdrew the league average.

Opening Day/Home Opener:

- The heading "Opening Day" (first game of the year) or "Home Opener" (first *home* game of the year) along with the date
- The list of teams and starting pitchers
- The weather; if available, the temperature is the game-time temperature at Wrigley Field. If not, it is from a newspaper weather chart at the hour or the hour before the first pitch. If available, the temperature is a lakefront temperature. Otherwise, it is from the official Chicago reporting station at the time.
- Attendance; due to varying counting procedures, it is the estimated attendance from 1914-1934, paid attendance from 1935-1992, and tickets sold from 1993 to date.

What's New:
- A listing of changes in and around the ballpark

What Happened:
- A collection of interesting and unusual occurrences

Game(s) of the Year:
- Highlights of one or more exciting, important, or emblematic games

Quote:
- A quote from that particular year

The following categories are presented sporadically:

Bear News:
- Information on Wrigley Field's other major tenant

War Happenings:
- Information presented during the heights of the world wars

Postseason, Pennant or World Series:
- Presented during appropriate years

This updated edition celebrates Wrigley Field's 100th anniversary. It weaves through the financial, political, and social battles to renovate the ballpark. Readers will get a glimpse of the fruits of renovation; Wrigley Field will never be the same. The Cubs went from being a 101-loss team in 2012 to a National League Division series winner just three years later. It's an exciting time to be a fan of Wrigley Field!

Most of the information for this book has been garnered from newspaper microfilm. Direct quotes are cited in the endnotes. All sources are mentioned in the bibliography. Any questions about sources or additions to the information presented can be directed to the author at pathy.sam@gmail.com.

PROLOGUE

By 1850, German immigrants settled the farmland we now call Chicago's North Side. These immigrants incorporated Lake View Township in 1857; they took the name from the township's proximity to Lake Michigan. Swedish immigrants moved north and joined the Germans, and Lake View prospered. Churches and businesses sprang up, turning Lake View into a small town—an alternative to congested Chicago to its south.

Chicago noticed the bucolic suburb and incorporated Lake View in 1889. Two years later, in 1891, the Chicago Lutheran Theological Seminary moved to the corner of Addison and Sheffield. The seminary and the neighborhood's growth paralleled each other for the next twenty years; the Lutherans erected buildings on the property, and the surrounding neighborhood rapidly developed.

The neighborhood's vibe flourished with the completion of the Addison Street station of the Northwest elevated line and the adjacent Milwaukee Road railroad tracks. Consequently, the Lutherans tired of the bustle and left in 1910. According to a letter in the school's archives, the seminary departed for these reasons: "Smoke, dust, grime, soot, dirt [and] foul gases; railroading by night and day; whistles, ding-donging of bells late and early and in between times, and the ceaselessness of undesirable traffic incidental thereto that is growing more unbearable every week."[1]

Mike Cantillon and Edmund Archambault purchased the land in hopes of organizing an American Association minor league team and building a ballpark there. It was a promising location; both the elevated train line and the Clark Street streetcar stopped near the property. But the American Association never came to Chicago.

A new baseball organization, the Federal League, began in 1913. They started small. Its Chicago franchise played at the De Paul University field on the North Side, a simple facility that held several thousand fans.

After the fledgling 1913 season, the Federal League expanded and competed head-on with the National and American Leagues. Chicago already had the major league Cubs and White Sox. If the Federals planned to compete, they'd need a better ballpark than a college field.

Charlie Weeghman, owner of the Chi–Feds (they were known as the Whales in 1915), got rich with a chain of low-priced restaurants. Weeghman was the perfect Federal League owner—a deep-pocketed gambler willing to spend money to stroke his ego.

Weeghman shopped the entire city for a stadium site, but the West Side Cubs and the South Side White Sox were well-established with deep fan bases. Weeghman was a gambler, but he wasn't crazy; battling nose-to-nose with them on their turf was suicidal. Logically, Weeghman looked north, eight miles from Comiskey Park and five miles from the West Side Grounds. While the North Side lacked the hardened baseball fans found in the rest of the city, the risk didn't deter Weeghman. It was his only option.

FIRST INNING
1914-1926
YOUTHFUL
EXUBERANCE

The Classic ballpark era began in 1909 with Shibe Park in Philadelphia. Classic ballparks were constructed predominately of steel and concrete, not wood. They were expensive and permanent, signaling that a team planned to be around a while. Most major league teams rushed to build them. Between 1909 and 1915, in fact, twelve of the sixteen teams replaced their wooden ballparks with concrete and steel edifices.

1909	Shibe Park	Philadelphia (AL)
1909	Forbes Field	Pittsburgh
1909	Sportsman's Park	St. Louis (AL)
1910	Comiskey Park	Chicago (AL)

1910	League Park	Cleveland
1911	Griffith Stadium	Washington
1911	Polo Grounds	New York (NL)
1912	Redland Field*	Cincinnati
1912	Navin Field**	Detroit
1912	Fenway Park	Boston (AL)
1913	Ebbets Field	Brooklyn
1915	Braves Field	Boston (NL)
*Redland Field became Crosley Field		
**Navin Field eventually became Tiger Stadium		

Comiskey Park was the largest Classic ballpark. The "Baseball Palace of the World" cost $750,000 and seated nearly 30,000 on two decks. The White Sox made a bold statement with Comiskey Park; they aggressively went head-to-head with the longer-established West Side Cubs.

The Cubs, on the other hand, played in West Side Grounds, which opened in 1893. Recent ownership—first with the egregious Charles Murphy, and since 1914, with Charles Taft—rested on the laurels of past success and a longtime West Side fan base. The team had fallen behind their South Side rivals, at least in terms of their ballpark.

Charlie Weeghman built his steel and concrete park on the North Side and joined the fight for Chicago's baseball heart. But the Chi-Feds/Whales and their league survived only two seasons. Weeghman bought the Cubs in 1916 and moved them to the North Side, saving the ballpark from extinction. In the process, Weeghman Park did what five of the eight other Federal League ballparks could not—successfully outlive its league. Chewing gum giant William Wrigley took over majority ownership of the Cubs in November 1918 and renamed the ballpark Cubs Park.

By 1920, baseball entered its modern era, where home run hitters dominated the game. Fan interest spiked. In 1923, the Cubs added 12,000 seats to the ballpark. In 1926, it became known as Wrigley Field. At the end of that season the Cubs announced plans to double-deck the park.

During its dizzying first thirteen years, the little outlaw ballpark on the North Side:

- Housed two different teams in two different baseball leagues
- Took three different names
- Spanned two eras of baseball: the Dead Ball era and the so-called modern era
- Survived a World War and the major league gambling scandal
- Expanded twice

1914

On December 29, 1913, President Weeghman announced the location of his new ballpark: the former seminary site at Clark and Addison Streets. On January 22, 1914, Weeghman signed a ninety-nine-year lease on the property. The terms called for $16,000 annually the first ten years, $18,000 the second ten years, and $20,000 the final seventy-nine years.

Resistance sprung up immediately. A 16-foot by 100-foot parcel of land on the property nearly broke the deal when someone tried to purchase it. Weeghman paid $15,000 to keep the site viable for his ballpark. Soon after, a petition against the proposed ballpark circulated throughout the neighborhood. Mr. Hermann Croon, of 3649 Sheffield Avenue, spoke for the neighbors, saying, "None of the property owners want the park. They know that a park of the kind will decrease the value of their real estate 25 to 50 per cent and practically kill good rental because of the kind of people that such a park will bring into the locality."[1]

In March, the property owners filed an injunction to stop construction.

Rumors spread that organized baseball drove much of the resistance. They feared the Federal League would take their players and drive up salaries. In early January, Cubs President Charles Murphy said, "It is my opinion that the Federal League will not start. There are some surprises in store for the promoters of the 'outlaw' circuit."[2] American League President Ban Johnson spoke with more candor, saying, "The Federal League must be exterminated."[3]

President Murphy was an accessory to major league baseball's plan to foil the Federals. It made sense. The Chi-Feds would compete for much of the same fan base. They'd do it in a newer ballpark. The upstarts also signed former Cub Joe Tinker to manage the club. While one understands the Cubs predicament at the time, it is staggering to think that the Cubs tried to stymie the construction of what would eventually become Wrigley Field.

Historians wonder why Weeghman's lease limited construction cost to $70,000, yet the park's building permit, submitted only nine weeks later, called for $250,000 in building costs. Weeghman provided an answer in the April 5, 1916, edition of the *Chicago Examiner*:

We had planned to build a big, wooden grand stand . . . then we went to the City hall for a building permit. Right there we hit an unexpected snag when the authorities informed us we could not build the wooden stands. This meant new plans, the ordering of steel and thousands of dollars of additional and unlooked-for expense.[4]

Zachary Taylor Davis designed the park, the same architect who designed Comiskey Park four years earlier. Although not nearly as extravagant as Comiskey Park (and costing only a third as much), Davis created a modern park for the Chi-Feds. In fact, of the eight Federal League ballparks, only Weeghman Park and Brooklyn's Washington Park (a near replica of Weeghman Park) used all concrete and steel construction. The other six Federal League stadiums, built in cities with laxer building laws or by teams with fewer means, employed at least some wood or all-wood construction.

On February 23, a wrecking crew razed buildings on the property. On March 4, with movie cameras rolling, Jack Bramhall's band playing, and a crowd of several thousand watching, Building Commissioner Henry Ericsson turned the first spade of dirt on the grounds. More than 100 workers were on-site that afternoon in a rush to complete construction by the April 23 opener.

A chronology of park construction:

- March 16—Workers drove the first rivets
- March 31—All steelwork commenced
- April 4—Roof and right field bleachers were completed
- April 6—Seats arrived at the ballpark
- April 7—Over 850 workers raced to finish by Opening Day

Construction at Weeghman Park. (Chicago History Museum, SDN-059261)

Depending on the source, the new park held between 14,000 and 16,000. It included a roofed grandstand, pavilions on either side of the grandstand, right field bleachers that seated 2,000. Field dimensions were 310 feet in left field, 345 feet in right, and 400 feet to center.

Weeghman did a masterful job foiling the baseball establishment and getting the park ready for the home opener. That alone left no guarantee fans would support the upstart league and pay major league prices: $1 for box seats, 75 cents for grandstands, and 50 cents for bleachers. Would curious baseball fans venture to the North Side to see an outlaw league? Would North Siders identify with and support "their" team?

The Season by the Numbers

87-67	.565 2nd 1.5 games out	366,555 est. attendance
43-34	.558 at home	unknown % of FL average

Home Opener

APRIL 23; CHI-FEDS (HENDRIX) VS. KANSAS CITY (JOHNSON); WINDY, 51 DEGREES; 21,000 ATTEND

Chi-Feds 9 Packers 1—The Chi-Feds pasted the Packers. Ex-New York Giant Art Wilson socked two home runs for the winners.

The day's crowd was more of a story than the game. Fans overwhelmed streetcars and the elevated trains. Numerous auto parades crept toward the park, while neighborhood booster groups in colorful costumes made their way on foot. Several thousand watched from the field and more than that never got in the park. Many of those fans saw the game from windows and roofs of the buildings across Waveland and Sheffield Avenues, beginning a fabled North Side tradition.

Each fan received a Chi-Feds hat or pennant upon entering the new park. Judge John Sexton threw out the first pitch. And when the Grand Army of the Republic raised the flag and the band trumpeted "Columbia, the Gem of the Ocean," North Side baseball was born.

What Happened

• During the first three games, eight home runs sailed over the short left field fence. On April 27, workers moved the outfield wall back to the three-story house along Waveland Avenue. To gain every possible inch, they removed the house's back porch. The new dimensions measured

327 feet down the left field line, almost twenty feet farther than before. In left center the dimensions increased nearly fifty feet.

For the rest of the season, the house beyond the left field wall was in play. On August 22, the Chi-Feds' Art Wilson hit a shot off its roof. The ball bounced back onto the field and Wilson settled for a double.

- Charlie Weeghman built a stable under the third base pavilion for his horse, Queen Bess, who formally pulled a pie wagon in the Loop. Now she pulled the lawn mower. At night she got the run of the field.

An overflow crowd watches the flag-raising ceremony at Weeghman Park. (Chicago History Museum, SDN-059322)

- Weeghman promoted the game to Chicago fans. By May, he discounted 1,000 of the best pavilion tickets. He reintroduced Ladies Day, which the National League outlawed in 1909. Weeghman also staged days for Germans, the Masons, and numerous booster groups. He brought in bands and singers. The *Chicago Tribune* commented that "there have been more feature entertainment at Weeghman Park than the Cubs and Sox together have staged in several years."[5]

The Chi-Feds warm up before an early-season game. Note the building between the left field wall and Waveland Avenue. (Chicago History Museum, SDN-059321)

- The 1914 Chi-Feds held their own, attendance-wise, with the White Sox and Cubs:

White Sox	469,290
Chi-Feds	366,555 (author estimate)
Cubs	202,516

Games of the Year

October 6—The Chi-Feds faced Kansas City in an important doubleheader. Chicago led Indianapolis by a half-game with only three to go. But Kansas City swept the Chi-Feds and dashed their hopes for a Federal League pennant. The Packers took the opener, 1-0, and the nightcap, 5-3. The second game was called after only seven innings on account of darkness. Sam Weller of the *Chicago Tribune* told what happened next:

> A robust woman bug who has been a steady customer at the park all season was the loudest in denouncing the umps. After the game she waited under the stand for half an hour, determined to swat her wrath on the heads of Messrs. McCormick and Cusack.
>
> Some one [sic] saw the unfortunate gentlemen escaping from a side exit and tipped off the belligerent woman. Although built for comfort rather than speed "Mrs. Irritation" dashed a block after the retreating umpires at almost ten second speed. The arbiters escaped only when the "L" station was reached.[6]

Indianapolis beat the Chi-Feds by a game and a half for the Federal League championship.

Quote of 1914

"Chicago took the Federal league [sic] to its bosom yesterday and claimed it as a mother would claim a long lost child. . . . Owners Weeghman and Walker of the north side club and President Gilmore of the new league were so overjoyed with the spectacle that they almost wept, and there is little doubt that it was an epochal day in the history of the national game."[7]

Sam Weller in the Chicago Tribune—*April 24, 1914—on Opening Day*

1915

The Chi-Feds became the Whales, a name suggested in a newspaper contest. The Whales name won out over 300 others, including the Chix, Tots, Colts, and Eagles.

The Season by the Numbers		
86-66	.566 1st .001 ahead	342,200 est. attendance
44-32	.667 at home	unknown % of FL average

Opening Day

APRIL 10; WHALES (HENDRIX) VS. TERRIERS (PLANK); SUNNY, 63 DEGREES; 16,000 ATTEND

Whales 3 Terriers 1—The Whales pushed across three runs in the eighth inning to clip the St. Louis Terriers. Claude Hendrix, Les Mann, and Art Wilson contributed hits during the rally. The Whales beat Eddie Plank, who jumped from the American League Athletics after leading Philadelphia to a pair of World Series championships.

Before the game, a several-hundred-car motorcade wound its way from downtown. The best-decorated vehicle went to Max Eitel of the Fed Fab Boosters, who won a silver cup. Members imbibed from it in President Weeghman's office after the victory.

The *Chicago Examiner* said this about the big day: "Politics, the European war, the hoped-for subway and the like passed into the great beyond for the time being. The 1915 baseball season was about to open and baseball was the only thought that occupied the mind of every man, woman and child in the grand stand."[8]

What's New

• Before the season, the team removed the bleachers in right field. In addition, they razed the houses along Waveland Avenue and moved the fence out to the sidewalk. In front of the fence they built a large bleacher section, adding over 1,500 seats.

• The scoreboard moved from left-center field to center field.

• The city rebuilt the Engine 78 firehouse across the street on Waveland Avenue. The brick firehouse still stands and serves the Lake View community.

Mayor-elect William H. "Big Bill" Thompson threw out the first ball. (Chicago History Museum, DN-0064356)

What Happened

- President Weeghman started a North Side tradition when he moved Ladies Day to Fridays. On one particular Friday women received chances to win a gold watch and a silk umbrella. Even so, the *Chicago Tribune* said this about women at Weeghman Park:

  Out in the bleacher, where the sun shone most of the time and where the back wall kept off the wind, one wise gentleman was discovered with friend wife and family. . . . Besides the savings in cash, that fellow picked out the most comfortable spot in the park, but in Chicago it is an unusual sight to see a woman in a bleacher.[9]

- Weeghman Park became multipurpose. First, Lane Tech and Senn high schools held track meets there. Next, on June 12 and occasionally thereafter, Weeghman opened a hippodrome. A ten- to thirty-cent admission provided circus acts, military bands, movies, and dancing under lights until midnight. Finally, on July 4 and 5 the park hosted fireworks shows. Pyrotechnics in the shape of President Wilson, the Liberty Bell, Niagara Falls, and Charlie Chaplin highlighted the $5,000 display.
- Celebration turned to tragedy on July 24. The Lake Michigan cruiser, the Eastland, capsized in the Chicago River drowning over 800 sightseers. As the horrific news spread across the city, the Whales cancelled their game against Baltimore. They called a doubleheader the next day at the request of Acting Mayor William Moorhouse and also one on July 28, the city's official day of mourning.

  President Weeghman offered his park as a theater for a film of the disaster's rescue efforts, with profits benefiting the survivors. Movie theaters instead showed the film, but a few days later, Weeghman donated all profits from a game against Buffalo to the Eastland Fund. Everyone including fans, players, and sportswriters paid to get in. But rain held attendance to 2,000, limiting contributions to $955.14, about $9,000 less than anticipated.
- "Less" became the operative word as the baseball war took its toll. To undercut the competition the Federal League teams dropped admission prices below the established leagues. In August, bleacher seats fell to ten cents, grandstands to twenty-five cents, and the last rows of box seats to seventy-five cents.

  Attendance improved slightly, especially with kids who could now afford to sit in the bleachers, but not nearly enough to offset big losses. President James A. Gilmore of the Federal League estimated that all three leagues would each lose about $200,000.

Attendance	1913	1914	1915
Whales	NA	366,555 (author est.)	342,200 (author est.)
White Sox	644,501	469,290	539,461
Cubs	419,000	202,516	217,058

Games of the Year

October 3—The Whales swept a dramatic doubleheader at Pittsburgh on October 2 to move four percentage points ahead of the Steel City team. The two met in a doubleheader at Weeghman Park the following day to decide the Federal League championship. A massive gathering of 34,212—twice the park's capacity—shoehorned into the North Side ballpark. Fans coveted every aisle and stood fifteen-deep in the outfield between the dugouts. Kids sat precariously on the right field wall and a group of 300 zealots took over the press box.

Pittsburgh scored three runs in the ninth inning and one in the eleventh to take the first game, 5-4. Umpire Bill Brennan warned both benches and the nervous throng that the second game, the season's deciding contest, would stop at sunset—5:24 P.M. The pitchers dominated until the sixth inning when the Whales pushed across three runs. After Pittsburgh went down in the seventh, the clock read 5:25. Brennan called the game; the Whales won the pennant by the slimmest margin on record, one percentage point (.566 to .565).

Delirious fans rained seat cushions down on fans carousing on the field. The field fans returned the fire and a playful war erupted with hundreds of cushions flying back and forth in celebration—the celebration of a championship.

James Clarkson of the *Chicago Examiner* spoke for the pennant-loving fans, saying, "Read it and weep you Feds of other cities, you Sox and Cubs, for there she is and there she'll fly for another year, and live in song and story as long as the ear rejoices in blooie of bat against ball or the eye delights in the jump or hook of the spinning sphere."[10]

The End

The irony would prove painful to Mr. Clarkson and to Federal League fans; the immense outpouring of support marked the last game in Whales' history. With all parties hemorrhaging red ink, on December 22 organized baseball agreed to compensate the Federal League to disband and end the baseball war. The deal allowed the most powerful Federal League teams to buy into the establishment. St. Louis Terriers owner Phil Ball bought the St. Louis Browns, and Charles Weeghman and associates purchased controlling interest in the Cubs. Among those buying in with Weeghman included meatpacker J. Ogden Armour, Sears Roebuck head Julius Rosenwald, and a chewing gum magnate named William Wrigley.

Quote of 1915

"The dollar sign, which was so greatly responsible for the wreckage that exists today, must be eliminated from the sport or crowded so far into the background that the public will come to believe again in the supremacy of pennants over coin and of victories over paychecks."[11]

I.E. Sanborn in the Chicago Tribune—*December 26, 1915*

1916

Charlie Weeghman now owned the remnants of his Whales and the West Side Cubs. He seemingly held leases on two ballparks: Weeghman Park on the North Side and West Side Grounds, the former home of the Cubs. Many felt the west side held more promise for the Cubs because of their rich history there. Weeghman disagreed. Weeghman Park surpassed the antiquated wood construction of West Side Grounds. And it was Weeghman himself who built the North Side ballpark. It was Weeghman who developed the North Side franchise. And it was Weeghman who seeded and nurtured the North Side fan base. To Charlie Weeghman, the decision was simple.

On the morning of January 21, Secretary Charlie Williams moved the lockers and uniforms from West Side Grounds to Weeghman Park. In these few hours the Cubs became Chicago's "North Side" baseball team.

Some still questioned the move. A Cubs fan wrote to the *Chicago Tribune,* saying, "All Cub fans I have talked to say they certainly will not follow them north—that when they leave the west side the team dies as far as we are concerned."[12]

After early season rainouts another suggested that West Siders had cursed the Cubs with poor weather, and the deluges would continue until the team moved back.

```
The Season by the Numbers
67-86          .438 5th 26.5 games out        453,685 (5,743 average)
37-41          .474 at home                   117% of NL average
```

Home Opener

APRIL 20; CUBS (HENDRIX) VS. REDS (SCHNEIDER); 74 DEGREES; 20,000 ATTEND

Cubs 7 Reds 6—The suspense of the Whales' 1915 pennant chase carried over to this year's opener. The Cubs scored twice in the eighth inning and tied it in the ninth. They won a dramatic victory in the eleventh on a double by Cy Williams and a single by Vic Saier.

Charlie Weeghman inaugurated the marriage of team and ballpark with a rousing pregame celebration. Ballplayers and a host of politicians led a mile-long auto parade that crept from Grant Park to the ballpark. The Democrats brought a live donkey and JOA, a bear cub (named for team stockholder J. Ogden Armour), frolicked before the game. Fireworks sent miniature American flags floating down on the field and bands proliferated. A local tailor offered a free suit to the first player to hit a home run (the Reds, John Beall onto Sheffield Avenue in the sixth inning).

North and West Sides seemed as one, as told in the *Chicago American*: "But this was as nothing to the shout that arose as [manager] Tinker and his men came trooping to the field. Those who had remained loyal to the West Siders in the war days and who were now in Weeghman Park for the first time greeted Joe as a long-lost friend."[13]

What's New

- The team purchased an infield tarp, 15 feet larger than any other in the National League.
- On June 17, JOA the bear cub returned to a permanent circular cage outside the park along Addison Street.
- President Weeghman let fans keep foul balls, a major league first. At other parks foul balls remained the property of the team and fans not willing to surrender them faced a showdown with security. Visiting teams also hedged at losing their practice balls at Weeghman Park and insisted on restitution from the Cubs.

  A week before Weeghman's generous move, a wire screen raised the right field wall by ten feet. Because home runs became scarcer (the Cubs drove two balls off the screen its first day of use), the team retained more of their baseballs.

  On the opposite side of the screen, facing Sheffield Avenue, hung the words CHICAGO NATIONAL LEAGUE BALL PARK. Symbolically the Cubs and Weeghman Park were one.
- In mid-season, the Cubs initiated a novel idea to post the official scorer's decisions on the scoreboard. When the official scorer ruled a hit or an error on a play he'd phone the scoreboard operator. The operator turned one of two rectangular slats on the scoreboard, one with an "H" or one with an "E" to let fans know the decision.

What Happened

- Secretary Charley Williams measured the baseline distances to squelch rumors that they were shorter than those at West Side Grounds.

	Right field line	Left field line
Weeghman Park	308 feet	342 feet, 9 inches
West Side Grounds	304 feet, 4 inches	312 feet

- Fans staged cushion fights after the opener and again three days later. Many spectators received cuts and bruises. The problem reoccurred on May 14 when a called third strike on Heinie

Zimmerman ended a rally in the ninth inning. *Chicago Tribune* writer I. E. Sanborn finished the story:

> The third strike on Zimmy was called by Umpire Rigler and Heinie stopped to expostulate with the arbitrator. This gave the overflow crowd the cue to rush in and chase Rigler off the lot. The umpire left at his normal gait, amid a shower of cushions, some of which hit him and with a band of fans throwing mud balls at him. The back of Rigler's uniform was a sight, and will be a souvenir emblematic of the low standard of sportsmanship in baseball.[14]

Weeghman threatened to increase security but did not end cushion rentals. The problem eventually diminished.

- News spread slowly before radio or television. For example, fans didn't know of rained-out games until getting to the park. This year the Cubs informed fans by hanging flags at the Board of Trade building. A white flag indicated a game. A blue flag indicated a rainout. Weeghman also hung signs in his restaurants.
- The North Side Cubs proved a rousing success. They more than doubled their 1915 West Side Grounds attendance.

1915	217,058
1916	453,685

Game of the Year

July 16—The Cubs forfeited their only game ever at the North Side ballpark. Home plate umpire Bill "Lord" Byron invoked a little-followed rule which limited hurlers to twenty seconds between pitches. In the tenth inning of a tied game against Brooklyn, Byron called a ball when Hippo Vaughn failed to pitch when ordered. When manager Tinker protested, Byron ordered him back to the bench. Tinker continued to argue and after five minutes Byron stopped the game, giving Brooklyn a 9-0 decision.

Quote of 1916

"Chicago fandom this afternoon will welcome a stranger to the North Side. . . .the unpleasant feud of two years' standing will be wafted into oblivion and, instead of one, there will be two sections of the greatest baseball town in the world to root for the amalgamated brotherhood, headed by Joe Tinker."[15]

G.W. Axelson in the Chicago Herald—*April 16, 1916—on Opening Day*

1917

On April 6, Congress declared war on Germany, dropping the nation into the World War. Baseball, at least early on, took the role of supporter and cheerleader.

The Season by the Numbers

| 74-80 | .481 5th 24 games out | 360,218 (4,589 average) |
| 35-42 | .455 at home | 126% of NL average |

Opening Day

APRIL 11; CUBS (VAUGHN) VS. PIRATES (JACOBS); DRIZZLE, 59 DEGREES; 20,000 ATTEND

Cubs 5 Pirates 3—Harry Wolter and Cy Williams hit run-scoring triples. Catcher Rowdy Elliott drove in a pair of runs with two singles.

The pregame ceremonies featured a patriotic show of fireworks, Naval cadets, and marching infantrymen. The team unveiled new white home uniforms with American flags on the left sleeves. They also set up a recruiting station in the park to enlist the numerous fans who hadn't registered for the war.

What's New

Contrary to popular belief, Pat Pieper was not the team's public address announcer when the Cubs moved north in 1916. Rather, according to Charles Dryden of the *Chicago Examiner*, Pieper began his public address job this year:

Like a crash of thunder out of a cloudless sky comes the announcement that Admiral Kingston, the silver-tongued megaphoner, has been slipped his unconditional release. He reported yesterday to have his uniform pressed and was shocked to learn that the green garments, the trumpet and the pallbearer's gloves had been conferred on Mr. Pat Pieper, well and favorably known as an expert purveyor of ball-park grub on the South, as well as on the North Side.[16]

Military men strut their stuff on Opening Day. (National Baseball Hall of Fame Library, Cooperstown, N.Y.)

What Happened

- On June 6, severe winds howled through the park and continuously shook the grandstand roof. The gales continued the next day. Rather than play consecutive games under what the *Chicago Tribune* called "hurricanic conditions,"[17] the Cubs cancelled the game with the Phillies. While the *Chicago Examiner* and the *Chicago Daily News* mentioned both wind and cold as reasons for postponement, the official Chicago temperature at game time was 61 degrees. It was the only game at the North Side ballpark ever called because of wind.
- On June 5, National Registration Day, the Cubs supported the war effort. Fans coming to the games registered at the makeshift recruiting station, and Liberty Bond salesmen were there to encourage fans to invest in the war. Over 300 Jackies from the Great Lakes Naval Station came by train and performed a pregame calisthenics and marching display. But when rain sent everyone home after the first inning, the navy men marched back to the Addison "L" station singing "How Dry I Am."

  Soldiers and military bands showed up at the park all summer. The cynic would accuse baseball of pushing patriotism to keep the government from raiding its players or worse, shutting down the game. The cynics were probably right.
- Later that month the Cubs donated a game's gate receipts to the Red Cross (7,155 attended, $3,858 collected).

Games of the Year

May 2—Hippo Vaughn and the Reds' Fred Toney staged the greatest pitching duel in major league history. Vaughn and Toney held each team hitless through nine innings—a feat unmatched before or since. With one out in the top of the tenth, Larry Kopf drove a single past first baseman Fred Merkle, ending Vaughn's gem. An error and an infield single by Jim Thorpe scored the lead run. Toney mopped up in the bottom of the tenth, preserving his 1-0 no-hitter.

September 11—Vaughn and Toney attempted to reprise their earlier masterpiece, but only Hippo came close, three-hitting Cincinnati, 5-1. Soldiers, sailors, marines, and their bands stirred the crowd of 7,000. The Cubs donated uniforms to the squads and theater women walked the grandstands soliciting money for the Ball and Bat fund that supplied baseball equipment to soldiers in France.

Quote of 1917

"Although the country is sober-minded and disturbed over the thought of bloodshed that is close at hand, there is no such desire to sidestep the pleasures of a summer's pastime or to interfere in any way with the recreation of a nation."[18]

George C. Rice in the Chicago Daily Journal—*April 11, 1917—on the eve of Opening Day*

1918

By year's end, nearly two million American soldiers saw action in Europe. The government dipped into major league rosters, taking dozens of ballplayers. The most important of the eight drafted Cubs was Grover Cleveland Alexander. The star pitcher, just purchased from the Phillies, threw only three games before heading for duty.

The Season by the Numbers		
84-45	.651 1st 10.5 games ahead	337,256 (5,149 average)
49-25	.662 at home	228% of NL average

Home Opener

APRIL 24; CUBS (VAUGHN) VS. CARDINALS (MEADOWS); 39 DEGREES; 10,000 ATTEND

Cubs 2 Cardinals 0—Only Rogers Hornsby's second inning single spoiled Hippo Vaughn's no-hit bid. The Cubs scratched across their runs on an error in the second and a single by Les Mann in the third. The Cubs not only played sharp, they looked sharp—wearing red, white, and blue socks.

The military showcased maneuvers during pregame ceremonies. The band played the National Anthem, a formal first at the park. Governor Frank Lowden threw out the first ball. These festivities and a parade in honor of Chicago native and Cardinal manager Jack Hendricks delayed the start of the game by an hour.

What's New

Nearly 100 influential Chicagoans organized the Cubs' Claws Club. The well-heeled fans sang and cheered at the games. Sometimes they met afterwards and hoisted a glass to their winning Cubs.

War News

- The national government imposed a 10 percent war tax on each baseball ticket. To limit confusion, the major leagues standardized admission prices.

Ticket Prices	1917	1918
Box seat	$1	$1.10
Grandstand	75 cents	85 cents
Bleachers	25 cents	30 cents
Passes	free	10 cents

- The team sold war savings stamps at the ballpark. Even players sold war bonds to fans at the game on April 25.
- Major league old-timers staged a two-inning benefit before a Cubs game on June 26, raising money for the Soldiers' Tobacco Fund.
- To conserve yarn and horsehide, owners asked fans to return foul balls, reversing a trend begun at Weeghman Park two years earlier. I. E. Sanborn of the *Chicago Tribune* added that "any one [sic] who fails to return such a ball, so it can be used again, will be considered a German sympathizer."[19]
- Government officials corralled eligible males as they exited games, searching for "slackers" who hadn't registered. The flash of a draft card served as proof of registration and men were expected to carry the card at all times. Due to a shortage of males, female ushers debuted on July 6.
- On July 14, Bastille Day, the French flag flew below the Stars and Stripes on the center field flagpole. Just four days later, the war reached its turning point. With the German army only fifty miles from Paris, the Allies counterattacked and drove them back. During the fifth inning on July 18, public address man Pat Pieper announced a bulletin describing the Allied success. The crowd erupted.

    The following day, Secretary of War Newton D. Baker issued a "work or fight" order to professional ballplayers. Baker deemed baseball "non-essential," forcing players to either enlist or enter productive work in a factory or shipyard. The edict would shut down the game. The Cubs seemingly finished their season with a 6-3 loss to Brooklyn on July 21, three games in front of the Giants.

Baseball owners petitioned to let their teams finish the season. On July 26, Baker compromised, extending the season to September 1. The owners greedily tacked on an extra day to play in front of large Labor Day crowds. The teams still lost over a month of income, yet the Cubs, scheduled to spend most of September on the road, forfeited only four regularly scheduled home dates, fewer than any other National League team.

A Pennant!

On September 2, the Cubs led by ten and a half games and were declared league champions. To determine World Series ticket recipients, fans had been writing their names on ticket stubs and dropping them in boxes as they left the ballpark. The more stubs, the better the chance of getting the prized tickets.

While manager Mitchell even balked at new uniforms for the World Series, thinking they'd take the team out of their familiar environment, Charlie Weeghman moved the first three World Series games to Comiskey Park to take advantage of its greater seating capacity. The decision proved costly. Not only did the Cubs lose home field advantage to the Red Sox (they dropped two of the first three games), only Game Three attracted a crowd (27,054) that wouldn't have fit into Weeghman Park. The Red Sox won the series in six games.

Games of the Year

April 26—Grover Cleveland Alexander made his last start of the season, a two-hit schooling of the Cardinals. Afterwards he boarded a train and reported to Camp Funston and then to Europe and the war. Before he left, team officials toasted him in President Weeghman's office. Alexander offered a few words, saying, "I am sorry to leave all of you fellows, but it looks like a tough fight over there. . . . I don't know whether I shall ever come back to play ball or not, but if I don't, I'll make it necessary for them to dig a lot of holes for the enemy before they get me."[20]

July 17—Lost in the war and World Series hoopla was the twenty-one inning marathon between the Cubs and the Phillies. Max Flack singled home the winning run as the Cubs won, 2-1. Both the Cubs' George Tyler and the Phillies' Milt Watson pitched complete games. There were no pitch counts available, but Watson faced seventy-five batters. If he averaged only three pitches per hitter, he'd have thrown 225 pitches.

Quote of 1918

"Chicago's once loyal fans had a feeling of relief that baseball was over, rather than a feeling of sorrow in the loss of a championship. When the ninth inning was posted on the various score boards [*sic*] about town the common expression among those present was: 'Well, it's all over. Now those fellows can go to work.'"[21]

In the Chicago Tribune—*September 12, 1918—after the Red Sox beat the Cubs to win the World Series*

1919

The Allies defeated the Axis powers in November 1918, ending the war. The nation returned to "normalcy."

```
The Season by the Numbers
75-65          .536 3rd 21 games out        424,430 (6,063 average)
40-31          .563 at home                 121% of NL average
```

Opening Day

April 24; Cubs (Vaughn) vs. Pirates (Cooper); sunny, 38 degrees; 8,000 attend

Cubs 5 Pirates 1—Rain cancelled the April 23 opener against the Pirates. Hippo Vaughn won the next day as the Cubs scored all their runs in the second inning on run-scoring singles by Bill Killefer and Max Flack.

Walter Eckersall of the *Chicago Tribune* said this about the cold conditions: "Wearing fur overcoats and carrying robes on their arms, the crowd which attended the frigid opening at the Cubs' park yesterday reminded one more of a football struggle between two leading college elevens."[22]

The four Cubs who saw military service—Grover Cleveland Alexander, Killefer, Tom Daly, and Pete Kilduff—carried Old Glory to the center field flagpole in pregame festivities. Alexander, just back from the war, threw out the first pitch.

What's New

• The exterior was painted bright green.

- A clock appeared on the center field scoreboard.
- The team raised box seat prices from $1.10 to $1.25 and $1.50, tax included. Grandstand seats remained eighty-five cents and the left field pavilion seats fetched fifty-five cents.
- Concessionaire Fred Chamberlain added a hot dog stand. He hoped to move his operation closer to the main entrance, but a $1,750 estimate for new lighting and plumbing relegated him to his old spot under the third base concourse.
- Bildad replaced JOA as the live bear in the cage outside the park. The team wanted a "north woods" cub but settled for the eight-year-old bear from the Malay Islands. Charles Dryden of the *Chicago Herald and Examiner* described Bildad as "small and wiry" and proclaimed, "If we are any judge of bears this Bildad had a baboon mixed up among his early ancestors."[23]

What Happened

- Last fall, Charlie Weeghman sold his interest in the ballclub after his restaurant business faltered. William Wrigley Jr. became majority owner of the Cubs. Consequently, the ballpark's name changed from Weeghman Park to Cubs Park.
- The Cubs fired their head groundskeeper. That night, he broke into Cubs Park and dismantled the furnace, shattered glass, destroyed furniture, and scattered the contents of a desk. The Cubs replaced him with Bobby Dorr. Bobby was a much better fit, becoming a fixture at the ballpark for the next thirty-eight years.
- The city endured a transit strike in late July. After the State Public Utilities raised fares in early August, fans paid seven cents to ride the Clark Street streetcar and eight cents to go by "L".
- At the same time a race riot exploded over much of the city. While the flare-ups cancelled a game between a Negro League team and a white amateur team, the biggest change at Cubs Park was the absence of new President Bill Veeck. Veeck Sr. served during the riots as a member of the Illinois Militia. When he got to the games, he appeared in militia khakis.
- Lacrosse and track events took over Cubs Park as part of a fundraiser for the city's poor. The Illinois Athletic Club's lacrosse team played and beat the Canadian champions, 9-6. Track events included a marathon that ran from suburban Lake Forest to the ballpark. The race finished inside the park as runners entered from the right field corner, ran along the box seat wall, and reached the finish line near the left field corner. Proceeds from the event benefited a fund that supplied ice for the city's underclass.
- The solemn crowds of the war years disappeared. On August 3, for example, bleacher fans disputed an umpire's call. They tossed so many bottles and cushions onto the field that the Cub outfielders vacated their positions.

The effects of the melee lingered beyond the doubleheader loss. Three days later, Boston's Ray Keating lined a one-hopper that bounced through a hole in the left field fence (ruled a home run by 1919 ground rules). The rowdy fans had broken the fence and no one fixed it. Keating's home run drove in Boston's only runs in their 2-0 win.

- Strange home runs seemed commonplace. On September 12, Fred Merkle of the Cubs drove a ball through a wire fence in the left field corner. On September 15, the Phillies' Lena Blackburne homered through an open gate down the left field line.

Game of the Year

September 21—This disappointing season mercifully ended on a quick note. The Cubs and Braves reeled off the final home game in only fifty-eight minutes—the shortest nine-inning game in park history. The teams combined for 15 hits, two walks, and five strikeouts. Grover Cleveland Alexander went the distance in the 3-0 win.

Football News

Football was considered a college game. But Walter Eckersall of the *Chicago Tribune* said, "Professional football teams are being organized in all parts of the country and numbers in Chicago. These are composed of former college men and in a great many cases by service men who played in camps . . . Practically every big city in the country will have a league composed of teams of different weights."[24]

In Chicago, it was the Hammond All-Stars, organized by Paul Parduhn. The team included former college player George Halas. The All-Stars leased Cubs Park and played half a dozen games there. The first, on October 26, saw Hammond defeat Minneapolis 45-0 before 3,000 fans.

After the inaugural contest, Parduhn dropped ticket prices and attendance increased. For example, on November 27, 10,000 saw Canton defeat Hammond, 7-0. But the Hammond All-Stars crashed soon after. Parduhn passed bogus checks to his players and ended up in jail.

Quote of 1919

"What has become of the boys out in the bleachers? Only a few years ago we found the real genuine 100 per cent baseball fans sitting out in the sun. Now the bleachers are too big and the grandstands are too small in nearly all ball parks [*sic*]. . . .

The same fellow who paid a quarter ten years ago for a baseball ticket paid a quarter for a dinner. Now he has to pay about 75 cents for a dinner, so he's willing to pay 75 cents for the ball game."[25]

James Crusinberry in the Chicago Tribune—*December 22, 1919*

1920

The Season by the Numbers			
75-79	.487 5th (t) 18 games out		480,783 (6,244 average)
43-34	.558 at home		95% of NL average

Home Opener

APRIL 22; CUBS (ALEXANDER) VS. REDS (RUETHER); SHOWERS, 61 DEGREES; 10,000 ATTEND

Cubs 4 Reds 3—The Cubs won it in the eleventh inning on Turner Barber's triple against the right field wall. The hit scored Buck Herzog who had singled. Grover Cleveland Alexander went the distance.

The Cubs dispensed with most pregame ceremonies, limiting it to a parade of marines, a brass band, and the two teams. According to Oscar C. Reichow of the *Chicago Daily News*, President Veeck felt "the ancient custom of having some official make a speech and throw the first ball has been tabooed."[26]

What's New

- Club presidents again standardized most major league ticket prices. All bleacher seats sold for 50 cents and grandstands went for $1. Box seat prices were left up to the individual teams.
- For the 1919 and 1920 seasons, a sign for Wilson Sporting Goods was affixed along the length of the right field wall.

What Happened

- Charles Murphy, former team owner and owner of West Side Grounds, remained a news item. In 1918, he repurchased stock in the Cubs. While just a minor stockholder, Murphy didn't hide his desire to bring the Cubs back to the West Side. "I hope and think the Cubs management

will eventually see the wisdom of returning to the west side location and building a modern, up to date plant."[27] Murphy's stance led the *Christian Science Monitor* to erroneously report on February 26 that the Cubs would move back to West Side Grounds before opening day.

In 1918, Murphy sued the Cubs for back rent. He claimed they broke a lease when they left the West Side in 1916 and owed him over $1 million. This year, Murphy filed another suit to keep the National League from scheduling games at Cubs Park.

Outside of a few amateur games and a rodeo in 1916, West Side Grounds sat idle. Murphy finally sold his rotting stadium to the state of Illinois for $400,000. The state razed the ballpark and constructed a hospital complex on the site; it ended talk of the "West Side Cubs."

- On June 26, New York Commerce High School met Chicago's Lane Tech in a battle of Public School league championships. The New Yorkers were led by a young lad named Lou Gehrig. New York won, 12-6, on the strength of a Gehrig grand slam onto Sheffield Avenue.

Game of the Year

May 30—Grover Cleveland Alexander continued his mastery over the Reds, winning 3-2 in the first game of a morning/afternoon Memorial Day doubleheader. Alexander even provided the game-winning clout, a tenth inning home run into the left field bleachers as the clock struck high noon. The Cubs dropped the nightcap, 4-2.

Scandal

Baseball couldn't quell the rumors that gamblers were influencing ballgames, including the outcome of the 1919 World Series. In May, major league bosses hired a detective agency to catch gamblers and keep them out of every big league ballpark. On May 24, during a game against Philadelphia, police and private detectives swept Cubs Park, arresting forty-seven people accused of betting on baseball.

On the morning of August 31, Bill Veeck Sr. got wind of a fix planned for that afternoon at Cubs Park. Rumors had Claude Hendrix, the Cubs scheduled pitcher, betting $5,000 on the Cubs to lose. Hendrix denied the allegation, but on that day, Veeck pulled him in favor of Grover Cleveland Alexander.

When the press heard the allegations later that week, the local chapter of the Baseball Writers' Association began an investigation. The enhanced scrutiny laid bare the depth of the problem and by the end of the month, eight White Sox players, dubbed the "Black Sox," were indicted for throwing the 1919 World Series.

The scrutiny became commonplace. Of a September 5 Cubs game against Pittsburgh, James Crusinberry of the *Chicago Tribune* wrote, "There were some rather significant yells from the bleachers regarding the fixing of games, but no one who watched the contest could pick a flaw in it."[28]

During the final weekend of the season, only 600 disheartened die-hards saw Alexander go the distance in a seventeen inning, 3-2 win over the Cardinals. By now, many fans were suspicious. Many more just didn't care. America's National Pastime seemed on the verge of self-destruction.

Football News

Professional football grew nationwide. This year, the Chicago Tigers, the Decatur Staleys, and the Racine/Chicago Cardinals played a half dozen home games at Cubs Park. On December 12, the Staleys met Akron for the hypothetical professional football championship. Over 12,000 fans, a Chicago pro football record, watched a 0-0 tie.

Quote of 1920

"The players on each side hustled and battled as if the grand jury was watching them."[29]
James Crusinberry in the Chicago Tribune—*October 3, 1920.*

1921

On November 12, 1920, Major League Baseball hired Chicago judge Kenesaw Mountain Landis as the game's first commissioner. His charge was simple yet monumental—to remove the gambling element from the game and restore the public's faith in the national pastime.

Landis forged the National Agreement, giving him far-reaching authority to investigate, fine, or ban owners, teams, or players who perform acts detrimental to the game. The commissioner would ban numerous suspected players, most importantly, the eight "Black Sox" just a day after being acquitted by a Chicago jury on August 2.

Judge Landis drew up new player contracts that included a strict code of conduct. Hippo Vaughn, who worked in the off-season at a delicatessen near Cubs Park, visited President Veeck's office on January 17. Before he left that afternoon, he became the first major leaguer to sign the new contract.

The Commissioner's moral crusade permeated the game. When the Cubs released Claude Hendrix and Buck Herzog, both implicated in 1920 gambling scandals, no other clubs claimed them, ending their baseball careers.

The Season by the Numbers		
64-89	.418 7th 30 games out	410,107 (5,361 average)
32-44	.421 at home	85% of NL average

Cub manager Johnny Evers welcomed Commissioner Landis to Opening Day. (Chicago History Museum, SDN-061907)

Opening Day

APRIL 13; CUBS (ALEXANDER) VS. CARDINALS (HAINES); CLOUDY, 50 DEGREES; 20,000 ATTEND

Cubs 5 Cardinals 2—The Cubs Bob O'Farrell whacked a second inning, two-run home run over the right field screen. Grover Cleveland Alexander got the win but needed help in the eighth from reliever Buck Freeman.

Cub fans bought into Landis's overhaul and came out in force. Scores watched from the field, on top of fences, or from the windows and roofs of buildings on Waveland and Sheffield Avenues. Hundreds got in for free after rushing through an undermanned bleacher gate. Commissioner Landis even watched the proceedings.

The forgiving crowd cheered almost everything. They cheered new manager Johnny Evers. They cheered Bob O'Farrell's Sheffield Avenue home run. They even cheered a black and tan dog that alluded efforts to get him off the field during the first inning.

George Phair of the *Chicago Herald and Examiner* penned this ode to Opening Day:

"Has gambling killed the game of ball?"
They often asked us in the fall,
When things looked dark and gray
With pop-eyed throngs on every side

The ancient baseball fan replied:
"The livest corpse that ever died
Is on the job today."[30]

What's New

- This spring, the cage along Addison Street held two bear cubs.

What Happened

- While Opening Day proved that Major League Baseball had a pulse, many fans remained skeptical. Attendance slipped in both leagues with the Cubs drawing their lowest North Side attendance outside the war years of 1917-1918. It didn't help that the team finished with its worst record between 1901 and 1948.

- Last year, Babe Ruth hit 54 home runs, more than any other American League team. This year, a "lively ball" controversy ensued as batters stroked more home runs than ever. James

Crusinberry wrote this after a game on July 3: "Three homers into the left field bleacher didn't even cause much of a stir. Homers are getting so common."[31]

Game of the Year

June 12—The Cubs collected 22 hits including four each by Max Flack and Charlie Hollocher, but still fell to the Braves, 12-9 in ten innings. Boston countered with fourteen hits, highlighted by Hank Gowdy's grand slam and a two-run, tenth inning homer into the left field bleachers by Tony Boeckel.

Bear News

The second bear outside Cubs Park foreshadowed new tenants that fall. The Decatur Staleys football team moved their games to Chicago and rented the park from the Cubs.

The Staleys paid the Cubs 15 percent of the gross receipts and all concession profits minus the scorecards. Their Cubs Park opener on October 16 drew 7,500 fans; the Staleys rushed past Rochester, 16-13. The Staleys played nine more games at Cubs Park and drew between 1,900 and 12,000 for each. The Staleys won the American Professional Football Association with a 9-1-1 record. But even with a championship, the team lost $71.63.

Quote of 1921

"The lively ball gave another exhibition of leaping fences and crashing its way about the field. . . . Walter Cruise poled two of the homers, one a lift over the right field wall and the other a stinging liner to center field that traveled so fast that Barber couldn't move thirty feet to get in front of it. It ripped its way clear to the far corner of the lot and still had so much life that it tore its way through the screened and picketed fence."[32]

James Crusinberry in the Chicago Tribune—*June 15, 1921*

1922

The Season by the Numbers		
80-74	.519 5th 13 games out	542,283 (6,952 average)
39-37	.513 at home	112% of NL average

Home Opener

April 20; Cubs (Alexander) vs. Reds (Donohue); 42 degrees; 20,000 attend

Cubs 3 Reds 1—The Reds held the Cubs to three hits. But the biggest one, a run-scoring double by Charlie Hollocher, keyed a three-run third inning. Gabby Hartnett made his Cubs Park debut and stroked a double.

An airplane dropped "beribboned bombs" during pregame ceremonies.[33] Despite the Opening Day excitement and a Cubs victory, the weather predominated. The *Chicago Tribune* reported that "the fans were frozen to their seats and even forgot to stand up in the seventh inning."[34]

What Happened

• The Cubs and Cardinals traded outfielders between games of a morning/afternoon double-header on May 30. Both the Cardinals' Cliff Heathcote and the Cubs' Max Flack went hitless in the opener. In the afternoon, Heathcote went 2-for-4 with the Cubs and Flack went 1-for-4 as a Cardinal. The two became the first to play for two teams in the same day.

• Serenity ruled Cubs Park on July 12. A 100-member symphony and local opera singers staged concerts on six consecutive Wednesday evenings. The concerts, sponsored by B'nai B'rith, benefited Eastern European orphans. The musicians performed on a platform over the field, the conductor standing above the pitcher's mound. A *Chicago Tribune* review said this about the unique setting: "The music had considerable audible competition; the 'New World' symphony was given additional new world sounds not contemplated by Dvořák; honking horns, grinding surface and elevated cars, the native cry of the candy butchers."[35]

• On July 12, police arrested forty suspected gamblers in the grandstand behind third base.

• Attendance grew 24 percent, in part because the Cubs improved by sixteen victories over 1921. Another factor was the passing of the gambling scandal. Commissioner Landis's hard-handed tactics cleaned up the game, at least in the minds of most fans, and many seemed ready to look forward, not back.

The Cubs drew more than 25,000 for an April 23 showdown against the Pirates. Nearly 10,000 fans couldn't get in the park. In mid-August, a three-game series against the Giants attracted 75,000 paid admissions.

On November 8, the team announced plans to expand Cubs Park. Led again by Zachary Taylor Davis, the project added 12,000 seats, bringing Cubs Park in line with most major league stadiums. (The expansion followed those in Washington, St. Louis, Detroit, and at the Polo Grounds in New York.)

Game of the Year

August 25—The Cubs outlasted the Phillies 26-23. Records and oddities that day:

- The 49 runs were and still are the most in a major league ballgame
- The 51 hits broke the major league record
- The Cubs' Marty Callaghan came to bat three times in the 14-run fourth inning
- In the fourth inning, the Cubs stroked 11 hits
- The Cubs scored 10 runs in the second inning
- Russell Wrightstone and Frank Parkinson of the Phillies were the first players in the twentieth century to come to bat eight times in a nine-inning game
- The Phillies came back from a 25-6 deficit and left the bases loaded in the ninth

Bear News

The Decatur Staleys officially became the Chicago Bears. George Halas chose the new nickname because his team played at Cubs Park. But the team failed to win the league title for the first time in its three-year existence. Attendance figures exist for seven of the team's eight home games. In those games, the Bears averaged 6,400 per contest.

In mid-season, the Bears cut ticket prices in half for boys under sixteen years old. Halas said the move allowed the team to "do our part to help make football a beneficial sport to every lad in Chicago."[36]

(From the Chicago Daily News, *April 25, 1922)*

Quote of 1922

"Bill Veeck packed 27,000 people into his undersized park for the Sunday conflict. When the stands bulged at the sides and the bleachers were filled and standing room behind the ropes was taken, Bill and his employees let the folks lie under the grand stand [sic] and peer through a wire barricade."[37]

In the New York Times—*August 21, 1922—on the Cubs/Giants game of August 20*

1923

The Season by the Numbers		
83-71	.539 4th 12.5 games out	703,705 (9,139 average)
46-31	.597 at home	146% of NL average

Opening Day

APRIL 17; CUBS (OSBORNE) VS. PIRATES (MORRISON); SUNNY, 41 DEGREES; 33,000 ATTEND

Pirates 3 Cubs 2—A record-breaking crowd watched the major's youngest team lose to Pittsburgh. Charlie Grimm drove in the Pirate runs with a bases-clearing double in front of the new right field bleachers.

The staff aces, the Pirates' Wilbur Cooper and the Cubs' Grover Cleveland Alexander, did not start because of the cold temperatures.

Chicago Mayor William Dever threw out the first pitch.

What's New

• The 1923 expansion launched a truism that follows the team to this day—the Cubs never skimp when renovating their ballpark. Rather than slap extra seats on the edge of the grandstand, Zachary Taylor Davis's expansion involved cutting the grandstand into thirds, separating the pieces, and filling in the gaps with new grandstands, like a giant jigsaw puzzle. *Popular Mechanics* magazine called the procedure "an altogether unprecedented engineering enterprise."[38]

Workers placed two of the three grandstand pieces on rollers. A team of horses pulled the left field piece 100 feet toward the northwest and the center section 100 feet south toward

*Cubs Park expands.
(National Baseball
Hall of Fame Library,
Cooperstown, N.Y.)*

Clark Street. Both pieces were set on new foundations. Not only did the park's size increase, but the right field line measured 354 feet, an increase of over 50 feet.

Workers lowered the playing field seven feet. This allowed fourteen new rows of box seats and a rebuilt diamond. It now featured a crowned field to aid drainage. The wooden bleachers in left field were razed and replaced with steel and concrete bleachers in both left and right field.

Final statistics of the project were impressive. The renovations cost over $200,000, nearly the price tag to build the whole park nine years earlier. The published capacity ranged from 29,300 to 32,000. The April 5 *Chicago Tribune* provided representative numbers: 9,300 box seats, 5,000 bleacher seats, and 17,000 grandstand seats for a capacity of 31,300—an increase of at least 12,000.

The 23,000 non-bleacher seats constituted the largest single-deck grandstand in the world. Davis's design, however, allowed for easy double-decking. For now, the single-deck concept provided open airy views and included only ramps—no stairs.

The exterior got spruced up, too. Stucco and wrought iron grillwork covered the outside. Nearly 100 colorful flags flew from its roof, a tradition that still holds today.

At the northwest corner of the park, along Waveland Avenue, William Wrigley constructed a six-room bungalow for grounds crew chief Bobby Dorr and his family. Wrigley offered the house rent-free as long as Bobby worked for the team.

- Public address man Pat Pieper unveiled a larger megaphone so fans could hear his announcements throughout the expanded ballpark. The megaphone stood almost as tall as Pieper and he needed an assistant to help hold it up.

What Happened

- Not everyone liked the finished product. Less than thirty-six hours before the April 17 home opener, vandals, in a union uprising, damaged $10,000 in plumbing throughout the park. Nearly forty plumbers came in the next morning and repaired enough of the breakage to make the park operable. Police and security personnel guarded the park that night, just hours before its opening.

  In the early morning hours of October 14, an explosion at the main entrance caused over $5,000 in damage. The bomb blew out nearby windows and downed telephone lines. Police claimed that union members, still smarting over the awarding of construction work last spring, were to blame.

- A new tradition swept the majors this year—the player who caught the last out of the game threw the ball into the stands. *The Sporting News* weighed in on the habit:

  > The practice has become a nuisance. At each park where the last ball is tossed into the air for a free-for-all scramble, more or less inconvenience is caused the spectators. When the ninth inning arrives boys begin piling into the lower boxes. . . . Spectators are bumped and trampled upon by the eager contestants. Two or three fights among the boys generally enliven the proceedings.[39]

  At Cubs Park, a tossed ball broke a man's glasses. In Pittsburgh, doctors amputated a boy's arm after he fell during a "last out" melee and landed on a broken bottle.

- Following President Warren Harding's death on August 2, major league baseball postponed games on August 3 and then on August 10, the day of his funeral. On August 6, the Cubs and Brooklyn held a memorial for Harding during their game. Frank Schreiber of the *Chicago Tribune* set the scene:

Players, umpires and fans stood with heads bared for five minutes starting at 4:15 in memory of the late President Warren G. Harding. It was at that hour that the funeral train bearing the former President's body was expected to arrive in Chicago. The big park was silent, save for the ticking of a lone telegraph instrument, and the bell in a steeple of a little church on Clark street [sic] tolled at half minute [sic] intervals.[40]

Game of the Year

April 20—Both Barney Friberg and Gabby Hartnett homered twice in a 12-11 win over the Pirates. It marked the first time in park history that two players hit multiple homers in a game. It was emblematic of the season. A total of 120 home runs were hit at Cubs Park. The new bleachers shortened both power alleys, providing targets to home run-conscious batters.

Quote of 1923

"The beauty of the new park is not confined to the spaciousness of the playing field. The stands themselves lend the idea of commodiousness. The wide aisles, the roominess of the seats and the sweeping lines of the stands all contribute to the impression. Although its actual seating capacity is less, the stand looks far larger than the one at Comiskey Park."[41]

Lambert G. Sullivan in the Chicago Herald and Examiner—*April 18, 1923*

1924

The Season by the Numbers
81-72   .529 5th 12 games out   716,922 (9,311 average)
46-31   .597 at home   142% of NL average

Home Opener

APRIL 23; CUBS (KEEN) VS. CARDINALS (PFEFFER); 63 DEGREES; 27,000 ATTEND

Cubs 12 Cardinals 1—The Cubs led 8-0 after two innings on the strength of five doubles. Jigger Statz stroked four hits and George Grantham and Ray Grimes homered.

In pregame ceremonies, the Senn High School ROTC raised the American flag up a new flagpole in center field.

What's New

- American League game scores replaced advertisements on the scoreboard. In fact, outside of the "Doublemint Twins" on top of the board, Cubs Park contained no advertisements.
- The team purchased striped seat cushions that were less aerodynamic when thrown.
- Ushers sported red caps.

What Happened

- William Wrigley purchased the land under Cubs Park for $295,000. Bought from A. J. Archambault and Mike Cantillon, Mr. Wrigley now owned the land but the team still owed eighty-eight years on the original lease negotiated by Charles Weeghman. The team now paid Mr. Wrigley each year.
- The Cubs lost two games to the Reds on Memorial Day before the largest crowd to date in Cubs history, 40,596 paid. The *Chicago Tribune* estimated that nearly 43,000 jammed into the 31,300-seat park. Irving Vaughan wrote that exuberant fans "filled every seat, every inch of standing room and made use of every inch of fence rail available, and four or five thousand who had no other place to go were forced on to the playing field. And at least 2,000 others with the cash and the desire to enter couldn't shoe-horn their way into the park."[42]

- The first baseball game ever transmitted by radio from Cubs Park occurred on October 1. It was Game 1 of the annual City Series between the Cubs and the White Sox. WGN's Sen Kaney broadcast the Cubs' 10-7 win from the press box. Elmer Douglass of the *Chicago Tribune* listened to the game on radio and reported hearing "the yelling by the crowd, the flying pigeons . . . the whistles, the chug-chug of railroad engines and passing trains a block or so to the west."[43]

Game of the Year

May 25—The Cubs stole seven bases including a steal of home by Cliff Heathcote in an 11-0 drubbing of the Braves. Right fielder Heathcote led the team with 26 steals. The Cubs swiped 137 bases during the season, a number they would not reach again until the 1984 team stole 154.

Quote of 1924

"Many persons decry the prominence given sporting events on a day originally set apart to do honor to our country's defenders. They call it desecration of the day. We cannot go that far. Acceptance of national holidays as a time for personal enjoyment is characteristic of this pleasure-seeking age. Our duties are so many and so complex, life's pace is so fast, that we welcome any respite as a period of diversion."[44]

  Editorial in the Chicago Tribune—*May 30, 1924—on Memorial Day baseball*

1925

The Season by the Numbers		
68-86	.442 8th 27.5 games out	622,610 (8,086 average)
37-40	.481 at home	117% of NL average

Opening Day

APRIL 14; CUBS (ALEXANDER) VS. PIRATES (YDE); 60 DEGREES; 38,000 ATTEND

Cubs 8 Pirates 2—Grover Cleveland Alexander hit a solo home run and went the distance. The Cubs cemented it away with a six-run seventh inning, the big blow a three-run home run by Gabby Hartnett.

In pregame festivities, the team raised a flag commemorating the fiftieth anniversary of the National League.

The *Chicago Herald and Examiner* reported: "As for incidents, only one occurred. . . . It was a fight in the west section of the grandstand. It was so far back the majority of the fans couldn't see it. They had to be satisfied with reports that it was a good fight."[45]

What's New

- The park was repainted—green with red and white trim.
- Picking up where they left off during last year's City Series, WGN broadcast Opening Day and frequent games throughout the season. Quin Ryan reported from the grandstand roof. He employed two microphones: one to capture his voice and the other to pick up the surrounding crowd noise.

What Happened

- A. D. Lasker sold his Cubs stock to the other large shareholder, William Wrigley, making the gum magnate the team's principal owner.

   William Wrigley also owned the Los Angeles team in the Pacific Coast League. He built a new ballpark for this minor league team—a near replica of the grandstand at Cubs Park. He named it Wrigley Field.
- Before double decking, foul balls frequently left the park, landing on Clark or Addison streets. During one game, a foul ball flew onto Clark Street and barely missed a motorman on a passing streetcar. A passenger on that streetcar wrote to a Chicago newspaper, suggesting that the team erect a fifteen-foot-high screen above the roof to protect pedestrians from foul balls.
- It wasn't foul balls that hurt the team this year, but opponents' home runs. Several teams beat the Cubs with drives into the two-year-old bleachers in left field. Dick Cox of Brooklyn, for example, beat the Cubs on consecutive days with "cheap" homers. Following Cox's heroics, on August 1 and 2, Bill Veeck Sr. ordered the removal of the left two-thirds of the left field bleachers. Afterwards, only a small 500-seat "jury box" bleacher remained to the left of the scoreboard.

   The park lost 1,500 bleacher seats but gained roomier dimensions. The distance down the left field line increased 51 feet to 370. Distance just to the left of the jury box increased to 406 feet. The added dimensions reduced home runs considerably. In the forty-nine games before August 5, batters hit 108 home runs (2.2 per game) at Cubs Park. In the twenty-eight home games beginning August 5, batters hit only six home runs (.21 per game). The drastic

Cub players in front of the troublesome left field bleachers. (Chicago History Museum, SDN-065326)

measures did not improve Cub fortunes. They finished in last place for the first time in their fifty-year history.

Game of the Year

July 4—Tony Kaufmann did it all; he threw a three-hitter and homered twice as the Cubs shattered the Cardinals, 9-1. Kaufmann became the first of only four pitchers to homer twice in a game at Wrigley Field. The others:

Glen Hobbie	July 2, 1961 vs. Cardinals
Fergie Jenkins	September 1, 1971 vs. Expos
Walt Terrell (Mets)	August 6, 1983 vs. Cubs

Bear News

College football star Red Grange was the biggest sports story of the year, surpassing Babe Ruth and boxer Jack Dempsey. Immediately after playing his last game with the University of Illinois, Grange signed with the Bears. His first professional game took place five days later on Thanksgiving Day morning against the Chicago Cardinals. A crowd of 36,000, a Cubs Park record, saw Red gain 36 yards on 14 runs from scrimmage. But he also returned three punts for 66 yards, had one tackle, and a touchdown-saving interception. His big defensive play proved vital as the score ended 0-0.

After the game, thousands rushed the field to get a close-up glance at the new superstar. For the day, Red received a black eye and about $12,000. Three days later, the Bears and Grange played the Columbus Tigers at Cubs Park. Another 28,000 watched in a snowstorm as the Bears won, 14-13. Grange gained 72 yards rushing.

Quote of 1925

"The Grange move will do much to settle the question of the future of pro football. If Grange can cary [sic] his following into his new venture, then thousands of dollars will be attracted to the box office and professional football as a business apparently will be assured."[46]

James S. Carolan in the New York Times—*November 23, 1925*

1926

The Season by the Numbers

82-72	.532 4th 7 games out	885,063 (11,420 average)
49-28	.636 at home	154% of NL average

Home Opener

APRIL 21; CUBS (ALEXANDER) VS. REDS (DONOHUE); 78 DEGREES; 32,000 ATTEND

Cubs 4 Reds 2—Cliff Heathcote hit two doubles and scored twice for the Cubs. Grover Cleveland Alexander pitched out of trouble the last two innings, putting two men on with no outs in each before retiring the sides. The victory marked the first home game for new manager Joe McCarthy.

What's New

- The team added a fence on the park's roof to keep photographers safe from falling into the seats below.
- The tarp was moved from the edge of the playing field to behind the fence adjacent to the right field bleachers.
- Ushers wore new red caps.

What Happened

- The Cubs acquired a short, stocky ballplayer off waivers from the New York Giants. Hack Wilson combined awesome power and a flare for the dramatic. He'd lead the National League with 21 home runs and supplant Grover Cleveland Alexander as the most popular Cub.

  Wilson's exciting play ignited the team and brought fans to Cubs Park. On May 2, a crowd of 36,000 saw the Cubs beat the Cardinals. A week later, 36,000 fans packed the park and another 5,000 were turned away. A half dozen more standing room turnouts proved that the park was too small, just three years since its most recent expansion. On November 16, the North Siders declared what was expected for months—Cubs Park would add a second deck for 1927.

- Last year's letter to the editor warning about the danger of foul balls landing outside the ballpark proved prophetic and tragic. Twelve-year-old Attillo Caprini went to see the Cubs battle Brooklyn on July 12. A batting practice foul flew over the grandstand and Caprini, outside the park along Addison Street, chased after it, knowing that returning it to park security meant a free ticket to the game. An automobile struck and killed the boy as he darted into the street.
- In late July, a doubleheader netted nearly $3,000 in concession money. The wife of concessionaire Fred Chamberlain took the cash home in a leather sack. Three men, at least one seen loitering around a concession stand earlier in the day, followed Mrs. Chamberlain, robbing her at gunpoint at her residence.
- Boxing came to Cubs Park on August 13. A crowd of 14,000, the largest since Illinois legalized the sport earlier this year, saw five bouts. The best had Joey Sangor battle bantamweight champion Charley Phil Rosenberg to a draw. Pugilists returned on September 6, but a lesser card attracted only 5,741 fans.

Game of the Year

May 23—The Cubs and Braves stroked 32 hits. The best was Hack Wilson's fifth inning line shot off the center field scoreboard, the first ever at the park. The Cubs scored seven runs in the eighth and overpowered the Braves, 14-8.

Quote of 1926

"The usual crowd waited after the game to escort Mr. Wilson out of the park. If this keeps up, it will be necessary to leave a big gate wide open until Hack gets out."[47]
    In the Chicago Tribune—May 12, 1926—on Hack Wilson's immense popularity.

SECOND INNING
1927-1939
LEAGUE LEADER

These were the best years in Wrigley Field history. William Wrigley and Bill Veeck Sr. achieved a near perfect business plan: a winning team and an expanded ballpark brought out record numbers of fans. The vast attendance, in turn, financed more elite players and more ballpark renovations.

The Cubs won four National League pennants—1929, 1932, 1935, and 1938—and could have won four more: 1927, 1928, 1930, and 1937. These teams included the greatest collection of stars in the Wrigley Field era: Riggs Stephenson, Charlie Grimm, Charlie Root, Phil Cavarretta, Bill Lee, Stan Hack, and Hall of Famers Gabby Hartnett, Hack Wilson, Kiki Cuyler, Rogers Hornsby, and Billy Herman.

The Cubs led the National League in attendance eight times and finished second every other year. Remarkably, in 1929, they broke a major league attendance record and tripled the average of the rest of the league.

Every team lost money during the depths of the Depression, but the Cubs did better than most. They actually made money in 1931, 1935, 1936, and 1937 and had capital to take risks. In 1929, they purchased Rogers Hornsby, the league's best hitter. He promptly won them a pennant. During the 1930s they purchased Chuck Klein and Dizzy Dean.

The Cubs tackled major renovations during this inning. They double decked Wrigley Field in 1927 and 1928. This wasn't unusual; many teams increased capacity coming out of the dead-ball era. Still, the Cubs were one of only four teams to undertake major renovations during the Depression, joining the Red Sox, Yankees, and Tigers. The 1936 box seat renovation, the 1937 bleacher rebuilding, and subsequent renovations in 1938 weren't done out of necessity or done with capacity in mind. Aesthetics drove these changes. Teams on the brink could never do this.

Although the Reds inaugurated night baseball in 1935, the Cubs did not pursue it. Only the most desperate teams at the time used the novelty to survive. Relative to the rest of major league baseball, the Cubs and Wrigley Field thrived. They were league leaders.

1927

The Season by the Numbers

85-68	.556 4th 8.5 games out	1,159,168 (15,153 average)
50-28	.641 at home	195% of NL average

Opening Day

APRIL 12; CUBS (ROOT) VS. CARDINALS (ALEXANDER); 54 DEGREES; 45,000 ATTEND

Cubs 10 Cardinals 1— Charlie Root and the North Siders savaged former Cub Grover Cleveland Alexander. Rookie Earl Webb smacked two home runs and newcomer Charlie Grimm added another.

Mayor Thompson threw out the first ball.

Jimmy Corcoran of the *Chicago American* called the field conditions "a trifle mangy" and blamed it on the Bears football the previous fall. He added, "The young men who will operate at shortstop . . . may have to wear masks and chest protectors when in pursuit of ground balls."[1]

What's New

- After a repainting, the park's color scheme was cream, green, and red.
- A January snowstorm and steel shipment delays limited upper deck expansion to just the third base-side. It increased seating capacity of the now lopsided ballpark to about 38,000.

    Yet, the spectacle still impressed Cub watchers. Gene Morgan of the *Chicago Daily News* captured the feeling on Opening Day:

    Double-Deck busses and pimento-cheese sandwiches are rivaled by that other architectural wonder, the new double-decked grandstand at Mr. Wrigley's pitching and pelting plaza. . . . Like the timid landlubber goes aloft for the first time to the gale-swept crow's nest, the coy Cub fan today scales the heights of the skyscraper stadium.[2]

- The Cubs christened their newly expanded ballpark, "Wrigley Field," in honor of team owner William Wrigley.

What Happened

- The expanded seating and a pennant chase brought out fans in stunning numbers. The team broke a National League attendance record and became the only club outside the Yankees to surpass the one million mark. The Cubs nearly doubled the White Sox attendance. Moreover, the South Siders became also-rans to the winning Cubs for the next twenty-three years.
- Fred Chamberlain retired following the 1926 season, ending his private concession business that served both Cubs Park and West Side Grounds. The Cubs didn't hire another concessionaire. Rather, they took over the business themselves, realizing the income potential of selling hot dogs and peanuts to hungry fans. John O. Seys oversaw the concessions at the park.
- Championship bouts highlighted three summer boxing cards. But boxing didn't attract large crowds at Wrigley Field. When Chicago Stadium opened in 1928, promoters preferred that smaller, less expensive venue. It kept professional boxing out of Wrigley Field for seven years.

Game of the Year

June 12—An overflow throng of 45,000 saw the Cubs clip the Giants 7-6. Earl Webb chipped in a home run and three singles while Hack Wilson stroked three doubles into the field crowd. The win marked the Cubs eighth straight win, seven of them by one run. The victory pulled the Cubs to within a game and a half of the Pirates.

Wrigley Field with half an upper deck—notice the original single-deck roof at left edge of photo. (Chicago History Museum, SDN-066556)

The Cubs rode a nine-game winning streak from June 29 to July 8. They did it again between July 31 and August 9 and moved into first place. Their lead expanded to six games by August 16. Pennant fever swept the North Side! But the Cubs went on a long road trip and collapsed. A September 1 defeat at Pittsburgh dropped them behind the Pirates. By the time they lost 13-1 to the Cardinals on September 6, they'd fallen to fourth place.

Quote of 1927

"[Umpire] Pfirman had hardly called out the last runner before he found it necessary to dance nimbly about to avoid being plunked. One missile did nick him on the ankle, but he stood his ground, dodging this way and that, and finally there weren't any more bottles to throw."[3]

Irving Vaughan in the Chicago Tribune—*September 13, 1927—on fans venting their frustrations over the season's disappointing ending.*

1928

The Season by the Numbers		
91-63	.591 3rd 4 games out	1,143,740 (14,854 average)
52-25	.675 at home	214% of NL average

Home Opener

APRIL 18; CUBS (NEHF) VS. REDS (KOLP); CLOUDY, 67 DEGREES; 46,000 ATTEND

Reds 9 Cubs 6—Pinch hitter Earl Webb cracked a three-run homer in the eighth inning, giving the Cubs a 6-5 lead. The dramatic drive went for naught as the Reds scored four in the ninth off Pat Malone and Charlie Root.

Over the winter, workers completed the right field upper deck expansion, increasing the park's capacity to 45,000. Nevertheless, thousands paid scalpers up to three times face value to get in the ballpark and many others stood on the field. The *Chicago Herald and Examiner* called this record-breaking opener the greatest in Chicago baseball history. The paper's Warren Brown remarked that "seldom in Cub history have players been accorded the roaring welcome that greeted [new Cub Kiki] Cuyler and [Hack] Wilson on their first appearances at the plate."[4]

What's New

- The upper deck eliminated the old rooftop press box. Newspaper writers used upper deck seats until workers built a glass-enclosed press box suspended under the second deck. Many considered it the best in baseball.
- Spurred on, no doubt, by the umpire Pfirman debacle last fall, the Cubs became the first major league team to stop selling soda in bottles. Instead, they dispensed liquids in paper cups. The change ended the practice of Wrigley Field fans throwing bottles at opposing players and umpires. The Cubs were forward thinkers on this issue; some teams dealt with bottle-throwing at their ballparks into the 1940s.
- Andy Frain took over security detail at the ballpark. His company would remain there for nearly sixty years.

What Happened

- On May 14, a car struck New York Giant manager John McGraw as he hailed a taxi after a game. McGraw suffered a wrenched knee and bruised right calf. He listened to the next day's game from his hotel room. To add insult to his injury, the Cubs won that game, their tenth in a row.
- In June, Amelia Earhart became the first woman to fly across the Atlantic Ocean. Shortly after, she and her flying companions, Wilmer Stultz and Lou Gordon, traveled to Chicago for a speaking engagement at Hull House. The trio received thunderous applause when they appeared at a game on July 22.

Games of the Year

July 21—The Cubs bewildered the Giants in two extra inning thrillers, 2-1 and 5-4. The Giants loaded the bases in the top of the fifteenth inning but could not score. In the Cubs half of the inning, Riggs Stevenson drove in Freddie Maguire with the winning run. In the nightcap, both teams traded runs in the ninth inning. The Cubs won it in the tenth on a Stephenson single and Gabby Hartnett's triple that went in and out of Les Mann's outstretched glove.

Irving Vaughan of the *Chicago Tribune* said this about the epic battles:

The enmity that has sent the Cubs and Giants down through the seasons as uncommon foes seems to gather fire as time moves along. The age-old bitterness, started by men long since departed from baseball's scenes of action, flared up furiously yesterday at Wrigley field [sic]. It flared through twenty-five sensational, gripping rounds of fighting and when the final hit had boomed forth in the gathering dusk to mark finis for the day, the haughty, ambitious Giants were groping about in fourth place under the sting of a double defeat.[5]

Unlike last year's collapse, the Cubs hung tough, going 19-12 in July, 16-11 in August, and 17-8 in September. After their final home game on September 13, they trailed St. Louis by two games. They went 9-5 on their last road trip but could not make up ground.

Quote of 1928

"In their efforts to give Chicago a team, in their attempts to provide adequate seating capacity, in their conduct of the sport at Wrigley field [sic], we think owners and officials of the Cubs deserve special mention."[6]

Harvey T. Woodruff in the Chicago Tribune—*April 19, 1928*

1929

The Season by the Numbers		
98-54	.645 1st 10.5 games ahead	1,485,166 (19,041 average)
52-25	.675 at home	302% of NL average

Opening Day

APRIL 16; CUBS (ROOT) VS. PIRATES (GRIMES); 47 DEGREES; 50,000 ATTEND

Pirates 4 Cubs 3—Pittsburgh scored three runs in the first inning and hung on to win. Burleigh Grimes, the old spitball pitcher, went the distance for the Pirates.

Team owner William Wrigley tossed the first pitch and Jack Bramhall's Band played at its fortieth opener. Many players received traditional floral displays; the most novel was a large baseball made of roses. When it opened, Charlie Root's son popped out.

What's New

• A fifteen-foot-high metal wall replaced a fence under and in front of the scoreboard.

- A 110-foot steel flagpole replaced the old wooden pole beyond center field. A ten-foot by twenty-foot American Flag flew from its mast.

- Workers erected ninety-foot flagpoles at the end of the right and left field foul lines, topped by **Wrigley Field** pennants. The flagpoles doubled as foul poles, necessitated by last year's home run ruling that balls were judged fair or foul not by where they landed, but by where they left the playing field. The poles were more than necessary, as home run frequency skyrocketed. In 1928, for example, 58 home runs were hit at Wrigley Field. In 1929, batters hit 117.

- Extra box seats increased park capacity by 3,000. Eight of the new, smaller folding chairs fit into the space that once held six larger chairs.

What Happened

- After falling short in recent years, William Wrigley tried to buy a pennant. Before the season, he sent five players and an astounding $200,000 to the Boston Braves for Rogers Hornsby, the National League's best hitter. Hornsby played up to expectations, compiling a .380 average, hitting 39 home runs, and driving in 149 runs.

- On June 21, Hack Wilson climbed into the stands after a fan who hurled obscenities at him. The agitator suffered a split lip, a wrenched back, and the audacity of being charged in the incident. He filed suit against Wilson, who claimed he rushed the stands to confront the belligerent fan but tripped and fell into him. The jury sided with the slugger, agreeing he acted in self-defense.

- On August 26, the Cubs' Norm McMillan hit the strangest grand slam in Wrigley Field history. In the eighth inning against the Reds, he drove a shot just inside the third base bag. The ball rolled into foul territory and disappeared. After McMillan and three other Cubs crossed the plate the ball was discovered—inside the sleeve of Ken Penner's warm-up jacket on the ground in the Cub bullpen. The slam proved a catalyst in an eight-run inning that gave the Cubs a 9-5 victory.

- A Labor Day doubleheader illustrated this year's level of fan excitement. The split games with the Cardinals drew 38,000 in the morning and another 43,000 that afternoon. The earlier gathering marked the largest morning attendance to date in baseball history. The 81,000 total surpassed any one-day crowd outside Yankee Stadium. The Cubs drew 1,485,166 fans this year, a major league record that stood until the 1946 Yankees drew 2,265,512.

  Fans attending the holiday doubleheader exhibited a curious custom. In summer, men sported straw hats. After Labor Day, they switched to wool or cotton ones for the colder months. Men celebrating big rallies that weekend hurled their soon-to-be-disposed-of skimmers onto the field. Hundreds of straw hats rained down from the stands, stopping play innu-merable times. The grounds crew gathered them on the edge of the diamond. The *Chicago Tribune* reported that the Cubs would sell the hats to "burlesque comedians who feature chapeau crushing skits."[7]

Game of the Year

June 15—The Phillies' Spud Davis and the Cubs' Rogers Hornsby hit grand slams in the Cubs' 8-7 win. It's the first time in park history that two players hit grand slams in the same game.

To the Pennant

The Cubs and Pirates shared time in first place into July. The Cubs captured first place for good on July 24 and built a fourteen and a half game lead by late August. They clinched the elusive pennant on September 18.

Labor Day 1929 (Chicago History Museum, SDN-069123)

As the Cubs drove toward the pennant, fans wondered if they might host World Series games at the larger Comiskey Park or perhaps even Soldier Field. But William Wrigley, more concerned with a championship than with profits, opted for Wrigley Field's home field advantage. To give more fans a chance to see games, Wrigley constructed 8,000 temporary bleacher seats over Waveland and Sheffield Avenues. At $1 per ticket, the team could realize only $24,000 for three World Series games, or about $1,000 less than the seats cost to erect.

Beginning September 10, fans ordered tickets by mail for the first World Series in Wrigley Field history. Box seats cost $6.60 and grandstands $5.50. Fans had to purchase reserved seats for all three games (One, Two, and Six). The team received almost 65,000 requests, or about twice what they could honor. Ticket processors picked the lucky winners the old-fashioned way—they pulled them by fistfuls from mailbags. Those not lucky enough to get reserved seats could still purchase 12,000 bleacher ($1) or 2,500 standing room tickets ($3) the day of each game.

To accommodate the World Series media, the team built a radio press box and a photographer catwalk under the upper deck. While the street bleachers came down after the series, these were permanent. Both stood until skybox construction in 1989.

GAME ONE; TUESDAY, OCTOBER 8; 63 DEGREES; 50,740 PAID

Die hard fans arrived outside the park two days before the opening game, and the line for bleacher tickets completely encircled the park seven hours before the first pitch. The game started fifteen minutes late to allow the overflow crowd into the ballpark.

The Athletics were 6-5 favorites to win the series. Connie Mack led a team of future Hall of Famers including Mickey Cochrane, Al Simmons, Jimmie Foxx, and Lefty Grove. But Mack surprised the baseball world by starting little used Howard Ehmke. The former Federal Leaguer, who scouted the Cubs the final month of the season, used a side-arm delivery and junk pitches to keep the Cubs off-kilter. He fanned 13, a World Series record. Jimmie Foxx's seventh inning home run off Charlie Root broke a scoreless tie and the A's went on to win, 3-1.

GAME TWO; WEDNESDAY, OCTOBER 9; 51 DEGREES; 49,987 PAID

The weather turned foul. Arch Ward of the *Chicago Tribune* wrote, "The breeze blowing in from Lake Michigan made the fans button up their overcoats and put on their gloves. It was good football weather."[8]

Jubilant Cubs fans wait in the wee hours to buy bleacher tickets to Game 1 of the World Series. (Chicago History Museum, SDN-069134)

The A's made it two in a row, winning easily, 9-3. Both Foxx and Simmons homered. Remarkably, George Earnshaw and Lefty Grove, the team's two 20-game winners, struck out 13 more Cubs.

Guy Bush won Game Three at Philadelphia's Shibe Park, 3-1, and the Cubs looked to even the series the next day, leading 8-0. But the A's championed the largest comeback in World Series history, scoring 10 runs in the seventh inning and won Game Four. The Cubs were three outs away from sending the series back to Wrigley Field for Game Six when Pat Malone allowed three runs in the bottom of the ninth. The A's won the fifth and final game of the series, 3-2. One of the most anticipated weeks in Cubs history ended swiftly, decisively, and miserably.

Quote of 1929

"Baseball, more than any other sport, unless perhaps pugilism has a diversified following composed of wealthy patrons and those of moderate or little means. In pugilism, the cheaper seats seldom offer a good view of the proceedings. In baseball, bleacher patrons can tell what it is all about."[9]

Harvey T. Woodruff in the Chicago Tribune—*August 1, 1929*

1930

The Season by the Numbers		
90-64	.584 2nd 2 games out	1,463,624 (18,764 average)
51-26	.662 at home	257% of NL average

Home Opener

APRIL 22; CUBS (MALONE) VS. CARDINALS (HALLAHAN); 44 DEGREES; 38,000 ATTEND

Cardinals 8 Cubs 3—Bill Hallahan, who two-hit the Cubs last week in St. Louis, scattered five hits. The Cubs lone runs came in the seventh inning on walks to Woody English and Kiki Cuyler, and a three-run Waveland Avenue home run by Hack Wilson.

What's New

• The park was repainted. The seats were still dark green and the exterior cream colored.

What Happened

• Des Moines of the Western League entertained Wichita under the lights on May 2—professional baseball's first night game. Irving Vaughan of the *Chicago Tribune* reported:

> As a spectacle the introduction was impressive. There is reason to believe that for the minor leagues, which are on a starvation diet, it may be a lifesaver, provided there are slight improvements. As for the Majors, it is a matter to be considered if evil days hit the big circuits or the magnates subordinate the competitive idea to gate receipts. At present they have an eye on each.[10]

The majors were still five years away from giving it a try. And the "lights" controversy at Wrigley Field wasn't even a glint in Cub fans' eyes.

- The Cubs' most loyal fan, Mary McCabe, died on May 5. Ms. McCabe, who attended virtually every Cub game in Wrigley Field, annually received the season's first tickets from team president Bill Veeck Sr.

- The Cubs' Hal Carlson died of a stomach hemorrhage at the nearby Hotel Carlos in the early hours of May 28. His sudden death proved all the more shocking considering that only a rainout canceled Carlson's scheduled start hours before. At 10:00 P.M. on May 27, he talked with teammate Kiki Cuyler in the hotel's lobby. Everything seemed normal. At 2:00 A.M. he called clubhouse attendant Eddie Froelich, also a Carlos resident, and complained of feeling ill. Carlson began bleeding from the mouth soon after and died by 3:30 A.M. He had a history of illness, the result of being gassed in World War I. Following that day's game, Cub players and team officials attended a memorial service at Linn's Funeral Home, a block from the ballpark. The thirty-eight-year-old Carlson left behind a wife and a four-year-old daughter.

- Hack Wilson treated Cubs fans to one of baseball's greatest offensive shows. A "juiced" ball toppled records throughout the majors, but no one hit them as often or as far as the stocky slugger. On May 6, Wilson sent a pitch off the field level scoreboard in center, equaling his 1926 clout. On August 26, he smacked his National League record 44th home run, breaking the mark set by Chuck Klein the previous season. By season's end Hack hit 56 home runs and knocked in 191 RBI, a record to this day.

- Wilson's heroics and the pennant contending Cubs continued the fans' love affair with the team. On June 27, 51,556 fans, the largest baseball gathering in Wrigley Field history, saw the Cubs beat the Dodgers, 7-5. Only 19,748, however, paid to watch. Over 30,400 women got in free for Ladies Day.

  The Cubs spent the 1930 season keeping women out of the ballpark after spending years encouraging them to attend games. The crush of women on Ladies Days kept paying customers from reaching the gates, and once there, left few available tickets. In May, the team required women to obtain tickets days before the Ladies Day game in hopes of lowering demand. After that didn't stop the rush, they required women to obtain tickets by mail. When nearly 100,000 requests arrived for an August Ladies Day game, the team capped each Ladies Day at 17,500 free tickets.

- Innovations like Ladies Day helped pique interest. So did William Wrigley's insistence on radio coverage for his team. In 1930, only three cities permitted radio broadcasts of home games. One radio station covered games in Boston and two stations covered games in St. Louis. Five

A coveted Ladies Day ticket from the 1930s.

stations broadcast Cubs home games. Wrigley Field also sported the league's only radio booth. Boston broadcasters reported from the press box and St. Louis relegated them to the grandstand.

• During a week in mid-August, the Cubs drew 243,400—the largest seven-day total to date in National League history. The four-game series with Brooklyn that week attracted 129,000 paying customers, another league record. Incredibly, those games took place during the week, without the benefit of a weekend or holiday date.

• On August 16, the Cubs won the first game of a doubleheader with the Phillies, 10-9, scoring two runs in the bottom of the ninth inning. They tallied three runs in the ninth inning of the nightcap to tie the Phillies before darkness ended the game two innings later. Veteran sportswriter Edward Burns of the *Chicago Tribune* called the overflow crowd the noisiest he'd ever heard.[11] The Cubs owned a two and a half game lead.

Games of the Year

May 12—The Cubs hit four home runs in the seventh inning to tie a National League record. Cliff Heathcote, Hack Wilson, Charlie Grimm, and Clyde Beck did the honors, but the Cubs still fell to the Giants, 14-12.

August 30—The Cubs smoked the Cardinals 16-4. Batting heroics went to Hack Wilson, who stroked his 45th and 46th home runs; George Kelly, who went 4-for-4 including a home run; and Kiki Cuyler, who got four walks and a double. The win maintained a five and a half game lead over the Giants, a seven game lead over the Brooklyn Robins, and a seven and a half game lead over the Cardinals.

The Cardinals ended the season 22-4 while the Cubs went only 13-14. St. Louis finished two games ahead. The Cubs, in fact, fell quicker than their infamous 1969 swoon. Their second collapse in four years cost manager McCarthy his job.

Regardless of the team's finish, 1929 and 1930 arguably marked the franchise's most popular two-year period in the Wrigley Field era, rivaled only by 1969-70 and 2007-08.

Quote of 1930

"At no time and at no place in the history of baseball has there been a display of interest and enthusiasm over the game as there has been here during the last two weeks. . . . All records for attendance have been shattered. . . . Each night the steel armored motor car carries the receipts away to a safe place. Visiting clubs leave here with checks such as they never got before."[12]

James Crusinberry in the Chicago Daily News—*August 21, 1930*

1931

The Season by the Numbers		
84-70	.545 3rd 17 games out	1,086,422 (13,928 average)
50-27	.649 at home	217% of NL average

Opening Day

APRIL 14; CUBS (ROOT) VS. PIRATES (FRENCH); SUNNY, 58 DEGREES; 43,000 ATTEND

Cubs 6 Pirates 2— Gabby Hartnett's two-run home run in the second inning scored the game's first runs. Veteran third baseman Les Bell drove a two-run double to left field in the eighth to put the game out of reach. Charlie Root tossed a four-hitter.

The *Chicago Daily Times* reported that a "six-foot floral horseshoe went to [manager] Hornsby, a floral bat and basket to Hack Wilson and baskets of flowers to Grimm and Malone."[13]

The *Chicago Tribune* said this about the band and the traditional Opening Day march to the center field flagpole: "It will be discovered that formations look better if the lines are in step. Yesterday it was every horn tooter for himself, while the players herded behind with every gait and waddle known to the art of human walking."[14]

What's New

• The park received more green paint. The newly painted telephone booths under the stands mimicked the park's traditional color scheme—green and cream.

- According to the *Chicago Daily News*, the team built a bar along the first base concourse. Although permitted to sell only near beer, the team saw the coming end of Prohibition and got a head start on anticipated beer sales.
- Concession vendors dressed in different color caps to distinguish what they sold.

    Peanut vendors—tan
    Popcorn men—blue
    Hot dog hawkers—red
    Ice cream men—white
    Pop sellers—green
    Lemonade men—yellow
    Candy barkers—wine
    Cigar and cigarette sellers—black
    Cushion renters—gray

- Andy Frain ushers wore their trademark blue and gold uniforms for the first time.
- The team added a first aid room done up in steel and white enamel.
- Baseball did away with cheap home runs. Previously, four-baggers could bounce over or through outfield walls. Beginning this year, balls had to go over a wall on a fly, otherwise, they were ground rule doubles. This new rule took away a few home runs each year at Wrigley Field when balls skipped over the six-foot screens in front of the outfield bleachers or over the walls down the left or right field lines.

What Happened

- It's incredible how far Hack Wilson's fortunes fell this season. He went from the league's premier slugger last September to a benchwarmer this June. A number of reasons contributed to his downfall.

    Wilson partied too much. After his record-breaking season, Hack lived life as the toast of baseball, arriving to spring training in poor physical and mental shape. Hack also claimed his eyesight deteriorated. If so, Cubs executives blamed it on too many late nights.

    Both leagues "deadened" the baseball. They raised the seams to improve pitching grips and the National League, over protests from President Veeck, thickened its cover. Home run frequency dropped in both leagues and plummeted 45 percent in the National League (Although a full 10 percent could be attributed to Hack himself).

	HOME RUNS		
	N.L.	A.L.	Wilson
1930	892	673	56
1931	493	576	13

Wilson played poorly under new manager Rogers Hornsby, who demanded a strict code of discipline that Wilson couldn't follow. Hornsby often reprimanded Hack and the slugger became sullen and drank excessively. Things spiraled out of control in August when Wilson scuffled with Pirate players at a Pittsburgh train station. Hornsby placed Hack on permanent leave. Wilson never played for the North Siders again.

- Wilson's about-face and the lingering Depression dropped attendance. The Cubs even took out newspaper ads promoting their July 4 doubleheader and games against the Cardinals and Giants, something unnecessary just last year.

The Cubs hosted their last morning/afternoon doubleheader on Labor Day, losing two games to the Cardinals before 17,000 at 10:15 A.M. and 26,000 at 3:00 P.M. It now cost more to stage two separate games with a total attendance at capacity than to fill the park once for a conventional doubleheader.

- Even though home attendance dropped almost 25 percent, scalpers still plied their trade outside Wrigley Field. The Cubs went so far as to get a restraining order against scalpers, calling them a public nuisance and claiming they damaged confidence in the franchise. The depth of scalper bravado showed when they posted signs advertising "choice baseball tickets" near the park at 1027 and 1039 Addison Street and 3607 Sheffield Avenue.[15]
- The Glasgow Celtics, the best soccer team in the world, beat the Chicago Bricklayers of the Western League, 6-3, before 11,000 on June 21. A bagpipe band and Irish and Scottish dancers highlighted the Gaelic pregame show.

Game of the Year

July 7—The Cubs routed the Cardinals twice, 14-2 and 6-3. Trailing 3-2 in the nightcap, pinch hitter Danny Taylor cleared the bases with an eighth inning double. Estimates set the crowd anywhere between 45,000 and 50,000, the largest paid attendance in park history to that point. In fact, almost 80,000 tried to see the game. The rush at the gates overcame fifteen fans and a fifty-year-old man died of a heart attack after working his way to his seat.

Bear News

The NFL's Chicago Cardinals moved their home games from Comiskey Park to Wrigley Field. The Cardinals hoped to exploit the Bears' popularity, since the South Siders averaged only 6,800 at Comiskey Park last year while the Bears averaged 11,500. It didn't work, at least for 1931. In three home games at Wrigley Field, the Cardinals averaged 4,833 while the Bears eight games averaged 17,187.

The Bears stole an idea from the Cubs and scheduled the NFL's first Ladies Day on October 25, a game against the Philadelphia Yellow Jackets. More than 28,000 requests came in for the 20,000 available tickets.

Quote of 1931

"Between games, Gabby Hartnett was presented with a three-carat diamond ring by his Catholic Order of Forester brothers. And they say there's a depression!"[16]

Wayne K. Otto in the Chicago Herald-Examiner—*September 21, 1931*

1932

The Season by the Numbers		
90-64	.584 1st 4 games ahead	974,688 (12,658 average)
53-24	.688 at home	238% of NL average

William Wrigley died on January 26 at his winter home in Phoenix, one week after suffering a stroke. The seventy-year-old patriarch oversaw some of the brightest days in team history. But he died without bringing the Cubs a world's championship.

A shrewd businessman, Wrigley made a fortune in the gum business. Most also considered him the most magnanimous baseball owner of his time; he paid his players well, nurtured fans, and kept Wrigley Field immaculately conditioned. His only son, P. K., took over club ownership.

"It's a terrible shock; it's like losing a parent. Mr. Wrigley was the finest man that ever lived."[17]

Bill Veeck Sr. in the *Chicago Tribune*—January 27, 1932

William Wrigley in 1929 (Chicago History Museum, SDN-069116)

Home Opener

APRIL 20; CUBS (MALONE) VS. REDS (LUCAS); CLOUDY, 59 DEGREES; 30,000 ATTEND

Reds 7 Cubs 2—The Cubs committed four errors and got only five hits, two of them by rookie Stan Hack. The Reds scored five times in the third inning.

The American flag flew at half-staff to honor Mr. Wrigley. Howard Mann of the *Chicago Daily News* said this about the twenty-one-year-old Hack: "It's a wonderful thing to have so much cheer bubbling out of your system in times like these . . . Our only fear is that somebody will discover that he has a soft, whispery voice as well as the smile and will make a radio crooner out of him."[18]

What's New

- The crush for Ladies Day passes continued as the Depression lingered. Seemingly unending requests forced the team to send out free tickets for games not on the original Ladies Day schedule. In all, the Cubs mailed out 280,000 free Ladies Day tickets this year.
- On June 22, National League President John Heydler ordered the Cubs and other league teams to add numerals to their uniforms. The Cubs wore them for the first time on June 30, their first game upon returning to Wrigley Field following a road trip.

What Happened

- Violet Popovich Valli shot her lover, Cub shortstop Billy Jurges, at the Hotel Carlos on July 6. Jurges allegedly ended his relationship with the showgirl that morning. Valli confronted him in his hotel room and bullets struck Jurges in his left wrist, right side, and ribs, presumably as he tried to keep Valli from shooting herself. Jurges refused to press charges, and Valli returned to Wrigley Field a week after the incident, sitting in the box seats near first base.
- The Hotel Carlos made the papers with the Jurges shooting and Hal Carlson's death in 1930. The small hotel, only two blocks north of Wrigley Field at 3834 Sheffield Avenue, was a popular summer residence for many Cubs players and staff. The hotel/rooming house still exists today as the Sheffield House.
- A solar eclipse on August 31 brought strange doings to the park. Kiki Cuyler hit the field level scoreboard on a fly for only the third time in Wrigley Field history. The Giants put across four runs in the tenth inning, but the Cubs answered with five of their own to win, 10-9.

To The Pennant

Acrimony between manager Hornsby and his players, along with Hornsby's growing gambling debts, ended his tenure on August 2. President Veeck replaced him with popular team captain Charlie Grimm. Veeck believed a lighter hand might bring the team back in contention. He proved right. Five games out at the time, the Cubs caught fire under Grimm and came home to Wrigley Field in first place on August 16.

That afternoon, over 32,000 celebrated "Charlie Grimm Day." The North Siders scored four in the ninth to beat Boston, 4-3, and went nineteen innings the following day to fluster the Braves again. When the Cubs swept New York on August 27, they had won nine straight and twelve of thirteen games on the homestand. Moreover, the team held a seven game lead over the Dodgers.

The Cubs clinched the pennant on September 20, taking the first game of a doubleheader with the Pirates, 5-2. Even as fans jammed the park for a chance to witness history, President Veeck insisted against an overflow field crowd, worried he couldn't control it in the heightened atmosphere. The decision left 15,000 fans outside the park scrambling for tickets. Police restored order after hundreds stormed the press gate.

The following day, the champs rode in an automobile parade from Wrigley Field to City Hall. The team alighted on La Salle Street and Mayor Anton Cermak introduced them in front of 100,000 admirers.

World Series

The Cubs faced the New York Yankees, led by ex-Cub manager, Joe McCarthy. A Depression-era crowd of only 41,459 saw the opener in Yankee Stadium. The Cubs outhit their American League rivals but fanned 10 times, left 11 men on base, and lost, 12-6. New York won the next day 5-2 before 50,709.

GAME THREE; SATURDAY, OCTOBER 1; 77 DEGREES; 49,459 PAID

Demand for series tickets didn't match that of 1929. The frenzy toward the Cubs had cooled and the Depression sapped pocketbooks. Scalpers sold ticket booklets for Games Three, Four, and Five for face value and a few grandstand seats even remained the morning of Game Three. Still, the team again erected temporary bleachers over Waveland and Sheffield Avenues and fans filled the cheap seats to capacity.

IRS agents roamed outside the park and charged scalpers a 10 percent tax on any ticket sold over face value. They also stationed officers near buildings on Waveland and Sheffield to collect a tax on roof viewers.

Adding fuel to the typical postseason fire was the Cubs' decision to award only a half of a World Series share to shortstop Mark Koenig. Koenig, a former Yankee, came to the Cubs in mid-season and provided key hits during their pennant surge. Because of this, Babe Ruth, Koenig's ex-teammate, called the Cubs "chiselers." The Babe pressed on, saying, "You ought to see Grimm burn when I round first and holler, 'Big hearted Charley.' Imagine those guys moaning about the small [Yankee Stadium] crowds [yielding small World's Series shares]."[19]

Before many fans reached their seats, Ruth hit a three-run homer off Charlie Root. Lou Gehrig and Kiki Cuyler traded home runs in the third inning, and the Cubs tied it up 4-4 in the fourth. As Ruth came to the plate in the fifth, the crowd erupted in a cacophony of cheers and hoots, an equal mix of adulation and detest that is reserved for the game's greatest personality. The Cub players didn't mix their allegiances; they stood at the edge of their dugout and blistered the Babe with verbal attacks. The amused Ruth shot right back, delivering smiles to the fans and retorts to the bench jockeys. Herbert Simons of the *Chicago Daily Times* told what happened next:

> Root threw a strike past him. The crowd roared. Good-naturedly the Babe lifted his right forefinger so all could see. Only strike one, he motioned. The next two pitches were balls. Another called strike and another razzing roar from the crowd! The Babe stuck up two fingers. And, if there was one of the 51,000 fans present who couldn't appreciate the full significance of this: "I've got a big one left" motion, he certainly did on the next pitch. Ruth took his stance and the ball took a ride, a 440-foot ride to the center field flagpole, a liner without equal in the history of Wrigley field.[20]

Gehrig hit the next Root pitch to the temporary bleachers in right. The Yankees won the game, 7-5, and for all practical purposes, won the series.

The question of Ruth calling his shot is still hotly debated today. Did he point to centerfield? Did he point to Root or the bench jockeys in the Cubs' dugout? Did he hold up a finger after each strike, indicating, "I got one left?" Or did he do some combination of the three? Most first-hand newspaper reports say Ruth gestured toward pitcher Root or to the Cubs dugout. Afterwards, Ruth wasn't helpful in sorting out the details. Sometimes he bragged about the feat. At other times he denied the heroics, as he did to Cub equipment manager Ed Froelich. "I may be dumb, but I'm not that dumb. I'm going to point to the center field bleachers with a barracuda like Root out there? On the next pitch they'd be picking it out of my ear with a pair of tweezers."[21]

Physical proof, a film of the action, didn't seem to exist. In 1994, however, a home movie surfaced. It showed Ruth pointing, but the poor quality and the angle of the footage shed little on Ruth's intent.

Remarkably, a better quality film, shot from a better angle, came to light in 1999. Harold Warp attended his first baseball game that day and shot the film of Ruth's home run. Not knowing its significance, he stored the tape for decades. Only after Warp's death did a relative discover the treasure. Mark Shapiro, a producer at ESPN who showcased Warp's footage on a television special, said, "It is obvious that the myth is dead. He was clearly pointing at the Cub dugout."[22]

Shapiro is probably right. But baseball scholars and fans still debate the facts. Regardless of any hyperbole, Ruth's home run, his 15th and last World Series four-bagger, was one of the most dynamic in baseball history. The scene was set—the World Series; Ruth gesturing and jawing with Root and the Cub bench before every pitch; the crowd whipped into a frenzy. Then, the Bambino hit the longest home run to date in Wrigley Field. It was pure Babe.

GAME FOUR; SUNDAY, OCTOBER 2; 75 DEGREES; 49,844 PAID

The Yankees won the anticlimactic Game 4, 13-6, to sweep the series. Because the Cubs failed to win a game, they returned over $200,000 in ticket money purchased for Game 5. Each Yankee took home $5,232 in World Series money. Each Cub got $4,245.

Bear News

On December 11, the Bears beat the Packers, 9-0. A snowstorm and near-zero degree weather limited the crowd to 5,000 stout souls. The victory tied the Bears for first place with Portsmouth and set up a championship game the following week with the Spartans at Wrigley Field.

With the temperatures still arctic-like and snow piling up, the Bears, fearing a financial freeze-out, moved the game indoors to the Chicago Stadium. The Bears and the Cardinals played a charity game there in 1930, but that was an exhibition. This one counted.

The indoor setting shortened the field to only eighty yards. A single goalpost stood on one end of the field. The team laid sod over a hay foundation that was left behind by a recent circus. The players didn't mind the change of venue, but the fans really appreciated it; over 11,000 attended the title game.

The Bears scored in the fourth quarter on a trick touchdown pass from Bronko Nagurski to Red Grange. They added a late safety for a 9-0 win and their first championship since 1921.

Quote of 1932

"I really think that in my best years I would have cracked that home run mark of sixty wide open with these fences to shoot at. I've said it before and I still think now that I could have knocked out seventy, easily."[23]

Babe Ruth to Edgar Munzel of the Chicago Herald and Examiner *—October 2, 1932—about the prospects of hitting at Wrigley Field*

1933

The Season by the Numbers		
86-68	.558 3rd 6 games out	594,112 (7,716 average)
56-23	.709 at home	162% of NL average

Opening Day

APRIL 12; CUBS (WARNEKE) VS. CARDINALS (DEAN); 41 DEGREES; 25,000 ATTEND

Cubs 3 Cardinals 0—Lon Warneke scattered just four singles. The Cubs scored all their runs in the third inning on singles by Frank Demaree, Charlie Grimm, Gabby Hartnett, and Warneke, and a walk to Billy Jurges. Frank Demaree started in center field for Kiki Cuyler, who missed most of the season with a broken ankle.

Acting Mayor Frank Corr threw out the first pitch. Corr served as Chicago's mayor for thirty-two days following the assassination of Anton Cermak.

It was so cold that Jack Bramhall's band played "Jingle Bells."

What's New

• On March 21, the U.S. House passed a bill permitting the brewing and selling of full-strength beer. President Roosevelt signed the bill, ending full National Prohibition on April 7. Five days later, at the opener, real beer flowed at Wrigley Field for the first time. The crowd imbibed at two bars under the stands, paying fifteen cents a cup. No vendors sold beer in the grandstand yet, but the day marked the marriage of beer and Chicago baseball.

- A vendor sold cigarettes to box seat fans on Opening Day. The woman, cloaked in a white dress and high heels, became the first female vendor at Wrigley Field.
- The Cubs added blue collars, pocket flaps, enlarged numbers, and controversy to their home uniforms. Newspapers sold their own scorecards outside the park for less than the club did inside. To foil the competition, Cub players frequently switched to uniforms with different numbers, rendering the knockoff scorecards worthless. The team went so far as to button on new numbers over the old ones. During a game on September 10, Kiki Cuyler's number fell off, exposing a big number 11, Charlie Root's number in the official scorecard.
- On July 4, the team unveiled a marble and bronze drinking fountain in memory of their late owner, William Wrigley Jr. The nine-foot-tall fountain, designed by Zachary Taylor Davis, stood inside the park's main entrance. Bill Veeck Sr. justified remembering Wrigley with a drinking fountain, saying, "We decided on a practical memorial to Mr. Wrigley in accordance with our understanding of his belief that usefulness was essential to the value of all things."[24]

  The fountain stood on the first base concourse until at least the 1970s when it was moved to the Friendly Confines Café after the Tribune Company bought the team. Sometime after, according to longtime Wrigley Field tour guide, Brian Bernardoni, it was moved to a storage building just south of the ballpark.

The first female vendor at Wrigley Field (www. ArgentaImages.com)

What Happened

- Undercover police arrested a former partner of Al Capone while he watched a Cubs game on May 21.
- The Century of Progress World's Fair opened in Chicago on May 27. The Cubs postponed their game that day so fans and players could attend the festivities. The Fair Queen and her court watched the Cubs–Braves game the next day and received a rousing ovation when they arrived.

When *Chicago Tribune* Sports Editor Arch Ward looked for a sporting event to coincide with the fair, he dreamt up a baseball game pitting elite players of the National and American Leagues. The game was scheduled for July 6 and its location decided by a coin toss in Judge Landis's Chicago office. American League President Will Harridge won the toss, calling heads. So Comiskey Park hosted the first baseball All-Star Game instead of Wrigley Field. The event proved such a hit that it became an annual rite of summer.

- Team President Bill Veeck Sr. died of leukemia on October 5. The former sportswriter guided the Cubs for fourteen years and built them into a power. Flags at both Game Two of the City Series at Wrigley Field and Game Four of the World Series in Washington flew at half-staff. Veeck was only fifty-six years old.

Game of the Year

July 23—The Cubs mashed the Phillies, 9-5 and 3-1 before 32,000 fans. With the wins they took sixteen of nineteen games on the homestand and pulled to within two games of the Giants. But that's as close as the Cubs got to consecutive pennants. They went on the road and lost six straight. The setbacks left them six and a half games behind.

Bear News

Dr. David L. Jones sold the Chicago Cardinals football team to Charles Bidwill for $50,000. Bidwell concentrated on drawing more football fans to Wrigley Field, saying, "Our appeal will be particularly to the popular fan—the everyday gent with no collegiate affiliation. We hope to attract letter carriers, streetcar conductors, clerks and above all, kids."[25]

The NFL divided into two divisions this year, and the Bears and the Giants, the division winners, met in Wrigley Field in the first real NFL "playoff" game. The Bears scored with only minutes left on a trick play (a forward pass, then a lateral to Bill Karr who stormed down the field untouched) for the 23-21 victory. Almost 26,000 fans saw the Bears take their second-straight title.

Quote of 1933

"This year's beer's back . . . and this should add considerable color to the trimmings—and perhaps to the cheeks of the clients."[26]

Jimmy Corcoran in the Chicago American—*April 11, 1933*

1934

The Season by the Numbers
86-65	.570 3rd 8 games out	707,525 (9,310 average)
47-30	.610 at home	199% of NL average

Home Opener

APRIL 24; CUBS (BUSH) VS. REDS (VANCE); 45 DEGREES; 16,000 ATTEND

Cubs 3 Reds 2—The Cubs knocked out forty-three-year-old Dazzy Vance in the first inning, scoring three runs on doubles by Woody English, Tuck Stainback, and newcomer Chuck Klein. They improved their season record to 6-0.

What's New

- William Walker became team president, replacing Bill Veeck, Sr. In one of Walker's first moves, he obtained a license to sell beer in the stands (in addition to the tap beer sold under the stands in 1933). But Walker objected to hard liquor at the park.
- Bill Veeck Jr. quit college and returned to Chicago after his father's death. He took an $18-a-week job as an office boy with the Cubs.
- The iconic marquee was hung above the main entrance at Clark and Addison Streets. It was originally light green, complementing the park's green exterior. It was also not originally lighted. The neon letters, outlining the words "WRIGLEY FIELD HOME OF THE CHICAGO CUBS," did not appear until 1936 or 1937.
- Wrigley Field added a public address system. Now Pat Pieper announced from a field seat near the backstop instead of walking the edge of the field belting out announcements through a megaphone. *The Sporting News* liked the modern touch, adding, "The antiquated one-man announcing system, employing a paper horn, belongs to the 'town ball' period."[27]
- To ration baseballs during the Depression, the Cubs installed a net from the top of the backstop to the top of the lower grandstand roof.
- To increase scorecard sales, the team numbered them and drew a number during the game. The lucky fan with the match received a season pass for all remaining home games.

What Happened

- A fire in a storage room destroyed the 2,000 seat cushions the team rented to fans. Management purchased new cushions by the home opener.
- On September 20, over 35,000 wrestling fans saw Jim Londos retain his heavyweight championship over Strangler Lewis. The card also included four boxing matches; former boxing champion Jack Dempsey refereed one of them.

Game of the Year

September 25—Phil Cavarretta made a stunning Wrigley Field debut. The eighteen-year-old Chicago native's home run led the Cubs to a 1-0 slicing of the Reds. Phil also walked twice and stole a base.

Quote of 1934

"You can't sell goods in a grimy package," William Wrigley often remarked and that is why he set about having the neatest and cleanest baseball plant in the majors. No woman ever leaves Wrigley Field with a soiled dress because of dirty seats or railings. The place is immaculate.

"The only drawback at Wrigley Field is the fact that customers . . . are in the shade . . . and cold winds come off Lake Michigan. If Wrigley had lived long enough he might have moved Lake Michigan. At least, he might have tried."[28]

Harry Neily in The Sporting News—*January 11, 1934*

1935

The Season by the Numbers

100-54	.649 1st 4 games ahead	692,604 (8,995 average)
56-21	.727 at home	164% of NL average

Opening Day

APRIL 16; CUBS (WARNEKE) VS. CARDINALS (D. DEAN); SUNNY, 33 DEGREES; 15,500 PAID

Cubs 4 Cardinals 3—Gabby Hartnett homered in the second inning and doubled in the winning run in the eighth. Dizzy Dean left in the first inning after Fred Lindstrom drove a shot off his shin.

Chicago Mayor Ed Kelly threw out the first pitch. Fans found remnants of snow in the grandstand. Herbert Simons of the *Chicago Daily Times* called today's temperature the coldest to date in Wrigley Field history.

Anna Woltz was the first person in line for a grandstand ticket. She claimed to have held this Opening Day title for the last twenty years.

What's New

- Upholstered chairs were added in the press box. Wayne K. Otto of the *Chicago Herald and Examiner* welcomed the change, saying, "Other press boxes have nothing to approach them in class, even remotely."[29]
- The Cubs ended their two-year experiment to color-code the vendors according to what they sold. This year all vendors wore green jackets, white pants, and white caps.
- The Cubs moved up the starting times for Saturday games from 3:00 P.M. to 2:00 P.M. The earlier start left less "dead time" between noon, when businesses traditionally closed on Saturday, and game time.
- Before ballgames, Pat Pieper spun records of popular songs over the public address system. He played "The Stars and Stripes Forever" as fans left the park. Pieper lost this job in May when Musicians' Union members insisted on turning the records. A professional disc jockey finished out the season but he and the music did not return in 1936.

- In an experiment to improve batting visibility, a green screen was placed in front of a portion of the left field bleacher jury box.

What Happened

- Ten of sixteen major league teams failed to draw even 400,000 fans last year. In response, the Cincinnati Reds played the majors' first night game on May 24. The league limited them to seven night games, but the experiment worked. The Reds averaged almost 20,000 per night game, more than doubling their season attendance to 450,000.
- In late July, over 35,000 boxing fans watched the Chicago CYO trump their counterparts from New York City. Boxing legends Joe Louis, Max Baer, and Benny Leonard attended the festivities.

To The Pennant

On July 6, the Cubs trailed the Giants by ten and a half games. But they turned it around with winning streaks of eight and eleven games, a 20-3 home stand, and four doubleheader sweeps in seven days. On July 27, they trailed the Giants by only a game.

Following a Labor Day split with Cincinnati, the Cubs trailed the Cardinals by two and a half games. The Cubs played eighteen of their last twenty-three games at Wrigley Field. But the Cardinals played their last thirty at home. The Cubs needed a mighty push to keep up with, let alone catch, St. Louis. They got more than a push. The Cubs reeled off twenty-one straight wins from September 4 to 27—the greatest stretch drive in major league history. They won eighteen in a row at home, outscoring their opponents 126-45. The Cubs took over first place on September 14 and clinched the pennant in St. Louis on September 27.

The remarkable streak galvanized Cub fans. About 7,000 a game witnessed the first seven home dates of the streak. The average ballooned to 33,000 for the last seven home dates.

World Series

A surprise pennant meant the Cubs couldn't conduct an organized, mail-in ticket lottery like those in 1929 and 1932. While the team reserved a small number of tickets for "regular" fans, they sold most box and grandstand seats on a first-come basis, the first time that happened in World Series history.

On the night of September 30, fans huddled outside the park. The *Chicago Herald-Examiner* set the scene:

Ten thousand rabid Cub fans camped out at Wrigley Field last night in a line blocks long to be on hand for the opening world series ticket sales . . . All around the ball park was the appearance of a gigantic bazaar as vendors offered everything from ancient overcoats—5 cents for the night—to old newspapers that would keep out the chill from the patient waiters. Scores of Cub supporters had built themselves rude shelters of canvas, paper or boards, but many were content to stretch out on the hard sidewalk.[30]

Scalpers also studded the lines. Many not only bought tickets once, but bribed ushers or police officers to run to the front of the line again and again. Fans a block away never realized the scam. All 37,000 tickets for Games Three, Four, and Five vanished by noon. Thousands went home disappointed, relegated to scalping seats they waited hours for or waiting in line again to purchase bleacher seats the day of the game. A couple days later, the police suspended six officers and the Cubs fired two ticket sellers who allegedly sold up to 100 tickets to scalpers.

The odds makers made the veteran Tigers a 7-10 favorite, perhaps because only three Cubs—Charlie Root, Gabby Hartnett, and Woody English—remained from the 1929 World Series team. The teams split the first two games in Detroit. Lon Warneke four-hit the Tigers and Frank Demaree homered in the 3-0 opening victory. Charlie Root failed to retire a batter in Game Two and the Tigers won easily, 8-3. Even so, Hank Greenberg, the American League's Most Valuable Player, broke his ankle in the seventh inning. Splitting two in Detroit and the loss of Greenberg buoyed Cub fans as the teams headed to Chicago for the next three games.

GAME THREE; FRIDAY, OCTOBER 4; 47 DEGREES, 45,532 PAID

By midnight 5,000 fans stood in line for the 12,000 bleacher seats that went on sale the morning of the game. Capitalism also flourished. According to the *Chicago Daily Times*:

Several hundred youngsters grabbed places in line, frankly for the purpose of selling out. The market at just before dawn was $5 bid and $10 asked. Ordinary dime sandwiches went for fifty cents and coffee was 25 cents a cup. Crates and boxes for sitting purposes brought peddlers as high as $2. Several young Negro entertainers from the south side collected a horde of nickels and dimes by their songs and tap dancing.[31]

More than 460 police patrolled in and around Wrigley Field. The officers kept fans off the rooftops on Waveland and Sheffield Avenues, claiming they posed a physical hazard. Actually, rooftop watchers had never been a problem. The real reason was to limit the already high stench of the scalping scandal, keeping building owners from selling roof spots to the highest bidders.

Sting operations outside the park arrested scalpers with up to $5,000 in fines under a new state law. But the scalping scandal created a backlash, leaving unsold seats in the temporary bleachers on Waveland and Sheffield Avenues.

The press box, however, filled to capacity and half of the 408 writers occupied an overflow section in the upper deck. The press wrote about the Cubs breaking tradition by raising their 1935 pennant up the center field flagpole in a pregame ceremony, not waiting until the following season. Tradition also ended when Armin Hand's band played the National Anthem that day. It marked the first time since 1893 that a non-military band other than Jack Bramhall's performed at a Cubs home game.

Frank Demaree homered and the Cubs took a 3-1 lead into the eighth inning. But Bill Lee and Lon Warneke faltered and the Tigers went ahead, 5-3. Three singles and an Augie Galan sacrifice fly scored two runs in the ninth, sending the game into extra innings. The Tigers won it in the eleventh on two singles either side of an error by third baseman Fred Lindstrom.

The real fireworks occurred in the sixth inning when umpire George Moriarty tossed manager Grimm, Woody English, and Tuck Stainback for arguing a call at second base. The bad blood actually began in the opener when Moriarty threatened to clear the Cub bench after players allegedly hurled anti-Semitic remarks at Hank Greenberg. The ugly encounters stained the rest of the series and psychologically took the Cubs out of their game, costing them in a close series.

Game Four; Saturday, October 5; 45 degrees; 49,350

With the score tied at 1-1 in the sixth inning, errors by Augie Galan and Billy Jurges gave the Tigers the lead for good. Gabby Hartnett's home run in the second inning produced the Cubs' only run in a 2-1 loss. The Cubs fell behind in the Series, three games to one.

Game Five; Sunday, October 6; 45 degrees; 49,237

The Cubs salvaged Game Five, 3-1. Billy Herman doubled and tripled, and Chuck Klein homered off Schoolboy Rowe. The first three Tigers singled in the ninth inning but Detroit scored only once as Bill Lee squelched the rally. It was Lon Warneke's second win of the series and the Cubs' first World Series victory at Wrigley Field after six losses.

Action during the third inning of Game Three of the 1935 World Series. Notice the temporary bleachers on Waveland Avenue and the distance markers on the outfield walls: 364 feet in front of the left field bleachers and 440 feet under the scoreboard. The markers first appeared this year. (Chicago History Museum, SDN-078094)

The teams headed to Detroit for Game Six. In the ninth inning, a seeing-eye single, a ground out, and a bloop single by Goose Goslin gave the Tigers a 4-3 win. It was Detroit's first World Championship, rendering the twenty-one game streak little more than a forgotten bit of trivia.

Quote of 1935

"I urge that everyone instead of paying the scalper his price remain at home and hear the game over the radio."[32]

Edward J. Geiger in the Chicago American—*October 2, 1935—prior to the 1935 World Series.*

1936

The Season by the Numbers		
87-67	.565 2nd (t) 5 games out	699,370 (9,083 average)
50-27	.649 at home	153% of NL average

Home Opener

APRIL 17; CUBS (CARLETON) VS. REDS (DERRINGER); 39 DEGREES; 10,000 PAID

Reds 12 Cubs 3—The Reds stroked eleven of their twelve hits and all their runs in the middle three innings. Ex-Cubs Kiki Cuyler and Babe Herman did much of the damage, with Herman hitting a two-run homer in the fifth inning off Tex Carleton.

Keeping with tradition, Jack Bramhall's Band performed and the Senn High School cadet corps marched with the players to center field to hoist the flag.

What's New

• In February, P. K. Wrigley announced a series of renovations designed to increase fan comfort. The two-year plan would replace 7,000 seats with larger ones (3,349 in the lower deck boxes and 3,650 grandstand seats), reducing capacity by 4,000 to 36,000. The plan also called for a scoreboard and bleacher renovation in 1937.

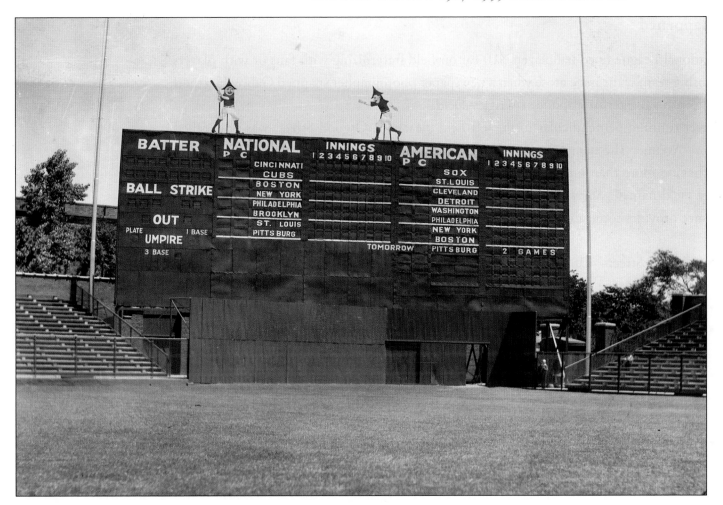

This is the last full year for the on-field scoreboard. Notice the "Doublemint Twins" atop the board. (www.ArgentaImages. com)

- The teams sold reserved tickets at 102 Western Union telegraph offices. Fans previously had three places to buy tickets: Wrigley Field, a downtown sporting goods store, and through scalpers. The new option damaged the scalping trade that thrived on limited ticket access.
- The Cubs reserved a room for baseball writers. The space included a table and lockers, like a mini clubhouse.
- Hal Berger re-created home games at 7:00 P.M. on radio station WIND. Berger attended each game and this perspective differed from re-creation broadcasters who only received play-by-play on a ticker tape. The Cubs hoped Berger's first-hand viewing added accuracy to the replay.

What Happened

- The National League fined ballplayers $10 for on-field fraternizing with fans or with players of opposing teams. The issue arose when a newspaper photographer snapped Gabby Hartnett chatting with gangster Al Capone at Wrigley Field.
- The street running perpendicular to the left field bleachers, Osgood Street, was now called Kenmore Avenue. The name change here and throughout the city ended the confusion of streets having more than one name. For who or what were the streets and avenues around Wrigley Field named? *Streetwise Chicago: A History of Chicago Street Names* by Hayner and McNamee provides some answers:

  - Addison Street—Dr. Thomas Addison, a London doctor who first described diseases of the endocrine gland
  - Clark Street—George Rogers Clark, the Revolutionary War hero
  - Kenmore Avenue—Kenmore, the home of Colonel Fielding Lewis and his wife Betty, George Washington's sister
  - Seminary Avenue—It was not named after the Lutheran Seminary that stood on the land before Wrigley Field, but rather, McCormick Theological Seminary located twelve blocks south of the ballpark
  - Sheffield Avenue—Joseph Sheffield, a farmer, land speculator, and founder of the Chicago, Rock Island and Pacific Railroad
  - Waveland Avenue—Joseph Sheffield named the street because its easternmost end was frequently submerged by Lake Michigan

Games of the Year

June 12—The Cubs won fifteen straight in June, including ten in a row at home. One was a 17-1 collaring of the Boston Bees. (The Boston Braves were nicknamed the Bees from 1936-1940.) Catcher Ken O'Dea had four hits. Both Phil Cavarretta and Tex Carleton homered in front of 22,000 Ladies Day fans.

August 28—The Cubs occupied first place from July 13-August 4. They recaptured the top spot again a week later but faltered soon after. Today, the Cubs ripped the Bees, 18-3 behind five hits by Frank Demaree. It was their sixth straight win, and they trailed the Giants by only three games.

August 30— The New Yorkers arrived for four games. Chicagoans fans dreamed of a series sweep and a return to first place. Instead, the Giants grabbed the first two in a doubleheader (6-1 and 8-6) sweep to open a five-game lead. Over 47,400 were there that day and management closed the park ninety minutes before game time. With bleacher expansion on the horizon, the overflow throng marked the last field crowd in Wrigley Field history.

Quote of 1936

"Baseball magnates could win wide favor from the fans by shutting off the sale of tickets on days when the seating capacity of the park is reached. Overflow crowds, such as the Cubs enjoyed Memorial day [sic] are in bad taste in a sport which is utterly dependent upon the good will of its customers."[33]

Arch Ward in the Chicago Tribune—*June 3, 1936*

1937

The Season by the Numbers		
93-61	.604 2nd 3 games out	895,020 (11,624 average)
46-32	.590 at home	189% of NL average

Home Opener

APRIL 20; CUBS (FRENCH) VS. PIRATES (BLANTON); CLOUDY, 54 DEGREES; 18,940 PAID

Pirates 5 Cubs 0—Cy Blanton held the Cubs to five singles, including two each by Augie Galan and Stan Hack. The game took only 1:33 to play, the quickest opener in Wrigley Field history.

Jack Bramhall's Band and the Senn High School ROTC led the players in a pregame march to the center field flagpole. Mayor Ed Kelly tossed the first pitch from his box seat.

What's New

• The Cubs sported new home uniforms; they included white shirts with a blue line running along each side of the zipper and a blue stripe down the outside of the pants. Most important was the return of the famous "C" surrounding "ubs" emblem. The storied logo has appeared on the home uniforms in some form every year since.

- A new backstop net measured 180-feet by 201-feet and weighed 1,000 pounds. It consisted of nearly forty-five miles of thread.
- The writers got a restaurant and restroom for the press box. The team selected the waitress for the parlor through a beauty contest.
- Wrigley and the Cubs made good on last year's promise to renovate the bleachers. The old field-level bleachers, both the full bleachers in right field and the small "jury box" in left field, were twenty-four years old. They were modest, one area of the ballpark that didn't live up to the team's hype as an up-to-date, comfortable venue.

The team hired Holabird & Root to design the renovation. Reconstruction preparation began on July 9. First, the old bleachers came down. Then, a temporary plywood wall went up between the playing field and the construction site (but because of safety and aesthetics,

Work begins; July 9, 1937
(www.ArgentaImages.com)

A temporary wall and the severed scoreboard; July 14. (www. Argentaimages.com)

construction workers finished thirty minutes before game time). Finally, one-third of the scoreboard, the portion displaying the American League scores, was cut from the scoreboard and discarded. The remaining two-thirds, the portion that displayed the batter, pitch count, umpires, and National League scores, was moved toward the left field line and used temporarily until the new scoreboard on top of the bleachers was operational.

The new left field bleachers opened on September 5. The upper center field bleachers opened on September 18. The next day, fans sat in the entire bleachers. The giant new scoreboard, built above the bleachers, became operable on October 1.

Bleacher facts:

- Cost $200,000
- Held 2,000 more seats than the old bleachers
- Bleacher benches made of cypress

Building the left field bleachers; August 2.
(www.ArgentaImages.com)

- Bleacher renovations changed dimensions: The left field line decreased six feet to 355 feet; center field dropped from 436 to 400 feet; right field increased from 321 to 353 feet. The dimensions haven't changed since.
- New bleachers made famous the "catwalks" (the walkway exit ramps down the left and right field lines), the "wells" (the areas where the bleacher wall curves), and the "wagon gates" (the six gates along the outfield walls).

Scoreboard facts:

- Cost $100,000
- Measures 27 feet by 75 feet; from 6 to 8 feet deep; three levels high
- Flagpole is forty feet above the scoreboard.
- Metal numbers and letters are 14.5 inches by 9.5 inches and weigh five pounds.
- First scoreboard to use yellow numbers to indicate an inning was still in progress.

The bleacher wall goes up; August 18.
(www.ArgentaImages.com)

- First scoreboard to use magnetic "eyelets" instead of lights. (If you sit nearby you can hear the eyelets "click" when numbers change.)
- Magnetic ball and strike numbers are 2.5 feet by 1.5 feet.
- One to four men work in it (depends on the number of games).
- Scores obtained by ticker-tape (computer since 2006)
- There is no toilet. Workers use a funnel connected to a pipe.
- It gets hot, cold, or wet inside depending on the weather.

Ed Burns, writing in *The Sporting News,* called the new scoreboard "the most elaborate and ingenious equipment of the kind in the country."[34]

According to Bill Veeck in his book, *Veeck as in Wreck,* inspiration for the new bleachers came from P. K. Wrigley. The Cub owner wanted an outdoorsy atmosphere to match his ads—Wrigley Field as a healthful diversion. Veeck claimed he suggested that P. K. Wrigley plant trees

The left and center field bleachers open; September 5. (www.ArgentaImages.com)

outside the bleachers, that would, over time, become a visible part of the scene. Instead, Wrigley wanted them planted in the park. And he got them—eight Chinese Elms, four to a side, planted on terraced steps to the top of the bleachers. The trees never took and were removed after the 1942 season. The treeless stair step remained, and over the years made good places to sit and watch the game.

Veeck claimed a liking to the vines at Perry Stadium, a minor league park in Indianapolis. The anecdote from his book about planting the ivy the night before the last home series of the season to fulfill a personal request from P. K. Wrigley, is a typically embellished Veeck tale. As his story goes, he and groundskeeper Bobby Dorr planted the first vines under the candescence of a string of light bulbs the night before the season's final series. That would be the night of September 30 or the early morning hours of October 1. But the above photo, taken by George Brace, is dated September 3. In addition, photos in the *Chicago Herald and Examiner* on September 8 and 9 clearly show vines crawling up the new outfield walls.

Grounds crew plants the ivy; September 3.
(www.ArgentaImages.com)

Initially, the grounds crew planted bittersweet ivy plants to climb up the outfield walls. Within the next two years, they planted 500 more bittersweet and Boston ivy sprigs. The latter took over and predominates along the walls today.

In order to secure the fledgling vines to the new brick wall, Bobby Dorr strung five pieces of copper wire a foot and a half apart up from the bottom. Since the outfield wall is 1,103 feet long, he used nearly a mile of wire.

The bleacher renovation stunned nearly everyone. The update turned a sturdy ballpark into the most attractive in baseball. A writer for the *Los Angeles Times* saw the bleacher renovation as an effort to "make the park the most symmetrically beautiful in the major leagues."[35] The Art Deco sweep to the bleachers, flowing from its ends to the top of the scoreboard, made it one of the few seating arrangements in sports that looked as beautiful empty as full of fans.

The full bleachers open. The old scoreboard is at the far left; September 21. (www. ArgentaImages.com)

In fact, the Wrigley Field bleacher renovation was the greatest ballpark remodeling job in the history of the sport. Almost seventy-five years later, seats in these same Wrigley Field bleachers are among the best-loved in baseball.

What Happened

• Beginning in 1934, the team gave radio stations free access to broadcast Cubs home games as long as the station advertised each game at least five times prior to airing.

    This year, stations paid a collective $45,000 to broadcast Cubs home games. P. K. Wrigley, still sharper than most owners on the benefit of radio, put this income back into advertising, including sponsorships of baseball pregame shows. The five stations that broadcast from Wrigley Field this year (and their announcers):

WCFL	Hal Totten
WBBM	Pat Flanagan
WGN	Bob Elson
WIND	Russ Hodges
WJJD	John Harrington

- When the bleacher reconstruction began on July 9, the Cubs owned a two game lead over the Giants. It was P. K. Wrigley's intention to finish the new bleachers on October 1, in time for the World Series. When the Cubs built a six and a half game lead on August 12, it looked like Wrigley might get his wish. But the Giants went 13-4 the rest of the month and the Cubs only 8-10. They passed the Cubs on September 2 and took the pennant.

Games of the Year

June 25—Augie Galan became the first National Leaguer to homer from both sides of the plate in an 11-2 chomping of the Dodgers.

August 6—Boston's Roy Johnson and Rabbit Warstler led off the game with back-to-back home runs. That never happened before in modern major league history.

Bear News

Professional football arrived as a big-time sport in Chicago on November 7. The defending champion Packers faced the undefeated Bears before 44,977 fans, marking the first time since Red Grange's 1925 debut that the Bears filled Wrigley Field beyond capacity. The Packers handed the Bears their only regular-season loss, 24-14, but the attendance topped the park record, set just two weeks earlier against the Lions.

The Bears and Cardinals met at Wrigley Field on December 5. It was so cold, a handful of the 7,313 fans built bonfires in the stands. With less than three minutes to play and the Bears ahead, the Cardinals scored on a 95-yard pass. Immediately after, the officials called the game on account of darkness and awarded the Cardinals the extra point without trying. The Bears won, 42-28, the most points scored to date in an NFL game.

The Bears hosted the Redskins for the NFL title on December 12. Workers spent two days thawing the field with kerosene torches. But a game time temperature of 15 degrees wrecked the effort. Players needed basketball shoes to keep their footing and only 16,000 die-hards braved the elements. The Bears lead 21-14 in the fourth quarter, but rookie quarterback Sammy Baugh tossed two Redskin touchdowns to win, 28-21. Washington won its first NFL title.

Quote of 1937

"Many commentators . . . have been libeling Wrigley field [*sic*] since midsummer, when workmen threw up a big pasteboard fence in left field and announced the move was the first in the construction of new bleachers.

None too willing to visualize the eventual permanent structure, perhaps, the aforesaid commentators and many others made a lot of cracks about 'elimination of the outfield,' the 'Cubs' pill box,' etc., etc. This erstwhile scoffer now is prepared to . . . emboss an apologetic scroll to P.K. Wrigley, owner of the most artistic ball park in the majors."[36]

Edward Burns in the Chicago Tribune—*September 12, 1937*

1938

The Season by the Numbers		
89-63	.586 1st 2 games ahead	951,640 (12,359 average)
44-33	.571 at home	185% of NL average

Home Opener

APRIL 22; CUBS (LEE) VS. CARDINALS (WARNEKE); 44 DEGREES; 15,669 PAID

Cardinals 6 Cubs 5—St. Louis scored four runs in the ninth inning to clip the Cubs. The big blow was a Jim Bucher single that rookie left fielder Coaker Triplett misplayed into a bases-clearing error. Joe Marty drove in four of the Cub runs; he homered in the second inning and tripled to right with the bases loaded in the third.

Every Opening Day since the Cubs moved to Wrigley Field, Jack Bramhall's Band played and a high school color guard marched with the teams to center field. There, the students raised Old Glory to the top of the flagpole. Today, Bramhall's band was there and the Lake View High School color guard accompanied the Cubs and Cardinals to center field. But instead of the students raising the flag, a grounds crew member hoisted it atop the new scoreboard.

Players and the color guard march to center field for the last time. (www. ArgentaImages.com)

In subsequent years, the flag flew above the scoreboard before Opening Day festivities began. Consequently, there was no reason for the teams and the students to march to center field. This longtime tradition ended today.

What's New

Renovations continued beyond bleacher reconstruction. Over the winter the Cubs:

- Extended the outfield brick wall around the whole park, giving Wrigley Field a more uniform, crisp look.
- Turned in and raised the left field grandstand and box seats toward home plate, providing better sight lines for nearly 3,000 fans. The seating area extended to Waveland Avenue, increasing capacity by 400.

- Added a new concession area beneath the turned-in seat section.
- Repainted the exterior and the underside of the upper deck from the traditional green to gray. The trim color inside and out changed from cream to an orange-red.
- Painted the park's famous marquee a bluish-gray. (It was originally green.)
- Added scoreboard yardarms that flew seven-foot pennants of all eight National League teams. The first four teams in the standings flew on the left side, the second four teams on the right. Warren Brown of the *Chicago Herald-Examiner* wrote that there were "so many pennants on the score-board [sic] the place looked like a wall in a freshman dormitory."[37]
- Added a twenty-four-foot crossbar to the scoreboard flagpole. On either end a light indicated to "L" riders and neighbors whether the Cubs won or lost that day. A blue light indicated a win, a white light a loss.
- Updated plumbing in both locker rooms and the umpires' room. The Cub clubhouse expanded to house an office for manager Grimm and space for trainer Andy Lotshaw.
- Added auxiliary scoreboards at the front entrance on the facing of both sides of the upper deck.

What Happened

- The Wright & Co. coal yard at 1106 Addison Street closed its doors. The 40,000 square foot plot on the northwest corner of Clark and Addison became a parking lot for 300 cars.
- John O. Seys, team Vice President and concessions chief, died of pneumonia at age sixty-four. Ray Kneip, who began as a vendor in 1906 at West Side Grounds, replaced Seys as head of concessions.
- The new bleachers poisoned the hitting background at the park. *The Sporting News* elaborated saying, "Batters are more jittery than ever at Wrigley Field . . . since the green-painted scoreboard was moved from center field to make way for new bleachers. Claim there's no background other than white and blue shirts on big days now."[38]

  Added the Giants' Bill Terry: "You couldn't have built a park more beautiful and at the same time worse as a playing field. The background is murder!"[39]
- Just before the season the Cubs made a blockbuster deal. They traded Curt Davis, Clyde Shoun, Tuck Stainback, and $185,000 to the Cardinals for pitcher Dizzy Dean. The twenty-eight-year-old Dean won 120 games between 1932 and 1936, including 30 in 1934. On paper, the Cubs became pennant favorites. Lost in the excitement of the moment, however, was Dean's shoulder trouble last season (he was only 13-10 in 1937).

Memorial Day, 1938 (National Baseball Hall of Fame Library, Cooperstown, N.Y.)

Games of the Year

June 8—The Cubs held a game and a half lead when the second-place Giants paid a visit. All tickets were sold an hour before game time. Many scaled the walls to get in, yet 25,000 were turned away. The Giants slashed the Cubs twice, 4-2 and 4-1.

After dropping a doubleheader in Cincinnati on September 3, the Cubs found themselves tied for third place, seven games behind Pittsburgh. On September 4, the Cubs beat the Reds in eleven innings. Beginning that day, the Cubs went on a 17-3-1 tear to close to within a game and a half of Pittsburgh. On September 27, the teams started a three-game "September World Series" in Wrigley Field, with the outcome providing clarity in the National League pennant race.

September 27—Dizzy Dean started for the first time in over a month and came up big, leading 2-0 going into the ninth inning. Dean gave up a run and the Pirates had the tying run on third base. Bill Lee came in and struck out Al Todd for the 2-1 win. The Cubs now trailed by only one-half game.

September 28—A back-and-forth battle had the Pirates in front, 5-3, going into the last of the eighth inning. A single by Ripper Collins, a double by Tony Lazzeri, and walks to Billy Jurges and Stan Hack got the Cubs within a run, bases loaded and no outs. Billy Herman singled, scoring Jurges but Paul Waner threw out pinch runner Joe Marty at the plate. Frank Demaree ended the rally by rapping into a double play. The teams were tied 5-5 going into the ninth inning.

It was 5:30. Darkness settled over Wrigley Field and the umpires agreed the ninth inning would be the last. If the game ended in a tie, it would be replayed as part of a doubleheader the next day. Charlie Root set the Pirates down in order and Pittsburgh's relief ace, Mace Brown, easily retired the first two Cubs: Phil Cavarretta and Carl Reynolds. That laid it on the shoulders of player-manager Gabby Hartnett. Brown snuck two knee-high fast balls past Gabby. His next offering wasn't a waste pitch and Hartnett was ready, driving it into the darkness. For those who saw it, it rifled into the back of the left field bleachers. Home Run! Teammates and fans raced onto the field. Hartnett claimed that once he reached third base his feet never touched the ground until he hit home plate. The Cubs were in first place!

September 29—The Cubs smacked the shell-shocked Pirates the next day, 10-1 for their tenth straight win. They held a game and a half lead with only four to play.

Two days later, the Cubs clinched the pennant in St. Louis. Hartnett's "homer in the gloaming" was one of the most important events in Wrigley Field history. It didn't win the pennant, but it propelled the Cubs to first place and demoralized the Pirates.

World Series

The park's normal capacity held 37,500 for baseball. The Cubs traded out the baseball box seats for the smaller football seats, increasing capacity to 40,070. Standing room left the final number of tickets at 43,660.

The team sold bleacher seats and standing room tickets the morning of each game. Art Felsch was the first one in line for a bleacher seat. The intrepid Milwaukeean spent six days and seven nights in front of the bleacher gate for a chance to see Game One.

GAME ONE, WEDNESDAY, OCTOBER 5; 62 DEGREES; 43,642 PAID

Nearly 2,000 fans already joined Flesch for bleacher seats the night before Game One. Yet, thousands of onlookers milled around the park, watching the waiters. One early bird fan said this about the gathering, "Yes, it does seem silly that we are here, but it's not as pointless as all of those folks gawking at us as though we were freaks in a side show."[40]

The swarm of overnight fans grew fivefold the next morning. They swallowed up the bleacher and standing room tickets in less than an hour. Latecomers had one additional option—apartment owners on Waveland and Sheffield Avenues sold views of the action out their windows. "Front row" seats cost up to $5.00. A spot in the residence, sometimes ten deep to the windows went for $2. One woman shoehorned fifty-seven fans into her two front rooms.

Prior to Game One, the Cubs and the Yankees made history when they both raised their pennants during the World Series. The Yankee flag went up the left field flagpole and the Cubs hoisted theirs in right field.

The Yankees scored two runs in the second inning and won, 3-1. Red Ruffing went the distance against Bill Lee.

GAME TWO, THURSDAY, OCTOBER 6; 53 DEGREES; 42,108 PAID

Fans bought 1,000 fewer standing room tickets today as an air of doom already permeated the city. Sore-armed Dizzy Dean, pitching on nothing but guile, got the Cubs into the eighth inning with a 3-2 lead. But Frank Crosetti hit a two-run homer and Joe DiMaggio matched him in the ninth. The Yankees continued their mockery of the Cubs, winning 6-3.

The teams went back to New York and the Yankees swept the final two games. The Bronx Bombers outscored the Cubs 22-9 in the series and captured their third straight World Series. As Cub pitcher Clay Bryant would later say of the Yankee dominance, "We came. We saw. And we went home."[41]

Quote of 1938

"There isn't a layout in either league to touch it for class."[42]
John Carmichael in the Chicago Daily News—*April 16, 1938—on renovated Wrigley Field*

1939

The Season by the Numbers

| 84-70 | .545 4th 13 games out | 726,663 (9,316 average) |
| 44-34 | .564 at home | 128% of NL average |

Opening Day/Home Opener

APRIL 24; CUBS (WHITEHILL) VS. PIRATES (TOBIN); 80 DEGREES; 15,844 PAID

Cubs 6 Pirates 2—Rain cancelled the first three home games against the Reds. The Cubs went to St. Louis and then returned home to play the Pirates. Forty-year-old Earl Whitehill, a sixteen-year American League veteran, tossed seven strong innings for his 215th career win.

The fourth try at the home opener produced neither pomp nor circumstance—no politicians, bands, or ceremonies. The 1938 pennant flew from the left field flagpole and the centennial baseball flag from the right field pole.

What's New

- Bill Veeck designed a $25,000 concession area on the concourse behind home plate. The new stand utilized ultra-modern materials: Formica, stainless steel, and fluorescent lighting. At eighty-five feet long, it was more than twice as long as its predecessor.
- The media lounge adjacent to the press box, dubbed "The Pink Poodle," opened for business.[43] Sportswriter Irving Vaughan gave it the catchy name because of its colorful motif.
- Screens to limit fan interference were added atop the outfield walls in front of the left and right field catwalks. Balls hitting the screen were in play. But umpires struggled to determine whether fly balls hit the screens or went beyond them and bounced back onto the field. A new ground rule, adopted on July 1, called balls that hit the screen a home run. Unfortunately, the change didn't end discrepancies, it made them worse. Umpires now had to judge whether a ball hit the screen or the wall below it. By opening day in 1940, the ground rule was changed back to the original ruling—off the screen equaled in play.

The problem continued for decades. Finally, in 1977, the team replaced the screens with green-painted plywood, ending the confusion.

Bill Veeck's new concession stand.
(www.ArgentaImages.com)

By August, more screens appeared at the park, this time to the field side of the foul poles. The new screens aided umpires in determining whether balls hit near the poles were fair or foul. A ball off the screen was a home run.

What Happened

- On August 14, the White Sox hosted their first night game at Comiskey Park. Over 35,000 fans, including Bill Veeck and Cub general manager Boots Weber, saw the Sox beat the Browns under the $140,000 lighting system. The White Sox became the sixth team and the fourth this year to inaugurate night baseball.

  Night games were immensely popular at Comiskey Park. During the Chicago City Series in October, for example, the first game at Comiskey, a night contest, drew almost 43,000 fans. The game the following afternoon attracted around 6,000.

What was P. K. Wrigley's take on after-dark baseball? "Where, when and if the public wants night games it will have night games."[44]

• A recent survey said 25 percent of fans attending Cubs games were women, an impressive number for the times.

Game of the Year

August 1—The Cubs beat the Phillies, 6-2. More important, Bill Nicholson hit his first major league home run, a solo shot off Bill Kerksieck.

Quote of 1939

"Beautiful in eyes of artist, horrible as viewed by baseballer. Dainty ivy growing along the buff brick wall is not enough protection from concussion. And insurance rates on N.L.'ers will increase as soon as companies get wise to the batting background."[45]

Hy Turkin in The Sporting News—*June 1, 1939—in his review of Wrigley Field*

THIRD INNING
1940-1949
STANDING STILL

This inning saw fewer changes at Wrigley Field than any other, in part because of World War II and the government's rationing of physical materials. The story of P. K. Wrigley donating lights intended for Wrigley Field to the war effort after the Pearl Harbor attack is true. It's also emblematic of the times.

Unlike World War I, the home front fully engaged in this war, baseball included. Gone were the incessant marching and calisthenics demonstrations. There was no need to convince anyone of the necessity of war or the part baseball would play in it.

The war permeated everything in the game: From the loss of players into the armed forces, to military fundraisers, and to rationing days at the ballpark. Baseball provided a diversion. Escaping the war, even for a few hours at the park, however, was impossible.

Wartime attendance improved at almost every National League park except at Wrigley Field. The great Cubs teams of the 1930s brought out fans, relative to the rest of the league, even during tough times. But the Cubs of the early forties couldn't compare to the teams of the thirties. The double play combination of Stringer and Sturgeon, for example, didn't have the ring of Herman and Jurges. The battery of Bithorn and McCullough didn't have the zing of Root and Hartnett.

In 1945, the Cubs captured their last National League pennant. It was unforeseen. The military draft took fewer Cubs than most teams. They finished three games ahead of the Cardinals who played the season without Stan Musial, Enos Slaughter, and Terry Moore.

Major League attendance skyrocketed in 1946 as Americans celebrated their hard-won victory. The 1946 Cubs recorded their highest attendance figure since 1930. After that, the team reverted to mediocrity, even finishing last in the standings for consecutive years in 1948 and 1949—the first time in franchise history.

How few changes occurred at Wrigley Field? The hitting background received more deliberations than any other portion of the park. During the decade, management temporarily closed off the center field bleachers, painted the bleachers and the scoreboard different colors on two occasions, hung a semitransparent blue screen to aid visibility, and finally, constructed a canopy to uniformly darken the area. As the standings attested, these improvements probably helped opponents at least as much as the North Siders.

1940

The Season by the Numbers

| 75-79 | .487 5th 25.5 games out | 534,878 (6,945 average) |
| 40-37 | .519 at home | 97% of NL average |

Home Opener

April 19; Cubs (French) vs. Cardinals (Cooper); cloudy, 43 degrees; 9,029 paid

Cubs 5 Cardinals 0—Larry French scattered six hits for the shutout. He also drove in a run in the second inning with a double. Rookie shortstop Bob Sturgeon committed two errors but stroked three hits. Umpire Ziggy Sears tossed manager Gabby Hartnett for arguing a ball/strike call in the eighth.

Jack Bramhall's Band entertained at its forty-eighth Cubs opener.

What's New

- Padding was added along the box seat wall near the right field corner.
- After a fourth place finish, P. K. Wrigley wanted to get closer to his team. They renovated an office for Mr. Wrigley, "a stream-lined suite featuring glass brick exterior."[1]
- The Cubs unveiled new vestlike home uniforms, the major's first.

What Happened

- The Polo Grounds in New York, Sportsman's Park in St. Louis, and Pittsburgh's Forbes Field installed lights. The addition of the Giants, Browns, Cardinals, and Pirates meant that a majority of major league teams (ten of sixteen) hosted night games.

    Attendance at night games continued strong. The White Sox's seven home night games averaged 32,000 fans, almost four times their daytime average. The St. Louis Browns attracted over 55,000 fans to their first four night games. In contrast, their 1939 attendance totaled just slightly more than 100,000.
- The team celebrated Pat Pieper's twenty-fifth year as the Wrigley Field public address announcer. (It was his twenty-fifth year working at Wrigley Field. As documented in 1917, it was only his twenty-fourth year as public address announcer.) Between games on September 22, he received platitudes from the fans and a travel bag from the team.

Jack Bramhall (www. ArgentaImages.com)

Game of the Year

July 19—Beanballs and a boxing match highlighted a Ladies Day drubbing of the Dodgers. After the Cubs built an eight run lead, Dodger pitcher Hugh Casey drilled Claude Passeau in the back. Passeau threw his bat at Casey and the two raced toward each other. Brooklyn's Joe Gallagher jumped Passeau. Stan Hack punched Gallagher, bloodying his face. When the umpires and police restored order, both Passeau and Gallagher were ejected. The ladies, no doubt, saw more than they expected in the 11-4 Cubs win.

Bear News

The Chicago Cardinals moved back to Comiskey Park after a decade at Wrigley Field. The underachieving Redbirds moved north in 1931 to share in the Bears' popularity. But not only did North Side fans not take to the team, many on the South Side refused to follow them to Wrigley Field. The move back south allowed the Cardinals to play home night games. In fact, the team opened the home season at night against the Bears. The Cardinals not only won, but drew 23,181, over 7,000 more than their 1939 home game with the Bears.

On November 3, a record 45,434 saw the Bears edge the Packers, 14-7. The Bears eventually played in the NFL final against the Redskins in Washington, where the Skins beat the Bears, 7-3, just a few weeks earlier. What happened defied logic; the Bears destroyed Washington, 73-0, in the most lopsided NFL game ever.

Quote of 1940

"Philip K. Wrigley, owner of the Chicago Cubs and the Los Angeles Angels may have learned that money cannot buy the best ball players in the land. However, he has proven that the same kind of heavy currency, plus high-class, artistic, ingenious, and at times, slightly revolutionary ideas can provide and maintain beautiful, comfortable and clean ball parks."[2]

J. G. Taylor Spink in The Sporting News—*August 1, 1940*

1941

The Season by the Numbers		
70-84	.455 6th 30 games out	545,159 (7,034 average)
38-39	.494 at home	90% of NL average

Opening Day

APRIL 15; CUBS (PASSEAU) VS. PIRATES (KLINGER); 66 DEGREES; 17,008 PAID

Cubs 7 Pirates 4—It wasn't an auspicious start. The game's first batter, Frank Gustine, lined a shot off Claude Passeau's leg. Passeau lay sprawled out on the ground and then hobbled around for a few minutes more. But he stayed in and went the distance. Bill Nicholson's three-run home run in the third inning provided the difference.

Cub fan W. T. Lillibridge attended his fortieth consecutive home opener.

For the first time in forty-nine years, Jack Bramhall's Band did not play at a Cub opener. Instead, a modern swing band entertained from the top of the center field bleachers.

What's New

- Charles Taubman, the only scoreboard operator in park history, died during the off-season. Taubman operated the Cubs' and White Sox' scoreboards for the last forty-six years. He claimed to have seen over 6,200 baseball games, more than anyone to that point. Al Balder replaced him.
- Wrigley Field improved its concessions, offering Virginia jumbo peanuts and South American popcorn. It also added a concession stand at the back of the grandstand behind home plate and portable carts that brought hamburgers to fans in their seats.
- Wrigley Field vendors wore all-white uniforms.
- Sometime between July 4 and August 5, the clock appeared atop the scoreboard. The ten-foot diameter, one-ton timepiece was originally green on white. It became white on green when the whole scoreboard was repainted before the 1944 season.
- On April 26, the Cubs provided organ music for the first time in major league history. Organist Roy Nelson played behind the screen in back of home plate. He had to finish a half-hour before game time so radio broadcasts wouldn't pick up restricted ASCAP songs. He played again the following day. Then the team went on a long road trip. Nelson planned to play only nonrestricted songs when the team returned, so he could entertain fans throughout the whole game. He never got the chance. The organ was gone when the Cubs came home on May 13 and didn't return. The team, it seemed, refused to oppose the musicians' union.

Still, the *Sporting News* said this about the short-term musical experiment: "What joy! A cushioned seat in a beautiful ball park [*sic*], delicious hamburgers with onions, a can of beer, victory and the

Popcorn poppers display their wares. (www. ArgentaImages.com)

Scoreboard with the new clock, August 5, 1941. (www.ArgentaImages.com)

restful, dulcet notes of a pipe organ. Baseball, indeed, has moved upward and onward since Abner Doubleday was a resident of Cooperstown!"[3]

The Opening Day swing band and the organ music were part of the plan to "loosen up" Wrigley Field after attendance dropped 200,000 between 1939 and 1940. The team also lifted a ban on pregame gift presentations to players.

What Happened

- Cubs batters still complained about the lack of a hitting background at Wrigley Field. The local media called it a convenient alibi for the team's lack of offensive punch. The press had a field day, blaming losses on a half dozen light-shirted bleacher fans or the vendors' new white uniforms. But an ironic ally spoke up after the Giants' Cliff Melton beaned Hank Lieber. On June 25, the *New York Daily News* sent the following letter to P. K. Wrigley:

Hank Lieber is going to recover from that beaning by Cliff Melton on Tuesday. That's the good news. Good news for his fans and the other players in the league. And, Mr. Wrigley, it is good news for you. It means that you are still lucky-lucky that a ball player hasn't been killed because of the poor batting background at your ball field. . . .How about installing a 20-foot dark green screen over those bleachers—before you have a real tragedy on your hands?[4]

After a recent streak where the Cubs scored only fourteen runs in eight games, general manager Jim Gallagher gathered pitchers with varying deliveries and white-shirted bleacher-ites to analyze the complaints first-hand. After the experiment, on July 1, Gallagher ordered three sections (2,000 seats) of the lower center field bleachers blocked off to fans. He also ordered the seats repainted dark green. Bleacher fans didn't sit in the area for the rest of the regular season, but took over the seats during the City Series games in October.

- Charlie Root closed out his sixteen-year career with the Cubs. On August 10, the team gave him his day. They presented him with a $2,200 check, a blanket with sixteen stars, a desk clock, and a pig. Cub fans gave him a station wagon while Chicago sportscasters presented him with a fishing rod. Even the White Sox gave him $50 in gas coupons. Charlie pitched and lost the game, 3-1 to Johnny Vander Meer and the Reds.

Root ended his career with 201 wins, still a team record. His playing career spanned three eras: he played in spring training with the 1925 team that finish in last place, he starred through the pennant years of 1929-1938, and finally, finished up with a team again mired in the second division. At forty-two years old, he was the oldest player in the majors and the last still playing who was born before 1900.

War Happenings

The war in Europe began to affect life in America and at Wrigley Field.

- Servicemen saw Cub games for free on Sundays, making the Cubs the first major league team to allow free admission to the armed forces.
- At 4 P.M. on July 4, the team halted their doubleheader with the Cardinals to allow the park's public address system to carry President Roosevelt's speech criticizing non-interventionists. Play resumed at the speech's conclusion.
- On July 22, women who brought a piece of aluminum to Wrigley Field received free admission.
- P. K. Wrigley purchased materials for an $185,000 lighting system for night baseball at Wrigley Field. The order included 165 tons of steel, 35,000 feet of copper wire, and 800

aluminum reflectors. Plans called for four light standards on top of the upper deck and two in the outfield. Just as the materials arrived at the park, Japan attacked Pearl Harbor on December 7 and brought the United States into World War II. Shortly after, Wrigley donated all the materials to the war effort, temporarily ending any thought of lights at Wrigley Field.

Game of the Year

May 19—The Cubs brought their bats in a 14-1 clubbing of the Dodgers. Of the Cubs fourteen hits, Phil Cavarretta stroked two doubles, Bill Nicholson homered, and Claude Passeau hit a grand slam in the nine-run second inning. Passeau went the distance, scattering four hits.

The Bears' John Siegal (6) slipped through the Giants' defense. (www.ArgentaImages.com)

Bear News

On December 14, in 16 degree weather, 43,000 fans saw the Bears and Packers play a division playoff at Wrigley Field. Oddly, one week later, only 13,341 turned out on a warm day to see the Bears rout the New York Giants 37-9 to win their second consecutive NFL title. Perhaps the ramifications of Pearl Harbor, on December 7, had finally sunk in. Perhaps the outcome of the Giants game was a foregone conclusion. Or perhaps the Bears' rivals, the Green Bay Packers, were the "real" championship opponents.

Quote of 1941

"The majority of parks in the major leagues are rather dismal places, badly in need of paint and repair. Wrigley Field, in Chicago, like Briggs Stadium [in Detroit], is an exception."[5]
  J.G. Taylor Spink in The Sporting News—*July 3, 1941*

1942

The Season by the Numbers		
68-86	.442 6th 38 games out	590,972 (7,625 average)
36-41	.468 at home	110% of NL average

Home Opener

APRIL 17; CUBS (LEE) VS. REDS (VANDER MEER); SUNNY, 51 DEGREES; 10,149 PAID

Cubs 3 Reds 2—The Reds outhit the Cubs, 10-5. But in the decisive seventh inning, the Cubs scored the tying and winning runs on a bases-loaded walk to Phil Cavarretta and a sacrifice fly by Lou Novikoff.

Over 400 sailors marched on the field. A naval band and Bob Strong's Band played in pregame ceremonies. After a speech by Mayor Kelly, the Cubs received a "Minute Man" flag for their efforts in purchasing Defense Bonds. Every Cub employee, from P. K. Wrigley to the groundskeepers, signed up to support the war effort.

The sunny weather sent many fans to the bleachers. Just before game time, management opened the blocked-off area to accommodate the rush. The area remained open the rest of the year, ending the half-season experiment to secure a hitting background.

What's New

The team installed a new public address system.

War Happenings

- Unlike during World War I, President Roosevelt endorsed baseball as a national morale booster. He suggested an increase in the number of night games to accommodate war workers. Accordingly, Commissioner Landis doubled the maximum number of night games per park from seven to fourteen. The Washington Senators were the exception; they could host up to twenty-one games because of the large number of war workers in the city.

    Without lights of their own, Cub general manager Jim Gallagher announced his desire to play night games at Comiskey Park. But the White Sox squelched the idea. They felt the additional night games would over-saturate demand. The Cubs had no leverage in the matter, and they capitulated. On February 12, the teams issued a joint statement claiming that both teams playing night games in one ballpark would hurt their rivalry.

    The following month, P. K. Wrigley hinted that the Cubs might construct a temporary lighting system for Wrigley Field. In an interview with the *Chicago Tribune,* Wrigley said that "eight 120 foot [wooden] poles are on their way from Oregon now, for use in the outfield."[6] He said that lights on the exterior of the Wrigley Building downtown were available as well as transformers once used in a casino on Wrigley's Catalina Island. Wrigley went so far as to get a building permit for the lighting system but he reiterated that he'd only go through with it if Cubs fans wanted to attend night games.

    In April, the team mailed questionnaires asking fans their preferences about game times. After compiling the results, the team dropped the idea of twilight or night games at Wrigley Field.

- Fans sang the "Star Spangled Banner" before each game. The song's lyrics appeared on the inside of the scorecard.

- Fans entering the pass gate were required to buy twenty-five cent war bonds. The team sold war bonds at the park and this year's scorecard cover urged fans to purchase them.

- The Cubs distributed at least 500 free tickets each game to area servicemen. According to the *Chicago Cubs News,* they also encouraged fans to donate foul balls to the armed forces. The team matched the fans' contribution, and by August, sent out more than 100 dozen baseballs.

    The team installed chain-link fencing behind the left and right field catwalks to keep home run balls off Waveland and Sheffield Avenues and into the hands of servicemen.

- All major league teams donated one game's receipts to Army and Navy relief funds. On May 27, the Cubs-Reds game followed a contest between Great Lakes Naval Station and Camp Grant. Over 10,000 fans contributed $10,400 to the funds. Even the players and umpires paid to get in.
- On September 1, women entered the park for free with two pounds of donated scrap metal. The team collected over 10,000 lbs. of brass, copper, and iron from things like baby carriages, sewing machines, and hand tools.
- The team donated 8,000 lbs. of rubber from the mats that covered the runways leading to the box seat sections. Made from old tire casings, the mats had been used at Wrigley Field since 1939.
- On September 2, an induction ceremony for the Army Cadets included Bob Wilson, son of Cub manager Jim Wilson. The war touched the team in a very big way when the younger Wilson died in action in December 1944.
- The Code of Wartime Practices for American Broadcasting forbade baseball radio announcers to mention the weather during games. Officials thought weather knowledge could theoretically benefit the enemy.

What Else Happened

- Negro League teams played at Wrigley Field for the first time. Blacks played at Comiskey Park because of its proximity to African-American neighborhoods on the South Side. But one wonders if the games at Wrigley Field this year were a "trial" for the inevitable integration of baseball.

  On May 24, Satchel Paige's Kansas City Monarchs met Dizzy Dean's All-Stars—a team of former major leaguers now in the service. The latter's best-known players included Zeke Bonura and Cecil Travis. Nearly 30,000 saw Paige stifle the All-Stars, 3-1.

  On June 21, almost 7,000 fans watched the Cincinnati Ethiopian Clowns, the Harlem Globetrotters of black baseball, play the House of David team and the Chicago Brown Bombers in a doubleheader.

  On July 31, nearly 18,000 fans celebrated Satchel Paige Day. Before he went out and tossed a complete game victory over Memphis, Paige received a gold watch, a bathrobe, a travel bag, a radio, and a new suit.

  The Negro Leagues scheduled Game 4 of their World Series between Kansas City and the Homestead Grays at Wrigley Field. Cold and wet weather canceled the game and they moved it to Philadelphia instead.

After the May 24 contest, Fay Young wrote this in the *Chicago Defender*:

It was a great game before close to 30,000 spectators and proved once and for all that America's baseball fandom wants to see a ball game regardless to the race, color or creed of the performers. And while the White Sox were taking a 14 to 0 licking in one game of the double header at Comiskey Park, here was Satchel Paige, Hilton Smith and the Monarchs performing in big league style but denied the right to play in the big leagues because of their color.[7]

• The first reference to a ball sticking in the outfield ivy occurred on August 13. Bill Nicholson's shot to right disappeared into the vines and he circled the bases for a two-run, inside-the-park homer against the Cardinals. The ground rule that limited a hit into the ivy to a double didn't come about for a few more years.

Game of the Year

July 15—The Cubs and Dodgers played one of the more manic games in park history. After fourth inning home runs by Lou Novikoff and Jimmie Foxx, Dodger pitcher Kirby Higbe threw the next pitch behind Bill Nicholson. The following half-inning, Cub reliever Hi Bithorn did some "dusting" of his own. The Dodger bench, led by manager Leo Durocher, rode Bithorn unmercifully. Hi loaded the bases and was removed for another pitcher. As he left the mound he rifled the ball at Durocher in the Dodgers' dugout. Continued dustings, seven errors, and three wild pitches provided enough hijinks for the 5,963 fans who witnessed the 10-5 Dodger win.

Quote of 1942

"There may be enough money raised at Wrigley Field this summer to buy a few tanks or even a bomber."[8]

General manager Jim Gallagher—in the Chicago Tribune, *April 12, 1942—on the sale of war bonds at the pass gate*

1943

```
The Season by the Numbers
74-79              .484 5ᵗʰ 30.5 games out          508,247 (6,601 average)
36-38              .486 at home                      106% of NL average
```

Opening Day

APRIL 21; CUBS (DERRINGER) VS. PIRATES (SEWELL); SUNNY, 57 DEGREES; 9,044 PAID

Pirates 6 Cubs 0—Rip Sewell shut down the Cubs on only three singles: two by Stan Hack and the other by catcher Clyde McCullough. The Cubs' backstop stole second base after his hit but broke an ankle on the play. Pirate rookie Frank Colman singled, doubled, and tripled off Paul Derringer, who replaced Claude Passeau, a victim of a bad cold.

Commissioner Landis threw out the first ball.

A fellow by the name of Emmett Wiggins was the first person to enter Wrigley Field this year, a feat he held for fifteen consecutive seasons.

What's New

- The team limited uniform numbers under "10" because they felt the "double numbers" looked better. According to *Cubs By the Numbers*, only veteran Stan Hack, who wore number 6, and Pete Elko, who wore number 8 for nine games at the end of the season, wore the lower numbers during 1943 and 1944. The Cubs also designated numbers 30-39 exclusively for pitchers.
- The Cubs bullpen pitchers utilized four full-length electric robes during the cooler months.
- In August, National League President Ford Frick ordered all teams to begin stating rulings and plays such as wild pitches and passed balls over the public address system. Before this, the official scorer only passed on the information to the press.

War Happenings

- The Cubs inaugurated a new slogan for their war-weary fans: "On your day off—Take the strain off."[9]

- The Cubs stopped wearing their vest-type uniforms after three years because of the rationing of the knitted material needed to make them. The team went back to the standard uniforms that every other club wore.

- Skinless hot dogs came to Wrigley Field. But due to a nationwide beef shortage, concession-aires stopped selling hamburgers.

- Government war regulations ended the team's ticket selling relationship with Western Union. Since 1936, Cub fans purchased over 400,000 reserved seats at Western Union offices, or 29 percent of the total sold. The team replaced the over 100 Western Union offices with a single ticket office at a department store in downtown Chicago. Scalpers rejoiced!

- The Cubs continued to sell war bonds and war stamps at Wrigley Field. At each game, buyers entered a drawing for an autographed baseball.

- During a July 26 game, fans cheered for five minutes after hearing over the park's public address system of Italian Dictator Benito Mussolini's ousting.

- To accommodate war workers on various shifts, the Cubs played two 11:00 A.M. games and a 6:00 P.M. twilight contest. The latter, played on June 25, attracted 10,070 fans and finished at 8:17 P.M., the latest ending Cub game at Wrigley Field before lights in 1988.

  In a five-day period beginning June 22, the Cubs played games at 11:00 A.M., a double-header beginning at 1:30 P.M., a 3:00 P.M. game, the 6:00 P.M. twi-night contest, and a Saturday 2:00 P.M. game.

  The Cub players requested that management "reblock" the centerfield bleachers for the twilight game because they were concerned about sun and shadows hampering vision. There was no indication that management honored the request.

- Attendance suffered during the war, so teams staged contests between ballplayers to attract fans. On September 5, Cubs and Pirates players competed in various skills, including a 70-yard dash, a fungo-hitting contest, a long distance throw, and a wheel barrel race. Each winner received a $25 war bond.

What Else Happened

- Elsie Dorr, wife of groundskeeper Bobby Dorr, died in the family apartment adjacent to the left field stands. Mrs. Dorr left behind her husband and two sons.

- On September 24, only 314 fans braved rain and cold to see a game against the Phillies, making it the least attended major league game in Wrigley Field history. Outfielder Andy Pafko made his major league debut and drove in four runs in the Cubs' 7-4 victory.
- Wrigley Field hosted a myriad of activities to provide diversions from the war.

1943 Police Baseball Game Ticket

On July 4, nearly 12,000 turned out for a double-header between North Side and South Side police teams. The North Siders won the day, 7-6 and 13-4, to sweep the best-of-three series for the second-straight year. Proceeds benefited the Police Benevolent Fund supporting families of slain officers.

On July 15, the Negro Leagues returned to Wrigley Field. Fans celebrated another Satchel Paige Day and honored the Kansas City Monarch pitcher for his 20 years in baseball. Nearly 25,000 saw Paige throw five shutout innings as a guest pitcher for the Memphis Red Sox. The nightcap pitted the Birmingham Black Barons against the Cincinnati Clowns.

Paige pitched two more times at Wrigley Field in 1943. On August 15, his Kansas City Monarchs met the Cleveland Buckeyes in a four-team doubleheader, complete with a beauty contest between games. On September 3, Paige faced Josh Gibson, the "Babe Ruth" of the Negro Leagues. Gibson homered and doubled. Other black baseball stars who appeared this year included Sam Jethroe, Lester Lockett, and Buck O'Neil.

In August, heavyweight Lee Savold knocked out Lou Nova in front of almost 13,000 boxing fans. Nova, who lost a championship bout to Joe Louis just two years ago, took a left hook to the chin in the second round.

Games of the Year

September 28—The Cubs swept the Giants, 3-2 and 2-1 on what may have been Old Timers' Day at Wrigley Field. Paul Derringer won his 200th game in the opener. Lon Warneke won the nightcap, his 192nd and final major league triumph.

Bear News

NFL teams also lost personnel to the war, including Bears' coach George Halas, who served in the Navy. To compensate, the Bears enticed Bronko Nagurski out of a five-year retirement.

Although he played tackle most of the year, he moved to running back the last quarter of the last regular season game and gained 84 yards, enough to carry the Bears to a 35-24 win over the Cardinals and a spot in their fourth straight NFL championship game.

On December 10, Sid Luckman threw five touchdowns and the Bears dismantled Washington, 41-21. Over 34,000 fans and George Halas, on leave from the Navy, cheered the victory.

Quote of 1943

"As a baseball magnate, P. K. Wrigley, who owns the Cubs, isn't very happy these days. His sole pleasure so far as his diamond chattels are concerned is derived from reading the National league [*sic*] standings upside down. This provides a delightful illusion. It put the Cubs in first place."[10]

Irving Vaughan in the Chicago Tribune—*May 20, 1943—as Cubs lost seven straight, residing now in last place*

1944

The Season by the Numbers		
75-79	.487 4th 30 games out	640,110 (8,154 average)
35-42	.455 at home	139% of NL average

Home Opener

APRIL 21; CUBS (DERRINGER) VS. CARDINALS (BRECHEEN); CLOUDY, 43 DEGREES; 4,783 PAID

Cardinals 4 Cubs 0—Marty Marion hit a solo home run in the eighth inning and the Cardinals added three more in the ninth. Harry Brecheen scattered four hits in front of the smallest Wrigley Field opening day crowd ever.

The Board of Trade American Legion Band played before the game and between innings. They were the day's only festivities.

What's New

• The Chicago Bears followed the Cubs when they moved their team offices from the Wrigley Building to Wrigley Field. The Cubs moved in 1942.

- Management again adjusted the hitting background. They painted the bleachers (and the scoreboard) a drabber green, hoping to cut down on reflected light.

War Happenings

- The Norge Ski Club of Cary, Illinois, moved its annual ski jumping tournament to Wrigley Field. Three variables convinced the War Production Board to support the meet:

  The need for limited travel, the use of rented scaffolding to build the ski ramp, and the decision to turn over profits to a war charity.

  Alpine skiers from as far away as Norway participated. But with a modified ramp that stood from the upper deck behind home plate to near second base, skiers jumped a maximum of only 125 feet, less than half the distance of a regulation ramp. Still, over 11,000 attended the two-day January meet.
- The only fans attending an April exhibition between the Cubs and the White Sox were 21,000 high school students who sold at least $25 in war bonds. Edgar Munzel of the *Chicago Sun* commented on the crowd that day, saying, "The youngsters kept up such a continuous din of screaming that it sounded like a giant gathering of the bobby socks brigade at a Frank Sinatra program."[11] The Cubs won, 7-6.
- Several ex-Cubs, including Three Finger Brown, Hippo Vaughn, Rogers Hornsby, and Woody English participated in a bond rally before a game on July 9. The event also recognized bond drive block captains whose neighborhoods surpassed their sales goals.
- To save leather, the Cubs requested that fans not ask for player's autographs on baseballs.
- At mid-season, Major League Baseball allowed teams to schedule an unlimited number of non-Sunday night games. The White Sox switched all September non-Sunday games, giving them twenty-two night games for the season.

  The War Production Board encouraged the Cubs to apply for the installation of lights during the 1944 season, believing night baseball at Wrigley Field could benefit war workers. The Cubs did apply but the board turned down the request. The materials were available but the team would not have lights installed before August, limiting them to a maximum of twenty-one night games, not enough to justify installation. The Board hinted that the team might receive an invitation to apply again in 1945.
- The All-American Girls Professional Baseball League staged a doubleheader on July 18 before almost 20,000 Red Cross workers, associates, and blood donors. The first game saw the Milwaukee Chicks beat the South Bend Blue Sox, 20-11. Darkness ended the nightcap between Racine and Kenosha after three and a half innings.

On September 10, the Navy honored 35,000 workers in the local radar industry with a rally at Wrigley Field. (Half of the radar instruments used in the war came from the Chicago area.) Navy entertainers put on a musical, and navy and swing bands provided music. Lt. Alexander Vraciu, a flying ace displayed his Grumman "Hellcat" airplane at the park's main entrance. He thanked the crowd, saying, "That plane out there could not have been built without your help."[12]

What Else Happened

- Oriole Park in Baltimore burned to the ground during a July 4 fireworks show. Although the home of the minor league Baltimore Orioles and the Negro American League Elite Giants, it originally opened in April 1914 as Terrapin Park, home of the Federal League's Baltimore Terrapins. Its sudden demise left Wrigley Field as the last remaining Federal League ballpark.
- Heavyweight Joe "the Polish Sensation" Baski won a split decision over Lee Savold in the featured ten-round boxing match on August 7. Over 7,600 paid to see six bouts. Nearly 5,000 servicemen watched for free.

Game of the Year

May 11—After winning their opening day game in Cincinnati, the Cubs lost thirteen straight. The losing streak chewed through three managers: the fired Jimmie Wilson, interim Roy Johnson, and now Charlie Grimm. Pitcher Ed Hanyzewski finally ended it with a 5-3, complete game glossing of the Phillies. A crowd of 3,878 paying fans and 250 servicemen saw the long-awaited victory.

Quote of 1944

"There is overwhelming evidence that Mr. Wrigley's foresight in demanding neatness, comfort and beauty as an essential (and profitable) adjunct of baseball entertainment has been proven a grand success. . . .It has occurred to us that he could do the fans outside Chicago a great service, and eventually fatten the purses of the nabobs, were he to invite all club owners, or at least a specially selected few, to a midsummer convention and inspection, with sessions each afternoon in Wrigley Field."[13]

Editorial in The Sporting News—*June 29, 1944*

1945

The Season by the Numbers		
98-56	.636 1st 3 games ahead	1,036,386 (13,373 average)
49-26	.653 at home	172% of NL average

Opening Day

APRIL 17; CUBS (DERRINGER) VS. CARDINALS (WILKS); 51 DEGREES; 11,788 PAID

Cubs 3 Cardinals 2—The Cubs had only four hits, but Don Johnson singled home Bill Nicholson with the winning run in the ninth inning. Nicholson walked and was sacrificed to second base by Ed Sauer. Earlier, Nicholson homered in the second.

What's New

- With men occupied in the armed services, females became a majority of Andy Frain's ushering squad.

War Happenings

- The War Production Board decided against putting baseball and other nighttime sports under their brownout order to conserve electricity. A positive recommendation would have curtailed night games for the 1945 season. The Board reasoned that if fans did not attend ballgames, they'd still use considerable electricity at home.
- The Cubs and White Sox moved up the traditional starting time of weekday games from 3:00 to 1:30 P.M. The earlier start allowed evening war plant workers to attend games and still get to their factories on time.
- Cubs returning from the service wore shoulder patches on their uniforms. The insignias resembled oversized pins that veterans wore on their lapels.
- On August 1, female fans were admitted free with a donation of a cake or cookies. The women donated 5,200 boxes of baked goods for the Chicago Service Centers.
- War regulations eliminated sleeper cars for train trips of less than 450 miles. The rule stopped a July 20 game after eight innings so Brooklyn could catch a 4:50 P.M. train to St. Louis,

and get there early enough to sleep a full night in their hotel. On September 3, the same regulation forced the Reds to leave Cincinnati the morning of a game at Wrigley Field rather than sleep the previous night on the train. Consequently, the Reds arrived late and the game started thirty-four minutes behind schedule.

What Else Happened

- The anticipated end of the war brought out fans in numbers not seen in years. The Cubs drew 42,568 paid on May 30 and 43,108 paid on June 24.

  The Cubs went 26-6 in July and took over first place on July 8. Attendance continued to grow. Eight more times this season the Cubs drew more than 40,000 paid, including a whopping 44,732 for a game against the Cardinals on August 24. The Cubs finished the year with their highest attendance average since 1931.

  The Cubs:

  - Went a remarkable 21-1 against the Reds, including an 11-0 record at home
  - Swept twenty of thirty-four doubleheaders, going 16-0-6 after July 1
  - Were led by Phil Cavarretta, who won the NL MVP award, and Hank Borowy, who came over from the Yankees on July 27 and went 11-2 down the stretch
  - Got lucky, losing fewer key players to the war than their rivals. The Cardinals, for example, pennant winners in 1942, 1943, 1944, and 1946, were without Stan Musial, Enos Slaughter, and Terry Moore for the entire 1945 season. The Cubs, on the other hand, lost no one of importance.

Games of the Year

September 3-9—The Cubs swept three doubleheaders in seven days, outscoring their opponents 42-8. Andy Pafko led the way with 11 RBI in six games. Cy Vandenberg, Hank Wyse, Ray Prim, and Claude Passeau tossed six complete games between them. By the end of the week the Cubs lead St. Louis by three and a half games.

September 25—The Cardinals came to Wrigley Field for one more crack at the Cubs, trailing by only a game and a half. Hank Borowy, with strong relief pitching by Ray Prim, won a tense 6-5 game. The Cubs took five of their last six games to seal the pennant and a date with the Detroit Tigers.

World Series

All seats except bleacher and standing room were sold in advance by mail. Fans purchased ticket booklets for three games (Games Four, Five, and Six). They cost:

Box seat—$21.95
Grandstand—$18.35

Day of game tickets cost:

Bleacher—$1.20
Standing room—$3.60

The team traded the baseball box seat chairs for the smaller football chairs, temporarily increasing seating capacity to well over 41,000.

Ticket scalpers asked upwards of $150 for a three-game set of box seats. During the series, the owner of a gas station at 3553 N. Clark Street, across from Wrigley Field, appeared in court to explain the charge that he sold a scalper access to the property for $25.

The gouging continued; parking lots charged up to $2 to park cars during the series. The Office of Price Administration won an injunction to drop the price to $1. But fans claimed that the only thing that dropped were the signs that said "$2." The lots continued to charge the higher amount when they could.

Even though America and its allies won World War II by August, war travel restrictions continued. Consequently, the Tigers hosted the first three games and the Cubs the last four. Hank Borowy shut out the Tigers, 9-0 in Game One. Virgil Trucks beat the Cubs, 4-1 in Game Two. In Game Three, Claude Passeau gave one of the greatest pitching performances in World Series history. He allowed only one hit for a 3-0 Cubs win. The North Siders came home with a 2-1 series lead.

GAME FOUR; SATURDAY, OCTOBER 6; DRIZZLE, 62 DEGREES; 42,923 ATTEND

Ex-Cubs Riggs Stephenson, Gabby Hartnett, Dizzy Dean, and Augie Galan attended the game. In addition, Mayor Kelly, boxer King Levinsky, and two hundred wounded soldiers saw the action, the latter partitioned off in the center field bleachers.

As another remembrance of the just finished war—Flags of the United Nations countries flapped in the breeze above and behind the left and right field bleachers.

Over 500 Andy Frain ushers kept order. They communicated with walkie-talkies, a first at the park. Bleacher vendors rented their beer and milk cartons for fifty cents so standees could get a better view.

Because of the rain, the grounds crew left the tarp on the field until just before game time. Without batting practice, the Cubs suffered. Dizzy Trout held them to five hits in a 4-1 Detroit victory. Don Johnson tripled and scored the Cubs' only run.

Game Five; Sunday, October 7; 68 degrees; 43,463 attend

Sunny weather meant fans bought more standing room tickets than the day before. In addition, the teams took batting practice for the first time in three games. The Tigers got to Hank Borowy for four runs in the sixth inning and pounded the Cubs, 8-4. It was a game of opposites—Hank Greenberg stroked three doubles and Andy Pafko struck out three times. The loss dropped the Cubs all-time World Series record at Wrigley Field to 1-10. Manager Grimm said this about the defeat: "We got the hell kicked out of us. It was just boom, boom, boom."[14]

Game Six; Monday, October 8; 49 degrees; 41,708 attend

The Cubs survived a twelve-inning marathon and the first three-plus hour game in World Series history, 8-7. Stan Hack and Phil Cavarretta singled in runs in a four-run fifth inning. The Tigers scored four runs themselves in the eighth, the last on a Hank Greenberg home run. But the Cubs prevailed in the twelfth on a freak double by Stan Hack. His left field drive fell in front of Hank Greenberg and took a wild hop over his head, allowing Billy Schuster to score all the way from first base. Hank Borowy pitched the final four innings for the win.

Game Seven; Wednesday, October 10; 52 degrees; 41,590 attend

The proverbial "if necessary" Game Seven was necessary. A few hours after the end of Game 6, fans gathered outside Wrigley Field to buy reserved seats. Edward Prell of the *Chicago Tribune* set the scene:

> Wrigley field's ticket corridors on Addison st. [sic] last night were illuminated by fires crackling inside tubs and garbage cans. At midnight the place was alive with more than 200 half frozen rabid baseball fans of all descriptions and ages . . . They established position rights at each window by being branded on their backs of their coats with chalk numerals.[15]

The crowd swelled to thousands when tickets went on sale at 8:00 A.M. All 36,000 reserved seats were gone before noon. The same scenario unfolded the following night as fans stayed for a chance at 5,000 bleacher tickets. The traditional day-of-game seats sold within minutes of being offered at 8:00 A.M.

Cub fans were ready for the most important game in Wrigley Field history, one that could provide their first World Championship since 1908. But the fans were quickly dispirited; the game was over soon after it began. A spent Borowy, fighting blisters and fatigue, failed to retire a batter as Detroit scored five first inning runs. The Cubs mustered only single runs in the first, fourth and eighth innings as Hal Newhouser pitched the Tigers to a 9-3 shredding of the North Siders and a world's title.

Postscript

The 1945 World Series produced historical precedents for the Cubs. The World Series loss stretched the Cubs non-championship streak to thirty-seven years. Ironically, the Cubs series appearance in 1945 probably contributed to the nearly seventy additional and still counting years of championship drought. The 1945 World Series gave P. K. Wrigley a false sense of the franchise's health. The Cubs lucked into this pennant. After the series, the aging team and their addled farm system couldn't keep up with the Cardinals, Giants, or Dodgers of the world. They spent the next twenty years in baseball purgatory.

The Cubs legendary Billy Goat curse also had its origins in the 1945 World Series. Here are the facts:

Billy Sianis, owner of the Billy Goat Tavern, did bring a goat to Game Four. The goat, named Murphy, had a legitimate ticket and did get into the park wearing a blanket that read, "WE GOT DETROIT'S GOAT".[16] As Sianis brought the goat to its seat—seat 6, box 65, tier 12— Chief Usher Andy Frain threw Murphy out of the park. Sianis dropped off the goat at a nearby parking lot, paid $1 to store him during the game, and went inside to watch the action. Afterwards Sianis said of the snub, "I'll sue for $100,000—no, I'll sue for a million."[17]

But outside of Sianis's threat to sue, there wasn't a contemporary reference to a curse placed on the Cubs. In fact, Will Leonard of the *Chicago Tribune* provided the first reference to a curse on December 26, 1967, twenty-two years after the incident. Leonard wrote:

"But Billy got even by putting a hex on the Cubs. The Cubs lost that World Series and their fortunes plummeted after the war. Finally, Phillip K. Wrigley, the owner, asked him to take the hex off. Sianis agreed. It did not seem to help the Cubs until recently."[18]

David Condon, also of the *Chicago Tribune,* and a personal acquaintance of Sianis, referenced the restaurateur over twenty times in newspaper articles in the sports section before first mentioning the supposed curse in 1969, fifteen months after Leonard's story. Condon ingrained the curse story in fans' minds, writing about it three more times in the next four years. The legend of the billy goat curse took off from there.

It's unlikely that Sianis, a rabid self-promoter, would keep quiet about his curse for over twenty years. It's unthinkable that the Chicago media of the 1950s and 1960s wouldn't latch on to it, especially since it coincided with some of the worst years in Cubs history.

The goat, entering and being thrown out of Game Four of the 1945 World Series, is factual. The subsequent story of Billy Sianis's curse, hatched over twenty years after the fact, is a great yarn, made greater by the Cubs' mediocre play. But logic says it never happened.

1946

The Season by the Numbers			
82-71	.536 3rd	14.5 games out	1,342,970 (17,329 average)
44-33	.571 at home		124% of NL average

Home Opener

APRIL 20; CUBS (BOROWY) VS. CARDINALS (BRECHEEN); SUNNY, 43 DEGREES; 40,887 PAID

Cardinals 2 Cubs 0—The Cardinals scratched across runs in the first and eighth innings. Harry Brecheen scattered six hits; Don Johnson stroked half of them, all singles.

National League President Ford Frick presented the 1945 league pennant to manager Grimm. The grounds crew hoisted it up the right field flagpole while Armin Hand's band played "God Bless America." The festivities took all of four minutes, to the delight of the chilled crowd.

During the opener, Ray Kneip's crew sold 40,000 hot dogs, 18,000 bags of peanuts, 12,000 bags of popcorn, 7,000 ham sandwiches, and 18,000 scorecards.

What's New

• The women's restroom on the lower concourse was doubled in size and remodeled.
• The scoreboard was repainted and rewired.

Concessionaire Ray Kneip and a few of his crew (www. ArgentaImages.com)

What Happened

- The Boston Braves hosted night baseball on May 11, leaving Wrigley Field as the only non-lighted National League ballpark. Boston and Detroit remained as "day-only" holdouts in the American League when Yankee Stadium was illuminated on May 28. The National League scheduled 128 night games, the most ever. For the first time, on August 9, all eight major league baseball games on a single date occurred at night. There was no turning back.

- WBKB, Chicago's only television station, attempted to broadcast its first baseball game, the April 20 home opener at Wrigley Field. While they shot the game, poor technical quality kept them from transmitting it to televisions.

   WBKB successfully telecast its first game on July 13. During Brooklyn's 4-3 win, a single camera in the upper deck focused on home plate, the pitcher's mound, and the right side of the field. The crude set-up left much of the diamond invisible to the television viewer. Commentator Jack Gibney described the action the camera missed.

   During the second inning, the station experimented with a slightly more powerful camera. But with it, the cameraman unsettlingly shifted back and forth between the pitcher and batter. Viewers phoned the station, preferring the earlier perspective, which WBKB returned to in the third inning. *Chicago Sun* sportswriter Tom Siler watched the game on television and said it provided "only a moderately clear image of the play."[19]

- World peace brought fans back to the ballparks. Add the popularity of the pennant winning Cubs and records fell at Wrigley Field. The largest paid crowd in team history to that point, 45,505, saw the Cubs and Phillies on May 5. On July 21, the same teams played in front of another record paid attendance of 45,615. The 1946 Cubs drew their third highest home attendance to that point, surpassed only in 1929 and 1930.

- Free from war and economic strife, the American public yearned for leisure activities:

  The Sunbrock Rodeo performed five days and nights at the ballpark. Over 900 cowboys and cowgirls competed in bronco riding, calf roping, and bull riding. Circus acts, Sioux Indians, and steeplechase horses also appeared. The rodeo would return again in 1947.

  The Chicago Maroons of the North American Pro Soccer League played its home games at Wrigley Field. Their first match, against the Toronto Greenbacks, attracted 2,200 onlookers. But the team and the league folded midway through the 1947 season.

  The inaugural game for the Chicago Rockets, the city's new All-American Football Conference team, drew a Chicago professional football attendance record of 51,962 to Soldier Field. The previous record saw 45,553 for a Bears-Packers game at Wrigley Field in 1944.

  The 1946 attendance marks for all three Chicago football teams:

  - Chicago Bears . . . 43,958 average for six games in Wrigley Field
  - Chicago Cardinals . . . 33,744 average for four games in Comiskey Park
  - Chicago Rockets . . . 27,707 average for seven games in Soldier Field

  The AAFC folded after the 1949 season, but the NFL absorbed the league's Cleveland Browns, Baltimore Colts, and San Francisco 49ers.

  Jake LaMotta knocked out Robert Satterfield in the seventh round of a bout on September 12. Even so, the crowd of less than 10,000 disappointed promoters and marked the last boxing card ever held at Wrigley Field. In the future, smaller venues hosted most of Chicago's boxing action (although Comiskey Park—larger and lighted—hosted Ezzard Charles vs. Joe Walcott in 1949 and Sonny Liston vs. Floyd Patterson in 1962).

Game of the Year

August 18—A sharp single in the seventh inning by the Pirates' Billy Cox accounted for the only hit off Paul Erickson in an 8-0 Cubs win. The 30,965 in attendance not only saw the pitching gem, but also witnessed something common then but unheard of today—a day given by fans to a merely average ballplayer. The player was Chicago-native Johnny Ostrowski. He totaled 131 hits in a seven-year career. Yet, fans presented him with a new car, luggage, and a wristwatch in a pregame ceremony.

Quote of 1946

"We have too much money invested in Wrigley Field to make such a move. And we're pretty well satisfied with it."[20]

P. K. Wrigley in the Chicago Tribune—August 8, 1946—squelching a rumor that he'd purchase the Riverview Amusement Park, raze it, and build a new ballpark on the site.

1947

The Season by the Numbers		
69-85	.448 6th 25 games out	1,364,039 (17,601 average)
36-43	.456 at home	106% of NL average

Opening Day

April 15; Cubs (Borowy) vs. Pirates (Sewell); cloudy, 59 degrees; 29,427 paid

Pirates 1 Cubs 0—Hank Borowy and Rip Sewell each tossed five-hitters. The difference was the Pirates' Hank Greenberg. In his National League debut, Hank ripped a sixth inning double to score Billy Cox with the game's only run. Ex-Cub Billy Herman made his managerial debut and got the win.

Pirates co-owner Bing Crosby sat in a box seat behind the visitor's dugout. He did not lead the crowd during the seventh inning stretch.

What's New

- WBKB televised every Cubs home game this year.
- Boston's Fenway Park hosted its first night game on June 13.
- The 1941 experiment to block out a portion of the center field bleachers lasted only half a season. Six years later, players still grumbled about the lack of a sufficient background. With the Cubs mired in sixth place and last in the league in batting average and home runs, management experimented again. Before a game on July 22, the grounds crew hung a 10-foot by 12-foot blue-tinted, semitransparent plastic screen in front of the center field bleachers. In theory, the screen would eliminate the white background for right-handed hitters and provide fans sitting behind it a clear view of the game. If the experiment worked, management planned to expand the screen to aid left-handed hitters. But the screen lasted only nine games. During that period, opponents outscored the Cubs 48 to 31.

What Happened

- Jackie Robinson, the first African-American major leaguer in the twentieth century, made his Wrigley Field debut on May 18. Brooklyn trimmed the Cubs, 4-2, despite Robinson going hitless to end a fourteen-game hitting streak. Bolstered by a large black audience, the paid crowd of 47,101 was the largest in Wrigley Field history.

   Beginning a month before the game, Fay Young of the *Chicago Defender*, the city's largest African-American newspaper, warned that black fans attending Robinson's first game would be more on trial than Jackie himself. Young understood the social significance that one ball-game carried. He wrote: "The Negro fan can help Robinson. The Negro fan can ruin him. Robinson is an American citizen, an ex-army officer, a ball player and a gentleman. Let us try and meet his qualifications as a gentleman. If you Chicagoans have got to raise a lot of hell, do a lot of cussing, go somewhere else."[21]

   The Cubs hired extra police for security, but the fans did their part. A Cub official called the historic gathering "the most orderly large crowd in the history of Wrigley Field."[22]

   Would Robinson's success sway the Cubs to sign a black player? John Ritchey, a catcher with the Chicago American League Giants of the Negro Leagues, received a late-season tryout in front of Cub coaches at Wrigley Field. Although the team took a look at Ritchey, almost six years passed before they signed a black player.

- The city took the owners of the building at 3701 Kenmore to court, claiming they charged visitors to watch Cubs and Bears games from their upstairs window. In addition, a city inspector claimed the owners erected a bleacher inside the window that threatened to collapse the building. The owners admitted they once charged fans. Now, they just allowed friends and residences to watch for free. The building still stands on the corner of Waveland and Kenmore Avenues. It's the one with the roof sign.

Bobby Dorr claimed that for $10, scouts of opposing NFL teams could view Chicago Bear practices from the windows of the buildings across Waveland and Sheffield avenues. Dorr said the coaches knew this and their insistence on practicing in areas out of view of the apartments made his spring field preparation more difficult.

- On August 30, the Cubs and 27,000 fans celebrated Stan Hack Day, honoring the third baseman's 16 years of service. Before the game, Stan received a Cadillac automobile, a $1,000 television set, a freezer, a fishing reel, a bronze cigarette box, a humidor filled with fifty-cent cigars, and a wristwatch. The team also presented him with a full-length portrait by Otis Shepard, with this inscription: "May life be as kind to you as you have been to other people."[23]
- On September 28, the Cubs released Hack, Claude Passeau, Billy Jurges, and Bill Lee. The quartet logged forty-six combined years with the team. But there would be no adequate replacements. The Cubs would spend the next two decades in the second division.

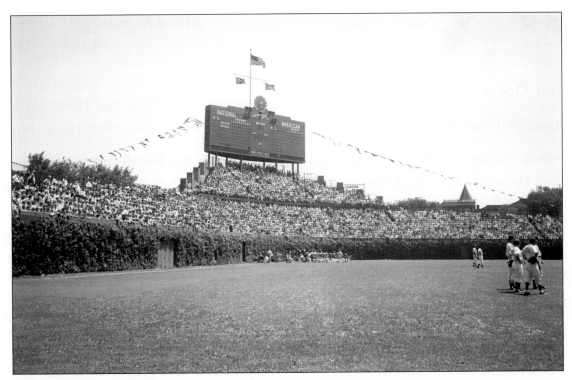

A band plays in the outfield before the All-Star game; note the lack of a hitting background. (www. ArgentaImages.com)

Game of the Year

July 8—Baseball's fourteenth All-Star game came to Wrigley Field. The American League squeaked out a 2-1 win in the lowest scoring game to date. The National League took the lead in the fourth inning on a Johnny Mize homer. The Americans tied it in the sixth when Luke Appling scored on a Joe DiMaggio double play ball. The final run came in the seventh when pinch hitter Stan Spence singled in Bobby Doerr.

Quote of 1947

"Baseball to me is a day time [*sic*] game and at Wrigley Field we have given customers a satisfactory sunshine outing and we'll continue to do so in the future, unless the patrons want it otherwise."[24]

P. K. Wrigley in the Chicago Tribune—*July 1, 1947*

1948

The Season by the Numbers

64-90	.416 8th 27.5 games out		1,237,792 (15,972 average)
35-42	.455 at home		94% of NL average

Home Opener

APRIL 23; CUBS (SCHMITZ) VS. CARDINALS (BRECHEEN); SUNNY, 81 DEGREES; 26,591 PAID

Cardinals 1 Cubs 0—Johnny Schmitz two-hit the Cardinals but lost the game in the ninth inning. He walked Erv Dusak who scored on a double by Ralph LaPointe. The Cubs managed nine hits off Brecheen but couldn't score.

Governor Dwight H. Green threw out the first pitch.

What's New

• Box seats increased in price from $1.80 to $2.00. That's the first price jump since the 1920s.

- The outside of the park, box seats, railings, and the first half dozen rows of grandstand seats were repainted. The scoreboard received another coat of green paint. In addition, its white letters and numerals received a bit of yellow paint to better distinguish them from a distance.
- WGN joined WBKB in telecasting each home game. Jack Brickhouse began a thirty-four-year career that made him the unofficial "voice of the Cubs." WGN used three cameras at Wrigley Field: one next to the Cub dugout, one on a ramp adjacent to the press box, and a third just outside the left field foul pole. The latter utilized a $7,500 Zoomar lens that allowed quick close-ups from a distance. The field level cameras for both stations required the removal of four feet of wall on either side of the Cub dugout.

  Even though two stations broadcast every home game, television sets were a novelty to most fans. In fact, bars housed nearly 30 percent of all the sets in Chicago. The team and WBKB donated televisions to area parks so "kids won't need to peer thru tavern windows to watch baseball games."[25]
- The Cubs condensed their sixteen-page scorecard to four pages. The downsizing favored flexibility, allowing the presumed starting lineups to be printed inside.
- During the 1948 All-Star Game in St. Louis, fans sat in the vacant hitting background. Afterwards, batters complained about pitch visibility. The Pirates' Dixie Walker spotted P. K. Wrigley there and warned him that the similar situation in Wrigley Field would eventually lead to a serious injury.

  It remains unclear whether Wrigley's All-Star Game encounter with Walker was the catalyst, but shortly thereafter, the team erected a canopy in three sections of the center field bleachers. The canopy consisted of plywood or metal sheets laid horizontally on the seventh row of the bleachers. Vertical piping on the bleacher side of the outfield wall held it up. It improved visibility, creating a permanent dark cavern up to twelve feet above the bleacher wall.

What Happened

- Detroit's Briggs Stadium (later Tiger Stadium) hosted its first night game, leaving Wrigley Field as the only major league park without lights.

First Night Games at Major League Parks

Crosley Field	Cincinnati	May 24, 1935
Ebbets Field	Brooklyn	June 15, 1938

Shibe Park	Philadelphia	May 16, 1939
Municipal Stadium	Cleveland	June 27, 1939
Comiskey Park	Chicago	August 14, 1939
Polo Grounds	New York	May 24, 1940
Sportsman's Park	St. Louis	May 24, 1940
Forbes Field	Pittsburgh	June 4, 1940
Griffith Stadium	Washington	May 28, 1941
Braves Field	Boston	May 11, 1946
Yankee Stadium	New York	May 28, 1946
Fenway Park	Boston	June 13, 1947
Briggs Stadium	Detroit	June 15, 1948

• On the night of September 14, Progressive Party presidential candidate Henry Wallace staged a rally at Wrigley Field. The former vice president's platform called for an end to segregation, an end to the Cold War, and universal healthcare. Nearly 400 police stood watch in and around the park. Outside of a few eggs tossed at him as he arrived, things remained calm. Over 16,000 supporters paid 60 cents to $2.40 to hear him orate from a stage over second base.

Game of the Year

July 25—Bill Nicholson slammed a home run off Alex Konikowski, the 200th of his career. Nicholson became the twelfth National Leaguer to reach the milestone. Only two other active NL players had reached it: Johnny Mize and Joe Medwick. The Cubs beat the Giants 6-3.

Bear News

After the baseball season, the Cubs erected a $125,000 bleacher section to accommodate Bears fans. The bleachers stood in the outfield, from the center field bleachers to the right field line. While the new stand obscured 3,500 bleacher and box seats, it added 4,000 total seats to the park's capacity. The Bears sold them as season ticket box seats, and they became some of the best vantage points for watching football.

The Bears and Cardinals met on December 12, tied for first in the Western Division; the winner would face the Eagles for the NFL championship. It was the Chicago sports event of the year, and a Wrigley Field record crowd of 51,283 saw the seesaw battle. The upstart Cardinals overcame a 21-10 deficit to win, 24-21.

With the new bleachers, competitive Bears teams, and a Wrigley Field before the 1960s downsizing, the Bears of this era drew the three biggest football crowds in park history:

51,283	Cardinals 24	Bears 21	December 12, 1948
51,065	Bears 28	Packers 14	October 15, 1950
50,286	Rams 42	Bears 17	December 2, 1951

Quote of 1948

"Cubs' sponsors and fans insist that an outing in Wrigley field [sic] is an interesting experience, regardless of the brand of baseball played there. Perhaps that is true . . . [But] it is difficult sometimes for an innocent bystander who doesn't eat hot dogs, sweats too much after a bottle of beer, and who already has a baseball cap, to see anything thrilling in one Cub flop after another."[26]
Edward Burns in the Chicago Tribune—*July 22, 1948*

1949

The Season by the Numbers
| 61-93 | .396 8th 36 games out | 1,143,139 (14,846 average) |
| 33-44 | .429 at home | 95% of NL average |

Opening Day

APRIL 19; CUBS (LEONARD) VS. PIRATES (SEWELL); 54 DEGREES; 29,392 PAID

Pirates 1 Cubs 0—Two old pitchers (Leonard, forty years old, Sewell, forty-one years old) met to open the new season. The Pirates scratched across their only run in the ninth inning on a fielder's choice. It was Sewell's third Wrigley Field home opener shutout in seven years. It also marked his thirty-fourth career win against the North Siders.

There were no Opening Day ceremonies outside of a dance orchestra that played throughout the game.

What's New

- The team added a miniature scoreboard to the left field upper deck façade. Bleacher fans could now see the score, the ball-strike count, and outs without having to continually look at the big board behind them.
- In July, the team extended the center field canopy by two additional sections in right center. The hitting background now covered five sections of the bleachers.
- A third station, WENR, joined WBKB and WGN in televising Cub home games. General manager Jim Gallagher said this about allowing stations free rein at Wrigley Field: "The Cubs realize that television is in its infancy, but we believe that someday video may play an important role in baseball. Therefore, the Cubs feel it is only fair to give television stations in Chicago every opportunity . . . in bringing the exciting drama of baseball into the home."[27]

What Happened

- The breakdown of the 179 scheduled National League night games:

St. Louis. 43	Brooklyn. 21
Boston. 32	New York. 14
Philadelphia. 30	Cincinnati. 14
Pittsburgh. 25	Chicago. 0

The Cubs' Board of Directors withheld dividends, leading many to think that the team planned to use the $141,000 profit for lights at Wrigley Field. P. K. Wrigley, however, squelched the rumors, saying most of the money had been reinvested in the Los Angeles minor league club.

• While P. K. Wrigley doted on his fans and players, he didn't do the same for Cub opponents. At a mid-season meeting of major league clubs, players requested that Wrigley Field and Sportsman's Park in St. Louis enlarge their visitor's locker rooms. The request gave some credence to Joe Garagiola's assertion that a locker at Wrigley Field consisted of only a nail on the wall.

• At the same meeting, owners agreed to erect ten-foot-wide warning tracks in their outfields. Only Shibe Park, Braves Field, and Wrigley Field already had them. Film of the 1945 World

The Marquee on September 21, 1949 (From the collection of Ray Medeiros)

Series at Wrigley Field showed only a chalk mark demarcation on the grass in front of the outfield wall. The 1947 All-Star game photo on page 127 clearly shows a warning track. So the Cubs added their warning track sometime during 1946 or 1947.

• On July 9, the *Chicago Herald-American* sponsored a fundraiser that featured two baseball games and a softball game. The schedule included a high school all-star baseball game and an old-timers' game with the likes of Gabby Hartnett and Charlie Grimm. A Hollywood softball game cast the comedians against the dramatists. The best-known actors that day were Eddie Bracken, Lloyd Bridges, and Sid Caesar. But the roster also included a virtually unknown starlet named Marilyn Monroe. About 15,000 attended the benefit.

Games of the Year

August 4—Johnny Schmitz ended the Cubs' eight-game losing streak with a 1-0, three-hit triumph over the Giants. Schmitz didn't allow a hit until Sid Gordon beat out an infield roller

Addison Street (From the collection of Ray Medeiros)

to start the eighth inning. Andy Pafko provided the only run the Cubs needed, a homer to left in the second.

September 22—Only 1,813 intrepid fans saw the Cubs beat the Phillies, 3-2. Luckily, one of those die-hards took the remarkable photographs that appear on pages 132–138, showing a day in the life of Wrigley Field in the post-World War II era.

Quote of 1949

"In my time as an athlete you could tell a ball player by his clear, sharp eyes and his ruddy skin. If things keep going in the night ball trend, the modern ball player can be identified by the thick-lensed glasses he wears and his squint when he ventures out into the sun. His sallow hide will be a further tipoff that he is a ball player, a fellow who eats irregularly during the day and has steaks just before going to bed."[28]

Cub manager Charlie Grimm in The Sporting News—*May 4, 1949*

Addison and Sheffield (From the collection of Ray Medeiros)

Waveland Avenue. The Dorr Family apartment is at the far right. (From the collection of Ray Medeiros)

The grounds crew prepares the field. (From the collection of Ray Medeiros)

The Phillies come to bat. (From the collection of Ray Medeiros)

The field level box seats were folding chairs until 1965. During each football season, the Bears replaced these seats with smaller folding chairs to increase capacity. (From the collection of Ray Medeiros)

The right field box seats stopped short of the right field wall. It provided space to house the batting cage. Also notice the stairs leading down to the right field "catwalk," a ramp leading to a convenient exit for bleacher fans. (From the collection of Ray Medeiros)

FOURTH INNING
1950-1959
MIDDLE AGE

At thirty-six years old and nearing middle age, Wrigley Field received its first major structural repairs. A series of projects strung out over more than twenty years replaced much of the steel, concrete, and seating of the grandstand. The long-term plan allowed Wrigley Field to serve fans for many more decades. P. K. Wrigley's far-sighted undertaking was unusual; few of Wrigley Field's peers received such care. Most, in fact, would be gone within twenty years.

P. K. Wrigley owned blueprints to raise the park's capacity to 50,000. But he would not need them. With a barren farm system and an unwillingness to sign black players early on, the team fell further behind the competition. P. K, two general managers—Wid Matthews and John Holland—and four field bosses—Frankie Frisch, Phil Cavarretta, Stan Hack, and Bob Scheffing—couldn't reverse the on-field slide.

In 1953, the Cubs finally signed Ernie Banks and Gene Baker, the team's first black players. But it didn't bring victories. Indeed, only Hank Sauer and Ernie Banks gave fans compelling reasons to watch the game at Wrigley Field.

Baseball attendance in both leagues dropped after the spike following World War II. Societal trends including television, the migration to the suburbs, and competition from the NFL lessened interest in the game. In 1953, baseball relocated the Boston Braves to Milwaukee. Not only was it baseball's first franchise shift in decades, the move cut into the Cubs' northern fan base.

Milwaukee County Stadium, while not modern by today's standards, broke from the Classic era ballparks. It was the first built with lights. All others to that time added lights after construction. In addition, parking completely surrounded the stadium, something unheard of at the Classic parks.

By decade's end, westward expansion brought the major leagues to San Francisco and Los Angeles. The Giants constructed Candlestick Park, baseball's first truly modern ballpark. The Modern stadium building boom commenced and wouldn't end until 1971.

1950

The Season by the Numbers		
64-89	.418 7th 26.5 games out	1,165,944 (15,152 average)
35-42	.455 at home	114% of NL average

Home Opener

APRIL 21; CUBS (RUSH) VS. CARDINALS (BRECHEEN); 51 DEGREES; 22,137 PAID

Cubs 2 Cardinals 0—The Cubs got only three hits, but both Hal Jeffcoat and Wayne Terwilliger tripled and scored. Bob Rush tossed a four-hit shutout.

The team started the new decade with only two players left from the 1945 pennant-winning team: Phil Cavarretta and Andy Pafko.

What's New

- A green-tinted backstop.
- New aluminum awnings over the ticket windows.

- Workers began a two-year project, replacing the concrete flooring beneath the box seats. This winter they completed the area from the left field corner to first base.
- Groundskeeper Bobby Dorr designed padding (actually wrapped bedsprings) along the wall down the left field line. The new pads complemented those that hung down the right field line since 1940.

What Happened

- The Cubs and a downtown hotel offered a package that included a ballgame and overnight accommodations. For $14.30 per couple, fans received two box seat tickets to any weekend game, a night at the Chicagoan Hotel, brunch in the hotel restaurant, and transportation to and from the game.
- Was Wrigley Field a cash cow? Visiting teams received 23 cents of every ticket sold no matter if it was a 60-cent bleacher seat or a $2 box seat. Since Wrigley Field had more box seats than any other major league park (@14,000) and twice as many as some, the Cubs realized a greater income per ticket than all other ballclubs.
- Police blotters and first responders got a workout at the park in 1950:

    February 9—An eleven-year-old boy confessed to a two-day arson spree in the neighborhood surrounding Wrigley Field. Among the casualties at the ballpark was a motorized cleaner.

    May 2—A foul off the bat of Stan Lopata hit the Phillies' batboy on the head, causing a concussion. Staff removed him unconscious on a stretcher.

    June 8—A fan tossed a bottle, narrowly missing Giants outfielder Bobby Thomson. Police officers arrested the fan but he escaped outside the park. In the ensuing chase, police fired shots and finally pistol-whipped and apprehended him near the Addison Street "L" station.

    June 27—A ten-year-old boy broke his wrist falling from the bleachers during a game against the Cardinals. Staff removed him by stretcher and sent him to the hospital.

    June 27—Two fans beat a cab driver near Irving Park Road and Sheffield Avenue after they questioned his driving route to the ballpark.

    August 27—A fifteen-year-old boy sustained injuries falling down a flight of stairs into a pile of garbage. The boy's family later sued the Cubs and received a $27,000 settlement. Their lawyer argued that the boy's fall was predicated on the team filling the park beyond a reasonable capacity that day.

Game of the Year

May 5—Hank Sauer drove a two-out, three-run homer in the ninth inning to tie the Dodgers, 6-6. In the bottom of the tenth, Randy Jackson won the game with a Waveland Avenue shot, his first major league home run.

Bear News

While the Cubs allowed fans to keep foul balls as far back as 1916, the Bears tried to get them back. With tight quarters at Wrigley Field, passed or kicked footballs frequently ended up in the stands. Andy Frain ushers didn't demand that fans return footballs, but if a ball ended up in the crowd and an usher pulled one out of a scrum pile, it went back to the team. During a game on October 15, over twenty-five balls landed in the stands. The ushers did not get a single one back.

Following the football season, a local car dealer stored several hundred new automobiles on Wrigley Field's concourses, ramps, and field. The dealer anticipated steel rationing during the Korean War and hoarded the 1950 models to sell next year.

Quote of 1950

"Wrigley Field has not blossomed in all its springtime glory yet. The field still showed some wear and tear from the demands of football and weather and the ivy on the bleacher wall was without greenery. But . . . the park is in no danger of losing its title as the most beautiful in baseball."[1]
John C. Hoffman in the Chicago Sun-Times*— April 17, 1950*

1951

The Season by the Numbers		
62-92	.403 8ᵗʰ 34.5 games out	894,415 (11,541 average)
32-45	.416 at home	99% of NL average

Opening Day

APRIL 17; CUBS (HILLER) VS. REDS (RAFFENSBERGER); SUNNY, 44 DEGREES; 18,211 PAID

Cubs 8 Reds 3—When rookie Dee Fondy tripled home three runs in the first inning, it marked the most runs scored by the Cubs in a home opener in six years. Fondy, Andy Pafko, and Frank Baumholtz had three hits in the convincing slaughter. Frank Hiller went the distance for the Cubs despite giving up 13 hits.

Chicago Mayor Martin Kennelly threw out the first pitch.

What's New

- The Cubs completed the re-flooring beneath the box seats, from first base to the right field corner. Workers poured concrete in exceptionally cold weather, aided by boilers underneath the flooring forms. The reconfigured box seat sections decreased capacity by 580 down to 38,703. In addition, the box seat area down the right field line was raised and turned toward home plate, just like the third base side had been in 1938. The two-year, $450,000 project was the most expensive to date in Wrigley Field history.
- Fixed seats replaced folding chairs in the upper boxes.
- The upper deck got four phone booths.
- Two drinking fountains were installed on the lower concourse behind first base.

What Happened

- Golfer Sam Snead did what no ballplayer has come close to doing—hit a ball over the Wrigley Field scoreboard. Of course, this ball was a golf ball. Snead, in town for an examination of a broken wrist, visited the ballpark before the Cubs opener. His first try, a four iron, hit the scoreboard. The next shot, a two-iron, cleared with no problem. No word on whom or what he hit on Waveland Avenue.
- The rodeo returned in July. Duncan Renaldo, television's Cisco Kid, starred in the show. The extravaganza featured horse riding, bullfighting, and a circus.
- A Turk Lown fastball beaned Brooklyn's Roy Campanella during the second inning of a late season game. Firefighters from Engine 78 across the street, watching the game unfold on television, were there when Campanella came out on a stretcher. The Dodger catcher suffered a lacerated ear and spent the night in the hospital.

Game of the Year

July 29—Player-manager Phil Cavarretta scorched the Phillies, 5-4 and 8-6. In the opener, Phil tripled in two runs in the sixth inning and tied the score with a sacrifice in the eighth. In the nightcap, Cavarretta came off the bench to hit a pinch-hit grand slam in the seventh, part of a six-run inning. Edgar Munzel of the *Chicago Sun-Times* called Cavvy's day the "most thrilling personal performance seen at the North Side Park since Gabby Hartnett's 'homer in the gloaming'".[2]

Quote of 1951

"The Cubs have come to the conclusion that it takes more than the mellifluous voice of Broadcaster Bert Wilson rapturously describing "beautiful Wrigley Field to bring fans out."

Edgar Munzel in *The Sporting News*—10/10/51—after Cubs attendance dropped 271,529 from 1950.[3]

In spite of the fact that . . .

"Bert is probably the greatest press agent any piece of real estate ever had. He worships Wrigley field [*sic*]. It's his personal Taj Mahal."[4]

Anton Remenih in the Chicago Tribune—*August 4, 1951*

Phil Cavarretta (www.ArgentaImages.com)

1952

The Season by the Numbers			
77-77	.500 5th 19.5 games out		1,024,826 (13,224 average)
42-35	.545 at home		134% of NL average

Home Opener

APRIL 18: CUBS (RUSH) VS. CARDINALS (BRECHEEN); SUNNY, 67 DEGREES; 20,396 PAID

Cubs 5 Cardinals 4—The Cubs scored four runs in the ninth inning before the Cardinals recorded an out. The scintillating rally went like this: Hank Sauer and Randy Jackson singled; Roy Smalley and Bruce Edwards walked, Sauer scoring on the second pass; Harry Chiti reached first on an error, scoring Smalley; pinch hitter Bill Serena doubled to center to score the tying and winning runs.

Eric Johnson, a fifty-three-year-old dairyman who had seen thirty-two Cub openers, threw out the first pitch. Johnson's toss started a string of fifteen of sixteen years that older fans, die-hard fans, or longtime Wrigley Field employees threw the first pitch at Wrigley Field openers.

What's New

- Box seat prices increased 50 cents to $2.50. Grandstands and bleacher tickets stayed the same, costing $1.25 and 60 cents respectively. The "Cubs" of 1876 charged 50 cents to see their games. So outside of the dime federal ticket tax, bleacher fans could still see a Cub game for the same price as seventy years ago.
- The team spent $50,000 rebuilding ramps in the ballpark.
- Management removed the four-year-old center field canopy sometime prior to the opener against the Cardinals. Before the third game of the series, on April 20, they roped off four sections of the lower center field bleachers, creating a new hitting background. The blocked-off seats have remained off limits to fans, except for a 1955 exhibition game with the White Sox and the 1962 All-Star Game.

  While it's unclear why the team removed the canopy, the *Chicago Tribune* credited Cardinal manager Eddie Stanky and outfielder Stan Musial with asking Cub management to improve the hitting background during that first series in April. Bob Broeg of the *St. Louis Post-Dispatch* concurred, saying, "With Musial and other Cardinals demanding it, the Cubs blocked off the center field bleacher at Stanky's request, relieving the white-shirt batting background."[5] If true, it marked the third time in eleven years the Cubs ignored complaints about the bad background from their own team but bowed to pressure from the opposition or outsiders.

What Happened

- A notice in the 1952 Chicago Cub scorecard reminded fans about Wrigley Field's ticket policies:

  Wrigley Field is NEVER sold out in advance!
  You may have heard that every box seat has been sold for the big game, but that doesn't mean ALL seats are sold. The Cubs always hold 25,000 unreserved grandstand and bleacher tickets until the day of the game.[6]

- During a June 8 Cubs-Braves game, Boston's Warren Spahn broke Frank Baumholtz's hand with an inside pitch. Spahn received a letter from an angry Cub fan, saying in part, "When you come back to Chicago, I'll see you and make good. . . . I'll get you somehow. You can be handled."[7] Two police detectives shadowed Spahn during the Braves' return to Wrigley Field in mid-July. He pitched the second game of the series and left Chicago without incident.

- Professional wrestlers invaded Wrigley Field again on June 27. Lou Thesz defended his championship belt against Pat O'Connor. Cold, damp weather kept away more than half the expected crowd of 25,000. Threatening skies forced the main participants into the ring at 9:30, a half an hour earlier than scheduled.

Game of the Year

June 11—Hank Sauer hit three home runs off Curt Simmons. His shots accounted for all the Cub runs in the 3-2 victory over the Phillies. Remarkably, Sauer also hit three home runs off Simmons in a game two years earlier at Wrigley Field.

Quote of 1952

"We get an occasional letter from a fan who says he'd like night ball because he can't get off during the day. I write him that if he must have night baseball he can witness it at Comiskey Park."[8]
P. K. Wrigley in The Sporting News—*February 20, 1952*

1953

The Season by the Numbers		
65-89	.442 7th 40 games out	763,658 (9,854 average)
43-34	.558 at home	80% of NL average

Opening Day

APRIL 14; CUBS (RUSH) VS. REDLEGS* (RAFFENSBERGER); CLOUDY, 59 DEGREES; 21,222 PAID

*The Reds were officially known as the Redlegs between 1953 and 1959. The change was in response to the nickname's negative connotation during the cold war.

Cubs 3 Redlegs 2—Randy Jackson's eighth inning double scored Dee Fondy and Bill Serena, putting the Cubs ahead for good. Bob Rush went all the way; the only Redleg runs came on home runs by Willard Marshall and Ted Kluszewski. Hank Sauer, last year's National League MVP, didn't start the game, as he recovered from a broken finger. Hank pinch hit in the eighth inning and popped out on the first pitch. Jackson followed with his game-winning double.

Adele Karstrom, a Cub fan since 1933, threw out the first pitch. Lou Diamond's band played the National Anthem.

What's New

- Yosh Kawano moved from the visitor's clubhouse attendant position to the Cub clubhouse attendant position. Kawano remained there through the 1999 season.
- The club added lockers for fans on the concourse under the grandstand.

What Happened

- Andy Lotshaw, trainer for the Cubs and the Bears, died at age 73. Lotshaw came to Cubs Park in 1921 when the Bears transferred to Chicago. A year later he also took over training duties with the Cubs. Considering he worked each April to December in Wrigley Field, he probably spent more time in the park to date than anyone of prominence except groundskeeper Bobby Dorr.
- The Boston Braves moved to Milwaukee after drawing only 281,278 fans the entire 1952 season. Consequently, the Cubs expected an attendance drop, estimating that more than 200,000 fans from Wisconsin visited Wrigley Field each year. The guess proved right. The Cubs attracted 763,658 customers for 1953, about 250,000 less than in 1952. The Braves drew a whopping 1.8 million that first year in Milwaukee, a National League record.
- The Cubs lost $410,690 in 1953, the second highest amount in National League history (behind last year's Boston Braves). The Cubs would have lost more, but their minor league team in Los Angeles showed a profit of $86,583.
- P. K. Wrigley dodged rumors all summer that he'd sell the Cubs. Wrigley denied it, but said if he did, he'd sell "to someone I'm sure is a baseball man at heart. I'm not going to dispose of them to anyone who is just looking for an investment."[9]
- On August 31, the Cubs took over the contract of shortstop Gene Baker from their Los Angeles farm team. Baker became the first African American on a Cubs official roster (although he didn't join the team until September 17). On September 14, Ernie Banks arrived at Wrigley Field via the Kansas City Monarchs of the Negro American League. He promptly hit his first batting practice pitch out of the ballpark. Rookies Banks, Don Elston, and Bill Moisan, saw their first action on September 17. (Baker didn't play. He pulled a muscle.) Banks went 0-3 and committed an error, but became the first African American to play for the Cubs.

Ernie Banks—his first day at Wrigley Field (www.ArgentaImages.com)

Game of the Year

September 6—The Cubs showed power, speed, and pitching in a doubleheader sweep. In the opener, Randy Jackson, Dee Fondy, Hank Sauer, and Ralph Kiner all homered. But Fondy's ninth inning steal of home helped the Cubs slip past the Redlegs, 7-6. The Cubs also took the nightcap, 7-2 behind rookie Jim Willis. The twenty-six-year-old schoolteacher went all the way for his first major league victory.

Bear News

A survey of season ticket holders convinced the Bears to move the starting time of their games up 25 minutes to 1:05 P.M. The earlier game time allowed fans extra time to get home before dark.

During the Bears-Cardinals game, someone stole the Bears' flag from the left field flagpole. The flag measured 9 feet by 16 feet and weighed over fifty pounds.

On October 18, twenty-three-year-old Willie Thrower became the first full-time African-American quarterback to play in an NFL game. Thrower replaced George Blanda during the second half against San Francisco and completed three passes for 27 yards. It was his only appearance for the Bears.

Quote of 1953

"If I had any sense I'd sell for the sake of peace and quiet."[10]
P. K. Wrigley in the Chicago Tribune—*July 23, 1953*

1954

The Season by the Numbers		
64-90	.416 7th 33 games out	748,183 (9,717 average)
40-37	.519 at home	72% of NL average

Home Opener

APRIL 15; CUBS (RUSH) VS. REDLEGS (BACZEWSKI); RAIN, 53 DEGREES; 17,271 PAID

Redlegs 11 Cubs 5—Rain delayed the start of the game for thirty minutes. Once it began, the Redlegs' Jim Greengrass hit a grand slam and former Cub Fred Baczewski pitched well enough for the win. Randy Jackson had four hits including a homer for the Cubs.

The game marked Stan Hack's first as manager at Wrigley Field. Hack replaced Phil Cavarretta, who was fired during spring training for admitting that the Cubs could not win the pennant. P. K. Wrigley accused Cavarretta of having a bad attitude and replaced him with Hack.

The Opening Day crowd made a nuisance of themselves. Fans repeatedly threw objects on the field and firecrackers exploded throughout the game.

Dan Kelly, an Assistant Supervisor at the Union Stockyards, tossed the first pitch. Kelly, a bleacher fan, missed only three Sunday games the last forty-six years. After the ceremony, he and his wife were treated to box seats. But Kelly confided that he'd be back in the bleachers during his next visit.

What's New

- A 200-car parking lot opened north of the park adjacent to the railroad tracks.
- The Cubs added a punching bag and a medicine ball to their clubhouse arsenal.

What Happened

- The misguided enthusiasm of the home opener carried over to an April 18 doubleheader. During the second game, a few fans entered the field near the Cardinal dugout, only to be confronted by ushers and Cardinal players. After a five-minute delay, order prevailed on the field. Edgar Munzel surmised that the ever-increasing mischief of a small group of fans could be blamed on long, drawn-out games and television. Drunken fans, it seemed, thought it was a good way to get famous. Munzel wrote, "Late afternoon fights have become prevalent at Sunday doubleheaders here that they are turning Wrigley Field into a brawl room even though it has some of the finest clientele in the major leagues."[11]

- As major league attendance dropped, even with the plethora of night games, some in the media began to support P. K. Wrigley's insistence on day baseball. Dan Daniel wrote, "The continual resistance of Phil Wrigley to urges from the other clubs to set up a lighting system on the Chicago North Side is regarded as a phenomenon in will power, and sturdy adherence to principal and aesthetic standards."[12]

  P. K. Wrigley himself piped in on the issue, saying:

  > Our bad year at the gate is not going to alter my thinking in the slightest. There will be no night baseball at Wrigley Field next season. In fact, there will never be any night baseball at Wrigley Field as long as I have the ball club, unless somebody can show me that I'm wrong about it. So far nobody has and it doesn't appear likely that anyone will.[13]

- The Cubs celebrated Hank Sauer Day on August 22. The slugger received over $6,000 in gifts including a Pontiac Catalina automobile, a hunting dog, and a year's supply of sauerkraut. The "tobacco shower" usually given to Sauer after home runs occurred throughout the game. Bleacher fans threw so much chewing tobacco that the game was delayed while Sauer and center fielder Bob Talbot stashed seventy-four packets of the stuff in the ivy for safekeeping.

  Sauer was one of baseball's great late-bloomers. In fact, he hit 97.6 percent of his home runs (281 of 288) after his 30th birthday. No other major leaguer with as many career home runs as Hank ever came close.

P. K. Wrigley enjoying a day at Wrigley Field (www.ArgentaImages.com)

• Over 14,000 watched the Harlem Globetrotters at Wrigley Field on August 21. The Trotters supplied their famous six-ton basketball court and put it to good use, beating a team of all-stars that included Red Holzman and Gene Shue. Portable lights illuminated the Saturday night contest that began at 8:30 P.M.

Game of the Year

April 17— The Cubs smoked the Cardinals 23-13. Randy Jackson got four hits and Gene Baker and Joe Garagiola stroked three each. The game broke a National League mark when the nine-inning contest took 3:43 minutes.

Quote of 1954

"The Cubs accent the "beautiful Wrigley Field" theme in all their advertising of the ball club, including Bert Wilson's fine "selling" job over the air. And it is thoroughly justified. With its ivy-clad walls, the amphitheater style construction down the foul lines, the comfortable roomy seats and the cleanliness of the park, no fans will challenge the adjective "beautiful" in connection with Mr. Wrigley's ball park."[14]

Edgar Munzel in The Sporting News—*June 23, 1954*

1955

The Season by the Numbers		
72-81	.471 6th 26 games out	875,800 (11,374 average)
43-33	.566 at home	90% of NL average

Home Opener

APRIL 12: CUBS (MINNER) VS. CARDINALS (LAWRENCE); 77 DEGREES; 26,153 PAID

Cubs 14 Cardinals 4—Opening Day fans hadn't enjoyed themselves like this in years. The Cubs led the Cardinals 11-1 after only two innings. They chewed through five Cardinal pitchers, slapping 18 hits. Hank Sauer had four while Randy Jackson and Paul Minner collected three apiece. Dee Fondy drove in five runs by the second inning: three on a bases clearing double and two more on a single.

Jacob Walter, a Cub fan for over fifty years, threw out the first ball. New Chicago Mayor Richard J. Daley also attended the game. A dance band played popular tunes.

What's New

• Workers repainted the lower exterior of the ballpark. They also repainted the scoreboard. In keeping with the game's increased specialization of pitchers, the column at the top of the board that had indicated each team's catcher, designated with a "C," now charted relief pitchers, indicated by "RP."

• Many seats were repainted and restrooms updated. Automatic hand dryers replaced paper towels. An outside sanitary service company inspected restrooms during each game.

- The team built a new $30,000 umpire quarters under the left field grandstand. The air-conditioned digs contained birch shelving, a shower room with three marble shower stalls, and a burgundy and coral painted parlor filled with Naugahyde furniture. Otis Shepard, the Wrigley Company artist, redesigned the room.
- In July, the team installed speakers in a 1,200-seat section of the left field grandstand to carry the audio portion of Jack Brickhouse's WGN telecast.
- The Cubs removed the fifteen-cent "Big Wedge of Pie" from their concession menu. Baseball and apple pie apparently did NOT go together!

What Happened

- On May 24, a violent rainstorm flooded the new umpires' room with a foot of water. Lightning struck the WGN-TV truck outside the ballpark and knocked out telephone service. Management called the Cubs-Cardinals game before it started.
- After a game on July 3, ballpark workers discovered a deceased male body underneath the right field bleachers. Police believed the man fell nearly thirty feet off a ramp leading from the bleacher seats.
- It was the hottest Chicago July on record with an average daily high of 91.5 degrees.
  During its first weekend, concession manager Ray Kneip ran three times as many pop vendors as normal. Sales of soft drinks increased tenfold.
- A *Chicago American* newspaper poll of 3,000 Chicago fans found that a majority had a greater interest in baseball since the war, but fewer said they attended games. When asked why, fans indicated parking problems and overall expense. In the same poll, only 46 percent of fans wanted the Cubs to host night games.
- Bert Wilson, the team's primary radio voice since 1945, died of a heart ailment on November 5. His trademark lines, the facetious "I don't care who wins as long as it's the Cubs" and "beautiful Wrigley Field" buoyed fans through very lean years. Wilson, forty-four years old, left behind a wife and three children.

Game of the Year

May 12—Sam Jones no-hit Pittsburgh, becoming the first to throw a no-hitter at Wrigley Field since the famous "double no-hitter" in 1917 and the first black man to toss one in major league history. Jones began the ninth inning by walking the first three Pirate batters: Gene Freese, Preston Ward, and Tom Saffell. Then, in miraculous fashion, Jones reared back and struck out the next three: Dick Groat, Roberto Clemente, and Frank Thomas. Jones was an all-or-nothing pitcher in 1955; he led the league in losses (20), walks (185), and strikeouts (198). But on this day, he treated 2,918 fans to the game of their lives.

Quote of 1955

"The time is coming when both the Sox and the Cubs will have to move away from their present crowded locations. . . .The population in the suburbs is growing by leaps and bounds. They'd better act before it's too late."[15]

Cub fan J. S. Krishack in the Chicago American—*July 6, 1955*

1956

The Season by the Numbers		
60-94	.390 8th 33 games out	720,118 (9,173 average)
39-38	.506 at home	64% of NL average

Home Opener

APRIL 20; CUBS (JONES) VS. REDLEGS (FOWLER); 41 DEGREES; 13,973 PAID

Cubs 12 Redlegs 1—Ernie Banks clubbed a two-run home run and the Cubs scored six times in the first inning. Monte Irvin also homered. Sam Jones struck out nine and carried a two-hit shutout into the ninth inning.

Everett Gregerson, a thirty-eight-year-old cab driver, threw out the first pitch (a replica of an 1876 baseball honoring the team's eightieth anniversary). Gregerson missed only a dozen Cub home games the past ten years.

The team observed a moment of silence for Bert Wilson.

What's New

The upper deck ramps were replaced. In addition, the team installed moving sidewalks on ramps along the first base side of the park. Plans called for a series of eight ramps to take fans from the concourse to the upper deck before games and back down afterwards. Mechanical problems, however, limited the sidewalks to just the upper deck ramps and they only brought fans up. After games, the fans walked down on their own power.

What Happened

- Two home run balls hit a parked car on the north side of Waveland Avenue during a Cubs-Giants game on June 13. Drives by Eddie Miksis and Willie Mays cracked the car's windshield and side window. The team paid for the damage.
- A storm on July 21 stopped a Cubs-Giants game after only five pitches. Lightning struck a flagpole on the roof and sent a portion of the pole into the box seats. A few customers suffered bruises and an umbrella got mangled, but no one received serious injuries.

Games of the Year

May 2—Records fell in the Giants' 6-5, seventeen-inning victory. The Giants used twenty-five players in the game, a major league record. The two teams totaled forty-eight players, besting the old mark by six. The Cubs' Don Hoak established a dubious major league record, striking out six times.

May 30—The Cubs and Braves split a doubleheader. The Cubs survived the opener, 10-9, and dropped the nightcap, 11-9. The teams combined for a major league record 15 home runs in a doubleheader. Bobby Thomson (4), Hank Aaron (2), Eddie Mathews (2), and Joe Adcock homered for the Braves. The Cub honors went to Gene Baker, Ernie Banks, Harry Chiti, Dee Fondy, Hobie Landrith, and Turk Lown. The Braves hit three consecutive home runs in the first inning of the opener. The trio of clouts precipitated a brushback pitch and then a beanball to Bill Bruton by the Cubs' Russ Meyer. The two fought and were ejected.

Bear News

Before the baseball season, the grounds crew collected ten wheelbarrows of broken glass in right field, left behind by Bear fans seated in the on-field bleachers.

The Bears scrubbed the Lions, 38-21, to win the Western Division and a date in the NFL title game. The vicious battle saw the Bears knock out Lions' quarterback Bobby Layne with a concussion. In the closing moments, the teams and several hundred fans sparred on the field. With order restored and the game over, the fans tore down the goal posts. They celebrated the team's best season in a decade.

The bravado didn't matter. Two weeks later at Yankee Stadium, the Giants whipped the Bears, 47-7 to win the NFL title.

Quote of 1956

"It is ridiculous for any fan to think that the Cubs take great pride in their baseball park but do not care about the team that plays in it. This would be no more consistent than displaying a platinum ring setting with a piece of beer bottle mounted on it."[16]

P. K. Wrigley in the Chicago Tribune—*May 18, 1956—on the dwindling on-field performance of his team*

1957

The Season by the Numbers		
62-92	.403 7th (t) 33 games out	670,629 (8,598 average)
31-46	.403 at home	58% of NL average

Opening Day

APRIL 16; CUBS (RUSH) VS. BRAVES (SPAHN); CLOUDY, 55 DEGREES; 23,674 PAID

Braves 4 Cubs 1—Johnny Logan homered in the Braves' four-run sixth inning. That's all Milwaukee needed as Warren Spahn scattered four hits for his 204th win. He beat a revamped Cub lineup, with rookies Bob Will, Dick Drott, and Cal Neeman making their major league debuts. The loss ruined Bob Scheffing's managerial debut.

William Klose, an eighty-one-year-old fan who saw his first Cub game in 1886, threw out the first pitch. Pete Palmer, a Broadway performer, sang the National Anthem.

What's New

• The scoreboard was repainted olive green with blue piping lines. The background color has remained the same since.
• Workers rebuilt the concession stand behind first base.
• The Cubs wore pinstriped home uniforms for the first time in twenty years.

- Wrigley Field's lack of lights frustrated schedule makers. In 1956, umpires called the second game of five doubleheaders because of darkness. In two cases, the Cubs and their opponents were tied, necessitating a replay of the entire game (and another doubleheader). This year, to stem the problem, the Cubs moved up the starting time of doubleheaders one-half hour to 1:00 P.M. It worked. Darkness didn't claim a single game.

What Happened

- Bobby Dorr, Wrigley Field grounds crew chief since 1919, died at age 71. Dorr oversaw the lowering of the playing field in 1923 and helped plant the famed ivy in 1937. His longevity and the fact his family lived in the apartment adjacent to the left field grandstand (at 1053 Waveland Avenue) provided Wrigley Field with one of its many nicknames, "Bobby Dorr's House." His obituary in the *Sporting News* bragged that "Dorr applied an artist's touch that made 'beautiful Wrigley Field' live up to its billing. He and his crew labored so painstakingly in grooming the field that seldom did even a blade of grass seem to be out of place."[17] Pete Marcantonio, a grounds crew member since 1934 and Dorr's assistant since 1947, took over as grounds crew chief.

  The use of Dorr's apartment after his death is sketchy. Retired team Traveling Secretary Bob Lewis lived in it for a time. Around 1980, it was a lounge for the players' wives. In 1982, the team's Marketing Department used the space. Sometime later, it became the Concession Department's headquarters. They still use it today.

- The Cubs and Redlegs played on NBC's "Game of the Week," marking the first ballgame televised "nationally" from Wrigley Field. Major League baseball broadcast the May 11 game to 120 stations in "non-major league" towns.

Bobby Dorr (www. ArgentaImages.com)

  The game was blacked out in major league cities because the commissioner and most team officials felt that televised baseball hurt major league attendance. P.K. Wrigley did not share the thought; he welcomed television, like radio, as a vehicle to promote his club and his ballpark. Housewives watched during the day and thousands of children rushed home from school to catch the last few innings of Cub home games on television. Those maternal and childhood habits produced generations of fans.

- On June 1 and 2, television stars Lassie and the Lone Ranger performed at a "Western Round-up" in Wrigley Field. The event included "trick riding, roping, and comedy numbers."[18]

Games of the Year

May 24 and 26—The Cubs' Frank Ernaga homered in his first major league at-bat, becoming the first Cub ever to accomplish this feat at Wrigley Field. The shot off Warren Spahn flushed the Braves, 5-1. Two days later, rookie Dick Drott fanned 15 Braves to set a modern Cub record. Frank Ernaga homered again in the twinbill. Those two home runs marked Ernaga's total 29-game career output.

Quote of 1957

"One of the prettiest parks in the Majors, with its vine-covered outfield walls and clean, neat interior. . . .The dozen or so restrooms are adequate (unless larger crowds start coming out to the park). . . . Andy Frain ushers are briskly efficient and are never tipped. . . . Best place to sit is behind home plate in the upper deck. . . . The whole park can get uncomfortably hot during Chicago's midsummer days."[19]

In Sports Illustrated—*April 15, 1957—the annual baseball issue not only critiqued the teams but their ballparks, too.*

1958

The Season by the Numbers		
72-82	.468 5th (t) 20 games out	979,904 (12,726 average)
35-42	.455 average	75% of NL average

Home Opener

APRIL 18; CUBS (DROTT) VS. CARDINALS (JONES); 69 DEGREES; 21,076 PAID

Cubs 11 Cardinals 6—The Cubs turned 13 hits, 5 walks, and 3 wild pitches into a convincing rout. Moose Moryn hit a two-run homer in the fourth inning. The Cubs feasted on former teammate Sam Jones and improved to 3-0. All their wins came against St. Louis.

Longtime Cub fan Frank Carter threw out the first ball.

What's New

- The Cubs raised grandstand tickets twenty-five cents and bleachers fifteen cents. This year's prices:

Box Seat . . . $2.50
Grandstand . . . $1.50
Bleacher . . . 75 cents

- The infield tarp was replaced.
- For the first time, on June 14, WGN-TV used a center field camera at Wrigley Field. Born out of necessity at a televised Little League game, the camera provided a clear shot of the ball from the pitcher's hand into the catcher's mitt. WGN used the same angle at Comiskey Park soon after and stations nationwide mimicked the discovery. This fourth Wrigley Field camera created the need for the center field camera shed. Over time the shed moved from the blocked-out hitting background to its present location near the upper center field bleachers.

What Happened

- In April, two boys got their clothing caught in the moving sidewalk. Ushers freed the first, an eight-year-old, when his shirt and jacket jammed in the machine. Moments later, a twelve-year-old's pants tangled when he tripped on the sidewalk. Firefighters from Engine 78 cut him loose.
- Stan Musial stroked his 3,000th hit on May 13. Cardinal manager Fred Hutchinson kept him out of the starting lineup in anticipation of Stan getting his hit at home the next night. But in the sixth inning, Musial pinch-hit and doubled down the left field line, becoming the eighth player to reach the milestone.
- Both Tony Taylor and the Cub bullpen got credit for an inside-the-park home run on July 1. In the first inning, Taylor drove a ground ball over third base that rolled in the vicinity of the Cub bullpen. As San Francisco left fielder Leon Wagner came over to retrieve it, he joined the Cub pitchers in a frantic search behind the bullpen bench. But the ball rested several feet beyond the bench in a gutter at the base of the wall. By the time Wagner realized the deception, Taylor scampered around the bases.
- In August, during a doubleheader with St. Louis, thieves stole a suit out of Jack Brickhouse's car in the press parking lot. Brickhouse hosted the television show "Playhouse" after the games that evening. The show went on, but work-weary Jack appeared in the wrinkled garment he wore at the ballpark.

Games of the Year

June 8—Moe Drabowsky held the Pirates to one hit. Ted Kluszewski knocked Pittsburgh's only safety, an infield topper in the second inning. Ernie Banks and Moose Moryn homered in the 4-0 win.

July 13—Lee Walls slapped seven straight hits, including his 19th home run in the 3-2 and 2-1 wins over the Phillies.

Quote of 1958

"To the blandishments of those who have sought to have him [P. K. Wrigley] install lights for the increased revenue of night ball, he has firmly said, "No.". . . .Can you imagine him going to the city of Chicago and threatening to move the Cubs unless the city provided him with parking space? Or can you imagine him talking out of one side of his mouth to the mayor of Chicago while talking out of the other side to another in a city 3,000 mile away? And then moving?"[20]

Oliver E. Kuechle in the Milwaukee Journal—*May 9, 1958*

1959

The Season by the Numbers		
74-80	.481 5th (t) 13 games out	858,255 (11,074 average)
38-39	.494 at home	66% of NL average

Opening Day

APRIL 11; CUBS (ANDERSON) VS. DODGERS (DRYSDALE); 42 DEGREES; 12,288 PAID

Snow cancelled the Cub opener on April 10, the earliest scheduled opener to date in Wrigley Field history. The postponement erased nearly $30,000 in advance ticket sales.

Cubs 6 Dodgers 1—Rookie George Altman reached base his first three at-bats and Bob Anderson went the distance. The Dodgers' only run came on a Don Drysdale home run.

Everett Lee, who saw his first Cub game in 1903, tossed the first pitch. To provide that "spring" feeling, the grounds crew dyed the grass green.

What's New

- The park's exterior got an extensive renovation. By July 1, workers added new aluminum-faced ticket windows on the Addison Street side of the park. In the same area, precast concrete panels replaced stucco and wire fencing. Exterior work on the Clark Street side continued into 1960.
- The Cubs moved the starting time of single, weekday games one-half hour later to 2:00 P.M. The new time allowed fans an extra half-hour to get from lunch to the ballpark. Weekend games and doubleheaders began at 1:00 P.M.

What Happened

- Over 375 vendors threatened to strike on Opening Day. The Cubs tried to sate them with new uniforms and a heated room beneath the stands, but the workers wanted a 25 percent commission and a $5 guarantee for cancelled games. The union and the team negotiated a new contract before the season began.
- Bill Veeck returned to Chicago when he purchased majority ownership of the White Sox. Veeck also brought the stunts he honed as a team owner in Milwaukee, Cleveland, and St. Louis. One of his frequent promotions was "Lucky Seat" night. During the game, he gave away prizes to random seat holders. Winners might win tickets for the remainder of the season. But more often than not they took home prizes like 50,000,000 celery seeds or a meal of eel, fried caterpillars, and French-fried ants delivered to the lucky fan's seat.

  Veeck had a plethora of novel ideas to promote his franchise. He scheduled music nights and gave away suntan lotion on hot days. With Veeck, Comiskey Park sold more than baseball; it was a funhouse full of surprises.

  Outside of Ladies Day, the Cubs, on the other hand, offered few promotions. They relied almost exclusively on Wrigley Field itself to attract fans. The White Sox, with a pennant and Veeck's unusual gimmicks, broke a Chicago baseball attendance record of 1,423,144. That's more than a half million better than this year's Cubs.
- Chicago hosted the third Pan American Games. Nine countries fielded baseball teams, including the United States, led by future Cubs Lou Brock and Ty Cline. Comiskey Park hosted three days of games and Wrigley Field hosted seven. Despite the novelty, on September 5, only 547 fans saw Venezuela defeat Puerto Rico for the gold medal at Wrigley Field.

Games of the Year

August 13—The Cubs made 19 hits, including five home runs, and thrashed the Giants, 20-9. George Altman went deep twice. Dale Long, Alvin Dark, and Tony Taylor also connected for home runs. Ed Donnelly threw one inning of relief to earn his only big league win. The game took 3:50 to complete, a new National League record for a nine-inning contest.

September 22-23—The Giants returned for a two-game series, immersed in one of the closest pennant races in National League history. With just five games to play, they trailed the Dodgers and the Braves by a game. In the opener, George Altman cracked a two-run, ninth inning homer off Sam Jones for a 5-4 win. The next day, third-string catcher Cal Neeman homered in the tenth to complete the sweep. Thanks to the Cubs, the Giants were done in 1959.

Quote of 1959

". . . From Wrigley Field where, according to the radio ads, you can have a picnic, to Comiskey Park where, nowadays, you can have a circus."[21]

Howard Roberts in the Chicago Daily News—*July 7, 1959*

FIFTH INNING
1960-1972
FALLING BEHIND

The Modern stadium era began in 1960 with Candlestick Park. It utilized cantilevered construction that eliminated most of the view-obstructing posts that came with every previous ballpark. Another convenience—acres of parking surrounded it. Modern stadiums followed in Los Angeles, Washington, New York, Houston, Atlanta, Anaheim, St. Louis, Oakland, San Diego, Cincinnati, Pittsburgh, and Philadelphia. Some were located downtown. Many replaced derelict Classic era parks in aging neighborhoods. All except the Los Angeles–area parks opened as multipurpose stadiums, designed to also meet the demands of professional football, fast replacing baseball as the country's most popular sport.

By 1963, pressure mounted for Chicago to build a multipurpose stadium to replace Wrigley Field and Comiskey Park. Newer was surely better, the prevailing thought went, and Wrigley Field's reputation suffered. Newspapermen penned words like "ancient"[1] and "rickety"[2] to describe the North Side ballpark. The prevailing wisdom nearly swept Wrigley Field and Comiskey Park away with most of the other Classic ballparks. But a combination of forces—financial, political, and philosophical—kept Chicago's old ballparks intact.

Regardless, changes occurred both inside and outside Wrigley Field. The Cubs completed the two-decade-long structural renovation, replacing more steel, concrete, and seating. The park completed its first major cosmetic updates since 1938, sheathing much of the exterior in pre-cast concrete panels. Today, the panels look out-of-place on the vintage ballpark. But in 1960, even the Cubs probably suspected that modern was better.

The neighborhood around Wrigley Field changed, too. The Lake View area became home for many first-and second-generation immigrants. Residents became more transient and the area showed signs of neglect. A 1963 newspaper article on Alta Vista Terrace, a Victorian-inspired block of homes a few blocks north of the ballpark, for example, called it "an island in the middle of a blighted area."[3]

The Cubs themselves continued to deteriorate and attendance reached its lowest levels since World War I. Yet, most unexpectedly, the long moribund franchise rebounded in 1967. Wrigley Field's rafters rocked again as a new generation of young people came to witness the "Cub Power" era. In fact, the last three years of the 1960s arguably produced as much excitement at Wrigley Field as the previous three decades combined.

1960

The Season by the Numbers		
60-94	.390 7th 35 games out	809,770 (10,382 average)
33-44	.429 at home	57% of NL average

Home Opener

APRIL 22; CUBS (HOBBIE) VS. GIANTS (JONES); 84 DEGREES; 26,753 PAID

Giants 10 Cubs 8—The largest opening day crowd since 1949 welcomed back Charlie Grimm as manager. The Cubs' Frank Thomas drove in three runs, but Jim Davenport homered twice and Willie McCovey added another, one of three Giant home runs in the fifth inning. Moose

Moryn gave the Cubs a lead in the seventh with a two-run double. But the Giants scored three runs in the final two innings for the win.

Eighty-three-year-old John Miller, a retired fireman, tossed the first pitch.

What's New

- Workers completed the exterior renovation project with new ticket booths at the Clark and Addison entrance and the continuation of the precast concrete panels on the Clark Street side of the park. Included in the new entrances were revolving gates guaranteed to keep fans from sneaking in.
- Fourteen flags now flew outside the main entrance, representing the eight National League cities and their six respective states. Today, just six flags fly there: the two competing teams, their cities, and their states.
- Almost 25 percent of the lower grandstand floor was replaced.
- A new backstop appeared behind home plate. Since it was shorter, the net to the upper deck took a steeper pitch than before.
- The Cub clubhouse was updated. Additions included new lighting, flooring, and a lounge between the clubhouse and manager Grimm's office. The clubhouse moved from behind the third base dugout to the left field corner. The change began the tradition of Cub players walking from the dugout to left field corner after games.
- Bowing to fan pressure, Pat Pieper announced batters during the entire game. For years, the public address man only announced the starters once through the batting order.

What Happened

- The city health department regulated the "excessive handling of hot dogs" at Chicago's two ballparks. Beginning May 13, all hot dogs were wrapped before being sold. Those sold by walking vendors required pre-wrapping and "pre-mustarding" at designated locations below the stands.[4]
- On April 30, a Cubs-Phillies game began fifteen minutes late because of a CONELRAD test. CONELRAD, a civil defense system designed to thwart Russian intelligence in the event of a nuclear attack, shut down all television stations and all but two low-power radio frequencies. Through CONELRAD (an acronym for "Control of Electromagnetic Radiation"), Americans received emergency information while Russia obtained no intelligence from commercial radio or television. The test, staged from 1:00-1:30 P.M., moved the television pregame show to 1:30 P.M., necessitating the later start.

- It wasn't the arms race, but a case of espionage that highlighted a June 30 game. Milwaukee pitchers Joey Jay and Bob Buhl sat in street clothes in the center field bleachers. One watched the signs that Cub catcher El Tappe flashed to pitcher Don Cardwell. The other waved a scorecard to tell the Braves batters what pitch was coming. A bleacher fan caught on to the shenanigans and informed players in the Cub bullpen. Trainer Al Scheuneman reached the bleachers just as Jay and Buhl abandoned their post. Their deceit didn't work. Ernie Banks cracked his 250th career home run and Richie Ashburn collected his 2,300th hit in an 11-5 Cub win.
- A coal car jumped the railroad tracks west of the ballpark and damaged autos in the team parking lot. The unlucky cars belonged to baseball scout Bill Prince, ex-player Phil Cavarretta, and a team photographer.
- The White Sox drew 1,644,460 fans this year. Their 834,690 attendance edge over the Cubs was their largest margin in team history.

Game of the Year

May 15—Don Cardwell no-hit the Cardinals, 4-0. Just traded from the Phillies, Cardwell became the first pitcher to throw a no-hitter in his first start with a new team. Moose Moryn's game ending, shoestring catch saved Don's masterpiece and sent thousands of fans onto the field. Richard Dozer of the *Chicago Tribune* called it the "wildest mob scene in Wrigley Field since Gabby Hartnett hit that legendary home run 'in the gloaming' twenty-two years ago."[5]

Bear Facts

Changing Wrigley Field to the home of the Bears each fall was time consuming and costly. Workers expended over 2,700 hours and $20,000 in wages to erect the 7,348-seat football bleachers. The baseball box seat chairs were switched out to the smaller football seats. The grounds crew also covered the dirt portion of the infield with 1,500 square feet of sod, costing over $1,000.

The Bears purchased a second tarp to "double-tarp" the field so it wouldn't freeze in very cold weather.

Quote of 1960

"Lights are a frill we can't afford now, but whenever we can afford them, I'd like to install them. . . .I want to make it clear that, lights or no lights, there will be no night baseball. The lights will be put in strictly as self-defense to assure completion of our day games."[6]

P. K. Wrigley in the Chicago Daily News—*October 12, 1960*

The on-field football bleachers in front of the center and right field bleachers (www.ArgentaImages. com)

1961

The Season by the Numbers

| 64-90 | .416 7th 29 games out | 673,057 (8,629 average) |
| 40-37 | .519 at home | 58% of NL average |

Home Opener

APRIL 14; CUBS (ANDERSON) VS. BRAVES (BUHL); FOGGY, 58 DEGREES; 11,299 PAID

Cubs 3 Braves 2—A Sammy Taylor two out, two-run, walk off home run vaulted the Cubs to the come from behind win. Hank Aaron homered in the seventh inning for the Braves. Relief ace Don Elston got the win.

Pat Pieper, now seventy-five years old, threw out the first ball.

It's a good thing the Cubs won. A group of long-suffering fans paraded through the stands with a sign saying, "Let's have a winner or lose our support."[7] Years of mediocrity were getting old.

What's New

The scoreboard changed with the game: The expansion Los Angeles Angels and Washington Senators added two teams to the American League side of the scoreboard. Space came two ways: Moving the words "NATIONAL" and "AMERICAN" higher and toward the center of the board, and condensing "innings" and the upper inning numerals (1-9) from two lines to one.

While the National League wouldn't expand until 1962, their new teams, Houston and New York, filled the extra two lines on the bottom of the National League side. Throughout the year, the line score in Houston's fourth through seventh innings said, "1962."

For easier viewing, red and green horizontal lines separated the games on the scoreboard. The Cubs' line score, which had stood at the top of the National League scores, was moved to the center (and the White Sox moved from the top of the American League scores to the center).

- Dimension distances appeared on the flagpoles for the first time.
- The Collins and Wiese coal yard, which stood since 1905 on the triangular piece of land immediately west of the park, was razed after the season. A Henry's Drive-in restaurant replaced it in 1962.
- The Cubs fired manager Lou Boudreau after the 1960 season. When he moved to the WGN radio booth in 1961, he was given a direct phone line to the Cub dugout. Boudreau could call down and relay information from his physical vantage point, inquire about strategy, or get clarification for his radio audience.

What Happened

- A bomb expert searched the press box after someone called in an anonymous threat during a May 19 game against the Cardinals. The device, reputedly stashed in a paper bag, was never found.
- A portable hot dog cart near the right field box seats caught fire during the sixth inning of a game on May 28. Wrigley Field staff could not extinguish the flames, so firefighters from Engine 78 put it out.

Wrigley Field in May 1961. Even when the coal yard was removed, the railroad tracks remained into the 1970s. (Chicago History Museum, ICHi-24209, photographer—John Spiro)

- Max Zang, a.k.a. "Gravel Gertie," died on July 15. Zang may have been the most famous vendor in Wrigley Field history. He developed his signature roughhewed voice from years of hawking his wares. Former radioman Bert Wilson gave him his nickname in 1946, probably after a character in *Dick Tracy.*
- Milwaukee manager Birdie Tebbetts retaliated for last year's espionage snafu. He believed the Cubs stole his catcher's signs from the open slats in the scoreboard and filed a formal protest after Ernie Banks homered in the third inning of a game on September 4.

Game of the Year

September 27—Nineteen-year-old Danny Murphy knocked his first two Wrigley Field home runs as the Cubs dumped the Cardinals, 5-2. Ken Hubbs, also nineteen, stroked his first major league home run. Richard Dozer of the *Chicago Tribune* wondered if "a silent crowd of 1,558 may have been witnessing the birth of a new era in Cub potency."[8] Murphy, it turned out, couldn't hit major league pitching. He retooled and returned as a reliever, fashioning a 4-4 career record with the forgettable White Sox teams of 1969-1970.

Quote of 1961

"In the last few years, the Cubs have spent an estimated million dollars on rehabilitating the ballpark. In general, the work was described as decorative. Actually, the ballpark was crumbling. Many of the steel beams in the park had rusted through and were very weak (Some workmen claim they could push their hands through the rusted remains of some beams)."[9]

Bill Furlong in the Chicago Daily News—*August 10, 1961*

1962

The Season by the Numbers

59-103	.364 9th 42.5 games out	609,802 (7,528 average)
32-49	.395 at home	51% of NL average

Home Opener

APRIL 13; CUBS (ELLSWORTH) VS. CARDINALS (WASHBURN); 43 DEGREES; 9,750 PAID

Cardinals 8 Cubs 5—The Cubs' Don Elston walked in the tying run in the ninth inning. Both teams scored in the fourteenth, but the Cardinals scored three more in the fifteenth for the win. The Cubs' Lou Brock stroked his first major league home run, a drive onto Sheffield Avenue. Stan Musial scored his 1,860th career run, breaking Mel Ott's league record.

In place of one manager, P. K. Wrigley tried the "College of Coaches," which consisted of eight coaches, five of which served as stints during the 1961 and 1962 seasons. Elvin Tappe was "manager" for the opener.

Bob Lewis, the team's retired traveling secretary, threw out the first ball.

What's New

- The main entrance exterior was painted dark blue. It remained that way until at least the late 1970s.
- Ray and Marge Meyer purchased "Eddie's Bleachers," a bar on the southeast corner of Waveland and Sheffield Avenues. It opened in the fall as "Ray's Bleachers" and later became the unofficial home of the "Bleacher Bums."

What Happened

- New stadium construction accelerated as Dodger Stadium and D.C. Stadium opened. The latter ushered in the era of multipurpose, publicly funded stadiums. Its impersonal, sterile design started a trend that would last for a decade. Their successful unveilings pushed the Modern stadium boom; by season's end the Mets broke ground on Shea Stadium and Houston revealed plans for the world's first domed stadium, the Astrodome.

- Telstar, a 170-pound, 34-inch satellite beamed the first transatlantic broadcast on July 23. Europeans got a glimpse of the Golden Gate Bridge, Niagara Falls, and ninety seconds of a game at Wrigley Field. Folks in the old country saw a panoramic view of the park and two Philadelphia batters facing the Cubs' Cal Koonce—the first flied to right and second singled, both on first pitches.

  Was it luck that the batters swung away, providing Europe an action-filled glimpse of the national pastime? According to Jack Brickhouse, home plate umpire Tony Venzon told them, "If the pitch is within two feet of the plate, swing or I'll call it a strike."[10]

- The Cubs sold fewer than 800 season tickets this year. While not unusual for the times, ticket manager Jack Maloney admitted, "We have no plan. The team had no sales drives or gimmicks to get fans into season tickets. People buy what they want, when they want it. That's long been the Cub practice."[11]

- Cub fans witnessed the team's sixteenth straight second-division finish. Moreover, the team finished last in attendance for the first time since moving to Wrigley Field. At the winter meetings, the National League owners took an extraordinary measure, asking P. K. Wrigley to install lights at Wrigley Field. The reason was simple—visitors received twenty-nine cents from each ticket sold, so road teams averaged only $2,185 per game. In contrast, visiting teams made $10,200 per game at new Dodger Stadium.

Games of the Year

July 30—The Major League All-Star Game returned to Wrigley Field. A crowd of 38,359 watched the American League post a 9-4 victory behind home runs by Pete Runnels, Leon Wagner, and Rocky Colavito. Interestingly, Warren Spahn and Stan Musial participated this year and also in the 1947 All-Star Game at Wrigley Field.

Fans sat in the lower center field bleachers for the first time since a 1955 exhibition game against the White Sox. Players complained that the lack of a suitable background provided the worst hitting conditions they ever saw.

Cub owner P. K. Wrigley caused a stir when he revealed he'd watch the All-Star Game at home on television. He told the *Chicago Daily News*, "Sometimes you get more out of the game by watching on TV than by being there in person." When asked if he'll miss the sunshine and fresh air that his team markets, Wrigley answered, "It all depends on where your TV set is."[12]

September 15—This miserable season reached a low point when the Cubs lost their tenth straight game, 6-4 to the Dodgers. The Cubs surrendered 11 walks, 3 errors, 2 hit batsmen, a wild pitch, and a passed ball. George Altman was picked off and doubled off, and the Dodgers stole five bases, including a triple steal in the ninth inning. The loss dropped the North Siders' record to 52-96.

Quote of 1962

"There's no sense having an exploding scoreboard if you don't have anything to explode it about."
P. K. Wrigley in the Chicago Daily News—*July 14, 1962—when asked if he'd consider a scoreboard like the one at Comiskey Park.*

1963

The Season by the Numbers		
82-80	.506 7th 17 games out	979,551 (12,093 average)
43-38	.531 at home	85% of NL average

Opening Day

APRIL 9; CUBS (JACKSON) VS. DODGERS (DRYSDALE); SUNNY, 35 DEGREES; 18,589 PAID

Dodgers 5 Cubs 1—The Cubs outhit the Dodgers 11-9. Ron Santo, Ernie Banks, and Andre Rodgers doubled, but it wasn't enough as Don Drysdale went the distance.

Linda Cody, Chicago's Easter Seal Child, threw out the first ball. She was the only thrower in a sixteen-year stretch who wasn't a longtime fan, a die-hard fan, or a longtime Wrigley Field employee.

What's New

- More green paint in the lower grandstand and more white paint on the flagpoles.
- The Cubs hired Robert Whitlow as baseball's first athletic director. The former athletic director at the Air Force Academy came aboard to maintain a consistency in training from the low minors through the major leagues. In short, the team hired Whitlow to clean up the inconsistencies in the desultory College of Coaches.

  Whitlow provided a sympathetic ear toward complaints about Wrigley Field's "fuzzy" hitting background. He erected a 64-foot by 8-foot green wire fence in front of the empty bleachers in center field. The ivy grew up the fence to provide a better hitting background.

What Happened

- Since 1959, the White Sox added 6,000 parking spaces around Comiskey Park. Their lots held 14,000 cars, nearly three times the public and private spaces around Wrigley Field. The Cubs looked to purchase nearby properties and turn them into parking lots. They also studied running a train along the tracks immediately west of the park to shuttle fans to and from satellite parking areas.

  In the intervening years, P. K. Wrigley had a chance to purchase the six-acre Convent of the Good Shepherd. The school for wayward girls stood at 1126 W. Grace Street, just two blocks north of the ballpark. Wrigley, however, had no interest. "I think it would be asinine for anybody to buy it just for a parking lot," he reasoned. At least now, Wrigley was right. Crowds at Cub games didn't necessitate additional parking.[14]

  The school parked 500 cars a game on their property for at least two decades. The Cubs finally purchased a portion of the school grounds in 1986 and ran a 700-car parking lot from the site.

- The sign stealing controversies of the past few years resurfaced again on June 5. During a Cubs doubleheader sweep, Giants manager Alvin Dark asked the umpires to shut the open slats through which the scoreboard operators watched the game. Instead, team Vice-President John Holland telephoned the scoreboard and ordered the operators to stay away from the openings.

- Anti-Castro demonstrators rushed the field during an August 4 game. They waved Cuban flags and a banner reading, "President Kennedy, please do not arrest anymore Cuban fighters."[15] Ushers and police ejected them from the park.

- During his third inaugural address, Mayor Richard J. Daley said that the city, like Washington and Houston, should build a modern stadium. His words planted the Chicago multipurpose stadium seed.

  Chicago White Sox owner Art Allyn came out categorically against such a project. Speaking two weeks after Daley's address, Allyn said, "If there is any possibility, however remote, of making use of the city's credit or utilizing the taxpayer's dollar, I'll not have a damn thing to do with it."[16] Allyn, an investment banker and fiscal conservative, believed new stadium financing must come from private funds. To make matters worse, everyone recognized that any multipurpose stadium, whether publicly or privately funded, needed his backing.

Games of the Year

June 5—The upstart Cubs swept the first place Giants, 9-5 and 5-4; their tenth win in twelve games. The victories pulled them within one game of the league leaders. Ernie Banks homered twice and Ken Hubbs, Billy Williams, and Lou Brock also went deep. Edward Prell of the *Chicago Tribune* said this about the exciting games:

> Perhaps not since the Cubs' last pennant days in 1945 was there such a wild demonstration of fans as the 19,710 put on during the five and a half hours of spectacular action. Most of the spectators still remained when Lindy McDaniel eliminated three dangerous batters with the tying run on second base. They gave the Cubs an uproarious standing ovation.[17]

The next day, the Cubs finished the four-game sweep. The anachronism was complete—with the season one-third over, the Cubs tied the Giants and Cardinals for first place!

August 31—Center fielder Ellis Burton stroked a ninth inning grand slam for a 6-5 defeat of Houston. The shot, into the second row of the left field bleachers, drove in Don Landrum, Andre Rodgers, and Leo Burke. Despite the heroics, the Cubs had fallen to a familiar position, seventh place and eleven games behind the Dodgers.

Bear Facts

On December 29, the Bears met the New York Giants for the NFL title, the first championship football game at Wrigley Field in twenty years. NFL Commissioner Pete Rozelle feared the 1:05 start time because of the potential of an overtime game in lightless Wrigley Field. Rozelle asked

1963 Football pass out ticket (championship game)

Halas to move the game to another venue. Halas instead moved the starting time up one hour to 12:05 P.M.

Air-blown heating units kept the field semi-thawed. But the temperature registered only nine degrees at kickoff. Fans didn't seem to care; 45,800 packed the ballpark.

The Giants took the lead when Y. A. Tittle passed fourteen yards to Frank Gifford. But the Bears dominated from then on. Their stifling defense intercepted Tittle five times, two of them leading to quarterback sneak touchdowns by Bill Wade. When Richie Petitbon intercepted a last desperation throw to the Chicago goal line, the Bears clinched a 14-10 victory and their first NFL title since 1946.

Quote of 1963 (Early 1964)

"I am in favor of building a community stadium in Chicago; something like a domed arena going up at Houston . . . The Cubs, White Sox and Chicago Bears would play there . . . We would tear down Wrigley Field and sub-divide it for residential use. But I don't think there is much chance of it."[18]

P. K. Wrigley in the Milwaukee Journal—*January 10, 1964—on building a Modern era stadium in Chicago.*

1964

The Season by the Numbers

| 76-86 | .469 8th 17 games out | 751, 647 (9,280 average) |
| 40-41 | .494 at home | 60% of NL average |

Home Opener

APRIL 17; CUBS (ELLSWORTH) VS. PHILLIES (MAHAFFEY); 82 DEGREES; 18,868 PAID

Phillies 10 Cubs 8—The teams combined for eight home runs; Billy Williams knocked two homers and Dick Allen hit the first of his career. The five in the fifth inning tied a major league record. Ron Santo went to the hospital with blurred vision after a collision with baserunner Danny Cater in the fifth inning.

Philip Clarke, a forty-year season ticket holder, tossed the first pitch. Louis Sudler sang the National Anthem accompanied by Henry Brandon's Band.

Warren Brown of the *Chicago's American* wondered, "If owner P. K. Wrigley will find time to sit in on Opening Day proceedings, and thus register THE upset of the season."[19]

What's New

- Renovated and enlarged restrooms on the lower concourse.

What Happened

- The Cubs celebrated "Ernie Banks Day" on August 15. During a pregame program, Ernie received platitudes and gifts. They included a proclamation scroll signed by Mayor Daley, a station wagon from the fans, a sterling silver tray, a transistor radio, a stereo, a color television, and a diamond ring. During the ceremony, Philip R. Clarke, the day's organizer, called Ernie "Mr. Cub," the first reference to a moniker that became as famous as Banks himself.
- Andy Frain, the man who started the ushering group that bore his name, died of a heart attack. Frain began at Wrigley Field in 1928 and his staff still served the park 40 years later. He was the perfect man to work the crowds, having sixteen siblings. Frain was only sixty years old.

- Wrigley Field reached its fifty-year anniversary. The team sponsored no recognitions or celebrations. No newspaper articles mentioned it. In an era when new equaled better, acknowledging advanced age was no virtue.

Game of the Year

June 30—A seventh inning single by Pete Rose kept Larry Jackson from tossing a perfect game. The Cubs beat the Reds, 1-0, and managed only two hits of their own. Shortstop Jim Stewart got them both: a double in the first inning and a run-scoring single in the sixth.

New Stadium

In February, Mayor Daley named a ten-man committee to investigate a Modern stadium in Chicago. The committee included P. K. Wrigley, Art Allyn, and George Halas. The Real Estate Research Corporation developed a report on preferred stadium designs, possible sites, and methods of financing.

The final report called for a 55,000-60,000 seat multipurpose stadium costing $22 million. Site purchase and preparation hiked the price from $34 to $49 million, depending on location. The stadium would have a grass field (the artificial surface was not yet invented) and an open roof.

The report recommended the site at Soldier Field over a Near West Side site and a South Loop location. At $34.5 million, the lakefront stadium cost 25 percent less than the Near West Side arena. The city owned the land and because a stadium already stood on the property, site preparation was minimal.

The report sighted three major sources of income. First, the Cubs, White Sox, and Bears would raise ticket prices and pay the city between 7 ½ to 10 percent of ticket sales. Second, each team forfeited concession income. Finally, the stadium would produce income from in-stadium advertising, team office rental, a 500-seat on-site restaurant, and a stadium sports club.

George Halas supported a new stadium. P. K. Wrigley, now with some doubts, publicly seemed willing to move forward. Art Allyn's earlier refusal to support a public stadium galvanized with the release of the report. He estimated the White Sox would lose $1.25 million a year off the gross income of concessions, parking, and rent. "I could not in good conscience support a program of the character suggested," said Allyn, and he resigned from the stadium committee shortly after the report's release.[20] Allyn's ferocious opposition doomed the project.

It's wildly ironic that Wrigley Field, the bane of many White Sox fans, still stands in part because a White Sox owner refused the chance to replace it.

The bleacher entrance at Waveland and Sheffield before 1965 (Chicago History Museum, ICHi-24309, photographer— F.S. Dauwalter)

Quote of 1964

"It may not necessarily be classified with the seven wonders of the world but there is no doubt that the domed arena now under construction in Houston will make the rest of the nation's baseball stadiums obsolete—even the new ones."[21]

Jerome Holtzman in the Chicago-Sun Times—*September 13, 1964—on the Astrodome*

1965

The Season by the Numbers		
72-90	.444 8th 25 games out	641,361 (7,521 average)
40-41	.494 at home	45% of NL average

Opening Day

APRIL 12; CUBS (JACKSON) VS. CARDINALS (GIBSON); CLOUDY, 47 DEGREES; 19,751 PAID

Cubs 10 Cardinals 10— Ernie Banks tantalized Cub fans with a two-strike, two-out, three-run, ninth inning homer (his 377th) to tie the game, 9-9. Darkness ended it after 10 innings, knotted at 10-10. The teams replayed the game on July 11, although the statistics from the original contest counted.

Albert Jorgenson threw out the first pitch. He toiled as an usher, an office boy, a member of the grounds crew, and since 1946, the scoreboard operator.

Louis Sudler sang the National Anthem accompanied by Henry Brandon's Band.

The fans observed a moment of silence for WGN broadcaster Jack Quinlan. He died the previous month in an automobile accident during spring training in Mesa, Arizona.

What's New

- Over 3,250 self-rising, plastic seats replaced folding chairs in the first 10 rows of box seats. The new seats sold for $3.50, 50 cents more than the box seats immediately behind them.
- This was the last season fans rented cushions. The addition of the more comfortable box seats lessened the need for the ten-cent concession rental.
- Bleacher seats increased 25 cents, finally reaching $1 a ticket.

- The cost of the four-page scorecard increased a nickel to fifteen cents, the first scorecard price hike in fifty years.

What Happened

- Robert Whitlow resigned as athletic director. The team didn't fill the position and removed the controversial "Whitlow Fence" hitting background. Between June 18, 1963, and the end of the 1964 season, ten batters lost home runs off the Whitlow Fence.

Date	Player	Team	Outcome	Additional Information
8/25/63	Santo	vs. Mets	triple	cost Santo a 100 RBI season
8/28/63	N. Matthews	vs. Phi	triple	cost Cubs a run in 8-7 loss
4/21/64	Mazeroski	Pitt	triple	
5/26/64	Cannizzaro	NY	double	
6/18/64	Banks	vs. Phi	double	
6/18/64	Dalrymple	Phi	double	
7/11/64	McCovey	SF	double	
7/31/64	Menke	Mil	triple	
8/14/64	Clendenon	Pitt	triple	
8/16/64	Santo	vs. Pitt	triple	

- While Mayor Daley plugged his multipurpose stadium plan, Houston's Astrodome, baseball's first domed stadium, opened for business. Its mind-numbing statistics included:

  - A playing field twenty-five feet below ground level
  - A translucent dome 208 feet high
  - A $4,500,000 air conditioning system
  - A $2,000,000, 474-foot-long electronic scoreboard
  - Skyboxes that rented for up to $90,000 a year
  - Parking for 30,000 cars

- The Cubs last *nine* home dates drew a *total* of 26,057 fans. Included were crowds of 892 and 550. During the latter, a Cubs-Dodgers game on September 16, the visitor's take, based on 29 cents per ticket, was only $151.25. Ron Santo said this about attendance: "It would be great to see at least 10,000 people in those seats, but we can't expect them to come out when we're playing this way. If we started to win, if we had a real good club, the people would come out. . . ."[22]

- P. K. Wrigley said he would never sell the Cubs. Wrigley's declaration squelched rumors that he would sell the Cubs and the new owners would move them to the Milwaukee to replace the Braves, who were moving to Atlanta in 1966.

Game of the Year

August 19—The Reds' Jim Maloney tossed an incomparable no-hitter; he struck out 12 and walked 10 in 10 innings. He threw 187 pitches before winning 1-0, thanks to Leo Cardenas's tenth inning homer off the left field foul pole. It marked the first of two no-hitters against the Cubs this year (Sandy Koufax tossed a perfect game in Los Angeles on September 9) and the first by a visitor since Fred Toney and the "double no-hit" game in 1917.

Bear News

The 3,253 new permanent box seats decreased the number of narrower folding chairs the Bears used during the football season. The loss of seats worried George Halas enough to consider moving the team elsewhere. In the end, the arrangement decreased football capacity by only 200, and Halas signed another three-year lease.

The Bears called Wrigley Field home, but not without consternation from the NFL. Commissioner Pete Rozelle said, "The Chicago Bears will be playing . . . in the smallest and most antiquated stadium in the National Football League."[23]

On December 12, rookie Gale Sayers went wild, scoring six touchdowns to tie an NFL record in the Bears' 61-20 rout of the 49ers. First, Sayers scampered 80 yards on a screen pass from Rudy Bukich. Then he scored on runs of 21 yards, 7 yards, 50 yards, and 1 yard. In the fourth quarter, he returned a punt 85 yards for his final score. The 61 points were the most the Bears scored in a regular season game to date.

Quote of 1965

"Wrigley Field, not so beautiful any more, but . . . where a better version of the Cubs and some night baseball might restore the roar of the crowd."[24]

Joe King in The Sporting News—*July 31, 1965*

1966

The Season by the Numbers

59-103	.364 10th 36 games out	635,891 (7,821 average)
32-49	.395 at home	40% NL average

Home Opener

APRIL 19; CUBS (BROGLIO) VS. GIANTS (HERBEL); CLOUDY, 63 DEGREES; 15,396 PAID

Giants 11 Cubs 10—The Giants' Willie Mays and Jesus Alou stroked four hits each. Mays whacked his 508th home run and drove in four runs. The Cubs' Randy Hundley and Byron Browne hit their first major league home runs in Leo Durocher's home managerial debut.

Al Bluhm attended his fiftieth consecutive opener and tossed out the first ball. Louis Sudler sang the National Anthem accompanied by Henry Brandon's Band.

The scoreboard during the home opener. The "next game" listings at the bottom of the board remained until major league expansion in 1969. (National Baseball Hall of Fame Library, Cooperstown, NY)

What's New

- The team added ten feet to the top of the screen behind the left field catwalk. The extra fencing came after complaints from Waveland Avenue neighbors of broken windows and unruly ball hawks. The addition remained for forty years until bleacher expansion in 2006.
- Eighty-year-old Pat Pieper continued as public address man but moved to the safety of the press box. Andy Frain usher Rick Ferrari took his place as on-field ballboy.
- Concessions sold pizzas at Wrigley Field. They were "Pro's Pizza," a small boxed pizza made for Ron Santo's fledgling pizza company.

What Happened

- Rain and cold postponed five games in the first month of the season. Through thirteen dates, the Cubs averaged only 6,700 fans per game.

  Fifteen games this season drew crowds under 4,000:

  2,566 on Thursday, April 21 vs. Giants

  3,076 on Thursday, April 28 vs. Pirates

  1,333 on Tuesday, May 10 vs. Cardinals

  3,813 on Wednesday, May 18 vs. Astros

  3,952 on Thursday, May 19 vs. Astros

  3,242 on Friday, May 27 vs. Braves

  3,778 on Friday, June 24 vs. Mets

  3,218 on Tuesday, September 6 vs. Phillies

  2,962 on Tuesday, September 13 vs. Braves

  961 on Wednesday, September 14 vs. Braves

  1,115 on Thursday, September 15 vs. Braves

  2,297 on Friday, September 16 vs. Cardinals

  1,041 on Tuesday, September 20 vs. Reds

  530 on Wednesday, September 21 vs. Reds

  1,257 on Thursday, September 22 vs. Reds

  The 530 fans that saw the Cubs and the Reds play out the string on September 21 marked the last time the Cubs failed to draw at least 1,000 fans at Wrigley Field. Twenty-three die-hards occupied the bleachers that day—fourteen sat in left field and nine in right field. No one sat in the center field bleachers.
- A dozen or so kids hung out in the bleachers during this, another lost season. They played catch with the players before the game. They razzed the opposition. One had a bugle. An older couple, Ma and Big Daddy Barker, showed up one day. She had a sheet with a hole in the middle, surrounded by the words, "Hit the Bleacher Bum."[25] The kids stuck their heads through the opening. The famous Bleacher Bums were born.
- On May 13, *Chicago Tribune* sportswriter Richard Dozer attended the opening of St. Louis' new Busch Stadium. Dozer seconded the feelings of many, saying, "The fact remains that

tonight Chicago fell another peg in its tumble towards the bottom of the list with its increasingly archaic north and south side baseball plants."[26]

- The Beatles played two shows at the International Amphitheater on August 12. Music producer Frank Fried confirmed that the group's first choice was Wrigley Field, but the team squelched the idea. During the band's tour this summer, they performed at Shea Stadium, Busch Stadium, Dodger Stadium, Candlestick Park, Crosley Field, Cleveland Municipal Stadium, and DC Stadium. But not Wrigley Field!

Games of the Year

April 23 and 24—Ferguson Jenkins made his Cubs debut as a relief pitcher in the third inning against the Dodgers. He got out of the inning with the bases loaded and pitched another five innings. Jenkins homered and drove in both runs in the Cubs' 2-0 win.

The next day, 20-year-old Ken Holtzman made his first major league start, limiting the Dodgers to three hits in six innings. The Cubs won again, 2-0.

September 15 and 25—Fergie Jenkins, now a starter, four-hit the Braves in an 8-2 win, his third victory in ten days. In the home finale, Ken Holtzman took a no-hitter into the ninth inning against the Dodgers. He settled for a two-hitter and out pitched Sandy Koufax.

Jenkins and Holtzman provided a ray of hope during a dismal season and a dire stretch of Cub futility. In fact, the years 1951-1966 marked one of only two times the White Sox dominated the Cubs in the Wrigley Field era. The South Siders were the model of consistency during this period, finishing in the first division each year. The Cubs were consistent too; they never reached the first division. Predictably, the White Sox outdrew the Cubs 18.9 million to 12.6 million. This scenario, however, was about to dramatically change.

Quote of 1966

"Fans who have been paying their way into Wrigley's park for years declare the Cub proxy could have been more zealous in providing for their comfort and enjoyment. As evidence, they cite the shabby appearance of a once immaculate ball park [sic] and the Cubs' perennial resting place near the bottom of the National League."[27]

In The Sporting News—*April 9, 1966*

In reality, Wrigley Field probably hadn't changed that much. Rather, most of the other major league ballparks had changed. When sportswriters saw Modern parks like Dodger

Stadium and the Astrodome, Wrigley Field paled in comparison. Perception, in this case is reality. The reputation of fifty-six-year-old Wrigley Field suffered.

1967

The Season by the Numbers		
87-74	.540 3rd 14 games out	977,226 (12,065 average)
49-34	.590 at home	73% of NL average

Opening Day

APRIL 11; CUBS (JENKINS) VS. PHILLIES (BUNNING); 41 DEGREES; 16,462 PAID

Cubs 4 Phillies 2—Fergie Jenkins didn't miss a beat as he stymied the Phillies on six hits. Glenn Beckert scored on a double steal in the sixth inning. He provided an insurance run with a solo home run in the eighth.

Ronald Centers, a twice-wounded Vietnam veteran, tossed out the first ball. Henry Brandon's Band played before the game.

What's New

- Wrigley Field received an updated public address system. In addition, organ music filled the park for the first time since 1941. Jack Kearney played the new keyboard in the football press box behind third base.

  The list of Wrigley Field organists:

Ray Nelson	1941
Jack Kearney	1967-1969
Frank Pellico	1970-1975
Vance Fothergill	1976-1978
John Henzl	1979-1981
Ed Vodicka	1982-1983
Bruce Miles	1984-1986
Gary Pressy	1987-date

- P. K. Wrigley refused to play the National Anthem before Cub games, believing the repetitive nature cheapened the song. The only exceptions were during World War II, on Opening Days, and on holidays. The team played the song before each game this year in response to the police action in Vietnam. "I don't care what Congress says," reasoned Wrigley, "We're at war in Vietnam."[28] They've played the song before virtually every game since.

Games of the Year

May 20—The Cubs swamped the Dodgers, 20-3. Heroes abounded: Randy Hundley hit a grand slam, Glenn Beckert drove an inside-the-park home run, Adolfo Phillips hit a three-run home run and a three-run double, Ted Savage stole home, and Ken Holtzman went the distance, raising his record to 5-0.

July 2—Ernie Banks called it his greatest thrill in baseball, even though he was injured and watched it from the radio booth. Pee Wee Reese of NBC-TV said the fans "gave me goose bumps. I've been in baseball a long time and it's hard to remember hearing a crowd cheer like they did out there today."[29]

Over 40,400 fans shoehorned into Wrigley Field—more than 10,000 were turned away. The Cubs sacked the Reds, 4-1, and moved into a first place tie with the Cardinals. It marked the team's sixth straight win and their sixteenth in nineteen games. It also marked the latest point in a season that the team resided in first place in over twenty years.

The Cubs hovered around first place through late July. Then they fell behind the Cardinals. Still, that magical day marked the rebirth of baseball on Chicago's North Side. Veterans like Banks, Williams, and Santo combined with the youthful newcomers: Jenkins, Hundley, and Beckert. It commenced the "Cub Power" era, one of the most explosive in franchise history.

What Happened

- According to the sales of player photos at the ballpark, Ernie Banks remained the most popular Cub. Ron Santo ran a close second. The photos, available each year since 1962, had a renewed popularity with the team's resurgence. Barney Sterling, the Cubs photographer, said, "We're actually selling pictures of the coaches. In previous years, we couldn't give away pictures of the managers and coaches."[30]

Concessionaires also did a brisk business selling shirts, buttons, and pennants—anything emblazoned with the "Cub Power" logo.

- Fans hungered to see the winning Cubs. Before a July 23 doubleheader against the Giants, for example, fanatics arrived outside Wrigley Field at 1:00 A.M. to wait for general admission seats. This was unthinkable the past twenty years.

Another Stadium Offer

During a press conference on June 15, Art Allyn revealed plans to build a $50 million sports complex on air rights over Dearborn Station. The fifty-acre project included a 46,000-seat ballpark, a 60,000-seat football/soccer stadium, and a 15,000-seat indoor arena. Allyn said construction would begin in 1969 with completion by 1972. To ensure team identity, he'd call the ballpark, patterned after Anaheim Stadium, "White Sox Park" when his Sox played there and "Cubs Park" when the North Siders played. He would name the football arena "Halas Stadium."

Allyn owned the White Sox and North American Soccer League Mustangs, his only certain tenants. He needed commitments from the Cubs and Bears to make it work. The Cubs' Bill Heymans and the Bears' George Halas Jr. attended the press conference. Both were non-committal. Arthur M. Wirtz, owner of the Blackhawks, did not attend. More noticeably absent was Mayor Daley.

Three months after the press conference, Allyn said leases were drawn on the property. The White Sox would be in the new park by 1972, no matter what the other teams did. He conceded the football stadium might not be built. "It will depend on whether George Halas wants to use it for his Bears. If not, we obviously cannot build it."[31] Although Halas wanted a larger stadium for his Bears, he couldn't support Allyn's long shot. And he couldn't offend Mayor Daley because Halas had few options. Daley, for his part, didn't want Allyn's stadiums and wouldn't cooperate in getting them built.

Quote of 1967

"If this team wins the pennant, those fans will tear the park apart."[32]

Don Larsen, former Cub pitcher in the Chicago Tribune—*August 21, 1975—reminiscing about the 1967 season*

1968

The Season by the Numbers

| 84-78 | .519 3rd 13 games out | 1,043,409 (12,803 average) |
| 47-34 | .580 at home | 87% of NL average |

Home Opener

APRIL 13; CUBS (NYE) VS. CARDINALS (CARLTON); RAIN, 72 DEGREES; 33,875 PAID

Cardinals 8 Cubs 5—The best-attended opener since 1946 saw the Cubs grab a 4-0 lead in the first inning (three runs came on Ron Santo's 200th career home run). But the Cubs squandered the lead as Curt Flood stroked five straight singles. Flood's second hit struck Rich Nye's pitching arm, forcing him to leave the game in the third inning.

Two wounded Vietnam veterans tossed and caught the first pitch.

The Ball State University Band and Henry Brandon's Band entertained before the game. Actor Forrest Tucker planned to sing the National Anthem, but a sore throat passed the duties to Louis Sudler.

The *Chicago Tribune* reported that during the opening ceremonies, manager "Leo Durocher got such a deafening, standing ovation that the public address man . . . had to delay the introduction of the rest of the Cubs for a few moments."[33]

What's New

- The brick wall from the Cubs' bullpen to the left field wall (water leaked under its foundation).
- A press ramp for photographers under the first base upper deck.
- The left field side of the upper deck received new floors and 1,265 self-rising contour box seats. The half-million dollar improvements also included a repaired and painted roof, and renovated ramp dormers on the exterior.

What Happened

- The White Sox drew only 7,756 for their home opener at Comiskey Park. Occurring less than a week after the Martin Luther King Jr. assassination riots, fans feared going to the Bridgeport neighborhood (even though the riots were seven miles from the park). These fears, the White

Sox's worst record since 1950, and the baseball renaissance on the North Side allowed the Cubs to outdraw the White Sox by nearly a quarter-million fans.

Art Allyn's ballpark plan went nowhere. Without Mayor Daley's help and with the White Sox floundering, Allyn's dream died; the Modern stadium era passed over Chicago. By April, Philadelphia, Cincinnati, and Pittsburgh broke ground on new stadiums. They marked the end of the Modern stadium building boom. Still, thirteen Modern era ballparks opened between 1960 and 1971.

CITY	STADIUM	YEAR	REPLACED
San Francisco	Candlestick Park	1960	Seals Stadium
Los Angeles	Dodger Stadium	1962	L.A. Coliseum
Washington	D.C. Stadium	1962	Griffith Stadium*
New York	Shea Stadium	1964	Polo Grounds*

Preseason work on the upper deck and the brick wall near the Cub bullpen (Chicago History Museum ICHi-67345)

Houston	Astrodome	1965	Colt Stadium
Oakland	Oakland-Alameda County Coliseum	1966 (football)	
Atlanta	Fulton County Stadium	1966	
St. Louis	Busch Stadium II	1966	Busch Stadium*
Anaheim	Anaheim Stadium	1966	
San Diego	San Diego Stadium	1967 (football)	
Cincinnati	Riverfront Stadium	1970	Crosley Field*
Pittsburgh	Three Rivers Stadium	1970	Forbes Field*
Philadelphia	Veterans Stadium	1971	Connie Mack Stadium*

- The demise of six Classic ballparks* between 1962 and 1971 left only four of the original 13 standing: Comiskey Park, Tiger Stadium, Fenway Park, and Wrigley Field.

Games of the Year

July 28—The Cubs took the Dodgers, 8-3 and 1-0 in front of 42,261, the largest Wrigley Field baseball crowd in twenty years. Randy Hundley caught both games and drove in four of the nine Cub runs.

September 10—Billy Williams hit three, two-run home runs in an 8-1 pasting of the Mets. Added to the two homers Williams hit the previous day, he became only the eighth player in major league history to total five home runs in consecutive games. The last to do that was Joe Adcock in 1954.

Quote of 1968

"The time is gone when the public is satisfied solely by beautiful vines and convenience to transportation. These are the 1960s. Even such fine ballparks as the ones built in the early 50s, in Milwaukee and Baltimore cannot be considered modern in light of 1960 developments. Wrigley field's [sic] scoreboard has value only to an antique dealer. Its press and radio facilities for football and baseball are bush league."[34]

David Condon in the Chicago Tribune— *April 6, 1968*

1969

The Season by the Numbers

92-70	.568 2nd 8 games out	1,674,993 (20,552 average)
49-32	.605 at home	137% of NL average

Opening Day

APRIL 8; CUBS (JENKINS) VS. PHILLIES (SHORT); PARTLY CLOUDY, 76 DEGREES; 40,796 PAID

Cubs 7 Phillies 6—Ernie Banks went deep his first two at bats (numbers 475 and 476), staking the Cubs to a 5-1 lead. But Phillies rookie Don Money homered twice himself, the second a three-run shot in the ninth inning to tie the score. Philadelphia scored in the eleventh inning on a double by Money, seemingly the game's hero. But in the Cubs' half of the inning, a belated hero emerged. After Ernie Banks flied out, Randy Hundley singled to left field. Willie Smith pinch hit for Jim Hickman and deposited Barry Lersch's second offering into the right field bleachers for the ecstatic win.

Ernie Banks received the loudest ovation during pregame ceremonies. Ron Santo presented entertainer Jimmy Durante with a Cubs jacket.

Sportswriter Edgar Munzel threw out the first pitch. The Loyola Academy High School Band performed, and after a boy scout gave the Pledge of Allegiance, the crowd observed a moment of silence for former president Dwight Eisenhower who died on March 28.

What's New

- In the second year of the three-year upper deck project, workers replaced the section from third base to home plate. Self-rising plastic seats replaced the old wooden seats in that area.
- Green indoor-outdoor carpeting on the dugout floors.
- Extended yardarms atop the scoreboard to include pennants for the expansion Montreal Expos and San Diego Padres.
- The scoreboard added the expansion teams in Montreal, San Diego, Seattle, and Kansas City. To allow for two additional games, the board lost the inning numerals at the top and the lines that advertised the next home game at the bottom.
- The elevated walkway that led visiting players from the dugout to the clubhouse was screened-in after a fan hit the Reds' Jose Pena with a baseball.

- The National League changed the rule on games called by darkness at Wrigley Field. Beginning June 27, all regulation tie games called by darkness would continue from the point it ended, not replayed in full.
- In July, the Cubs set up an autograph booth to accommodate their burgeoning fandom. Before every home game, three Cubs signed between 12:15-12:45 P.M. in a booth under the third base grandstand.

What Happened

Longtime Cubs fans know what happened—only the most celebrated collapse in team history. Here is a condensed version of the infamous season played out at Wrigley Field.

April 8—"One game was more than enough and many fans in the huge Opening Day crowd were talking about the possibility of a pennant in 1969."[35]—Jerome Holtzman, *Chicago Sun-Times*

April 9—Billy Williams hit four doubles in an 11-3 trouncing of the Phillies. He became the first National Leaguer to do this in 15 years.

"Of course, we think we can win it all."[36] —Ron Santo

April 12—After four straight wins, the Expos beat the Cubs, 7-3. Even team owner P. K. Wrigley watched the game from a box seat. "It is possible that this was Wrigley's first Wrigley Field appearance in about 20 years."[37]—Jerome Holtzman, *Chicago Sun-Times*

April 13—The Cubs scored three runs in the ninth inning to clip the Expos, 7-6. The win sent hundreds of fans swarming onto the field. "Most Wrigley Field veterans said they had never seen such a wild post-game melee by fans on the field. Others said it was close but not equal to the demonstration that erupted when Walt Moryn's running catch clinched Don Cardwell's no-hit game against St Louis in 1960."[38]—George Langford, *Chicago Tribune*

May 4—A series of brushback pitches started by Tom Seaver set the stage for a Mets sweep of the Cubs by identical 3-2 scores. A crowd of 40,484 saw the game and nearly 20,000 couldn't get in to the park. (two games ahead)

May 13—Newcomer Dick Selma blanked the Padres, 19-0. Two more home runs by Ernie Banks led the charge. The win was the Cubs' third consecutive shutout, something they had not done since 1909. It also equaled the most lopsided shutout in team history. (four games ahead)

"The Cubs are 20 per cent home free. That's right. Already, one fifth of the baseball season is complete and the bubble isn't even scratched."[39] —Rick Talley, *Chicago Today*

June 5—"I just can't see how this team is going to fold. The Cubs have not one but three pitchers who are stoppers, who will keep them from going into any prolonged losing streak."[40]—Astros manager Harry Walker (eight and a half games ahead)

June 6—"A strange thing happened . . . in Wrigley Field. A fan in the left field bleachers caught a home run ball and immediately threw it back on the field-scornfully. 'We don't want it! We don't want it!' chanted a motley looking crew calling themselves the Bleacher Bums."[41] —Donna Gill, *Chicago Tribune*

June 23— "The New York Mets are having the month of their lives, and only the greedy or foolhardy would want to look too far ahead. What is so rare as a June in which the Mets have won 15 of 20 games? For Met fans who have not seen their team win more than it lost in only two months of their eight-year history, the moment should be sufficient unto itself."[42]—Leonard Koppett, *New York Times* (five games ahead)

June 28—"I say you ought to put a cage over 'em."[43]—Jim Grant, Cardinals pitcher after being hit in the face with a handball thrown from the bleachers.

"Those persons who throw things at the players are not Bleacher Bums," [71 year-old Bleacher Bum, Lou] Blatz said, "They're just plain bums."[44]

June 29—The Cubs celebrated "Billy Williams Day" as the slugger played in his 896th consecutive game to break Stan Musial's National League record. Between games of a double-header Billy received a car, a boat, a gold watch, a hunting dog, a suit of clothes, and a pool table. Williams had four hits and the Cubs swept the Cardinals, 3-1 and 12-1. (eight and a half games ahead)

"The Cubs just kicked the hell out of us."[45]—Cardinal manager Red Schoendienst

July 11—"The only team with enough talent to take the Eastern division flag away from the Cubs is St. Louis. St Louis is too far behind to do it. Ergo, the Cubs win. It's that simple. Of course, the New York Mets have some fine young pitching. But it is not that much better than the Cubs'. And it's a cinch that the Mets aren't going to win on pitching alone."[46] —Robert Markus, *Chicago Tribune* (four and a half games ahead)

August 2—"Jack Brickhouse of the Cubs' broadcasting team predicted when his favorites would clinch the National League East Division title. According to Brickhouse, that grand happening will be on Tuesday, September 23 at 4:04 P.M." [47] (six and a half games ahead)

August 19—Ken Holtzman no-hit Atlanta, 3-0—the team's emotional apex this year. A crowd of 41,033 erupted when Hank Aaron grounded out to Glenn Beckert for the final out. Ken's gem was the first of an eleven-game home stand; it's a span many thought would cement the Cubs' hold on first place. (eight games ahead)

August 21—The Braves checked the Cubs for the second straight day, a 3-1 victory in front of a season-high Ladies Day crowd of 42,364. Although their magic number stood at only 35, a sour feeling was evident. Richard Dozer of the *Chicago Tribune* laid it on the line: "It must be said, with considerable concern, that the Chicago Cubs have quit hitting."[48] (seven games ahead)

August 28—What about that important eleven-game homestand? The Cubs went 4-7. The Mets, during the same period, went 8-1. (three games ahead)

September 5—Steve Blass four-hit the Cubs and stroked his only major league home run in the Pirates' 9-2 win. Billy Williams homered twice and doubled twice, the team's only hits. (four and a half games ahead)

September 7—The Cubs dropped three straight. They hoped to salvage a game against the Pirates before a road trip to New York. Things looked bad, trailing 4-3 in the eighth inning. But Jim Hickman stepped to the plate and hit a two-run home run for a 5-4 lead. In the ninth inning, Willie Stargell crushed a two-out, two-strike shot onto Sheffield Avenue to tie the score. Pittsburgh added two unearned runs in the eleventh for the win. (two and a half games ahead)

The exhausted, frazzled club went to New York and lost two games to the Mets.

September 9—"It appears to be a ball club coming apart, gradually, slowly, inexplicably like a man being poisoned from an infected hangnail."[49] —Jimmy Cannon, *Chicago Daily News* (one-half game ahead)

When the Cubs lost at Philadelphia the next day and the Mets swept a doubleheader from the Expos, the Cubs, who had led the division for 156 days, fell to second place.

September 11—"Somebody said they [the Mets] drank champagne in their locker room last night. That party could have been a little premature."[50] —Leo Durocher (one game back)

September 15—"The bugler keeps blowing 'Charge.' But the sound that comes out is 'Taps.'"[51] —George Vass, *Chicago Daily News* (four and a half games back)

The Cubs went 1-11 from September 3-15. In the same period, the Mets went 12-3.

September 19—"There was an ugly stirring among a number of the 15,376 in Wrigley field [*sic*]. Fights began breaking out here and

Jack Brickhouse in June 1969 (www. ArgentaImages.com)

there throughout the crowd. . . . The wind was sour with the smell of spilled beer and a highly vocal minority of patrons in the box seats were venting the stored anger and frustrations built over the last three weeks."[52] George Langford, *Chicago Tribune* (four games back)

September 21—"When the dazed Cubs swung blindly thru two more innings, the Cardinals had put their official seal on a 4 to 1 triumph, and another had slipped away thru the hourglass that is taking the Cubs closer to the long winter of remembering what might have been."[53] —Richard Dozer, *Chicago Tribune*

"Whatever became of that gay Hey, Hey Holy Mackerel theme song the Cubs used to sing?"[54] James Enright, *Chicago Today* (four and a half games back)

October 2—"The Bums, and others caught up in the exhibitionism of the irresponsible few, got into the act in the eighth inning. . . . As they swarmed onto the second aisle of the lower deck, they. . . .stormed onto the Cubs' dugout roof, chanting their cheers. Then, with a complete disregard for the law and order people, they put on a similar demonstration atop the Mets' dugout."[55] —Edward Prell, *Chicago Tribune* (eight games back)

"After the game the Bums and their ladies dropped into the playing field from the 11 ½ feet high wall. At least one of the girls was removed in a fire department ambulance that entered the park through the large door in the right field wall."[56] —Bill Gleason, *Chicago Sun-Times*

Quotes of 1969

"Sure, I'll admit we played some terrible baseball, some of the worst I've seen in years."[57]
—Leo Durocher

"I gave it everything I had. So did 24 other guys. We all tried. It doesn't matter what anyone says."[58]—Ron Santo

"So they flopped. But we had a great time while it lasted."[59] —George Vass, *Chicago Daily News*

1970

The Season by the Numbers		
84-78	.519 2nd 5 games out	1,642,705 (20,280 average)
46-34	.575 at home	120% of NL average

Home Opener

APRIL 14; HOLTZMAN (CUBS) VS. SHORT (PHILLIES); SUNNY, 54 DEGREES; 36,316 PAID

Cubs 5 Phillies 4—Newcomer Johnny Callison smacked a two-run double in the first inning. The Cubs added two more in the seventh on a Billy Williams single and a wild pitch. Ken Holtzman gave up four runs in the ninth, yet pitched a complete game.

Hall of Famer-elect Lou Boudreau threw out the first pitch to another Hall of Famer, Gabby Hartnett. The crowd observed a moment of silence for the stricken Apollo 13 spacecraft. Louis Sudler sang the National Anthem. Ron Santo and Ernie Banks presented comedian Milton Berle with a Cub jacket.

Much of the action didn't involve the players. In a carryover from last season, fans brawled throughout the game. After the last out, a fan fell out of the bleachers and tussled with Andy Frain ushers. Soon after, hundreds of bleacher fans stormed the field and joined in a melee in the right field corner. An Andy Frain usher said the rioting crowd "didn't come out here to watch a ballgame. They were the kinds who were just looking for trouble."[60]

Jack Griffin of the *Chicago Sun-Times* put the Opening Day riot in perspective, saying, "The Cubs no longer have fans. They have bred a cult."[61]

What's New

- After Opening Day, the team made the following changes:

    - Reduced the number of bleacher tickets from 4,000 to 3,200
    - Opened the bleachers at 9:00, a full hour before the rest of the park
    - Sold beer in the bleachers from stands only—no beer vendors
    - Installed closed-circuit cameras in bleachers; security carried walkie-talkies
    - Installed the bleacher basket
    - Added a triangular-shaped top to the bleacher wall to keep first-row fans from standing on it
    - Added signs in the bleachers saying, "Spectators forbidden to enter or throw objects on playing field. Violators will be prosecuted."[62]
    - Chicago Police patrolled the park on busy days.

- Replaced the flooring and 1,500 seats in the upper deck boxes
- Added 6,000 self-rising plastic seats in the lower deck. All lower deck box seats now were fixed plastic seats and sold for $3.50. The upper deck boxes remained at $3.00.

- General admission grandstand seats increased 25 cents to $1.75.
- A new organ
- In a nod to the women's movement, female ushers, who hadn't worked at the park since World War II, began on Memorial Day.

What Happened

- The Cubs made a $1.2 million in profit in 1969. P. K. Wrigley's wish list included lights for football (if the Bears stayed at the park), elevators and escalators, brighter and more convenient concessions, and updated restrooms. Profits never reached that level again, and from his wish list, only the restrooms were renovated during the rest of P. K.'s tenure.
- On May 9, Ernie Banks hit his 499th career home run. The next day, a Sunday, over 32,000 came to Wrigley Field as Banks hung on the cusp of history. Ernie received massive ovations before each at-bat, but could only leg out a triple. On Monday, he tripled and singled against the Braves. Fewer than 6,000 fans attended. Life, it seemed, took precedence over history.

  Tuesday, May 12, began with heavy storms, but they stopped in time for baseball; only 5,264 showed up in the gloom. Banks came up in the second inning against Pat Jarvis. On a one and one count, he lined a chest-high pitch into the first row of the left field bleachers. Number 500! With it, he joined a nine-member fraternity that included the likes of Ruth, Aaron, Mays, and Mantle. But Ernie Banks was different. He carried the Cubs during years of desolation. His milestone vindicated long suffering Cub fans. Ernie reached number 500—The years of near nothing were worth it!

Games of the Year

May 30—On Memorial Day, the Cubs formally celebrated Banks's feat along with Billy Williams's extension of his National League consecutive games record to 1,025 games. Banks hit his 501st home run in the nightcap. It made the difference in an 8-7 win.

September 3—Billy Williams hadn't missed a game since September 22, 1963—1,117 straight. The strain of this season, however, showed; he'd been hitless in his last thirteen at-bats. With the Cubs within a half game of the Pirates, Billy asked to sit. He did not play for the first time in almost seven years. During the ninth inning, chants of "We want Billy" went unanswered.[63] Finally, Billy gave one to himself.

The Cubs went only 12-13 the rest of the way and finished five games out. The proverbial missive of last season's cry of "wait 'til next year" went for naught. Next year had come and gone.

Bear News

The Bears scheduled their September 27 home opener at Northwestern University's Dyche Stadium. They did it for three reasons. First, baseball's new divisional lineup added a playoff series and the improved Cubs had a reasonable chance to make the playoffs, potentially delaying the start of the Bears' home season. Second, Dyche Stadium held 55,000 fans or about 9,000 more than Wrigley Field. Finally, the NFL put pressure on the Bears to vacate Wrigley Field, the smallest NFL venue. The Bears used this game as a trial balloon for permanent relocation.

The City of Evanston filed suit to stop the game and the Bears countersued. After months of friction the game went on. The Bears beat the Eagles, 20-16 before 53,643 fans.

Quote of 1970

"I'm angry that we're living in a society so depraved that a baseball fan can't even go to the ball park [*sic*] in broad daylight with assurances that he won't be physically brutalized before it's over."[64]

Robert Markus in the Chicago Tribune—*April 16, 1970—after the Opening Day riot at Wrigley Field*

1971

The Season by the Numbers

83-79	.512 3rd (t) 14 games out	1,653,007 (20,407 average)
44-37	.543 at home	116% of NL average

Opening Day

APRIL 6; CUBS (JENKINS) VS. CARDINALS (GIBSON); SUNNY, 40 DEGREES; 39,079 PAID

Cubs 2 Cardinals 1—Billy Williams parked one on the right field catwalk off Bob Gibson, providing a euphoric ending to a 2-1, 10-inning win. The Cardinals lone run came on a seventh inning home run by Joe Torre. Fergie Jenkins went the distance, retiring twenty of the final twenty-one batters.

The Chicago Fire Department Band played before the game. Fire Lieutenant Frank Becka threw out the first pitch. Since Ernie Banks sat out the game with arthritic knees, Billy Williams received the biggest pregame ovation.

No beer flowed because of Election Day in Chicago. Maybe that's why fans behaved better than last year. But it was still Opening Day; there were stories to share. A twenty-one-year-old Andy Frain usher told the *Chicago Today* of a few fainting spells in the crush to get bleacher seats. He also reported four torn buttons and a gold stripe appliqué ripped from his uniform. "I think I can remember when the buttons went. But I have no idea who went after the gold stripe on my pants."[65]

What's New

- Plastic grandstand seats behind third base and in the upper deck behind first base.
- An upgraded first aid station.
- The custom of selling 22,000 non-reserved seats the day of the game ended. Management reserved the first six rows of grandstands—1,892 seats called "reserved grandstands"—and sold them for $2.75, a dollar more than regular grandstand seats.
- Baseball Commissioner Bowie Kuhn announced a first—an after-dark World Series game. The fourth game of the series, scheduled at the National League ballpark, would be played at night, unless the Cubs were involved. Then it would be a day game after all.

What Happened

- This was the last year the Baby Ruth candy sign sat atop the building at 3649 Sheffield Ave (it is not evident in any photo after March 31, 1971). It stood since the mid-1930s, presumably in the line of Babe Ruth's called home run in the 1932 World Series. Early photographs show it atop the building at 3653 Sheffield. It moved two buildings south, to 3649 Sheffield after the 1937 bleacher expansion. The new scoreboard above the bleachers obstructed its visibility to fans, necessitating the move.
- The block of Victorian-style row houses two blocks north of the ballpark, called Alta Vista Terrace, became the city's first landmark street. Newspaper articles described its environs as a "rather shabby neighborhood."[66] But the area's strong housing stock and location near the lake, downtown transportation, and Wrigley Field would be coveted by gentrifying home-owners and developers before the end of the decade.

The famous Baby Ruth sign visible beyond right field in 1941 (www.ArgentaImages.com)

- The Cubs celebrated Ron Santo Day on August 28. In pregame ceremonies, the third baseman received a mountain of gifts including a car, a boat, vacations to Jamaica and Italy, a color television, stereo system, a pool table, typewriter, an adding machine, a golf cart, a dune buggy, and a snowmobile. There was even a congratulatory letter from President Nixon. A $25,000 check went to the Diabetes Association of Chicago in honor of Santo, a diabetic his whole playing career. Phil Niekro ruined the day, stifling the Cubs, 4-3. Ron was held to a single.

Game of the Year

June 17—Don Kessinger went 6-for-6. His fifth and final single led off the tenth inning. Ron Santo singled him home and the Cubs denied the Cardinals, 7-6. Burt Hooton made his major league debut, pitching into the fourth inning. Bill Bonham got his first major league win with three shutout innings in relief.

Bear News

The Bears signed a five-year lease to use Northwestern University's Dyche Stadium. But just two weeks later, the Big 10 Conference voided the lease, adhering to its tradition of denying professionals the long-term use of facilities.

With only four months before the first home game, the Bears signed a three-year lease with the Chicago Park District to use Soldier Field. Rapid updates included an artificial playing surface and reinstallation of the football bleachers used at Wrigley Field. The renovated stadium held about 55,000 fans and an informal poll in mid-season found most fans satisfied with the change. The poll results identified three improvements over Wrigley Field: parking, more and better-placed seating, and accessibility.

The Bears compiled a 221-89-22 record at Wrigley Field. The 332 home games stood as the most ever at one stadium by an NFL team until 2007, when the Packers broke the record at Lambeau Field.

Quote of 1971

"Nothing that transpires in Soldier Field, or any other place the Bears may eventually call home for that matter, can be counted on to titillate the susceptibility of future historians as much as the success, the heartbreak and the glory that went into the record at Clark and Addison."[67]
George Strickler in the Chicago Tribune— *September 19, 1971*

1972

The Season by the Numbers
85-70   .548 2nd 11 games out   1,229,163 (16,656 average)
46-31   .597 at home   100% of NL average

Opening Day

APRIL 15; CUBS (JENKINS) VS. PHILLIES (CARLTON); 55 DEGREES; 17,401 PAID

Phillies 4 Cubs 2—A strike interrupted the start of a baseball season for the first time as players walked out for improved pensions. When the owners capitulated, the season shortened by eight games and the Cubs and the Phillies opened on a Saturday. No bunting or ceremonies marked the occasion. The drab day ended when Jose Cardenal dropped a Tim McCarver fly in the ninth inning, allowing the lead runs to score.

Andy Frain usher Seymour Balcher said this about the strike-delayed season, "I don't feel the opening-day spirit. You can look at the people. They don't feel it. Maybe they're a little disgusted."[68]

The Cubs wore new home uniforms—double-knits that featured pullover shirts and a built-in belt.

What's New

• $500,000 spent on 1,000 additional grandstand seats in the right field corner of the park, increasing capacity to 38,000.

What Happened

• On Father's Day, infielder/trumpeter Carmen Fanzone played the National Anthem. He went 0-for-2 but the Cubs beat the Dodgers, 5-4 in eleven innings.
• Manager Leo Durocher stepped down at mid-season, replaced by ex-minor league manager Whitey Lockman, who had been serving as the team's director of player development. Durocher's Cubs went 46-44. The team rallied under Lockman, finishing the season 39-26. Their 85-70 record and .548 winning percentage was their third-best since 1938, behind only 1945 and 1969.

Games of the Year

April 16—In just his fourth major league start, Burt Hooton no-hit the Phillies, 4-0. The young Texan walked seven and struck out seven. When he fanned Greg Luzinski to finish the game, he became the first National League rookie to toss a no-hitter in 60 years.

July 11—Billy Williams went 8-for-8 in a doubleheader. He homered twice, doubled, and hit five singles as the Cubs split with the Astros. Williams went on to hit .333 and win the National League batting title. He finished third in home runs, second in RBIs and was named the Sporting News Player of the Year.

September 2—Milt Pappas needed one more strike for the tenth perfect game in major league history. He had Padre pinch-hitter Larry Stahl down 1 and 2 in the count, but walked him on three close pitches. The next hitter, Garry Jestadt, popped to second base and Pappas settled for an 8-0 no-hitter. Remarkably, Cub pitchers tossed four no-hitters in three years (Holtzman in '69 and '71; Hooton and Pappas this year). They waited 36 years before the next one (Carlos Zambrano in 2008).

September 16—The Cubs slashed New York 18-5. Ellie Hendricks received five of the Cubs' 15 walks, tying a National League record. Burt Hooton hit a grand slam, Jose Cardenal hit two home runs, and Billy Williams poled the 350th of his career. Glenn Beckert had the indignity of making two outs in an inning twice (in the seven-run third and in the five-run seventh).

The classiest Cub— Billy Williams (www. ArgentaImages.com)

Quote of 1972

"The customers chose to observe the passing of the season in different ways—some with Olympian quantities of malt brew, others with a dance, a sob, amateur pugilism, an illegal foot-race across the diamond or lavishing long ovations on everyone from batting champion Billy Williams, to Coach Ernie Banks for snaring a foul ball."[69]

George Langford in the Chicago Tribune—*October 5, 1972—on the season's last game*

SIXTH INNING
1973-1984
NEW APPRECIATION

Fans took a look at the multipurpose stadium blitz and didn't like what they saw. Most of the Modern era stadiums were too large, their sightlines better for football than for baseball. The last three—in Cincinnati, Pittsburgh, and Philadelphia—all looked the same, resembling concrete donuts with playing fields of dyed green plastic.

Rick Talley of the *Chicago Tribune* said what many were thinking:

At one time I couldn't understand why Chicago couldn't have a spiffy new edifice when Philadelphia could. But in the last four years I've spent a lot of time in those concrete blobs called stadiums. . . .They all have artificial turf . . . Please. I'll take grass. . . .You say Chicago needs a modern stadium in which it can be proud? I say be proud of ballparks which are ballparks.[1]

In comparison to the Modern era stadiums, Wrigley Field came out on top. Its scale was more human, sitting fans closer to the field. And it still had God's grass, Bill Veeck's ivy, and the familiar neighborhood over its outfield walls. This new appreciation didn't translate into increased ticket sales just yet, in fact, the team still regularly closed off the upper deck for many weekday games. But at least those who attended Cub games, no doubt, were happier to be in Wrigley Field than in one of the sterile "cookie cutters."

Cub fans took a roller coaster ride during this inning—some ups, lots of downs. The early part was marked by P.K. Wrigley's unwillingness to spend on free agents. After his death in 1977, his family's estate tax burden further limited big time spending on the team and on the park.

In spite of Wrigley Field's rediscovered appeal, fans grew weary of the Wrigley ownership. The once innovative leadership of the 1920s and '30s was a distant memory. The final years, 1980 and 1981, marked some of the darkest days in team history.

That changed in June of 1981. The Tribune Company purchased the team and a corporate mentality took over. A flurry of renovations and upgrades infused the ballpark with new life. These, and eventual improvements to the team put the park on the cusp of a renewed love affair with fans. In addition, the lights issue, kept dormant for decades by P. K. Wrigley's stubborn insistence on day baseball, came to the forefront.

1973

The Season by the Numbers

| 77-84 | .478 5th 5 games out | 1,351,705 (16,791 average) |
| 41-39 | .513 at home | 97% of NL average |

Opening Day

APRIL 6; CUBS (JENKINS) VS. EXPOS (TORREZ); SUNNY, 65 DEGREES; 40,273 PAID

Cubs 3 Expos 2—A single by Joe Pepitone, an error, and three walks accounted for the two-run ninth inning rally. The final walk to Rick Monday sent pinch runner Tony LaRussa (yes, *that* Tony LaRussa) home with the winning run. It marked Tony's only appearance in a Cub uniform.

Former POW, Lieutenant Commander Robert Naughton, threw out the first pitch.

What's New

The Cubs raised reserved grandstand and box seats prices 25 cents to $3.00 and $3.75 respectively. Still, the Cubs had the lowest priced box seats in the major leagues.

What Happened

- The major leagues played 1,185 night games this year, or about 61 percent of the schedule. Commissioner Bowie Kuhn investigated limiting night baseball due to the nation's energy crisis. Commonwealth Edison, for example, estimated that a three-hour night game in Comiskey Park used over 5,600 pounds of coal energy or nearly 130 gallons of fuel oil.
- A billboard on the roof of 3631 Sheffield Avenue stood since the park opened in 1914. This year, Torco Oil rented it and eventually became its longest-running advertiser. The following lists the known advertisers and the verified years their ads stood across from Wrigley Field's right field fence.

  - Bismark/Marigold Garden—1914-1926
  - Atlas Beer—1929-1933
  - Prager Beer—1936-1941
  - Blatz Beer—1945-1951
  - Fox Head Beer—1952 and/or/through 1954
  - Miller High Life Beer—1957-1963
  - Schlitz Beer—1969-1970
  - Buick—1972 (For at least a portion of season)
  - Torco Oil—1973-April 22, 1996
  - Southwest Airlines—April 22, 1996-September 29, 1996
  - Torco Oil—1997-2000
  - Sears 2001-2002
  - Miller Lite Beer—2003-2014 (Unlike previous advertisers, Miller Lite frequently changed their sign, sometimes as often as every few games.)
  - MB Financial Bank—early 2015
  - Gilbert's Craft Sausage—July 24, 2015 to October 21, 2015

- Fans at Comiskey Park drank standard 3.5 percent alcohol beer while the Wrigley Field brew was a weaker 3.2 percent. Ballparks sold the lighter beer after Prohibition and the Cubs never switched to the stronger stuff, in part to make fans behave better.

Coach Ernie Banks and Lieutenant Commander Naughton before the opener (www. ArgentaImages.com)

- The Cubs' Gonzalo Marquez hit his only major league home run on September 21. The Venezuelan nestled an opposite field shot off the Expos' Steve Rogers into the left field basket. Gonzalo can thank the rowdy Bleacher Bums for his basket home run!

Games of the Year

May 31—The Cubs hung a ten-spot on the Astros in the first inning and won, 16-8. Remarkably they started their rally after two outs, scoring their runs on six singles, four walks, an error, a hit batsman, and a wild pitch. No one got more than one hit in the prodigious inning.

On July 1, the Cubs led the Cardinals by seven and a half games. After July 4, the Cubs lost twelve of their next fifteen and were out of first place by the All-Star break. In early August, they suffered through an eleven-game losing streak. They lost fifty-one of their last eighty games.

Had they even gone .500 during the twenty-six games in their two big losing streaks, they'd have finished the season 87-74, five games ahead of the Mets, who finished with the worst first place record to date in baseball history (82-79 .509).

Quote of 1973

"With everything going artificial, it's nice to come to Wrigley Field. I guess this is like old-time baseball—grass and dirt."[2]

Houston Astro Roger Metzger in the Chicago Tribune—*May 31, 1973*

1974

The Season by the Numbers		
66-96	.407 6th 22 games out	1,015,378 (12,536 average)
32-49	.395 at home	70% of NL average

Opening Day

The Cubs broke up the remnants of their "Cub Power" team, trading away Fergie Jenkins, Glenn Beckert, Randy Hundley, Ron Santo, Jim Hickman, and Paul Popovich. In their stead, newcomers like Bill Madlock, Vic Harris, Jerry Morales, George Mitterwald, Steve Stone, Steve Swisher, and Tom Dettore filled the roster. The team now averaged twenty-six years old, one of the youngest in the majors.

APRIL 9; CUBS (BONHAM) VS. PHILLIES (SCHUELER); 37 DEGREES; 30,601 PAID

Cubs 2 Phillies 0—Bill Bonham went the distance, four-hitting the Phillies. He loaded the bases in the ninth but got Greg Luzinski to hit into a double play. Bonham fanned nine, including Luzinski and Mike Schmidt three times each. Bill Madlock made his Wrigley Field debut, getting two hits and a stolen base.

On the turnover of the team's roster, a young bleacher fan was overheard saying, "I don't recognize nobody."[3]

There were no streakers at the opener, unlike the half-dozen naked men and topless women cavorting at the White Sox opener the previous week.

The Proviso East High School state championship basketball team threw out the first ball. Sarah Vaughan sung the National Anthem.

1974 Game Ticket

What's New

- $385,000 spent on upper deck renovations, including new restrooms
- Inflation spiked throughout the country and prices rose at the park:

    - Scorecards from 15 to 20 cents
    - Hot dogs from 40 to 45 cents
    - Beer from 55 to 60 cents
    - Hats from $1.75 to $2
    - Box seats from $3.75 to $4

What Happened

- The World Football League began play in 1974, including a team in Chicago. Early speculation had Wrigley Field as the "probable playing site"[4] for the Chicago Fire. When the league announced that the schedule included weeknight games, the Fire settled on Soldier Field. The Fire and the league, however, soon fizzled. The WFL ceased to exist halfway through its second season.
- Pat Pieper, the longtime baritone-voiced public address man died on October 22. Pieper felt ill before a game on September 8 and left the park. He never returned, dying of acute jaundice. Pieper first sold peanuts at West Side Park in 1904 and he moved north with the Cubs in 1916. The next year he became the park's public address man. Pieper claimed to have missed only sixteen games since 1904 and none since 1924. He was eighty-eight years old.

Game of the Year

April 17—The Cubs new catcher, George Mitterwald, hit three home runs and drove in eight runs in an 18-9 thrashing of Pittsburgh. As an added oddity, Burt Hooton went the distance for the Cubs despite giving up 16 hits.

Quote of 1974

"The bleacher bums may fade away. The manager and the players may come and go. Even the likes of Ernie Banks and Billy Williams eventually have to leave. But Pat Pieper has always been at Wrigley Field. He's as much a part of the old park as the great scoreboard in center field, the vines on the wall, and the smell of mustard and hot dogs."[5]

William E. Carsley (Letter to the Editor) in the Chicago Tribune—*October 30, 1974*

Pat Pieper (www.ArgentaImages.com)

1975

The Season by the Numbers

75-87	.463 5th (t) 17.5 games out	1,034,819 (12,776 average)
42-39	.519 at home	73% of NL average

Opening Day

APRIL 10; CUBS (BONHAM) VS. PIRATES (ELLIS); 37 DEGREES; 19,239 PAID

Pirates 8 Cubs 4—A nine-inch snowfall on April 2 snarled the city. The subsequent cold and slush delayed the Cubs opener twice, on April 8 and April 9. The next day wasn't much better. But the "Lumber Company," as the Pirates were nicknamed, hit four home runs into a brisk north wind. The Cubs scored all their runs in the fifth inning, thanks to doubles by Steve Swisher, Bill Madlock, and Rick Monday. Bill Bonham replaced Rick Reuschel who had the flu.

Billy Herman, newly elected to the Hall of Fame, was scheduled to throw out the first pitch. But the two-day delay cancelled his appearance. The team also postponed an on-field presentation of Pat Pieper's memorabilia to the Baseball Hall of Fame.

What's New

- The Cubs increased children's general admission tickets and bleacher seats 25 cents to $1.25.
- Jim Enright, the former Chicago sportswriter, became the permanent public address replacement for Pat Pieper.

The list of Cubs P. A. announcers at Wrigley Field:

1916	Admiral Kingston
1917-1974	Pat Pieper
1974	Chuck Shriver
1975-1981	Jim Enright
1981	Peter Mead
1982-1983	Lee Pelty
1984	Walt Jacobs
1985-1994	Wayne Messmer
1994	Chuck Swirsky

1995-2010	Paul Friedman (all games 1995-1999; nights and weekends 2000-2004; nights 2005-2008; nights and weekends 2009-2010)
2000-2010	Wayne Messmer (weekdays)
2005-2008	Mike Terson (weekends)
2011 to date	Andrew Belleson

What Happened

Bookies made the Cubs 50-1 long shots to reach the World Series. But they started fast, going 18-9 through mid-May and enjoying a four game lead over Pittsburgh. Steve Stone, at 4-0, led the staff and Darold Knowles, who came over with Manny Trillo from Oakland for Billy Williams, saved six of the Cubs first eighteen wins. But the North Siders fell to earth soon after and were out of first place by June.

Games of the Year

August 21—The newspaper headline screamed, "Oh Brother!"[6] The Cubs' Rick and Paul Reuschel became the first siblings to throw a combined shutout in at least fifty years. Rick drubbed the Dodgers for 6 1/3 innings but left with a blister. Older brother Paul came in and mopped up for a 7-0 win in front of 8,377 fans.

September 16—The scoreboard never lies: Pirates 22 Cubs 0. The 22 runs marked the widest shutout margin in baseball history. Rennie Stennett went 7-for-7—the most hits in a nine-inning game this century. Stennett also tied a major league record, getting two hits in an inning twice in the game. He singled and doubled in the first, singled in the third, singled and doubled in the fifth, singled in the seventh, and tripled in the eighth inning. The Cubs managed only three hits off Pirate pitching.

Quote of 1975

"The Cubs still offer one of the better entertainment buys in all of professional sports. There's something about going to Wrigley Field on a summer afternoon."[7]

Rick Talley in the Chicago Tribune—*August 7, 1975*

1976

The Season by the Numbers

75-87	.463 4th 26 games out	1,026,217 (12,669 average)
42-39	.519 at home	72% of NL average

Home Opener

APRIL 13; CUBS (REUSCHEL) VS. METS (SWAN); SUNNY, 66 DEGREES; 44,818 PAID

Cubs 5 Mets 4—A record Opening Day crowd saw Jerry Morales hit two home runs off Craig Swan. But it took Rick Monday's bloop single in the ninth inning to score Manny Trillo with the game winner.

Fans received numbered certificates commemorating their attendance at the team's first home game of their second century. The game's historical significance and the beautiful weather brought out the largest Cub Opening Day crowd to that point. In fact, thousands never got in the park.

James Darren sang the National Anthem. The seventy-seven-year-old granddaughter of former Cub Cap Anson threw out the first ball.

What's New

- The Cubs tried their hand at promotions, perhaps to keep within shouting distance of Bill Veeck, who returned this year as owner of the White Sox. The team sponsored a Jacket Day and gave out disposable razors on Mother's Day.

What Happened

- Cub pitching went south. The Mets' Dave Kingman hit two tape-measure home runs on consecutive days. On April 14, Kingman hit perhaps the longest ball in Wrigley Field history, at least 530 feet up Kenmore Avenue.

  Just two days later, on April 16, Mike Schmidt became the first National Leaguer to hit four consecutive home runs in one game. The Phillies trailed 13-2 early on but pulled out a mind-blowing 18-16 victory.

The certificate given to every fan at the home opener. (author's collection)

Cincinnati overwhelmed the Cubs on consecutive afternoons, 14-4 and 14-2. The second day, May 9, the Reds hit six home runs. Tony Perez (twice), George Foster, Ken Griffey Sr., Pete Rose, and Dan Driessen all connected off Cub pitching.

By the end of April, Cub pitchers carried a robust 7.78 ERA at Wrigley Field. Things improved later in the season, yet when Mike Phillips homered in the Mets' 11-0 drubbing on September 7, it marked just his fourth home run of the year—all at Wrigley Field.

• While the long ball got the Wrigley Field headlines, it took a bevy of singles to bring the year to an exciting conclusion. The Cubs' Bill Madlock trailed Ken Griffey Sr. .339 to .336 as the race for the National League batting title entered its last day. Griffey sat out the finale in Cincinnati while Madlock went on a tear, hitting four singles his first four at bats. When Griffey caught wind of Madlock's exploits, he came into his game and struck out twice in a futile attempt to hold the lead. The Cub third baseman won his second consecutive batting title that day by the slimmest of margins, .3385 to .3363.

Game of the Year

April 21—The Cubs and Expos waited through a Wrigley Field record five rain delays (fourteen minutes prior to the game; thirty minutes in the second; thity-one minutes in the fourth; twenty minutes in the fifth; twenty-seven minutes in the sixth). Montreal rushed through the fifth inning to get the game to regulation. (Tim Foli was an easy out trying to stretch a triple into a home run, and Woodie Fryman jogged into a tag at second base.) The Cubs, on the other hand, stalled to get to the next rain delay. (Holding conferences on the mound, tarring and retarring bats, requesting that the grounds crew spread sand on the infield, and arguing with umpires.) It wasn't rain, but darkness that finally halted the game at 5:45 P.M. Montreal won the completed game the following day, 12-6.

Quote of 1976

"Cubs' fans go to the park because they genuinely love the game of baseball and they genuinely love Wrigley Field."[8]

Tom Fitzpatrick in the Chicago Sun-Times—*April 4, 1976*

1977

The Season by the Numbers		
81-81	.500 4th 20 games out	1,439,834 (17,776 average)
46-35	.568 at home	90% of NL average

Philip K. Wrigley, eighty-two years old, died on April 12 of gastrointestinal hemorrhaging at his home in Lake Geneva, Wisconsin. Wrigley left a fortune worth nearly $100 million, amassed while expertly marketing the chewing gum company willed to him upon his father's death in 1932. P. K. Wrigley passed the gum company presidency to his son, William, in 1961 but held on as CEO and chairman of the board of the Cubs until his death. P. K. lived two baseball worlds—his Cubs achieved embarrassing little on-field success, but his stubborn refusal to add lights at Wrigley Field built a loyal fan base drawn to day baseball, Cub games on television, and the ballpark as a comfortable destination. In short, his greatest baseball legacy would be caretaker of Wrigley Field. The continual renovations and updates allowed the ballpark on Chicago's North Side to thrive for 100 years.

Opening Day

APRIL 7; CUBS (BURRIS) VS. METS (SEAVER); SUNNY, 63 DEGREES; 39,937 PAID

Mets 5 Cubs 3—Steve Ontiveros homered in his first game as a Cub. But outfielders Jerry Morales and Bobby Murcer collided, keying a Mets' four-run sixth inning.

Ernie Banks, newly elected to the Hall of Fame, threw the first ball to the Cubs other Hall of Famer, radioman Lou Boudreau. John Gary replaced Frank Sinatra Jr. in singing the National Anthem. Henry Brandon's Band played at their twenty-second Cub Opener.

What's New

• To meet increased demand, the Cubs added a second telephone number that gave recorded information about tickets and promotions. Ironically, when the Cubs could finally sell winning baseball, 1977 marked the team's most ambitious promotional slate ever with the likes of Cap Day, an Old Timers' game, and Bonnet Day dotting the schedule.

Yet, Bonnet Day demonstrated just how staid the Cubs franchise had become under the Wrigley ownership. To get a free hat, women needed to be accompanied by a paying *male* adult. Patriarchy had waned in America, but it was still standard fare at Wrigley Field. To further illustrate the team's backwardness, the 1977 scorecard had these words above the list of concessions: "You'll enjoy a snack at Wrigley Field, where we serve only the best food and drinks, and at prices lower than you'll pay elsewhere. Pay no more than these listed prices."[9]

These were the exact words that accompanied the concession list in the 1948 scorecard, thirty seasons ago.

• The team did have one sliver of creativity in the souvenir department. Dawn Hopkins, a former Cub employee-turned-landscaper, took cuttings from the outfield ivy and sold them at the park for $1 a sprig.

What Happened

Trades bringing Bill Buckner, Ivan DeJesus, and others got the surprising Cubs going. Before the last out against Pittsburgh on May 28, the faithful stood and chanted, "we're number 1, we're number 1"[10]—something rarely heard in Wrigley Field. The 6-3 victory moved the Cubs into first place and fans began a daily ritual of standing ovations when the team ran onto the field before each game.

Former Cub Paul Popovich returned for the Old Timers' game on June 25 and recognized the heightened atmosphere, saying, "It sure looks like shades of 1969 around here."[11] It was like 1969, only doubled. Both the Cubs and White Sox led their divisions and the city percolated with excitement. On July 27, the Cubs drew 42,342 for a doubleheader with the Reds and the White Sox 39,177 for a game against Detroit. The 81,519 fans at Chicago's two ballparks broke a one-day city attendance record.

A crowd of 25,963 at Wrigley Field on July 24, 1977. The old football press box is visible to the right. (National Baseball Hall of Fame Library, Cooperstown, N.Y.)

Games of the Year

June 25—A group of former Cubs fractured a team of Hall of Famers, 5-1, in a pregame exhibition. The ex-Cubs included the likes of Billy Jurges, Stan Hack, and Ron Santo. The twenty-four Hall of Famers that day included perhaps the largest collection outside of Cooperstown. Men like Joe DiMaggio, Ralph Kiner, and Warren Spahn came back to play at Wrigley Field one final time.

In the regular game, the Cubs scored four runs in the ninth inning to overcome the Mets, 5-4. The win improved the Cubs' record to 44-22, seven games over Pittsburgh.

July 28—The Cubs came back three times to edge the Reds in a heart-pounding 16-15, thirteen-inning battle. The teams combined for 43 hits and a record-tying 11 home runs. Rick Reuschel pitched relief, scored the winning run, and got the win. Herman Franks concocted bizarre defensive shifts to save players. Right fielder Bobby Murcer played shortstop on five occasions and second base on four. Shortstop Dave Rosello moved to second base six times and Jose Cardenal spent time at second, short, and in right field.

Afterwards, however, an injury to Bruce Sutter sent the team into a tailspin. They dropped out of first place on August 6 and continued dropping, finishing 20 games behind the Phillies. Philadelphia clinched the title at Wrigley Field on September 27. Pitcher Larry Christenson hit a grand slam in their 15-9 coronation.

Quote of 1977

"People turn out to see the Sox if they're winnin'. People turn out to see Wrigley Field no matter what the Cubs are doin'."[12]

Jim Bendas, a vendor at both Comiskey Park and Wrigley Field in the Chicago Tribune Magazine—*June 26, 1977*

1978

The Season by the Numbers

79-83	.488 3rd 11 games out	1,525,311 (18,831 average)
44-38	.537 at home	90% of NL average

Home Opener

APRIL 14; CUBS (FRYMAN) VS. PIRATES (REUSS); CLOUDY, 53 DEGREES; 45,777 PAID

Cubs 5 Pirates 4—A record Opening Day throng (and third largest in park history) saw Woody Fryman toss a no-hitter through 5 2/3 innings. Ivan DeJesus drove in two runs while Gene Clines contributed an RBI single. The Cubs won in dramatic fashion on a walk off home run by Larry Biittner.

Jerry Vale sang the National Anthem. Charlie Grimm tossed the first ball.

The team pre-sold 3,500 more grandstand seats this season. They also sold 5,000 additional reserved seats for the opener. A loss of nearly 9,000 unreserved seats for the opener caused a near riot outside the park. Fans fainted in the crush at the bleacher entrance. Those unable to purchase seats smashed ticket windows at Clark and Addison while others tried to force open entrance gates or scale walls.

For the third straight opener, teenagers jammed the park. "'I'm not really much of a base-ball fan,' said one fourteen-year-old as he crouched near the fence down the left-field line. 'But opening day is opening day—time to cut school and come to the ballpark.'"[13] Longtime bleacher fan Carl Leone added, "This is the rowdiest crowd I've ever seen, and I've been coming here since Hack Wilson, Kiki Cuyler and the rest."[14]

Exhibit "A": The *Chicago Tribune* described the mayhem: "By 9:30, the bleachers were filled and a battle of food erupted in the stands. People were pelted with doughnuts and yogurt. Oranges were hurled between the left and right field seats. By noon, the center-field grass was a carpet of mushy fruit."[15]

Exhibit "B": About fifty youths were caught urinating from the upper deck onto fans below.

What's New

- Baseball free agency commenced in 1976. In November 1977, the Cubs signed Dave Kingman, agreeing to pay the enigmatic slugger a guaranteed $260,000 for each of the next two years.

With free agency, baseball economics changed forever. The Cubs raised revenue, not by hiking everyday prices, but by increasing the number of higher-priced reserved seats.

	General grandstand	Reserved grandstand
	($1.50-3.00)	($4.50)
1977	18,017	2,150
1978	14,458	5,707

The change seemed innocent enough in a more demanding economic environment. But it accelerated the trend that eliminated all day-of-game seats by 1985.

- Beer vendors returned to the bleachers for the first time since being ousted in 1970.
- In a move that shook up moms, the Cubs stopped selling milk at Wrigley Field. They also charged women $1 to attend Ladies Day games. Outside of a small tax, Ladies Days were always free.

What Happened

- The Chicago Sting played its first three years of soccer at Soldier Field. Now they hoped to reach a new audience, playing eight of fifteen home games at Wrigley Field. The move proved a minor success. The Sting attracted their largest crowd to a game not involving Pele when 9,345 saw them beat Dallas on July 23.

  Unlike the Bears, who arranged the gridiron from first base to left field, the Sting set up their soccer pitch from third base to right field. Either way, Cub players claimed the soccer matches chewed up the field. And unlike the Bears, the damage occurred during the baseball season, not after.

Games of the Year

May 19-25—In a perfect five-game home stand against the Cardinals and Phillies, the Cubs hit 11 triples. Three-base honors went to Greg Gross (four), Bobby Murcer, Dave Rader, Ivan DeJesus, Ray Burris, Dave Kingman, Gene Clines, and Steve Ontiveros.

1978 Bleacher Tickets (pair)

Quote of 1978

"I just love pitching in this park. Day games make me perspire, and I enjoy that. Plus, the fans are always in the game here. Chicago has baseball fever every time you come in. Fans are high even if the Cubs aren't. The place has atmosphere."[16]

Phil Niekro of the Braves, in the Chicago Tribune—*August 17, 1978*

1979

The Season by the Numbers

| 80-82 | .494 5th 18 games out | 1,648,587 (20,407 average) |
| 45-36 | .556 at home | (93% of NL average) |

Opening Day

APRIL 5; CUBS (REUSCHEL) VS. METS (SWAN); 53 DEGREES; 35,615 PAID

Mets 10 Cubs 6—Thirty-miles-per-hour wind gusts made fly balls an adventure. Dave Kingman homered for the Cubs. Richie Hebner homered and doubled twice for the Mets.

The Cubs learned from the riot at last year's home opener and sold every ticket in advance: box seat, bleacher, and even standing room. It marked the first time in park history that bleacher seats weren't available the day of the game. It ended the time-honored Opening Day tradition of "camping out" around the park to get a seat. Consequently, teenagers never came back to Opening Day en masse and this year's opener drew 10,000 less than last year's.

Stan Hack threw out the first pitch and Freddy Fender sang the National Anthem. Regular National League umpires boycotted the game in an attempt to renegotiate their contracts. Substitutes included a sporting goods storeowner and two area teachers.

What's New

• Even though the Cubs spent $300,000 to lengthen the dugouts, there were numerous problems. First, the roof was too low; players bumped their heads on the ceiling. Next, the floor and footrests were too low; players' feet dangled like little leaguers. Finally, the fence in front of the dugouts was too high, blocking players' view of the field.

During the team's first road trip, workers adjusted the dugouts, raising the floors and foot rests. They cut the dugout fence in half and lopped off cement from the dugout roof. Even though the latter improved head clearance, today you can still see protective pads on the roof edge near the dugout entrances.

- The grounds crew got new uniforms, as did the infield, with a tarpaulin featuring two large Cub logos. But the howling Opening Day winds treated it like gossamer, tearing it after the game.

What Happened

- Jack Brickhouse called his 5,000th WGN-televised game on August 5. Brickhouse worked all Cub and White Sox home games from 1948-1967 and all Cub games beginning in 1968. That's a record as secure as DiMaggio's 56-game hitting streak or Cy Young's 511 wins. The on-field ceremony that day included proclamations from Illinois Governor Jim Thompson and Chicago Mayor Jane Byrne. Among Jack's gifts included a chair made of bats from famous Cubs and a stained glass art piece of Wrigley Field with the names of over 600 Cub players etched in it.

  A Nielsen survey indicated that 566,000 adults in the Chicago area watched the Cubs on weekday afternoons on WGN. That's 176,000 more than in 1976. Competitive, exciting Cub teams accounted for the increase. In addition, 226,000 or 40 percent were women, continuing the historical truism that female fans supported the Cubs.
- A decade ago, baseball stadiums tried to look as different from Wrigley Field as possible, with plastic grass and exploding scoreboards. A first salute to Wrigley Field, however small, occurred in San Diego. San Diego Stadium added ivy along its outer outfield wall.

Game of the Year

May 17—A south wind howled toward center field. But even after the Phillies led the Cubs, 7-6 in the first inning, few of the 15,000 in attendance could have imagined what was in store. Over four hours later, Philadelphia outlasted the Cubs, 23-22 in ten innings. Records set or tied that day included:

- Most home runs in game—11 (tied)
- Most total bases by both teams—97
- Most total bases by the Cubs—49

- Most total bases by the Phillies—48
- Most home runs given up by the Phillies—6
- Most runs scored by the Phillies—23

Individual honors went to:

- Bill Buckner—grand slam and seven RBI
- Garry Maddox—home run and double in the third inning
- Mike Schmidt—two home runs including the game winner in the tenth
- Dave Kingman—three home runs including one off the third house down Kenmore Avenue and one off a Waveland Avenue building. Kingman, in fact, hit two of the sixty longest home runs in Wrigley Field history in one afternoon!

Dave Kingman (www. ArgentaImages.com)

David Israel of the *Chicago Tribune* wrote: "Thursday's game was also eloquent and irrefutable testimony before any commission investigating the possibility of building a multipurpose stadium in Chicago. The Cubs do not need one. Cub fans do not want one. And National League baseball players would not have half as much fun in their lives with one."[17]

Wrigley Field stirred whenever Dave Kingman came to bat this season. He led the National League with 48 home runs and hit numerous clouts completely out of the ballpark. Although Kingman's star fell the next year, for 1979 at least, his blasts eclipsed memories of Wilson, Sauer, and Banks. No Cub had ever hit them as high or as far as Dave Kingman.

Quote of 1979

"I love Wrigley Field. If I were bringing a friend here from China, I would bring him to Wrigley Field."[18]

Bill Lee, Montreal pitcher in the Chicago Tribune—*July 5, 1979*

1980

> The Season by the Numbers
>
> | | | |
> |---|---|---|
> | 64-98 | .395 6th 27 games out | 1,206,776 (14,898 average) |
> | 37-44 | .457 at home | 67% of NL average |

Home Opener

APRIL 17; CUBS (LAMP) VS. METS (HAUSMAN); 56 DEGREES; 33,313 PAID

Cubs 4 Mets 1—Dennis Lamp and Bruce Sutter scattered eight hits. Rookie Carlos Lezcano hit his first major league home run, a two-run shot in the fifth inning. The game took only 1:58.

George Halas threw out the first pitch. Bernard Izzo, a member of the Chicago Lyric Opera Company, sang the National Anthem.

What Happened

- The Sting split its games between Wrigley Field and Comiskey Park, bypassing Soldier Field. The ballparks proved better venues; fans sat closer to the action and natural grass proved superior to Soldier Field's artificial surface.

   With the Cubs and White Sox reeling on the field, the Sting's Wrigley Field attendance average (16,037) beat both the Cubs' (14,898) and White Sox's (14,819) home averages.

- Jim Murphy purchased Ray's Bleachers and renamed the bar, "Murphy's Bleachers." Ray's was simple: twelve bar stools, a pinball machine, and a pool table with a plywood cover. Murphy's would evolve into something much more, eventually adding a beer garden, Irish bar, enclosed grill, an upper deck party room, and a rooftop pavilion. Ray's wasn't the first establishment at that address. In the 1930s, a hot dog stand called "Ernie's Bleachers" occupied the property. In 1940, Ernie built a more substantial brick building under the same name. A few years later, Ernie sold the bar and it became "J. B.'s." J. B. sold it back to Ernie and in 1962, Ray and Marge Meyer took it over.

   This map charts some of the longtime businesses around Wrigley Field, their names, and their dates of operation:

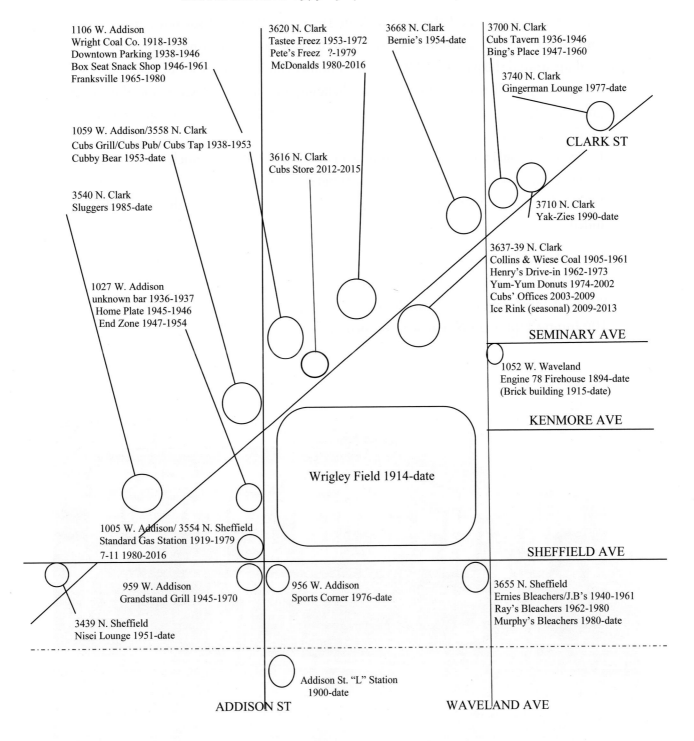

1106 W. Addison
Wright Coal Co. 1918-1938
Downtown Parking 1938-1946
Box Seat Snack Shop 1946-1961
Franksville 1965-1980

3620 N. Clark
Tastee Freez 1953-1972
Pete's Freez   ?-1979
McDonalds 1980-2016

3668 N. Clark
Bernie's 1954-date

3700 N. Clark
Cubs Tavern 1936-1946
Bing's Place 1947-1960

3740 N. Clark
Gingerman Lounge 1977-date

CLARK ST

1059 W. Addison/3558 N. Clark
Cubs Grill/Cubs Pub/ Cubs Tap 1938-1953
Cubby Bear 1953-date

3616 N. Clark
Cubs Store 2012-2015

3540 N. Clark
Sluggers 1985-date

3710 N. Clark
Yak-Zies 1990-date

3637-39 N. Clark
Collins & Wiese Coal 1905-1961
Henry's Drive-in 1962-1973
Yum-Yum Donuts 1974-2002
Cubs' Offices 2003-2009
Ice Rink (seasonal) 2009-2013

1027 W. Addison
unknown bar 1936-1937
Home Plate 1945-1946
End Zone 1947-1954

SEMINARY AVE

1052 W. Waveland
Engine 78 Firehouse 1894-date
(Brick building 1915-date)

KENMORE AVE

Wrigley Field 1914-date

1005 W. Addison/ 3554 N. Sheffield
Standard Gas Station 1919-1979
7-11 1980-2016

SHEFFIELD AVE

959 W. Addison
Grandstand Grill 1945-1970

956 W. Addison
Sports Corner 1976-date

3655 N. Sheffield
Ernies Bleachers/J.B's 1940-1961
Ray's Bleachers 1962-1980
Murphy's Bleachers 1980-date

3439 N. Sheffield
Nisei Lounge 1951-date

Addison St. "L" Station
1900-date

ADDISON ST

WAVELAND AVE

Seven bars stood around the new park in 1914. In 1919, at least ten bars existed. No saloons, at least legal establishments, existed from 1920 to 1932 during Prohibition. Six bars popped up around the park by 1936, and the number climbed to at least fifteen by 1945. The numbers dropped thereafter, mirroring the changing fortunes of the Cubs and the changing neighborhood. For example, the immediate area housed a minimum of eight bars in 1950 and only six in 1965.

The numbers again increased beginning in the late 1970s. So much so, that by 2009, twenty-five bars stood within two blocks of Wrigley Field.

Not all the establishments around Wrigley Field succeeded. Some of the shorter-lived bars included:

Tavern Inn; 3438 N. Clark (late teens)
The Clubhouse; 1035 W. Addison (mid-thirties)
Sheffield Tavern; 3454 N. Sheffield (early forties)
10th Inning Tap; 3733 N. Clark (mid-forties)

Cubs Grill (became Cubby Bear), circa 1938, 1059 W. Addison (www. ArgentaImages.com)

The Bighouse; 3710 N. Clark (early fifties)

Phil's Half Note; 3471 N. Clark (late fifties)

Extra Alarm Club; 3714 N. Clark (early sixties)

Ten-Four Club; 3714 N. Clark (mid-sixties)

Copa Sabana; 3714 N. Clark (late seventies)

Studio 69 LTD; 3474 N. Clark (early eighties)

Wild Hare Singing Armadillo Frog Sanctuary; 3530 Clark (late eighties)

Players on Clark; 3714 N. Clark (early nineties)

• Beginning in 1978, just as the neighborhood began to gentrify, realtors called the area Wrigleyville. This year, recognizing the developing relationship between the park and the surrounding area, the Cubs urged fans over the public address system to show consideration for the neighborhood when they went home.

Cubs Grill, interior, circa 1938 (www. ArgentaImages.com)

Game of the Year

April 22—The Cubs throttled the Cardinals, 16-12 as Ivan De Jesus hit for the cycle by the fifth inning: he homered in the first, doubled in the third, singled in the fourth, and tripled in the fifth. Barry Foote homered twice in the last two innings, including a grand slam into the right field basket to win it in front of 18,899 fans. Foote's shot drove in Lenny Randle, Bill Buckner, and Jerry Martin.

Quote of 1980

"We have a unique facility that should be preserved . . . I do not think that lights, advertising and such would add enough revenue to warrant disrupting a rather unique atmosphere."[19]

Team owner William Wrigley—in the Chicago Tribune, *August 2, 1980— when asked about the possibility of raising revenue with lights or gimmicks*

1981

The Season by the Numbers

38-65	.369 6th 21.5 games out	565,637 (10,672 average)
27-30	.474 at home	52% of NL average

Opening Day

APRIL 9; CUBS (REUSCHEL) VS. METS (ZACHRY); SUNNY, 53 DEGREES; 37,030 PAID

Mets 2 Cubs 0—The Cubs' Ken Reitz hit two doubles and a triple. But Lee Mazzilli and Rusty Staub stroked solo homers in the fourth inning.

Eighty-two-year-old Riggs Stephenson, a Cub star fifty years ago, threw out the first pitch. Florence Henderson sang the National Anthem.

What's New

The Cubs reported a $1.7 million deficit for 1980. The financial weary team received some good news. A car lost control on Sheffield Avenue and slammed into the park, damaging three of the preformed concrete slabs. But the team had planned to construct an additional gate in the exact area. The price of the gate cost only 1/3 of what a repair job would have run.

What Happened

- "Lightless" Wrigley Field racked up less than $30,000 each year in electric bills. The Yankees, on the other hand, paid $400,000 to power their ballpark.

- The Cubs began the season with a dismal 1-13 record. 1980-1981, in fact, marked the worst two-year record to date in team history. It's no wonder fans stayed away. Six of the first fourteen games failed to draw 5,000 fans and twelve attracted less than 13,000.

- Things could hardly have gotten worse, but they did. On June 12, the player's union announced a walkout that lasted fifty days. The strike not only cancelled twenty-two home games that the masochistic Cub fan could never get back, but left vendors, ushers, and area merchants scrambling for income. Luckily, the Sting still played at Wrigley Field. They drew a team-record 30,501 for a 6-5 win over the Cosmos on June 28.

  Less than a week after the strike began, on June 16, William Wrigley agreed to sell his 81 percent share of the Cubs to the Tribune Company for $20.5 million in cash. Wrigley needed the money to help pay off family estate taxes and the Tribune Company received guaranteed baseball programming for their cable station, WGN.

  The deal ended the family's association with the team that began in 1915, months before the Cubs played their first game in what would eventually become Wrigley Field. The sale included the ballpark. Near the time of the sale, the Wrigley family also sold the land under Wrigley Field to the Tribune Company for $600,000. William Wrigley's father bought the land in 1924 and had leased it to the team since.

- Neighbors worried that the Tribune Company would install lights at the ballpark. A group of 25 East Lakeview residents met on June 23 and mapped a strategy to squelch night baseball, including direct appeals to Mayor Byrne and Commissioner Bowie Kuhn. The grassroots group circulated petitions and organized a drive to pay for legal fees.

  On August 2, the team said they would not immediately install lights. Andy McKenna, the Cub chairman remained noncommittal on night baseball, claiming that while the incoming executives discussed the issue, they made no final decisions.

- The *Chicago Tribune* leaked ideas proposed by the new Cub management. Wrigley Field, they hinted, might get taller outfield walls, more scoreboards, new home locker facilities, parking, and higher-priced seating. The team even discussed adding a digital clock to the scoreboard and turning the old clock into advertising space.

- In August, public address man Jim Enright became seriously ill. Enright died of kidney failure on December 20. He was seventy-one years old.

- Jack Brickhouse stepped down at the end of the season, concluding an amazing run as WGN-TV broadcaster. The eternally optimistic Brickhouse witnessed more Cub games at Wrigley Field than anyone except Pat Pieper or Yosh Kawano. In the off-season, Harry Caray, who clashed with the new White Sox ownership, dropped a bombshell, announcing that he'd be the WGN television man in 1982.

Game of the Year

August 10—A post-strike gathering of only 7,551 saw the Cubs drop the season's second opener, 7-5 to the Mets. The game went into extra innings tied 1-1, but the Mets scored in the eleventh, twelfth, and thirteenth innings off Lee Smith, Doug Capilla, Rawly Eastwick, and Lynn McGlothen.

Quote of 1981

"The infield is a disgrace. Do you hear me? It's a disgrace. The grass is so long I could feed my whole herd of cattle. . . . I figure it must be another Cub economy move. They're going to let the infield grass grow until it's time to bring in a combine for it. After all, hay is going for $100 a ton these days. That revenue could help balance the team budget."[20]

First baseman Bill Buckner in the Chicago Tribune—*April 30, 1981—getting in on the frustrating atmosphere surrounding the team*

1982

> The Season by the Numbers
> 73-89   .451 5th 19 games out   1,249,278 (15,423 average)
> 38-43   .469 at home   68% of NL average

Home Opener

APRIL 9; CUBS (JENKINS) VS. METS (SCOTT); 34 DEGREES; 26,712 PAID

Cubs 5 Mets 0—The "new tradition" Cubs opened with an old name, Fergie Jenkins, who returned after an eight-year absence. Jenkins lasted into the seventh inning, long enough to quiet the Mets behind a Bill Buckner home run. New public address man Lee Pelty kept busy warning fans to refrain from tossing snowballs onto the field and at their favorite target, ex-Cub Dave Kingman.

Other newcomers joined Pelty that day. Ryne Sandberg appeared in a Cub home uniform for the first time. Harry Caray sang his inaugural rendition of "Take Me Out to the Ballgame." But a week later, after just seven tries, Bob Verdi of the *Chicago Tribune* called fan reaction to Harry's singing as "at best, tepid." Even Harry himself admitted, "It's not working out." He added, "And if we don't do it right, we might as well not do it at all."[21]

The problem was a lack of harmony. Harry and new organist Ed Vodicka, who was stationed in the old football press box down the left field line, couldn't see each other. So either Harry started before Ed or Ed before Harry. They finally developed a cueing system that got them on the same musical page. From that point on, Harry always introduced his famous Wrigley rendition with, "a one, a two, a three. . . ."

What's New

- A corporate mentality and aggressive competition from the new White Sox owners swept the franchise and Wrigley Field toward modern times. A myriad of changes in and around the park included:

  - computerized telephone system
  - trash compactor and vacuum system
  - improved lighting inside and out
  - a hall-of-fame on the main concourse featuring plaques of forty-two former Cubs
  - carpeting and heating in the press box
  - new heating and air conditioning in the visitor's clubhouse
  - lots of paint including "Building a New Tradition" splashed above the bleacher entrance and logos of National League teams on the visitor's dugout roof
  - team logos on the on-deck circles
  - new players' wives lounge
  - new Andy Frain usher uniforms
  - a 104-page program/magazine sold at the park
  - catered parties in the bleachers
  - an expanded marketing department hoping to add to last year's 973 season tickets (The Sox sold 5,400 season tickets in 1982. The Cubs hoped for 2,000.)
  - an electronic message board below the scoreboard

- The Cubs hired a ballgirl. Marla Collins, twenty-four years old, sat on the field between the backstop and the first base dugout. She shagged fouls and supplied the umpire with baseballs. Collins wore a Cub uniform that, during suitable weather, included short pants. She made $150 per game.
- On June 25, the Cubs moved their bullpen from left to right field, giving manager Lee Elia a clear view of his relief pitchers from the third base dugout. The *Chicago Sun-Times* theorized that Elia wanted to keep his pitchers from ducking into the clubhouse entrance down the left field line. But before the 1984 season, new Cub manager Jim Frey moved the Cub bullpen back to the third base side.[22]

What Happened

- The lights issue permeated the neighborhood. In February, a Cub marketing aide tried to soothe area residents, saying, "lights in Wrigley Field are a very low priority for us."[23] Executive Vice President and General Manager Dallas Green backed off earlier declarations, saying, "While lights are an eventually, they are not a priority at this time."[24]

  Neighborhood groups, including the newly formed C.U.B.S. (Citizens United for Baseball in Sunshine) claimed night baseball would exacerbate parking problems, increase vandalism, and drive down property values. Alderman John Merlo spoke for many when he said, "We must take every possible precaution to prohibit the installation of lights."[25]

April 28, 1982. Notice the electronic message board and the soccer time clock below the scoreboard. (National Baseball Hall of Fame Library, Cooperstown, N.Y.)

The neighbors lobbied hard and made themselves heard. Both the Illinois House and Senate passed bills banning high-decibel, nighttime sporting events in Chicago. Comiskey Park and Soldier Field were grandfathered in because they played night games before July 1, 1982. Governor Thompson signed the bill into law on August 23, temporarily ending talk of night baseball at the park.

• A permanent recognition came to Mr. Cub when the team retired Ernie Banks's uniform number on August 22. Banks's number 14, the first retired by the team, flew from the left field flagpole.

• Examples abound of the passing of the Cubs from the Wrigley family to corporate ownership, more aggressively concerned with the bottom line. Management experimented with 12:05 P.M. game times and sold all non-bleacher seats in advance for two June dates against the Cardinals. On October 4, they cleaned house of most of Bill Wrigley's front office staff, firing the ticket manager, promotions director, director of publications, traveling secretary, three general secretaries, visiting clubhouse attendant, manager of group sales, and head of security. The massacre spared few. Getting the ax a few days earlier was Cub coach and legend Billy Williams.

Games of the Year

August 17-18—Even "Let's Play Two" Ernie Banks probably wouldn't have wanted to take part in the 2-1, twenty-one-inning marathon between the Cubs and Dodgers. Darkness stopped the game after eighteen innings, tied 1-1. The Dodgers won it the next day. Highlights included:

- Tied record for longest Wrigley Field game in innings, first set in 1918
- Wrigley Field record game time of 6:10 (the twenty-one-inning marathon in 1918 lasted only 4:00)
- Dodgers ran out of position players, necessitating pitchers Fernando Valenzuela and Bob Welch to duties as outfielders
- Five ejected, including managers Tommy Lasorda and Lee Elia

Quote of 1982

"It's weird in Chicago. There are people out there who are actually disappointed when the Cubs win. It's like the thing to do is come to Wrigley Field, have a party and watch the Cubs lose. That's what's expected."[26]
New Cub Larry Bowa in the Chicago Tribune—*June 11, 1982*

1983

The Season by the Numbers

| 71-91 | .438 5ᵗʰ 19 games out | 1,479,717 (18,268 average) |
| 43-38 | .531 at home | 81% of NL average |

Opening Day

APRIL 6; CUBS (JENKINS) VS. EXPOS (ROGERS); CLOUDY, 45 DEGREES; 4,802 PAID

Expos 3 Cubs 0—The Cubs should have realized this wasn't their year. They went through the 1982 season, home and away, without a rainout. During Opening Day ceremonies on April 5, rains came and sent home a near-capacity crowd. The following afternoon they lost the new opener, 3-0. The Expos' Al Oliver hit two homers in front of the second smallest opening day crowd in Wrigley Field history.

What's New

- Changes at the ballpark included a new manager's office, ticket offices at the Clark and Addison Street entrance, rebuilt concession stands, and remodeled restrooms.

  By June, two businesses opened along the right field concourse: a Cub gift shop and The Friendly Confines Café. Both were open year-round, necessitating outside entrances off Addison Street. One can't overlook their significance; the park now generated income when there was no game and even during the off-season.

  The year-old Cubs Hall of Fame was squeezed into the gift shop. The twenty-nine plaques of famous Cubs would now entice fans into the shop to spend money.

  The Stadium Club stood directly above the new shops. Established to provide a perk for season ticket holders, the Stadium Club brought fine dining, including prime rib, into the old ballpark.

- Before mid-season, two beer ads hung below the scoreboard and another from the marquee at the main entrance. The former marked the first commercialism of the park's interior since the Wrigley "Doublemint" stick figures stood atop the pre-1938 scoreboard.

- Marla Collins began her second year as the Cub ballgirl. Because of her growing popularity, the team required her to wear shorts at every game, even during cold weather.

What Happened

- Cub fans assumed new ownership would bring instant success. It didn't. On April 29, after a heartbreaking loss, a 5-14 record, and poor treatment of his players by Wrigley Field fans, Manager Lee Elia belted out the most fabled meltdown in park history. His tirade that day defended his players' effort but tore into the discontented fans coming to the ballpark. A part of the three-minute exhibition included:

  "What the **** am I supposed to do, go out there and let my players get destroyed every day and be quiet? For the nickel-dime people who turn up? They don't even work. That's why they're out at the game."

  Elia said more as a tape recorder ran:

  "I'll tell you one thing, I hope we get hotter that , just to stuff it up them 3,000 people that show up every day, because if they're the real Chicago fans, they can kiss my ass right downtown. Hope we get hot—just to stuff it up those 3,000 people who show up every day. If those are the real Chicago fans they can kiss my ass. . . ."[27]

  The Cubs improved somewhat afterwards, but never enough to save Elia's job. The passionate manager was dismissed on August 22 and replaced by Charlie Fox.

- The night game question lingered, even in light of the state law prohibiting them. Dallas Green said the team could bypass the decibel curfew by starting games at 7:00 P.M., assuming most would end before curfew or at worse, turning off the organ and p.a. system at 10:00 P.M.

  Meanwhile, the opposition pushed on, staging a "No-Lights Day" on June 11. Banners hung from buildings across Waveland and Sheffield Avenues and a "No Lights" balloon flew above the left field bleachers.[28] The rabble-rousers left little to chance and their hard work triumphed again. On August 25, the Chicago City Council voted 42-2 to pass a zoning code amendment that further prevented night games at the ballpark. The carefully worded proposal singled out Wrigley Field by prohibiting sports contests that occurred between 8:00 P.M. and 8:00 A.M. in a stadium holding more than 10,000 seats that stood within 500 feet of 100 living quarters.

  Even before the city law, Dallas Green reasoned that the Cubs, lights or no lights, might need a larger park to raise revenues to compete in the 1980s and beyond. Cub Chief Executive Officer Jim Finks added, "People have narrowed the issue down to do we put lights in Wrigley Field or not. The day-night issue is important. But I feel to leave it at that, as most people do, is missing a significant option for us—a new stadium."[29]

Game of the Year

June 10-12—The Cubs took two of three from the Cardinals. The exciting contests attracted a Wrigley Field three-game record of 116,107 paid, besting the previous mark set in 1969 against the Mets. Catcher Jody Davis became a hero that weekend, homering in each game. The throngs responded, beginning the "JO-DY, JO-DY" chant that accompanied Davis's at-bats the rest of his Cub career.

Quote of 1983

"Eighty-five percent of the **** world is working. The other fifteen come out here."[30]
Manager Lee Elia on the fans at Wrigley Field—April 29, 1983

1984

Only a crazy man or a seer would pick the Cubs to win big in 1984. So readers of the January 1 *Chicago Tribune* thought that astrologer Bob Marks's prediction of a Cub pennant was a New Year's resolution to become "overly optimistic."

The Season by the Numbers		
96-65	.596 1st 6.5 games ahead	2,107,655 (26,182 average)
51-29	.638 at home	124% of NL average

Home Opener

APRIL 13; CUBS (TROUT) VS. METS (GOODEN); 56 DEGREES; 33,436 PAID

Cubs 11 Mets 2—Home runs by Gary Matthews, Ron Cey, and Jody Davis helped club the Mets. The North Siders got 14 hits off Dwight Gooden and three relievers, including three each by Matthews and Davis. Steve Trout pitched a complete game. The biggest pregame ovation went to first baseman Bill Buckner, who watched the game from the bench after losing his starting job to Leon Durham.

DePaul basketball coach Ray Meyer threw out the first pitch. The cast of the musical "Dreamgirls" sang the National Anthem.

What's New

- A renovated Cubs' locker room.
- After being denied lights by both the state and the city, the team moved eighteen games to a 3:05 P.M. starting time. They treated them like a party, scheduling postgame concerts with the likes of Chuck Berry and Sha-Na-Na (the concerts also alleviated traffic—widening the timeframe when fans left the ballpark). But the neighbors weren't thrilled; the late-starting games exasperated parking issues for residents coming home from work. In response, the team added remote parking from the WGN studios and DeVry University, two miles west of the park.

    The 3:05 P.M. games aggravated more than just the neighbors. Upper deck shadows made it hard for batters, catchers, and umpires to see pitches. "It's ridiculous to play that time of day," said Jody Davis. "I tried to knock balls down. No way I could catch 'em. It's just a matter of time before somebody gets hurt."[31]
- Even before Opening Day, season ticket sales grew 46 percent to over 6,500. Part of the increase came from extensive marketing by the Tribune Company. Around this time, corporate culture also invaded sports. Season ticket sales rose in most cities as corporations purchased seats for their customers. The wealthier season ticket holders became the teams' most coveted fans.

What Happened

- The Cubs lost eighteen of its first twenty-one exhibition games, forcing Dallas Green into action. On March 27, he picked up two-thirds of an outfield from Philadelphia: Gary Matthews and Bob Denier. The change improved team chemistry immediately.

    But Green didn't stop there. The day he pried Dennis Eckersley from Boston, May 25, the Cubs were two games in front of the Phillies. Green also got pitcher Rick Sutcliffe from Cleveland on June 13. Sutcliffe promptly won his first start and kept on winning.
- Steve Goodman wrote the team's new theme song, "Go Cubs Go." The complete opposite of his earlier "A Dying Cubs Fan's Last Request" that lamented the team as losers, the new song's lyrics predicted a Cub victory. Initially, the buoyant song blared over the public address system before each game. It proved prophetic; the Cubs won this year. But tragically, Goodman, a long-time leukemia sufferer, died of the disease on September 20, just days before the Cubs reached the playoffs.

Games of the Year

June 23—America took notice of the vastly improved Cubs. In front of a national television audience and a packed Wrigley Field, Ryne Sandberg homered twice off ex-Cub Bruce Sutter—a solo homer in the ninth and a two-run shot in the tenth to save the Cubs from defeat. They scrapped the Cardinals, 12-11 in eleven innings on an RBI single by Dave Owen. When Sutcliffe fanned 14 the following day, that astrologer seemed to be onto something.

August 6-8—On August 1, the Cubs beat the Phillies and moved back into the Eastern Division lead. The second place Mets came to town with visions of 1969 in Cub fans' minds. But this year was different. The Cubs swept four from the New Yorkers behind three game-winning RBI by Keith Moreland. Their lead reached four and a half games.

Ryne Sandberg (www. ArgentaImages.com)

To the Playoffs

The team's success created a problem. If the Cubs won the division or more, would they install lights for nighttime playoff and World Series games? In July, Cub President Jim Finks answered, saying, "we started the year without lights and will finish the year without lights. We have no plans on using them no matter who asks. If we do, we'd break faith with too many people."[32] The "people" were Wrigleyville residents. They met at the park on August 19 to map strategy, including the threat of legal action if necessary.

If the Cubs played World Series afternoon games instead of at night, NBC stood to lose at least $13 million in advertising revenue. Since baseball guaranteed the amount, each major league team would reimburse the network up to $700,000 to address the shortfall. Certainly, baseball wanted to force night games on the Cubs. Yet, state and local laws forbade them, and baseball didn't have the time to pursue it before the end of the season.

Beginning September 17, Cub fans sent in ticket applications for the five playoffs and World Series games scheduled at Wrigley Field. Nearly 1.8 million fans applied for a chance to be the lucky 17,500 to actually get two tickets to a game.

The Cubs clinched the National League East on September 24 in Pittsburgh. That night, thousands gathered at Clark and Addison to celebrate. But before the team met the Padres in the playoffs, they had one final piece of business. Following the last regular season home game, a 2-1 win over the Cardinals, manager Jim Frey led the players around the field as they thanked the fans for their support. The Cubs smashed their all-time attendance record, beating the 1969 season by nearly 400,000.

October 2 marked the first Cub postseason game in 39 years. To celebrate such an auspicious occasion, the weather cooperated perfectly—bright and sunny, temperatures in the mid-sixties with a strong breeze toward the bleachers. After Rick Sutcliffe set down the Padres in the first inning, Bob Denier led off the Cub half with a home run. Two batters later, Gary Matthews also homered. Matthews homered again. Ron Cey did too. But the star was Sutcliffe. He pitched two-hit ball for seven innings and drove a mammoth shot to Sheffield Avenue in the third inning. The final record-filled score was 13-0. The *Chicago Tribune* described the near-indescribable scene: "Fans screamed, hugged one another, danced and even wept while the action on the field fulfilled nearly four decades of their dreams . . . People stood and cheered as the Cubs hammered away at the Padres. There was shock, disbelief, then ecstasy. It was all too good to be true."[33]

Two generations of Cubs fans never experienced anything like this at Wrigley Field. The long-anticipated day was, in fact, one of the greatest in park history.

The euphoria grew the next day when Steve Trout and Lee Smith handcuffed San Diego, 4-2. Afterwards, fans wouldn't leave the ballpark. Ushers finally pried them out nearly an hour later. There, the throngs joined in the streets, celebrating the Cubs, on the brink of history.

Cub fans know what happened next. The Padres swept three straight in San Diego, crushing the dream. There would be no pennant in 1984.

Quote of 1984

"That was the beginning of Wrigley Field merging with Wrigleyville. Before 1984, this wasn't a weekend destination point and a place where people would socialize after games. There were some small corner taverns that people happened upon and that was it."[34]

John McDonough, Senior Vice President of Marketing and Broadcasting

SEVENTH INNING
1985-1998
LOVE AFFAIR

The memorable 1984 season, capped by the most perfect game in park history—Game One of the National League playoffs—changed Wrigley Field forever. The appreciation afforded the ballpark the last decade turned into a love affair.

Cubs fans came back to Wrigley Field—the team broke their attendance record again in 1985. And although attendance ebbed and flowed during the inning, fans came to Wrigley Field like never before and watched the Cubs, win or lose. For example, the eight seasons before 1984, the team averaged 16,111 fans per game. During the eight years after 1984, they averaged 26,811 per game.

While occasional winning seasons were a catalyst to increased fan interest, the pure joy evident at last year's playoff game—the mix of the park's subtle beauty, history, and the special relationship between the fans and the park—kept fans coming back.

The Wrigley Field love affair seduced more than just Cubs fans. Accolades from across the country would become the norm. In the twenty-five years before 1984, architects consciously designed stadiums to not resemble Wrigley Field. After 1984 they built ballparks inspired by Wrigley Field and other Classic ballparks. Beginning in 1992 with Oriole Park at Camden Yards, over twenty Neoclassic ballparks, averaging more than one a year, went up nationwide, with Wrigley Field and Fenway Park as models.

While the city and the state of Illinois passed laws to keep lights out of Wrigley Field, network television threatened to keep future playoff games out of Chicago without night games. The potential financial losses spurred the state to reverse course. With the White Sox on the verge of fleeing to Florida and the Cubs making overtures towards the suburbs, Chicago politicians allowed lights at the park. The more than fifty-year lights debate ended rather quickly, decided finally not by neighborhood desires, but solely by outside money interests.

1985

The Season by the Numbers		
77-84	.478 4th 23.5 games out	2,161,534 (26,686 average)
41-39	.513 at home	118% of NL average

Opening Day

APRIL 9; CUBS (SUTCLIFFE) VS. PIRATES (RHODEN); SUNNY, 35 DEGREES; 34,551 PAID

Cubs 2 Pirates 0—Keith Moreland drove in both runs with a home run and a single. Rick Sutcliffe and Lee Smith combined on a six-hitter. The win marked Sutcliffe's fifteenth straight regular-season victory, breaking Ed Reulbach's 1909 team record. Shortstop Shawon Dunston made his major league debut, singling in four at-bats.

Equipment manager Yosh Kawano threw out the first pitch following a ceremony naming the Cub clubhouse in his honor. Diane Fratantoni, star of the musical "Cats," sang the National Anthem.

What's New

• Wayne Messmer replaced Walt Jacobs as public address announcer and sang the National Anthem before selected games. Wayne was a busy man. He now handled public address duties at Wrigley Field, Comiskey Park, Soldier Field, and Chicago Stadium.

- Last October's disappointment didn't hurt interest in the Cubs. In fact, on January 25, the Cubs suspended season ticket sales after selling 25,000 full or partial packages, shattering last year's record of 7,500. Remarkably, in less than four years, the team increased their season ticket base by more than twenty-five fold.

- In late March, the team sold all bleacher seats in advance, ending the day-of-game tradition dating to the beginning of the franchise in 1876. No longer could fans guarantee a seat by arriving early in the day. Instead of seats going to the heartiest fans, they went to those buying months in advance or those paying top dollar to a scalper. After Opening Day, Bill Veeck never returned to the bleachers. In July, he sat in the Comiskey Park bleachers and voiced his opposition to the Cub policy. "Someone has to say it's wrong. It's wrong for the scalpers to have control of the bleacher tickets. It's wrong that the going rate is $10 to $20 on weekends."[1]

  Last year, the bleachers and the back section of the upper deck were the final 8,370 general admission seats in the park. This year, every seat in the park was reserved.

- The ever-increasing popularity of Wrigley Field necessitated physical changes. In late May, the team added 225 seats in the catwalks in left and right field (and extended the baskets under those areas). A month later, nearly 575 seats were added in the aisle behind the terrace box seats. The 800 new seats provided a potential ticket income of $6,000 per game, or about Ryne Sandberg's salary.

  The Cubs broke a Chicago attendance record that the White Sox held for one year. The Cubs drew 2,161,534, about 25,000 more tickets than the White Sox sold in 1984.

- It's not new and it's odd that it happened again, but just as bleacher die-hards were being squeezed out, two San Diego home run balls found their way back onto the field during a game on May 4. The "throw-it-back" phenomena that started in 1969 and ebbed thereafter returned for good this year.

What Happened

In December 1984, the Cubs filed a suit claiming the recent city and state laws against night baseball were unconstitutional because they singled out Wrigley Field. On March 25, Circuit Court Judge Richard L. Curry upheld the laws, saying that night games would prove detrimental to the neighborhood around the park. He chastised the team and baseball commissioner Peter Ueberroth, saying they, "lost their grasp on reality and perspective on values. . . .they ask for a reversal of the status quo which has existed at this ballpark for 70 years."[2] He finished with a spicy retort to the team, "You're out. O.U.T. The Cubs are out. The inning is over. The contest is lost."[3]

Jerome Holtzman of the *Chicago Tribune* thought the ruling was actually a blessing for the team. "Like it or not, Chicago has been and continues to be a Cub town. In my view, there are two reasons for this popularity: [1] the location and easier access to Wrigley Field, and [2] the fact that with daytime baseball mothers are willing to ship their kids off for an afternoon at Wrigley Field."[4]

Assumed blessing or not, shortly after, the big guys got in the picture. ABC television, which would televise the 1985 World Series, exercised a clause requiring all games be played in prime time. Dallas Green added that if the Cubs made it that far, he'd move the games to another National League city. That scenario, he said, would be "the death blow." Tribune Company Executive Vice President John Madigan, minus the hyperbole, said, "it would be very difficult to remain in Wrigley Field without lights."[5] Anticipating a loss of upwards of $150 million in income if the games moved out of Illinois, the state senate quickly voted to allow up to eighteen night games a year at Wrigley Field. The state house and local neighbors, however, offered only portable lights for postseason, something the Cubs wouldn't accept.

By the time the Cubs lost thirteen straight in June, there was no discussion of postseason night games this year. But the forces-to-be ramped up the lights issue at Wrigley Field. It now went beyond neighborhood emotion. Big money was at stake and those who figured to gain came to the center of the controversy.

In late June, Cub management name-dropped Schaumburg and Arlington Heights, two northwest suburbs they'd consider moving to if they failed to get lights in Wrigley Field. The Tribune Company owned 100 acres in Schaumburg and met with the village manager about a possible move. They spoke with engineering firms concerning cost estimates for various stadium options.

The White Sox, on the other hand, didn't mince words; they wanted out of aging Comiskey Park. Owner Jerry Reinsdorf purchased 100 acres in west suburban Addison, about five miles south of the Tribune property. These moves, along with private pitches for domed stadiums south of the Loop and in nearby Cicero constituted the greatest threat to abandonment of the Chicago ballparks in more than twenty years.

Game of the Year

September 8—Pete Rose's second hit of the game, a fifth inning single off Reggie Patterson, marked the 4,191st hit of his career, equaling Ty Cobb's all-time major league record. After the hit, Pete received a three-minute standing ovation. He bounced out to short in the seventh inning, and after a two-hour rain delay, he swung through a Lee Smith fastball in the ninth.

Darkness ended baseball that day in a 5-5 tie. But the games' statistics counted. (Rose got his record-breaking 4,192nd hit on September 11.)

Quote of 1985

"Now you hear people saying Wrigley Field and Comiskey Park have to go to make room for progress. It's shameful when places that provide so much pleasure suddenly become inadequate because there's a few more bucks to be made elsewhere."[6]

Bill Veeck in the Chicago Tribune—*June 28, 1985*

1986

The Season by the Numbers		
70-90	.438 5th 37 games out	1,859,102 (23,239 average)
42-38	.525 at home	100% of NL average

Home Opener

APRIL 18; CUBS (SUTCLIFFE) VS. PIRATES (RHODEN); SUNNY, 53 DEGREES; 38,151 PAID

Pirates 4 Cubs 0—Pittsburgh's Jim Morrison went 4-for-4 with a home run and two RBI. The Cubs collected nine hits but could not score; after eight games they were hitting just .193. Rick Sutcliffe fell to 0-3.

Walter Payton of the Super Bowl Champion Bears threw out the first "football." His five-year-old son, Jarrett, donning a Cub uniform, then threw out the season's first pitch. The Stanley Paul Orchestra and the Ft. Sheridan Color Guard assisted with opening ceremonies. Sam Sianis's goat also made an appearance.

What's New

• The team built a new outdoor restaurant at Addison near Sheffield. The 150-seat establishment served food before and after games.
• The first ATM was installed at the park.
• The removal of the two beer signs below the center field scoreboard in May left Wrigley Field's interior free of permanent advertisement. The team did not renew the three-year contract

with Anheuser-Busch, concluding that an ad-free park provided more intrinsic value than the revenue from the two intrusive signs.

What Happened

• Bill Veeck defied death for decades. He lost a leg in World War II, he drank, he slept only a few hours each night, and he chain-smoked. He finally succumbed on January 2, the result of cardiac arrest brought on by emphysema. Both sides of town mourned the passing of the people's owner.

Veeck arrived at Cubs Park in 1919 when his dad became club president. He grew up at the park and become a peanut vendor before entering Kenyon College. He returned to the Cubs in 1933 following his father's death. He signed on as an office boy, worked concessions, and sold tickets—learning the business of baseball at Clark and Addison Streets. Outside of P. K. Wrigley, Veeck more than anyone made the park the celebrated place it is today. In 1937, Bill literally wired the scoreboard and purchased the ivy.

He bought the then minor league Milwaukee Brewers in 1941. After stops in Cleveland and St. Louis, he purchased the White Sox on two occasions—in 1959 when they won a pennant, and again after the 1975 season, stitching together a last-minute syndicate of investors that saved the franchise from moving to Seattle.

Bill Veeck in 1959 at Comiskey Park (www. ArgentaImages.com)

Veeck spent his retirement in the Wrigley Field bleachers and claimed his biggest wish was to have owned the Cubs. That would have been quite a time—the people's owner holding court at America's favorite ballpark.

• The White Sox and the city began negotiations on a $250 million, open-air stadium on the near South Side. To advance the project, the White Sox offered the Cubs the stadium for eighteen night games a year. Dallas Green, however, still anticipating lights in Wrigley Field, told the *Chicago Sun-Times*, "'We're not interested in that. . . . By the time the stadium is built, it would be moot.'"[7]

The Cubs confirmed that when lights are installed, they'd expand Wrigley Field by at least 5,000 seats. The team would either add seats to the upper deck or double-deck the bleachers.

• On July 22, Marla Collins, the ballgirl with the short shorts, lost her job after posing partially nude in Playboy magazine. The firing was understandable, but somewhat of the Cubs' own doing as they sold Marla's sex appeal: Harry Caray constantly extolled her virtues and WGN-TV moved Collins's chair toward the first base dugout to maximize exposure to their television cameras. After the firing, Collins said, "The Cubs wished me all the best but couldn't condone what I did. . . . There is no embarrassment on my part. It was very tastefully done."[8]

The team received over 100 applications to replace Collins, and soon after, hired two females who signed "code of conduct" agreements. Roger Baird, a member of the grounds crew who subbed during the interim, occasionally worked as ballboy. Baird, it seemed, wasn't required to wear short pants.

• Vince Lloyd retired after the season, ending a nearly forty-year run as the team's television color man and radio broadcaster. Lloyd hit his stride when teamed with Lou Boudreau on radio in 1965. Lloyd's seamless delivery and Lou's baseball expertise melded into a remarkably authoritative yet homey product that felt as comfortable as the Friendly Confines itself. In the sixties and seventies, it wasn't unusual to hear Vince's and Lou's voices anywhere in Wrigley Field, coming from the transistor radios brought by Cub fans eager to both see the game in person and hear the "Vince and Lou Show."

Games of the Year

April 20 and August 11—The Cubs and Pirates took seventeen innings and two days to decide this game. Pittsburgh scored two runs in the seventeenth to outpace the Cubs, 10-8. The teams used a league record seventeen pitchers, with the Cubs tying a major league mark with ten. The list included the great and the long forgotten: Dennis Eckersley, Jay Baller, Matt Keough, George Frazier, Lee Smith, Dick Ruthven, Rick Sutcliffe, Steve Trout, Frank DiPino, and Dave Gumpert.

September 2 and 3—The Cubs and Astros played an eighteen-inning marathon that used fifty-three players, a major league record. Included was Greg Maddux, who made his major league debut. Maddux pitched the eighteenth inning and took the loss after giving up a home run to Billy Hatcher. Yet, manager Gene Michael had this to say about his young pitcher, "I like what I saw. . . . I want to see what he can do as a starter."[9]

Quote of 1986

"My answer to the National League is who the hell are you to be telling us where our team should play?"[10]

Mayor Harold Washington in the Chicago Tribune—*May 21, 1986—after the National League said Cub home playoff games would take place in St. Louis instead of Wrigley Field.*

1987

The Season by the Numbers

76-85	.472 6th 18.5 games out	2,035,130 (25,281 average)
40-40	.500 at home	99% of NL average

Opening Day

APRIL 7; CUBS (SUTCLIFFE) VS. CARDINALS (TUDOR); SUNNY, 46 DEGREES; 38,240 PAID

Cardinals 9 Cubs 3—The Cubs scored their runs in the first two innings on an error, a walk, and a sacrifice fly. The Cardinals scored in only two innings, but they put across five in the third and four more in the seventh. Andre Dawson made his Cub debut, going 0-for-4 with an RBI.

In January, Billy Williams was elected to the Baseball of Fame. Billy's wife Shirley threw out the first ball. Wayne Messmer sang the National Anthem.

What's New

- The Stadium Club and Friendly Confines restaurants expanded.
- Two new gift shops opened near the Clark and Addison entrance.
- With security in mind, the team ended beer sales after the eighth inning. They also reduced the maximum number of beer vendors from 200 to 90 and shrank the largest beer from 20 to 16 ounces.
- The Cubs' own security force replaced the Andy Frain ushers, a park staple since 1928. Recently the Frains only seated fans while the Cubs' men took care of security issues. The team enlarged their own force and rehired many of the older Frain workers. But the ushers in the blue serge suits disappeared into history.
- When the scoreboard was repainted in mid-season, a white "tic-tac-toe" design was added so fans could better read the line scores.
- For the past couple of seasons, when the Cubs took the field to start the game, the Van Halen song "Jump" was played over the public address system. This year the song "You're My Cubs" replaced it (but both "Jump" and another Van Halen hit, "Dreams," returned sporadically over the years).

August 27, 1987. The Cubs' line score moved to the bottom of the National League line scores in 1984. The White Sox score moved to the bottom the same year, but with collegial P. K. Wrigley long gone, their name changed from "Sox" to "Chicago." (National Baseball Hall of Fame Library, Cooperstown, N.Y.)

What Happened

- The year started poorly for two fans caught in the Wrigley Field press box during the early hours of January 5. Police officers found the interlopers with Harry Caray's net and seat cushion. The perpetrators received the sympathies of Caray, who was reached by telephone in California. "'All they had to do was ask me and I'd have given them the items. . . . I hope they come before a very kind-hearted judge.'"[11]

  Caray suffered a stroke that kept him out of the broadcast booth until May. While fans heard a tape of Harry singing the seventh inning stretch, thirty-two celebrities filled in for him in the television booth. Among those working home games at Wrigley Field included Brent Musburger, Ernie Banks, and Bill Murray.

- Billy Williams entered the Baseball Hall of Fame and the Cubs retired his number 26 uniform on August 13. Williams's number now hung on the right-field flagpole. Ernie Banks's number 14 flew in left field.

Games of the Year

May 19—Harry Caray's triumphant return, on Mug Day no less, proved a fitting tribute to Chicago's favorite beer-loving broadcaster. Not only did the Cubs whip the Reds, 9-2, but Caray received an on-air telephone call from President Ronald Reagan. Harry's seventh inning rendition of "Take Me Out to the Ballgame" infused the crowd.

June 2 and 3—The Cubs dismantled the Astros in consecutive games, winning 13-2 and 22-7. In the latter, they opened with a nine-run first inning. The Astros' Billy Hatcher and the Cubs' Brian Dayett and Keith Moreland hit grand slams, the first time in major league history that two teams hit three in a game.

The 1987 Cubs finished in last place. But thanks in part to Andre Dawson's MVP season, they were the first cellar-dwellers to draw more than 2,000,000 fans.

Quote of 1987

"I didn't practice singing. I don't wanna get on key."[12]

Harry Caray in the New York Times—*May 20, 1987—when asked if he sang while recovering from a stroke*

Seventh Inning Stretch—Postscript

The city's Economic Development Commission conducted a poll on night baseball at Wrigley Field. The survey of 1,140 Chicagoans asked whether they favored lights. Citywide, 49 percent said yes. Households from a half to one mile from the park favored it 33 percent and those within a halfmile 32 percent. When asked whether they favor lights with restrictions (only eighteen night games a year, limited beer sales, and fewer 3:00 P.M. games), the numbers jumped to 83 percent citywide, 70 percent one-half to one mile away, and 59 percent within a half mile from the park.

Mayor Washington, long opposed to night baseball at Wrigley Field, rethought his position. First, the poll numbers showed citywide support for lights. Second, keeping the status quo meant huge economic losses if the Cubs hosted postseason games in St. Louis. Finally, there was the Cubs' threatened move to the suburbs and the White Sox stalled stadium deal with the state of Illinois. The loss of one or even both teams, at least an outside possibility, would devastate the mayor politically. While Washington had limited control over the White Sox situation, he did have a say in the lights issue.

On November 13, the mayor, in an attempt to head off political losses and buoyed by the poll numbers, came out in support of a compromise on lights at Wrigley Field. He would bring the issue to vote in the city council if the team agreed to only eighteen night games a year and to reduce the number of the annoying 3:05 P.M. start times. The mayor had the votes to repeal the five-year-old city noise laws. Lights seemed assured.

On November 25, a heart attack killed Mayor Washington. While the city mourned its loss, both sides of the lights debut scrambled for leverage.

1988

The Season by the Numbers

77-85	.475 4th 24 games out	2,089,034 (25,632 average)
39-42	.481 at home	103% of NL average

Opening Day

APRIL 15; CUBS (SUTCLIFFE) VS. PIRATES (SMILEY); SUNNY, 43 DEGREES; 35,084 PAID

Cubs 6 Pirates 0—Rick Sutcliffe went the distance and scattered just six hits. Andre Dawson, Shawon Dunston, and Dave Martinez homered for the Cubs.

Andre Dawson received his 1987 National League MVP award before the game. Chicago's new mayor, Eugene Sawyer, threw out the first pitch.

What's New

The Cubs once again eliminated beer vendors in the bleachers. The action stemmed from a Commissioner's office initiative to curb excessive drinking at all ballparks. Beer still flowed at concession stands, but fans had to leave their seats for the alcohol. One harried bleacher fan on Opening Day said, "I'm missing the game standing in line. Maybe I'll have to cut down on the beer, or maybe I'll have to start drinking with both hands."[13]

What Happened

By the time Mayor Sawyer came out in favor of lights, on January 25, neighborhood forces succeeded in getting a nonbinding referendum on the March 15 ballot. The late Mayor Washington's council votes, enough to repeal the lights ban last fall, had crumbled. Aldermen reopened talks on the issue and proposed their own plans.

Adding to the mess was a *Chicago Tribune* editorial that called these flip-flopping aldermen "boneheads" and "political bums." A powerful Chicago alderman questioned the piece, saying, "It doesn't make sense. It certainly doesn't help their [Tribune Co./Cubs] case. Right now, passing this through the council has about as much chance as the Cubs winning the World Series."[14]

But Mayor Sawyer pulled everything together. Within two weeks, the lights issue passed a key council committee, 7-2. Outside the chambers that day, a leading anti-lights activist said of the changing fortunes, "I can't believe this is happening. . . .If you go through with this, there will be hell to pay." He later hinted that Wrigley Field "will not be known as the friendly confines anymore. I think you will find some real problems when fans start coming into Lake View, especially if they are wearing Cub hats. They will be marked."[15]

On February 25, two days after the committee vote, the Cubs were granted the 1990 All-star game, contingent, of course that the team has lights in Wrigley Field. The game offered the city a windfall of up to $35 million.

Later that day, the Chicago City Council repealed the six-year-old noise law, voting 29-19 to allow lights in Wrigley Field. Under the agreement, the Cubs could stage a maximum of seven night games in 1988 and eighteen a year through 2002. They could not schedule more than seven 3:05 games. Beer sales would stop at 9:20 P.M. or the end of the seventh inning, whichever came first. The city also had to address traffic and security issues and develop a neighborhood parking plan by June 1.

Anti-lights aldermen called the agreement "bare-bones" and "lightweight"[16] because it provided no forcible safeguards or escape clauses for the neighborhood. Alderman Bernard Hansen, who represented the Wrigleyville area, wondered about the quick turn of events. "Are we going to vote for the Cubs because they got awarded an All-star game this morning or are we going to wait until after the March 15 primary when the people of Lake View can express their views?"[17]

Others charged politics as usual. One area activist said, "This is like the old days of patronage. They are all getting something from the mayor, I don't know what, but we know who changed their positions."[18] Alderman Hansen added, "I think there was some very heavy, intense lobbying. Call it what you want, that's what I call it. Rumors have been flying about a lot of things."[19]

Subsequently, the anti-lights defenses shriveled. They threatened to vote the Wrigley Field precinct dry. It never happened. They sued the Cubs. Nothing came of it. Their nonbinding, anti-lights resolution passed 4,007 to 1,292. But it led nowhere. The neighbors now had to change their mindset, from fighting to keep lights out to coping with their existence.

The Cubs, for their part, moved faster than light. Architectural plans that were drawn up in 1985 for the $5 million project came out of mothballs. On the morning of April 7, a helicopter lifted the first light tower girders to the third base roof. Workers erected all six light towers and banks of lights by June 21. Wiring made them operable by mid-July.

The roof lights, however, were only part of the whole project. Exterior lights and lights in Cub-owned parking lots were needed. Inside, electricians wired lights on concourses, stairs, and ramps. Eight halide lights illuminated the scoreboard. Two shone on the American flag. A two-day test proved the whole system worked. It also provided a chance to redirect any of the 540 bulbs to eliminate "dark spots" on the field. The goal, according to an engineer, was to make sure light from two directions shone on every spot on the field.

Ever since the Cubs received permission to install lights last February, the odds pegged July 18 as the likely evening for the first night game. It made sense. It occurred after July 1, the first legal night for lights. It allowed a reasonable amount of time to construct the lighting system. It was also a scheduled 3:05 P.M. start time.

On June 20, the Cubs ended the suspense. The first night game would occur on August 8 against the Phillies. It too was a 3:05 game but it provided an extra two weeks as a buffer against construction delays. The team froze the remaining 13,000 tickets available for the game and sold them over the phone on June 28. Nearly 1.5 million callers dialed in that morning.

The public saw the first fruits of the six-year lights battle on the night of July 25. Patrons paid $100 to attend the annual Cubs Care benefit to watch the team practice under the stars. The event was a relative bargain. Not only could you be the first to see Cubs baseball at night, but Ernie Banks, Billy Williams, Ryne Sandberg, and Andre Dawson staged a home run hitting contest.

Night baseball and the ballpark's small size brought one additional problem. Wrigley Field lacked enough storage space, refrigeration, and electrical outlets to heat the coffee and hot chocolate that nighttime fans craved. John Doncrank, general manager at Wrigley Field for the ARA concession vendor, admitted that "we must have 15 different hiding places under the stands" just for cups.[20]

Games of the Year

August 8—On this night, 39,008 fans joined ninety-one-year-old season ticket holder Harry Grossman in a pregame chant, "Let there be light!"[21] Grossman flipped a switch and the lights

First night game at Wrigley Field (Associated Press/John Swart)

came on. With that, a streak of over 5,687 consecutive day games ended at Wrigley Field. Thanks to a two-run Ryne Sandberg home run, the Cubs lead the Phillies 3-1 in the fourth inning. Then, as if visited by the memory of Gabby Hartnett's "Homer in the Gloamin," clouds thickened and then it rained. It rained for over two hours before the umpires called the game. The spirit of day baseball won out, at least temporarily.

The Mets came to town and the official first night game took place on August 9. The Cubs handled the New Yorkers, 6-4, behind three hits by Rafael Palmeiro. Frank DiPino got the win.

September 30—Producing far less hoopla but as much historical intrigue was the surprise visit of President Reagan to Wrigley Field. Reagan, in town to support Vice President George H. W. Bush's presidential campaign, threw out the first pitch and called an inning-and a-half of television play-by-play with Harry Caray. Few fans realized what was going on, especially when workers hung tarps on the ramps to screen the President's path from the Cub dugout to the press box. Reagan's visit marked the first presidential visit to Wrigley Field and the first to a Cub game since William Howard Taft came to West Side Grounds in 1909.

Quote of 1988

"It is not within the power of architecture to guarantee that we have a good time—except perhaps, at Wrigley Field. For this extraordinary baseball park, this amiable pile of steel and bricks and concrete . . . seems to radiate more joy than all the domed stadiums of the last generation put together."[22]

Paul Goldberger in the New York Times—*September 18, 1988*

President Reagan throwing out first pitch. (AP Photo/Charles Tasnadi)

1989

The Season by the Numbers

93-69	.574 (1st)	2,491,942 (30,765 average)
48-33	.593 at home	120% of NL average

Opening Day

APRIL 4; CUBS (SUTCLIFFE) VS. PHILLIES (YOUMANS); 57 DEGREES; 33,661 PAID

Cubs 5 Phillies 4—A home run by Andre Dawson and two hits each by rookies Jerome Walton and Joe Girardi put the Cubs in front of the Phillies, 5-3. Mike Schmidt's eighth inning home run brought in a new closer, Mitch Williams. He loaded the bases in the ninth but struck out the side to save the game. Williams's heroics earned a victory for Rick Sutcliffe, the first Cub to win back-to-back home openers since Grover Cleveland Alexander in 1925-26.

Former Cub vice-president Salty Saltwell threw out the first pitch. Wayne and Kathleen Messmer sang the National Anthem.

What's New

- After the Cubs secured lights, they renovated Wrigley Field to the tune of $14 million. Beyond increasing capacity by 600, the improvements included:

  - Sixty-seven skyboxes. The skyboxes in total held 850 fans and rented for an average of $55,000 per year. Skybox occupants had many game time options: $125 bottle wines, slabs of ribs, and a dessert cart. All sixty-four yearly rentals sold out before Opening Day. Three rented on a game-to-game basis for up to $1,500.
  - A new press box in the top portion of the upper deck behind home plate, displacing 700 seats. The organ, originally in the football press box, moved to the western end of the new press box.
  - Two permanent concession stands behind the press box, the upper deck's first.
  - An additional front row in the upper deck, adding about 500 seats.
  - Plastic seats in the upper deck, replacing the last 4,600 wooden grandstand seats.
  - The "Food Court," an open-air restaurant above the Clark and Addison marquee.

- The first permanent concession stand on the ground floor of the bleachers.
- A new sound system.

The renovations did register a few complaints. The skyboxes hid the scoreboard from some lower deck grandstand seats. In response, management installed televisions and mini-scoreboards above these areas. Also, the Baseball Writers' Association of America protested that Wrigley Field was the only National League ballpark without a press box elevator. But the Cubs refused to install one for fear it would mar the exterior architecture near the Clark and Addison Street entrance.

- The best box seat tickets increased $1 to $11.50. Bleachers now cost $5.00. For $30, groups could hire their own vendor for a game.

What Happened

Anyone questioning the logic of night baseball at Wrigley Field need only compare the first non-opener weekday games of 1988 and 1989. On Tuesday, April 19, 1988, the Cubs drew 7,293 to an afternoon game against the Expos. On Wednesday, April 5, 1989, the Cubs sold 25,000 tickets and drew 18,674 for the season's first night game.

One problem with night games: many fans found the 7:00 P.M. start time inconveniently early. Nearly half the fans missed the first pitch while rushing to get to the park after work. But a later starting time wasn't an option. The city ordinance allowing lights dictated the earlier starting time.

The city expanded the original residential night parking permit area, adding streets west of Ashland Avenue and north of Irving Park Road.

Games of the Year

July 30—Mark Grace hit a game-winning two-run home run to trip the Mets, 6-4. Grace's shot off Randy Myers drove in Jerome Walton to complete a three-game sweep. The Cubs won eight of their last nine in July and finished the month 18-9. By then they trailed the Expos by only two games.

August 29—The Cubs erased a 9-0 deficit, scoring two in the sixth inning, three in the seventh, four in the eighth, and the winning run in the tenth when Dwight Smith drove in Jerome Walton. The 10-9, ten-inning burst against the Astros represented the largest Cub comeback in the twentieth century. The win helped maintain a two and a half game lead over the Cardinals.

To the Playoffs

The Cubs stayed hot down the stretch. The Expos, swept in a three-game Wrigley series from August 7-9, returned in mid-September, just in time to be swept again, part of a Cub six-game winning streak. Another sweep of the Pirates on September 22-24, the team's final regular-season home games, reduced their magic number to three. Just like in 1984, the team returned to the field after the last out to give and receive thanks for a magical season, one that broke another single-season attendance record at the park.

When the Cubs clinched the Eastern Division in Montreal on September 26, the *Chicago Sun-Times* reported that "the intersection of Clark and Addison filled with more than 2,000 joyous fans who held up traffic and shot off fireworks."[23] But the crowd seemed smaller and more orderly

than the one that toasted the Cubs clincher in 1984. Maybe a five-year wait between titles paled compared to the thirty-nine years between 1945 and 1984. Or maybe fans were waiting for a pennant or a World Series championship to really let loose.

Wrigley Field hosted the first two National League Championship Series games between the Cubs and the Giants. In Game 1, the Giants schooled the Cubs, 11-3. Will Clark hit two home runs including a grand slam off Greg Maddux. Clark drove in six runs, the most in a postseason game since Bobby Richardson in the 1960 World Series.

A chilly all-day rain ended just before the start of Game 2. The uncomfortable conditions dropped scalpers' prices in half. The Cubs faced Rick Reuschel, their former teammate. Reuschel didn't last the first inning this night as the Cubs scored six runs and thumped the Giants, 9-5. Mark Grace socked three hits including two doubles and drove in four runs. Les Lancaster pitched the final four innings for the win.

With the playoff series now a best of seven, the Cubs hoped to win at least one of the next three games in San Francisco and bring the series back to Wrigley Field. They didn't and lost the series, four games to one. For the second time in five years, a brilliant season ended bitterly on the west coast.

Quote of 1989

"Cub management threw a 75th anniversary party for Wrigley Field, and when it was over my only thought was that I hope it stands for 75 more years."[24]

Jerome Holtzman in the Chicago Tribune—*April 16, 1989*

1990

The Season by the Numbers

77-85	.475 4th (t) 18 games out	2,243,791 (27,701 average)
39-42	.481 at home	111% of NL average

Opening Day

APRIL 10; CUBS (BIELECKI) VS. PHILLIES (RUFFIN); 36 DEGREES; 7,791 PAID

Baseball owners locked out players over stalled labor talks. An agreement on March 18 ended the delay, but spring training's late start postponed the first week of play. Subsequently, the Cubs' home opener against the Mets on April 6 never happened. The new opening day, Monday April 9, became opening night, the first night game on this year's schedule and the first opening night in team history.

During player introductions umbrellas dotted the ballpark. Shortly after the Phillies' Len Dykstra's second inning home run off Greg Maddux, the rain intensified and the umpires stopped the game. Less than two hours later they called it. Was the season ever going to begin?

Cubs 2 Phillies 1—The season commenced the following afternoon amid swirling 25 mph winds. Three Cub pitchers yielded only four hits. Marvell Wynne's eighth inning single drove home Mark Grace with the winning run.

What's New

- A new roof and gutters.
- An extensively remodeled visitor's clubhouse.
- A new telephone system.
- A new restaurant in the right field corner.
- Restrooms were updated.

What Happened

- On May 29, the Cubs and White Sox played simultaneous home *night* games for the first time. The Cubs outdrew the Sox, 28,925 to 15,353.
- The neighborhood concern that lights would damage property values proved unfounded. A three-story gray stone at 3627 N. Sheffield, the building south of the Torco Oil sign, sold in 1978 for $174,000. In 1990 it went on the market for $419,000, a 240 percent increase. A real estate firm purchased it and rehabbed the building into four condos. The basement garden condo sold for $239,000 and the other three for $299,900.

The condo renovation plan accelerated the wave of bleachers and mini-skyboxes on the roofs of the buildings along Waveland and Sheffield avenues that began in 1988 at the Lakeview Baseball Club, 3633 N. Sheffield Ave. Cub President Don Grenesko felt that selling rooftop access to watch games constituted theft. As early as 1989 he hinted that the Cubs might erect a barrier to protect the team's product.

Game of the Year

July 10—The Cubs chose a mail lottery to distribute the 6,000 public tickets for the sixty-first annual All-Star Game. Management didn't want a repeat of the telephone disruptions that occurred during phone lotteries for the first night game and last year's playoffs.

Fans who couldn't score tickets attended the All-Star workout a day earlier. For no more than $7.50, they watched batting practice, a home run hitting contest, and an Old Timers' game. The longball derby pitted the American League's Ken Griffey Jr., Cecil Fielder, Jose Canseco, and Mark McGwire against their National League counterparts: Matt Williams, Bobby Bonilla, Darryl Strawberry, and Ryne Sandberg.

McGwire and Williams hit the only homers until Sandberg came to the plate. Ryne Sandberg won the contest, slamming three: two into the left field bleachers and one amongst the ball hawks on Waveland Avenue.

Players still salivated at the possibilities of hitting at the Friendly Confines. Jose Canseco said this: "I've seen some games on TV. You hit fly balls, and they're home runs. You get a guy who weighs 235—if he gets a hold of one, you might see some monster shots. Fans are going to see some 500-, 600-foot shots."[25]

But the game provided few thrills. The National League broke an All-Star Game record with just two hits. The only extra base hit—a double by Julio Franco—drove in both runs in a 2-0 American League win. Add a one-hour rain delay and the game bored everyone. Jack Buck, who called the game for CBS said, "I wish the wind had blown out."[26]

Quote of 1990

"How bad had Cub pitching been this year? So bad that Bleacher Bums are getting rotator cuff injuries from throwing the opposing team's homers back on the field."[27]

Mike Conklin, in the Chicago Tribune—*July 16, 1990—on the Cubs' porous pitching*

1991

The Season by the Numbers

77-83	.481 4th 20 games out	2,314,250 (28,928 average)
46-37	.554 at home	114% of NL average

Opening Day

APRIL 9; CUBS (JACKSON) VS. CARDINALS (B. SMITH); 42 DEGREES; 31,622 PAID

Cardinals 4 Cubs 1—The Cubs trotted out three former MVPs: Ryne Sandberg, Andre Dawson, and George Bell. Add high-priced free agent pitcher Danny Jackson, and the day was a major disappointment. Over 7,000 no-shows skipped the damp spring day. The Smiths ruled; Bryn Smith got the win and Lee Smith the save.

Cub outfielder Dwight Smith sang the National Anthem. Sergeant First Class Garnell Fryer, who served in the Gulf War, threw out the first ball.

What's New

- The Cubs raised ticket prices $1 for all seats except the lower boxes, which increased $2. Tickets ranged from $6 for bleachers to $15 for box seats.
- The Cubs didn't offer Ladies Day this year, ending the tradition that dated to the opening of the ballpark in 1914. But women probably didn't miss much. Last year's Ladies Day promotion offered only $2 off a $7 terrace reserved seat.
- New green-colored signage along the concourses. New awnings hung over concession stands.
- Additional televisions were added to the upper and lower grandstands.
- By mid-season, the Cubs opened a parking lot along the "L" tracks, three blocks north of Wrigley Field. For two years, a neighborhood group and the Cubs clashed over the half-mile strip. The neighbors wanted the eyesore turned into green space. The Cubs wanted a 400-car

lot. The two sides compromised: a 200-car, landscaped parking lot on the southern half and a park on the northern half, built with $50,000 from the team.

- Management banned smoking in the press box.
- The White Sox played their final game in eighty-year-old Comiskey Park on September 30, 1990. Their new ballpark, right across the street, opened on April 18; the new and the old differed 180 degrees. The new Comiskey Park eliminated the myriad of poles that obstructed vision in the old park. Its forty-foot wide concourse tripled the width of the caverns of its predecessor. Modern conveniences in the new park included elevators and escalators, coat checks, and a children's play area. Newspaper quotes gathered from writers sitting in the press box or from players on the field called the city's first new sports facility in sixty years, "beautiful"[28] and a "winner."[29]

But the double-decked skyboxes and press box behind home plate forced the upper deck seats to a fifth level. Subsequently, the front of the upper deck sat 160 feet from home plate, farther away than the last upper deck row in the old ballpark. To pull fans as close to the field as possible, the upper deck pitched at a dizzying 35 degrees. The effects left most of the upper deck seats too high and too far from the field.

New Comiskey Park, in fact, was the first ballpark literally designed around its skyboxes. The ninety suites signaled the sport's new financial realities. Renting from $55,000 to $90,000 a year, the suites, although seating less than 2,000, accounted for nearly 25 percent of the park's admission revenue. A worker who helped construct the $135 million park knew the team's motives. "We install ventilators in the skyboxes. This park is really for those people."[30]

Comments calling the stadium a "throwback" to the Classic parks were also misguided. New Comiskey was a suburban stadium put down in an urban setting. It looked jarring and uncomfortable in its Bridgeport neighborhood. Wrigley Field, on the other hand, connected with its surroundings, its architecture at peace with its community. The buildings on Waveland and Sheffield seemed an actual extension of the park.

Moreover, Wrigley Field's neighborhood percolated on game days with its unique housing, bars, and shops, adding excitement before fans even entered the stadium. New Comiskey Park, surrounded by acres of parking with nothing else of interest around it, approximated all the excitement of a trip to a shopping mall: distant and impersonal.

Was this new stadium really a "home run"? The *average* fan, destined for the upper deck wouldn't think so. They'd call the place a "single" or at best a "two-base error." Just a few years later, after the newness and the curiosity factor wore off, fans stayed away in droves. By then, *Chicago Sun-Times* writer Jay Mariotti said this about Chicago's two ballparks: "Comparing Wrigley to Comiskey is like comparing the art museum to McDonald's."[31] The fans agreed.

After the park's first two years in which the White Sox outdrew the Cubs, the North Side park outdrew new Comiskey Park for twenty consecutive years and counting.

What Happened

- Fans expected big things from these Cubs. The addition of Bell, Jackson, and reliever Dave Smith doubled the payroll to $26 million. When the team struggled, fans grew impatient. They booed, especially Jackson, Smith, and new manager Jim Essian. In fact, this marked the first time in Wrigley Field history that Cubs fans, known for their leniency, regularly booed the team.
- Harry Grossman, who turned on the lights before Wrigley Field's first scheduled night game, died on April 15. Grossman, 94, attended over 4,000 Cub games since 1906. He lived most of his life in walking distance of West Side Grounds or Wrigley Field.

Game of the Year

July 23—Should Harry Caray have sung "Buy me some peanuts and Valium?" The Cubs beat the Reds, 8-5, but two out-of-control players stole the show. In the seventh inning, umpire Joe West called a third strike against Andre Dawson. The normally sedate Dawson argued the call. Things escalated and West ejected Dawson. Andre bumped West and emptied the Cub bat rack—thirteen ended up on the field.

In the eighth inning, after the Cubs already scored on Reds reliever Rod Dibble, Doug Dascenzo squeezed home Rick Wilkins. On the play, instead of throwing to first base to get Dascenzo, Dibble threw at Dascenzo. Umpire West also ejected Dibble.

What did each perpetrator think of their actions? Dawson said he "lost it a little bit." Dibble claimed the ball "slipped out of my hand." And what was Reds manager Lou Piniella's take on it all? "It wasn't very pretty."[32]

Quote of 1991

"Marvin is going to be so mad. Marvin died in the hospital. Les died at the game."[33]

Linda Eisenberg in the Chicago Tribune—*October 11, 1991 (Bleacherite Marvin Rich died in 1989. Les Wolper, his best friend, died on September 5, 1991. A bleacher regular since the 1940s, Les collapsed in the first row of the right field seats and never regained consciousness. Linda Eisenberg, Marvin's niece, sat next to Les when he died.)*

1992

The Season by the Numbers

78-84	.481 4th 18 games out		2,126,720 (26,256 average)
43-38	.531 at home		106% of NL average

Home Opener

APRIL 10; CUBS (CASTILLO) VS. CARDINALS (TEWKSBURY); 47 DEGREES; 32,659 PAID

Cardinals 2 Cubs 1—Five Cubs pitchers gave up only five hits, but the Cardinals hit back-to-back doubles off Paul Assenmacher in the eleventh inning. Frank Castillo, twenty-three, became the youngest Cub to start a home opener since Bob Anderson in 1959.

Bears coach Mike Ditka threw out the first pitch.

What's New

• Cub fans elected Ernie Banks, Billy Williams, Ron Santo, and Fergie Jenkins as the first inductees into the Cubs Walk of Fame, a permanent display outside the entrance at Clark and Addison Streets. At the ceremony on June 12, each honoree was immortalized with a marble sidewalk plaque etched with their name and years of service.

• Illinois Governor Jim Edgar signed into law the Baseball Facility Liability Act. The first of its kind legislation thwarted lawsuits by fans struck by balls or bats in any public or private ballpark in Illinois. Legislatures sponsored the law on behalf of both the Cubs and White Sox who recently lost judgments against injured fans.

Historically, courts denied claims by fans injured by foul balls, citing an assumed level of risk. That changed when a fan, hit by a foul ball at Wrigley Field in 1983, won a $67,000 judgment. The fan sat just outside the screen behind home plate. Court testimony showed the screen at Wrigley Field was not as wide as in other parks. The jury ruled against the Cubs, believing their screen provided insufficient protection.

What Happened

• The Cubs acquired Sammy Sosa, a fleet, raw outfielder from the White Sox. On May 7, Sosa, playing center field and batting leadoff, drove a Ryan Bowen pitch onto Waveland Avenue for his first Wrigley Field home run. Few realized what Sosa would accomplish. He'd eventually hit more Wrigley Field home runs than anyone.

Wrigley Field Home Runs	
Most by a Cub	Most by a Visitor
Sammy Sosa 293	Willie Mays 54
Ernie Banks 290	Mike Schmidt 50
Billy Williams 231	Hank Aaron 50
Ron Santo 212	Mel Ott 38
Ryne Sandberg 164	Eddie Mathews 36

A young Sammy Sosa (www.ArgentaImages. com)

- Sosa's long balls aside, a ten-year study showed that the wind blew in more days than it blew out at Wrigley Field. Specifically, between 1983 and 1992, the wind blew in 51 percent of the time and blew out only 32 percent.
- Baltimore opened Oriole Park at Camden Yards, major league baseball's first Neoclassic ballpark. While sharing new Comiskey Park's preponderance for luxury boxes, the Orioles design team made this park look "old," relenting that the Classic parks were more visually and emotionally pleasing than those that followed them. Built with a brick exterior, the designers also ingeniously utilized the old B&O Warehouse as an outside border along right field. The extension of the park to the neighboring building was a direct nod to Wrigley Field and its Waveland and Sheffield Avenue environs.

Over the next twenty years, more than twenty of these "new-old" parks sprang up all over the country. Whether open air or with retractable roofs (the permanent dome concept never appeared again), they all tried to recapture some of the nostalgia of Wrigley Field and its fellow Classic ballparks. Houston's Enron Field, for example, mimicked Crosley Field's outfield incline. The Ballpark at Arlington and San Diego's Petco Park shared old Tiger's Stadium's outfield upper deck overhang. Many ringed a portion of the field with stone or brick walls, just like Wrigley Field.

The new parks were more fan-friendly. Architects designed them as baseball-only, so they were relatively smaller than the multipurpose stadiums before them. Lower deck fans sat closer to the field. The parks' footprints, less confined by the city grid than the Classic ballparks, had wider concourses and more options for revenue-enhancing gimmicks—Hall of Fames, batting cages, playgrounds, dining areas, and swimming pools.

The initial success of the Neoclassic and the fact that most were designed by one architectural firm—HOK, meant they began looking very much alike and, relenting to baseball's new economics, all included lofts of luxury boxes that left almost all the upper deck seats too far from the action.

But most importantly, the war against Wrigley Field and the Classic ballparks, begun in 1960, had ended. Architectural principals that determined that stadiums, *not* look like Wrigley Field faded away. While the last two decades brought an appreciation of Chicago's North Side ballpark, it wasn't until this year that actual brick and steel began to recognize and replicate its charms.

The following lists the Neoclassic ballparks in chronological order. Outside the fact that all the ballparks were baseball-only facilities, all the new parks, even the roofed ones, had real grass and traits that mimicked Wrigley Field and its Classic brethren.

YEAR	BALLPARK	CITY	CLASSIC BALLPARK DISTINCTION
1992	Oriole Park at Camden Yards	Baltimore	brick interior wall; brick warehouse beyond RF
1994	Jacobs Field	Cleveland	granite, limestone and brick exterior
1994	Ballpark in Arlington	Arlington, TX	brick interior wall; outfield overhang like Tiger Stadium
1995	Coors Field	Denver	brick exterior
1997	Turner Field	Atlanta	brick exterior
1998	Bank One Ballpark	Phoenix	partial brick exterior; grass field under retractable roof
1999	Safeco Field	Seattle	brick exterior; hand-operated scoreboard
2000	Enron Field	Houston	center field incline, grass field under retractable roof
2000	PacBell Park	San Francisco	brick exterior; accessible by five modes of transportation

2000	Comerica Park	Detroit	brick exterior
2001	Miller Park	Milwaukee	grass field under retractable roof
2001	PNC Park	Pittsburgh	stone exterior and interior walls
2003	Great American Ballpark	Cincinnati	brick interior wall; "sundeck" seats like Crosley Field
2004	Citizens Bank Park	Philadelphia	brick interior wall
2004	Petco Park	San Diego	left field warehouse; outfield over-hang like Tiger Stadium
2006	Busch Stadium III	St. Louis	brick exterior, exposed steel
2008	Nationals Park	Washington	stone interior wall
2009	Citi Field	New York	brick exterior; rotunda modeled after Ebbets Field
2009	Yankee Stadium II	New York	modeled after old Yankee Stadium
2010	Target Field	Minneapolis	limestone and green steel exterior
2012	Marlins Park	Miami	retractable roof with real grass

Game of the Year

September 30—Greg Maddux got his 20th win of the year as he flustered Pittsburgh, 6-0. Maddux became the Cubs first 20-game winner since Rick Reuschel in 1977. Ryne Sandberg went 4-for-4 and scored half of the Cub runs.

Quote of 1992

"I've left Wrigley early when there were thousands of people in the streets outside who couldn't get a ticket. They just wanted to be there. After the game, people hang around, go to the bars. It really is an event."[34]
    Former Cub Rick Sutcliffe in the Chicago Sun-Times—*April 19, 1992*

1993

The Season by the Numbers
84-78	.519 4th 13 games out	2,653,763 (32,562 average)
43-38	.531 at home	101% of NL average

Opening Day

APRIL 5; CUBS (MORGAN) VS. BRAVES (MADDUX);
SUNNY, 39 DEGREES; 38,218 PAID

Braves 1 Cubs 0—The Cubs faced *their* 1992 Cy Young winner, free agent Greg Maddux, who continued his winning ways, handcuffing the Cubs on five hits. Fans showed their displeasure with Maddux's move to Atlanta, booing him at every opportunity. They even "threw back" a foul ball he hit into the stands.

Ernie Banks threw out the first pitch, replacing First Lady Hillary Clinton who attended to her ailing father. The Maine South High School band, Clinton's alma mater, performed before the game. Wayne Messmer sang the National Anthem.

What's New

- The Cubs sold bleacher season tickets for the first time. The new policy gave die-hard fans a chance at tickets without fighting the casual fan or scalpers. Management interviewed each applicant to determine his or her intentions. If they

1993 Season Schedule cover

planned on reselling the tickets they were denied. In the end, the team sold fewer than 100 of the $614 passes.

- For the first time, fans purchased Cub tickets from their personal computers.
- League-wide no-shows the past few seasons embarrassed Major League Baseball. To that end, the National League now counted tickets sold as the daily attendance figure, not the number of fans attending games. (The American League began this practice in 1966.) The procedural change increased Cub "attendance" by more than 500,000 over last year, the approximate number of no-shows in 1992.
- Each team pennant on the yardarms above the scoreboard grew slightly smaller to accommodate the pennants of the expansion Marlins and Rockies. But the scoreboard itself did not change. Each side still showed only six games, with two National League and one American League contest missing on days with a full schedule.
- The Cub home uniforms included names on the players' backs for the first time in team history.
- The Cubs purchased the Yum-Yum donut shop and the car wash immediately west of the ballpark. The team coveted the land the two stood on for future expansion. In the meantime they leased the donut shop but ran the car wash and made money on each. By now the donut shop sold hot dogs and beer, sharing the space with Byron's Hot Dogs.

What Happened

- Wrigley Field continued as the only major league ballpark without interior ads visible from the stands. The league averaged eighteen signs per park. Candlestick Park led the majors with forty-one.
- During a game on July 7, WGN-TV cameras caught Reds pitcher Tom Browning on the roof of 3643 Sheffield Avenue in full uniform, hobnobbing with fans and waving to his teammates in the Reds bullpen. Browning, who pitched a perfect game in 1988, claimed to get more fan interest about his Sheffield Avenue escapade than about his pitching gem.

  Wrigley Field and its neighborhood captured the nation's attention. The protagonist in a new CBS television series, *The Building*, lived in an apartment on Sheffield Avenue, as did a character from the movie, *Blink*.

  The list of recent films or television shows that showcased Wrigley Field included:

  - *Ferris Bueller's Day Off* (1986)
  - *About Last Night* (1986)

- *Taking Care of Business* (1991)
- *Rookie of the Year* (1993)
- *The Building* television (1993)
- *Blink* (1993)
- *Chicago Sons* television (1996)

Game of the Year

August 15—Barry Bonds and Matt Williams went back-to-back twice in a 9-7 rattling of the Cubs. Bonds and Williams homered off Mike Morgan in the third inning and Randy Myers in the eleventh inning. "Double doubles" occurred six times before in National League history and once before at Wrigley Field. On October 3, 1972, Don Money and Greg Luzinski of the Phillies went back-to-back twice against Dan McGinn and Larry Gura.

Quote of 1993

"Those people gave the Cubs their fourth straight full house. They also gave them their first serious booing of the year—which, all things considered, shows remarkable restraint."[35]
Alan Solomon in the Chicago Tribune*—June 21, 1993—after a 7-4 loss to St. Louis*

1994

> The Season by the Numbers
>
> | 49-64 | .434 5th 16.5 games out | 1,845,208 (32,659 average) |
> |-------|-------------------------|----------------------------|
> | 20-39 | .339 at home | 100% of NL average |

Opening Day

APRIL 4; CUBS (MORGAN) VS. METS (GOODEN); 53 DEGREES; 38,413 PAID

Mets 12 Cubs 8—Tuffy Rhodes pounded three home runs, becoming the first major leaguer in history to homer his first three at-bats on Opening Day. A ten-minute delay followed Rhodes's third home run in the fifth inning as groundskeepers cleared hats and debris that fans threw on the field in celebration. Nevertheless, the Mets' twelve runs were the most scored by a Cub Opening Day opponent this century.

First Lady Hillary Clinton threw out the first pitch. She also sang the seventh-inning stretch with Harry Caray (who planted a kiss on her cheek). Olympic speed skater Bonnie Blair was also honored before the game, receiving a gold bat from Ernie Banks.

Attending her thirtieth opener was ninety-two-year-old Carmella Hartigan. She told the *Chicago Sun-Times*, "The people, they keep me young, especially in the bleachers. You can talk and say anything you want and nobody takes offense."[36]

What's New

- After banning smoking in the press box three years ago, the team banned it in seating areas. Fans could still light up in the restrooms and concourses.
- Vendors sported new red, white, and blue uniforms.
- The CTA enlarged the platform of the Addison Street "L" station. The renovated station included paintings of Ernie Banks, Ryne Sandberg, Fergie Jenkins, and Billy Williams. The Addison Street "L" station was busy, in the top 10 percent in usage of the city's 156 stations. In addition, the #22 Clark Street bus route was the third busiest in the city.

First Lady Hillary Clinton and Harry Caray sing "Take Me Out to the Ball Game" on opening day. (Associated Press/John Zich)

What Happened

- Public address man Wayne Messmer was shot outside a west side restaurant in the early morning of April 9. The 15-year-old robber's bullet entered Messmer's neck, nearly killing him. Besides his public address duties, Messmer sang a stunning rendition of the National Anthem at sporting events throughout town, including Wrigley Field and at Chicago Blackhawk hockey games, which he did just a few hours earlier.

  Chuck Swirsky replaced Messmer as public address man. Fans heard a tape of Wayne singing the National Anthem before a game with the Braves on April 15. Messmer's wife, Kathleen, was there to thank the fans for supporting them through the ordeal.

  Messmer returned on Memorial Day and threw out the first pitch. He received a hero's welcome: a standing ovation and a pennant bearing his initials on the ballpark's roof. He couldn't sing yet. He finally performed his signature song prior to a Chicago Wolves hockey game on October 14.

- It was tough enough to manage the Cubs this year, which on April 29 fell to 6-15 for the season. But it was tougher to face 200 angry Cub fans who just witnessed the team's ninth straight home loss. Manager Tom Trebelhorn promised to meet with the fans after the game, and did, standing on a bench outside Engine 78 on Waveland Avenue. The fans pulled no punches. But Trebelhorn point blankly answered over thirty questions in thirty minutes. The heated discussion settled little, but at the very least, frustrated Cub fans had their say.

  The home losing streak reached twelve, the longest in team history. Some squeamish fans wore paper bags on their heads. After complaints that security personnel made them remove the bags, Cub executive Mark McGuire set the record straight, saying, "As long as a person is not blocking the view of the person behind them and we don't have a complaint, they are free to wear bags over their heads."[37]

- A potential baseball strike hung like a black cloud over every major league ballpark. The players wanted relaxed free agency and arbitration rules. Owners pushed for revenue sharing and a salary cap; without them, they said, the game's finances could not survive. The players walked on August 12 when owners refused to take the salary cap off the table. The Cubs lost forty-four games to the strike, including twenty home games. Consequently, virtually everyone associated with the game on and around Clark and Addison suffered. Vendors and parking jockeys lost their livelihood. Sportsworld, a sports apparel store across the street from Wrigley Field, lost 75 percent of its business. A nearby pizzeria lost an estimated $200,000 in sales.

  The season never resumed. Two world wars and the Depression couldn't stop the World Series, but the strike did. The World Series wasn't played for the first time in ninety years. The black cloud had stamped a permanent black mark on the game.

Game of the Year

July 22—The Wayne Messmer tragedy—The losses—The impending strike. Could the season have been worse? It was worse. Ryne Sandberg abruptly retired on June 13 while going through a difficult divorce. In addition, Harry Caray collapsed in the Miami heat and humidity before a Cubs-Marlins game on June 23. He spent two weeks in a hospital bed and missed twenty-six games.

But the season of horrors temporarily subsided when Sandberg and Caray returned to Wrigley Field. Sandberg attended ceremonies marking his enshrinement in the Cubs Walk of Fame. A healthy Harry resumed his announcing duties. The magic lifted the Cubs, too. Mark Grace homered in the seventh and the Cubs bopped the Reds, 7-6. It was a momentary return to better times and a season's best 40,001 fans loved every minute of it!

Quote of 1994

"Go ahead and strike today. . . . Everything is already bad enough."[38]
Young Cubs fan in the Chicago Tribune—*August 8, 1994—prior to the year-ending strike*

1995

The Season by the Numbers

73-71	.507 3rd 12 games out	1,918,265 (26,643 average)
34-38	.472 at home	108% of NL average

Every major league team entered the season in a quandary—how to entice fans to buy tickets to watch players who refused to play. The Cubs offered money back guarantees on season tickets and rebates if replacement players competed.

Eighty percent of Cubs season ticket holders reordered for this uncertain season. But would the average fan come back? A *Chicago Tribune* telephone poll revealed that 60 percent of Cub fans would follow the team, even if it consisted of replacement players.

Major League baseball teams signed replacement players and sent them to spring training for a full schedule of games. Men like Dana Ridenour, a nine-year minor leaguer and a waiter this off-season signed with the Cubs in hopes of pitching in Wrigley Field.

Days before an opening day with replacement players, U.S. District Judge Sonia Sotomayor ruled the owners weren't negotiating in good faith. The players union seized the opportunity to save face and get their players back on the field. They offered to play without an agreement. The owners concurred and the major leaguers returned with little being settled except a promise from both sides to negotiate. After an abbreviated spring training, the season began on April 25, with each team playing 144 games.

Baseball damaged its public trust during the 234-day strike and now faced a cynical fan base. But the game returned and players could only repair the damage by being on the field, not in the courtroom. The game was back and that was a good thing.

Home Opener

APRIL 28; CUBS (FOSTER) VS. EXPOS (HENRY); SUNNY, 59 DEGREES; 32,909 PAID

Cubs 4 Expos 3—Sammy Sosa hit a mammoth two-run homer over the center field television camera shed. Shawon Dunston, Rey Sanchez, and Brian McRae scored the other Cub runs. Kevin Foster pitched six strong innings for the win.

Nearly 10,000 seats remained the morning of the game. Cub Ticket Director Frank Maloney tried to make lemonade from lemons, saying, "It will be the chance of a lifetime to get good seats of all types for a Cub opener."[39]

To hearken back to better days, Andy Pafko threw out the first pitch.

Wayne Messmer sang the National Anthem at the park for the first time since being shot last April.

Umpires, striking for better wages, picketed outside before the game. Replacements took their place on the field.

What's New

• Paul Friedman replaced Wayne Messmer as the permanent public address announcer. On July 26, Dyane Karp subbed for Friedman, becoming the first female p.a. announcer in Wrigley Field history.

What Happened

• A preseason fan poll indicated what most Chicagoans already knew; Cub fans outnumbered White Sox fans, 42 percent to 29 percent (while an uncommitted 17 percent supported both equally). More interestingly, nearly twice as many female fans (50 percent to 26 percent) preferred the Cubs to the White Sox.

- Temperatures on July 13 reached 103 degrees and the Friendly Confines Café doubled as a first aid room to handle stricken fans. The heat index hit 116 on July 14. That day, Cub players Jamie Navarro and Brian McRae sprayed bleacher fans with a hose before the game.
- Wrigley Field head groundskeeper Roger O'Connor died on August 25. He was fifty-three years old and had worked at the park for twenty-eight seasons. Two days later, the grounds crew and the Cub team led the fans in a moment of silence. A flag commemorating O'Connor hung beneath the Ernie Banks flag on the left field flagpole. Roger Baird replaced O'Connor.

Games of the Year

September 25—The Cubs' Frank Castillo came within one pitch of a no-hitter against the Cardinals. Bernard Gilkey hit a two-strike triple to end the gem. Castillo, who had struck out 13, retired the next batter.

September 28—Cubs pitcher Randy Myers surrendered a two-run, eighth inning homer to James Mouton, giving the Astros a 9-7 lead. Soon after, an inebriated box seat fan ran onto the field and confronted Myers. The reliever wrestled down the fan and held him until security arrived. Remarkably, Myers pitched to another batter, giving up a single.

The Cubs tied the game later that inning. They tied it again in the tenth. The Astros scored in the eleventh but the Cubs came back with two of their own on hits by Shawon Dunston, Scott Bullett, and Mark Parent. The jaw-dropping 12-11 defeat of the Astros marked the first time since 1900 that a major league team battled back from six deficits to win a game.

Quote of 1995

"The return of baseball deserves no applause. It ought to ask permission to be allowed back into our lives. . . .It expects to find us still sitting behind the third base dugout, full of summer and good cheer. We are the one thing over which baseball was not divided. It was a shared arrogance and a mutual indifference. We simply did not matter, nor do we yet."[40]

Bernie Lincicome—in the Chicago Tribune—*April 3, 1995*

1996

The Season by the Numbers		
76-86	.469 4th 12 games out	2,219,110 (27,228 average)
43-38	.531 at home	102% of NL average

Opening Day

APRIL 1; CUBS (NAVARRO) VS. PADRES (ASHBY); 38 DEGREES; 38,734 PAID

Cubs 5 Padres 4—The Cubs celebrated their earliest home opener to date. Ryne Sandberg returned after a nearly two-year retirement to numerous standing ovations, but it was the other Cub veteran, Mark Grace, who played the hero's role. His tenth inning cue shot past third base drove in the winning run. Rey Sanchez and Scott Servais each hit two-run home runs but new closer Doug Jones failed, leaving the heroics to Grace.

Northwestern football coach Gary Barnett threw out the first pitch.

What's New

- The Cubs settled a lawsuit that made Wrigley Field more accessible to the disabled. The team doubled the number of handicapped reserved seats to eighty-eight, installed an elevator to the terrace seats, and brought bathrooms, concessions, and parking up to ADA code.
- A local advertising company sponsored cup holders attached to every seat, becoming the only commercial advertisement visible from the stands.

What Happened

It was so cold at Wrigley Field on April 4 that:

- The game temperature stood at 34 degrees; the wind chill was 12 degrees
- Intermittent snow showers blew throughout the game
- The grounds crew spread salt in the aisles to prevent icing
- The Bears provided winter caps for many Cub players; other players purchased ski caps at concession stands
- Five hundred sixteen fans bought tickets the day of the game. Less than 2,000 fans dared to attend.

Regardless, Ryne Sandberg hit his first home run since June 1, 1994 and the Cubs chilled the Dodgers, 9-4.

- Fog rolled in off Lake Michigan and created havoc at the Cubs-Expos game on June 8. First, Sammy Sosa lost a fifth inning fly for a double. Later in that inning, as the fog intensified, the umpires conferred but decided to keep playing. In the bottom of the sixth, play stopped again and the umpires ordered Cub coach Mako Oliveras to hit fungoes into the outfield to test visibility. Harry Caray introduced his seventh-inning stretch, saying, "I can't see ya—but let me hear you."[41] By the time the game ended and the Cubs had won, 6-4, the fog pulled back over the lake.

• The gentrification of Lake View continued. Southport Avenue, just a few blocks west of the ballpark, lived a working class life: lined with mom-and-pop businesses like taverns, a barbershop, and a bowling alley. Between 1994 and 1996, however, eleven upscale restaurants moved in, making the street a popular nighttime destination.

Game of the Year

May 16—Amaury Telemaco, three days removed from Triple-A, threw a no-hitter through 5 2/3 innings, helping the Cubs slaughter Houston, 13-1. After a sixth inning single spoiled the gem, nearly 16,000 fans gave the 22-year-old Dominican a standing ovation. The Cubs put the game away in the seventh inning with eight runs. Included in the onslaught were a bases-clearing double by Mark Grace and two home runs by Sammy Sosa. His two shots made Sosa the first Cub to homer twice in an inning.

Quote of 1996

"We'd have to be some kind of stupid to leave this place just so we could put a microbrewery in a new stadium."[42]

Cubs President Andy MacPhail in the Chicago Tribune—*November 29, 1996*

1997

The Season by the Numbers		
68-94	.420 5th 16 games out	2,190,308 (27,041 average)
42-39	.519 at home	96% of NL average

Home Opener (and Beyond)

APRIL 8; CUBS (TRACHSEL) VS. MARLINS (LEITER); 29 DEGREES; 35,393 PAID

Florida 5 Cubs 3—The Cubs came home with an 0-6 record. Sammy Sosa's second inning home run and Doug Glanville's two hits weren't enough as Steve Trachsel lost a 3-2 lead in the seventh.

Their seventh straight loss to open the season equaled the club mark from 1962. The weather that day shared billing with the team's futility. The wind chill dipped to one degree.

Actor Chris O'Donnell tossed the first pitch.

Their tenth-straight defeat came against the Braves, 6-4 on April 13. To add to the misery, Ryne Sandberg needed fourteen stitches after a fourth inning shot off the bat of teammate Brant Brown entered the Cub dugout and clipped Ryne in his right ear.

The streak reached twelve games on April 16 after a 4-0 loss to the Rockies, breaking the all-time National League record for losses to start the season. (After fourteen straight losses, the Cubs beat the Mets in New York on April 20.)

What's New

- When Brant Brown's shot cuffed Ryne Sandberg's ear, the ball cleared the half-sized fence in front of the dugout. In 1977, Cub manager Herman Franks ordered the fence cut in half because he could not see over it. Immediately after the Sandberg incident, management rebuilt the fence to its original full height.
- Juniper bushes occupied the center field hitter's background, adding to the park's natural motif. In recent times, the hitting background went from green Astroturf (1967-81), to no Astroturf (1982-92), to no Astroturf and no bleacher seats (1993-96), to juniper bushes (1997-2005), to juniper bushes and the Batter's Eye Lounge (2006-date).

What's Happened

- Opening Day, with its one-degree wind chill, was probably the coldest Cub game in Wrigley Field history. A generation or two ago, the game would have been postponed. With today's emphasis on advance ticket sales, the team would suffer too big of a financial loss if they called the game and rescheduled it.
- Wrigleyville Alderman Bernard Hansen added a revision to the state's ticket scalping law, prohibiting scalping within 2,000 feet of the ballpark. Charlotte Newfeld, chairwoman of C.U.B.S., a grassroots community group, argued that the ordinance was advanced without public input. "We have homeless people and pollution. We need more libraries," she said. "Ticket scalping is not high on our list."[43] The law, however, was seldom regularly enforced.
- Young Cub fans caught the Beanie Baby craze when the team handed out 10,000 of the prized toys twice during the season. "Cubbie" the bear caused such a stir on May 18 that extra security was needed. Eager fans began arriving at 6:30 A.M. and the team opened the park

thirty minutes earlier than usual. Cub officials claimed the Beanie Baby toys drew the largest percentage of children to the park for any game in Wrigley Field history.

Game of the Year

May 15—The Cubs hit four triples and scalded the Padres, 8-2. Jose Hernandez tripled in the fourth inning. Brian McRae, Doug Glanville, and Sammy Sosa tripled in the four-run seventh. The Cubs hadn't hit that many triples in a game since 1968.

Quote of 1997

"It's a Wrigley Field."[44]

Detroit Tiger President John McHale in the Detroit News—*October 30, 1997—at the ground-breaking of the team's new Neoclassic ballpark, Comerica Park.*

1998

The Season by the Numbers		
90-73	.552 2nd 12.5 games out	2,623,000 (32,186 average)
51-31	.622 at home	110% of NL average

The year was the most emotional in Cub history. It started on Valentine's night when Harry Caray collapsed at a restaurant in Rancho Mirage, California. He remained unconscious for four days and died on February 18. Harry—the man of the people, the life of the party, everyone's friend—was gone.

Fans outside Wrigley Field held a vigil. A shrine, populated with mostly flowers and beer bottles, grew near the main gates. There, one tearful fan said of Harry, "He gave this stadium life. He was the spirit."[45]

Cub officials had to decide what to do with Caray's trademark singing of "Take Me Out to the Ballgame" during the seventh inning stretch. They could end the tradition. They could play a tape of Harry singing, like they would during spring training games this year. They decided to use guest conductors to lead the song. "For now, it's a one-year deal,"[46] said Cub marketing chief John McDonough. Fan acceptance would dictate the future of the substitute singers. But the choice of the Opening Day singer was obvious—Harry's widow, Dutchie.

Opening Day

APRIL 3; CUBS (TRACHSEL) VS. EXPOS (VAZQUEZ); CLOUDY, 41 DEGREES; 39,102 PAID

Cubs 6 Expos 2—Opening Day healed emotional wounds. Players wore a Harry Caray caricature patch on their right sleeves, the same image that now hung permanently in glass above the WGN television booth. Harry's grandson, Chip, began his stint as WGN play-by-play man. And all eyes focused on Dutchie Caray when she led Cub fans during the seventh inning stretch. It was a fitting way to say goodbye to the man, who, since his arrival in 1982, arguably meant more to the franchise than any ballplayer.

The game itself was almost an afterthought. But for the record, Steve Trachsel drove in half the runs and pitched into the eighth inning for the win.

Cammi Granato and Sarah Tueting of the USA women's Olympic gold medal hockey team threw out the first pitches.

Harry Caray—back in the day. (www. ArgentaImages.com)

What Happened

- Ernie Banks conducted the seventh inning stretch during the second game, followed by a lineup of former Cubs, local heroes, and national celebrities. The guest singers allowed fans to remember Harry and continue the celebratory event. The concept became so successful, in fact, that the quasi–famous were calling the Cubs, trying to get the gig.
- On March 3, Jack Brickhouse underwent surgery to remove a benign, nickel-sized brain tumor. The surgery succeeded. But Jack suffered cardiac arrest and died on August 6. In less than six months, Cub fans lost two beloved telecasters who called games for over fifth years. After Brickhouse's death, the Cubs added a patch with his famous home run call, "Hey, Hey" on their left sleeves, just above the Cub insignia.

Games of the Year

May 6—Making only his fifth major league start, 20-year-old Kerry Wood struck out the first five Houston Astros. In the fourth and fifth innings, he struck out five consecutive batters and struck out the sides in the seventh and eighth innings. When he struck out Bill Spiers to lead off the ninth inning, Wood had fanned 19, tying a National League record. After a ground out, he struck out Derek Bell to end the game. Wood's 20 strikeouts tied a major league record, set twice by Roger Clemens. In the game, he gave up only a scratch single and walked no one. Baseball statistician Bill James's "Game Score" system ranked Wood's masterpiece as the greatest pitching performance in big league history.

Wood was dominant much of the season. He won the National League Rookie of the Year award and his appearances at Wrigley Field were highly anticipated events. But foreshadowing much of his career, Wood missed the last month of the regular season with arm soreness.

September 13—Sammy Sosa homered twice, his 61st and 62nd as he tied and passed Roger Maris's 1961 home run mark. His second home run precipitated a near riot, and three curtain calls were needed to sate delirious fans. The Cubs dumped Milwaukee, 11-10. With it, the Cubs scored ten or more runs for the third consecutive game for the first time since 1930.

Sosa's dramatic home runs that day landed on Waveland Avenue. John Witt scooped up the first (he later sold it for $7,500). The second, the record breaker, caused a melee; its outcome still disputed today. Ball hawk Moe Mullins claimed to have caught the ball, only to have it pried free by the scratching and biting mob. Brendan Cunningham grabbed it, ran down an alley behind Waveland Avenue and found refuge in a police van. Both men retained lawyers and Mullins obtained a restraining order against Cunningham selling the ball. They settled out of court and presented the ball to Sosa, who gave it to the Baseball Hall of Fame.

Following the near-riot on Waveland Avenue, security increased the rest of the season. More than fifty uniformed officers on foot and on horseback kept order. Barricades forced fans to just the north side of the street.

September 20—The team celebrated Sammy Sosa Day before the last regular season home game. To honor Sosa's heritage, Dominican flags flew from Wrigley Field's roof. Fans heard the Dominican National Anthem along with the "The Star Spangled Banner." Sosa joined his family, Commissioner Bud Selig, and Roger Maris's children at home plate. Billy Williams and Ernie Banks presented Sammy with a crystal trophy and a painted portrait from the Cub team. Sammy then ran the perimeter of the field, doffing his cap to the adoring fans. He passed a huge sign attached to the left field bleacher fence reading, "Sammy, You're The Man."[47]

The season legitimized Sosa as a Cub superstar, joining the ranks of Banks and Williams before him. He finished with 66 home runs, four short of Mark McGwire. The home run race with McGwire enthralled the nation and produced good will for baseball, just three years removed from the crippling strike. Sosa won the National League MVP award.

To the Playoffs

With one day left in the season, the Cubs and Giants were tied for the Wild Card playoff spot. The Cubs lost in Houston, 4-3 in eleven innings. The Giants took a 7-0 lead in Colorado, but the spirit of Harry and Jack went to work and the Rockies chopped away at the lead. Just after the Cubs hit the clubhouse following their loss, the Rockies caught and beat the Giants, 9-8, setting up a one-game playoff between the Cubs and the Giants. An earlier coin toss determined that the game would be played in the Friendly Confines the next day, Monday, September 28.

Many fans waited outside Wrigley Field on Sunday in case there would be an extra playoff game. After the Giants lost, thousands joined them and the ticket line nearly encircled the park. The game sold out that night.

The 39,556 who shoehorned into Wrigley Field saw a classic. Steve Trachsel and Mark Gardner of the Giants were in control through four innings. After Henry Rodriguez singled in the fifth inning, Gary Gaetti drove one into the night air. It nestled into the bleachers—2-0 Cubs. Pinch hitter Matt Mieske's two-run single in the sixth doubled the score. After a wild pitch provided an insurance run in the eighth inning, the ghosts, the tears, the emotions of the season seemed ready to vault the Cubs into the playoffs. But this was 1998. Nothing came easy. The Giants scored three runs in the ninth inning and had the tying run at the plate. But Rod Beck ended the threat when ex-Cub Joe Carter popped to Mark Grace. The Cubs were on their way.

How ironic that the actual playoffs provided none of the drama and intrigue of this marvelous season. The Braves swept the Cubs in three games with the North Siders managing only four runs. In the finale at Wrigley Field, which the Braves won 6-2, Terry Mulholland and Rod Beck gave up five eighth inning runs, the last coming on an Eddie Perez grand slam.

Quote of 1998

"This is baseball."[48]

Cleveland's Jim Thome in the Chicago Sun-Times—*June 24, 1998—before his first game at Wrigley Field*

EIGHTH INNING
1999-2010
GLORIOUS
UNCERTAINTY

The 1998 season brought Wrigley Field icon status. With the playoff run, the home run chase, Sammy, Kerry, and the memories of Harry and Jack, the ballpark cemented deep emotional ties with Cub fans. The faithful not only loved the park, they found an uncontrollable pull to come and take part in its stew of emotions, drama, and charms.

The die hards, the marginal fans, and even the non-fans came. They came for the joy that oozed out of every crevice of the ballpark. They came to experience the Wrigleyville neighborhood. They came and joined in life's celebration at Clark and Addison Streets.

You couldn't get that experience at Chicago's new South Side ballpark. Only Fenway Park and perhaps football's Lambeau Field could provide a similar experience. It meant fans would come to the ballpark in greater numbers, regardless of the Cubs' record or the time of the season. It was a seemingly enviable position for the North Side franchise.

But for all the joy, an underlining reality simmered. The ballpark was nearly ninety years old. From 1950-71, P. K. Wrigley rebuilt the grandstand, replacing every inch of concrete, every seat, and much of the steel. At some point, the ballpark would again need this care. The Tribune Company, with its corporate mentality, focused on short-term profits first, would be unwilling and unable to make these renovations.

Moreover, even though the Cubs set their all-time attendance record in 1999, the next year, 2000, their attendance total finished behind smaller market teams in Cleveland, Baltimore, San Francisco, Denver, Atlanta, Houston, Phoenix, and Seattle. These cities had *new* stadiums. They accessed vast "revenue streams" unheard of in 1914, let alone 1990. These parks had exclusive seating, plush skyboxes, state-of-the-art concessions, and greater parking and advertising potentials. They were self-contained entertainment venues with batting cages, playgrounds, and even a swimming pool.

Could Wrigley Field compete financially with these new ballparks and the plethora of Neo-classic ballparks yet to come? The Cubs tried, adding a few dozen on-field seats this coming year. Rumors also leaked that the team commissioned architectural drawings to expand the bleachers, add more expensive seats, and a parking garage. Would they succumb to in-stadium advertising? Could they keep Wrigley Field from literally falling apart? It promised to be an interesting decade at the North Side ballpark.

1999

The Season by the Numbers

67-95	.414 6th 30 games out	2,813,854 (34,739 average)
34-47	.420 at home	119% of NL average

Home Opener

APRIL 12; CUBS (TAPANI) VS. REDS (AVERY); SUNNY, 50 DEGREES; 39,092 PAID

Reds 7 Cubs 2—Two home runs by Mike Cameron and round trippers by Barry Larkin and Eddie Taubensee led the Reds. Cub starter Kevin Tapani left after three innings with shoulder tightness.

Walter Payton, visibly thin from a rare kidney disease, threw out the first ball. Tragically, he died later in the year.

What's New

- Before the opener, the Cubs unveiled tributes to their fallen telecasters: a Harry Caray statue along Addison Street and Jack Brickhouse's HEY HEY signs on the foul poles.
- To thwart scalpers, the Cubs initiated a lottery for single game tickets. Cub fans bought 300,000 single game tickets that first day, or about a quarter of the tickets available for the whole season. It was easily the most tickets sold in one day to date in team history.
- Forty-eight field seats were added near the visitor's bullpen. The Cubs used the seats for player families, staff, and businesses. None were sold to the public.

(author's collection)

What Happened

- In response to a series of unruly fan incidents, management limited beer sales to two at a time per buyer (down from four). They doubled security in the bleachers and added cameras to aid the prosecution of troublemakers. The bleachers also received its own public address system that piped in messages, some by Cub players, reminding fans to be on their best behavior.
- It was nearly fifty years ago that Cub fans saluted Hank Sauer with "tobacco showers" in left field. This year, fans revived the tradition, tossing Oh Henry candy bars after home runs by new outfielder Henry Rodriquez. But the salute became a casualty of the tougher security policy. On May 30, five fans were arrested for disorderly conduct after "celebrating" a Rodriguez home run. Ironically, hundreds of Oh Henry

bars rained down from the bleachers that day; the candy maker distributed free samples outside the park before the game.

The Cubs eventually dropped all charges against the "Oh Henry Five" and the arrests were expunged from their records. The overzealous prosecutions, the result of the earlier security issues, brought the team unwanted negative publicity.

• *Sports Illustrated* named its 25 favorite sports venues. Wrigley Field finished sixth behind Yankee Stadium, Augusta National Golf Course, Michie Stadium at West Point, Duke's Cameron Indoor Stadium, and Bislett Stadium in Norway. It said this about the Friendly Confines: "It's impossible to feel blue at Wrigley Field, even though your beloved Cubs are losing again. The place has grown a bit larger and, amazingly enough, even more graceful since it was built in seven weeks in 1914 for $250,000. It's a national treasure, a true American original."[1]

The other major league ballparks on the list included Fenway Park (ninth) and Camden Yards (fifteenth).

Game of the Year

May 5—Colorado scored in every inning (1-1-1-1-2-1-2-2-2) and burned the Cubs 13-6. Dante Bichette had four of the team's 18 hits and Larry Walker scored four runs. The Cubs contributed to the rout, providing six walks, three errors, and two wild pitches. Three of the five Cub pitchers that day—Richie Barker, Dan Serafini, and Brad Woodall— had forgettable careers with the team, pitching only this season as Cubs.

Quote of 1999

"You are in a shrine. Sit back, absorb and worship. Drink two beers instead of four. Check the frat-boy angst at the gate."[2]

Jay Mariotti in the Chicago Sun-Times—*May 15, 1999*

2000

```
The Season by the Numbers
65-97              .401 6ᵗʰ 30 games out          2,734,511 (34,438 average)
38-42              .475 at home                    112% of NL average
```

Home Opener

APRIL 10; CUBS (LIEBER) VS. BRAVES (MILLWOOD); 39 DEGREES; 38,655 PAID

Cubs 4 Braves 3—The Cubs trailed 3-0 in the ninth inning, but early season magic beckoned. Mark Grace and Glenallen Hill walked and Shane Andrews promptly homered to tie the score. After Damon Buford singled and Joe Girardi sacrificed him to second base, pinch hitter Jeff Reed singled Buford home for the incomparable win.

The team, along with Ernie Banks, Billy Williams, and Ron Santo honored Mark Grace before the game, recognizing Grace's feat of leading the majors in hits and doubles during the 1990s. They were admirable feats; the only others who could claim the "most hits in a decade" distinction were Honus Wagner, Ty Cobb, Rogers Hornsby, Paul Waner, Lou Boudreau, Richie Ashburn, Roberto Clemente, Pete Rose, and Robin Yount.

Sharon Grace, Mark's mother, threw the first pitch to her son. Wayne Messmer sang the National Anthem.

What's New

- After a six-year absence, Wayne Messmer returned as public address man, sharing duties with Paul Friedman.

What Happened

- Hooliganism struck again at Wrigley Field. A fan stole Chad Kreuter's hat off his head in the visitor's bullpen. Dodger players entered the seating area and a melee ensued. No one was seriously injured in the May 16 dustup, but three fans were charged with disorderly conduct and nineteen Dodger players and coaches received suspensions.

In the now too common "team response," officials increased security near the bullpens, where players and fans sat inches apart. They also reduced by 10 percent the number of beer vendors and ended night game beer vendors a half inning earlier.

- Sammy Sosa and Glenallen Hill hit two of the longest home runs in Wrigley Field history this year. On May 11, Hill walloped a home run on the *roof* of 1032 Waveland Avenue, the three-story building at the southwest corner of Waveland and Kenmore. On June 7, Sammy Sosa homered into the upper center field bleachers. For a list of the longest home runs in Wrigley Field history, see the Appendix.

Game of the Year

July 8— Eric Young and Sammy Sosa homered in the first inning. Jon Lieber struck out 12 and shut down the White Sox, 9-2.

Quote of 2000

"It's all about enforcement. If trouble breaks out, you've got to have the muscle and authority to stop it. The only new rule anyone should be talking about is an ordinance mandating that ushers in Wrigley Field should not be so frail and aged they look like Bob Hope's older siblings."[3]
Richard Roeper in the Chicago Sun-Times—*June 5, 2000*

2001

The Season by the Numbers

88-74	.543 3rd 5 games out	2,779,465 (35,183 average)
48-33	.593 at home	113% of NL average

Opening Day

APRIL 2; CUBS (LIEBER) VS. EXPOS (VAZQUEZ); SUNNY, 49 DEGREES; 38,466 PAID

Expos 5 Cubs 4—The Cubs restocked to improve on last season's last place finish. But newcomers Bill Mueller, Matt Stairs, Todd Hundley, and Ron Coomer went 0-for-11 in the loss. The Expos got three singles off Mark Fyhrie and Todd Van Poppel to win it in the tenth inning.

Ex-Cub pitcher and broadcaster Steve Stone threw out the first pitch.

What's New

- Only six rooftops held fans on opening day. The others had not completed renovations that complied with a new safety ordinance. The city required the rooftop owners to install guardrails, washrooms, and extra exits. Some owners estimated the renovations would cost upwards of $100,000.
- Even after two straight last-place finishes, the Cubs raised ticket prices an average of 16 percent. Bleachers climbed from $15 to $20 and club boxes, the most expensive in the park, increased from $25 to $30. Cub President Andy McPhail said the increase was necessary to stay competitive with Central Division rivals; Houston opened Enron Field in 2000 and both Pittsburgh and Milwaukee got new ballparks this year.

What Happened

- An informal *Chicago Tribune* poll asked Cub fans to choose between keeping Wrigley Field or winning a World Series. While 178 wanted the World Series win, a remarkable 158 opted to keep Wrigley Field instead. Here are some responses:

  "Keep Wrigley. With so many new parks attempting to recreate the ambiance, the bricks and the intimacy, it would be folly to dispense with the blueprint." (Bob Kimbell)

  "The sunshine, beer, and tubetops are proof that God loves us and he loves baseball at Wrigley. He, in his boundless wisdom and glory knows that winning isn't everything."[4] (Lee Mueller)
- Arne Harris, the longtime producer and director of Cubs' baseball on WGN-TV died of a heart attack the last weekend of the season. Harris made Wrigley Field an important part of the telecasts. Said cameraman Joe Amigleo: "He wanted to show people having fun. He always said, 'If you can't sell the team, sell the ballpark.'"[5]
- After months of speculation, the Cubs unveiled an $11 million plan to update Wrigley Field. The centerpiece was a 2,100 bleacher seat expansion; it would hang halfway over the Waveland and Sheffield Avenue sidewalks, supported by pillars. In addition, the update included 215 new box seats in three rows between the dugouts, complete with a private lounge and restrooms. The team also planned for a new structure immediately west of the park for a parking garage, a team Hall of Fame, and a restaurant.

  Public reaction was mixed. Area residents balked, believing it added too many seats and too many assaults to the character of the park and the neighborhood. The bleacher overhang was the flashpoint. One local called it a "dark cave."[6] Another wondered if it would shelter the homeless. Still another told Cub executives at a town hall meeting, "I'm concerned with [the Tribune Co.] encroaching city sidewalks so you can make more money."[7]

The rooftop owners led the rally against sidewalk pillars, which allowed a larger bleacher renovation. The larger the renovation meant the larger the visual obstruction from the rooftops. The rooftop owners hired lawyers to fight the changes. They even floated their own compromise that limited bleacher expansion to just 921 seats.

In July, the Mayor's office claimed the city, not the Cubs, owned a parcel of land immediately west of the park. That parcel, an extension of Seminary Avenue, sat adjacent to the land on which the Cubs wanted to build their parking garage, Hall of Fame, and restaurant. The Cubs asserted they purchased the strip of land from a railroad in 1982. The city claimed the railroad had rights to lay track on the land, but did not own the land. The Cubs, therefore, purchased nothing and could not legally build on it.

The restrictions against the Cubs kept growing: legal challenges from the rooftop owners, pending landmark legislation by the city that might limit Wrigley Field expansion, required city approval to play more night games, and now the Cubs intending to build on land they didn't own.

Short of threatening to move out of Wrigley Field, the only leverage the Cubs owned was their product. So in December, they erected windscreens on the fencing behind the bleachers to obstruct rooftop views. The team was now warring with their neighbors. It wasn't an enviable position, but one the Cubs thought was necessary. First the rooftops were stealing their product, the Cubs felt, and now the rooftop owners were keeping the team from pursuing their better interests.

Games of the Year

September 27—As the nation contemplated and remembered the September 11 terrorist attacks, Major League Baseball postponed a week of games, tacking them on the end of the season. The Cubs' six home games against the Reds and Pirates, scheduled for September 11-16, would now be played October 2-7.

The team's first home game after the attacks came with changes geared toward more vigilant times. Police closed off Waveland and Sheffield avenues to auto traffic. Backpacks and coolers were not allowed in the park and security checked smaller bags and purses.

That night, called "We Will Remember,"[8] provided Wrigley Field with a patriotic air not seen since the world wars. American flags replaced the rooftop pennants that honored past players and seasons. American flags also hung from buildings across Waveland and Sheffield avenues. Ex-Cubs Ernie Banks, Andy Pafko, Randy Hundley, Steve Stone, Scott Sanderson, Steve Trout, Mike Bielecki, Dave Otto, and Mickey Morandini helped raise over $275,000 selling hats for a victim relief fund. All fans received small American flags and Sammy Sosa rounded the bases with a flag in hand after homering in the first inning.

Ceremonies that night included a tribute to firefighters and rescue workers. Area school children lead the crowd in the Pledge of Allegiance while Wayne Messmer sang "America the Beautiful" and the "Star Spangled Banner." During the seventh-inning stretch, he sang "God Bless America." In fact, for the remainder of the season, the latter, sung by Messmer and others, replaced "Take Me Out to the Ballgame." The Astros clipped the Cubs, 6-5.

Quote of 2001

"Do you want to win? Make up your mind. You can't pound on me for not winning and then restrict my ability to run it like a business."[9]

Andy MacPhail, Cubs president-general manager in the Chicago Sun-Times—*September 11, 2001—on resistance to expansion*

2002

The Season by the Numbers		
67-95	.414 5th 30 games out	2,693,071 (33,248 average)
36-45	.456 at home	118% of NL average

Opening Day

APRIL 5; CUBS (BERE) VS. PIRATES (D.WILLIAMS); 40 DEGREES; 40,155 PAID

Pirates 2 Cubs 1—Snow showers and seven Pirate pitchers held the Cubs in check. Their only score came on Sammy Sosa's controversial sixth inning home run into the right field basket. Umpires originally called it a fair ball, saying it hit the top of the basket and bounced back on the field. Manager Don Baylor convinced them that the ball hit the wall beyond the basket. The Pirates pushed across their two runs in the seventh, in part on back-to-back doubles.

Ron Santo threw out the first pitch.

What's New

- While the Cubs sold 2.8 million tickets in 2001, it ranked only thirteenth in the majors, in large part due to increased attendance at newer stadiums. To enhance revenue, the Cubs raised ticket prices for the second straight season. The across the board increases included bleacher seats from $20 to $24 and club boxes from $30 to $36.
- After decades of fighting an increasing plethora of scalpers and ticket brokers, the Cubs joined them. First, they allowed season ticket holders to resell game tickets for more than face value on the team's website. This kept more unsold tickets out of scalpers' hands.

  More importantly, the Cubs became the first professional sports team to open their own ticket brokerage. The subsidiary corporation, called "Wrigley Field Premium Ticket Services, Inc.," held aside 200 tickets a game, selling them for up to four times equivalent face value. Now the team competed with the half dozen neighborhood ticket brokers, with the Cubs holding some of the most desired seats in the ballpark.

  Fans filed a class action suit, accusing the Cubs and their brokerage of fraud, deceptive practices, and violating the Illinois Ticket Scalping Act. A Cook County circuit judge found the team not guilty in November 2003 and the added revenue stream continues to this day.
- New lockers and carpeting were installed in the Cub clubhouse.
- The Cubs removed their sidewalk Walk of Fame near the main entrance because the stone plaques were deteriorating. In their place, a collection of banners hung on the main concourse. Those enshrined on the Walk of Fame (and now on the banners) were Cap Anson, Gabby Hartnett, Rogers Hornsby, Hack Wilson, Phil Cavarretta, Stan Hack, Andy Pafko, Hank Sauer, Ernie Banks, Billy Williams, Ron Santo, Fergie Jenkins, Don Kessinger, Glenn Beckert, Rick Reuschel, Bill Buckner, Ryne Sandberg, Rick Sutcliffe, Andre Dawson, Jack Brickhouse, Lou Boudreau, Harry Caray, Pat Pieper, and Yosh Kawano.
- In light of last year's terrorist attacks, the team revamped security procedures. Entry gates now had a bag search lane and an express lane for those without a bag or purse.

What Happened

- In February, the Cubs presented a revised expansion plan, addressing concerns with the bleacher overhang on Waveland and Sheffield Avenues. The new plan eliminated 100 seats and about half the overhang and half the pillars.

Green windscreens cover the left field catwalk fence. (author's collection)

While the city and the Landmarks Commission commended the effort, locals weren't impressed. They felt the team sidestepped their concerns. "The complaints from the neighbors are that they don't want pillars in the sidewalk. They don't want it looking like . . . underneath the [CTA] elevated or Lower Wacker Drive,"[10] said Alderman Bernard Hansen. As the Cub management continued to hit foul balls, resistance stiffened. The new mantra in the neighborhood was, "No seats on our streets."[11]

The green windscreens put up last December remained throughout the baseball season. Their installation symbolized the continued divide between the Cubs and their neighbors.

• St. Louis pitcher Darryl Kile was found dead in his Chicago hotel room on Saturday, June 22. At the 2:05 scheduled game time, no players had come out to warm up and no one had sung the National Anthem. At 2:35, with rumors and confusion swirling in the stands, Cub captain Joe Girardi, flanked by his team and Cardinal manager Tony LaRussa, addressed the crowd. "We regret to inform you, because of a tragedy in the Cardinals family, the commissioner has canceled the game." Amid murmurs from the stands, he continued, "Please be respectful when you find out eventually what has happened," Girardi said. "I ask that you say a prayer for the St. Louis Cardinal family."[12]

The Cubs and Cardinals played the next night. It's a game Kile himself was scheduled to pitch. Darryl Kile's name and number "57" showed on the auxiliary message board throughout the game. Wayne and Kathleen Messmer sang the National Anthem unaccompanied and no other music played until the seventh inning stretch. The Cubs won the game, 8-3, but it was of little importance. Baseball took second stage that evening.

Game of the Year

June 18— Four players with more than 400 home runs met on the playing field for the first time in major league history. The Cubs' Sammy Sosa (475) and Fred McGriff (459) went against the Rangers Rafael Palmeiro (460) and Juan Gonzalez (401). Palmeiro homered in the second inning. But shortstop Alex Gonzalez homered off John Rocker in the ninth inning to propel the Cubs, 4-3.

Quote of 2002

"If you put a babushka on an animal, I guess it's an improvement."[13]

Alderman Bernard Hansen in the Chicago Sun-Times—*February 26, 2002—on the updated bleacher renovation proposal from the Cubs*

2003

The Season by the Numbers		
88-74	.543 1st 1 game ahead	2,962,630 (37,032 average)
44-37	.543 at home	131% of NL average

Home Opener

APRIL 8; CUBS (CLEMENT) VS. EXPOS (DAY); CLOUDY, 32 DEGREES; 29,138 PAID

Cubs 6 Expos 1—Shovels replaced fungo bats as four inches of snow and ice canceled the April 7 opener. The Cubs and Expos played the next day with snow still visible on the vines and a

13-degree wind chill. Perhaps that's why only 15,000 hardy fans actually came to the park. Matt Clement pitched 7 1/3 innings for the win. Shortstop Alex Gonzalez got three hits and scored half the Cub runs.

Students from Lemoyne Elementary School led the crowd in the Pledge of Allegiance. Wayne Messmer sang the Canadian and American National Anthems.

Sammy Sosa hit his 500th home run the previous weekend in Cincinnati. Today, Sammy threw a first pitch to Ryne Sandberg, while Ernie Banks tossed one to Billy Williams.

What's New

- The team raised ticket prices up to 25 percent for nineteen "prime" games. The increase, to see teams like the Cardinals, White Sox, and Yankees gave the Cubs an avenue to enhance revenue without a general price increase.
- Video boards were added along the left and right field upper decks. The screens displayed additional information like out-of-town scores and pitch speed.
- Beginning in July, fans pedaling to games could check their bikes at the old car wash on the corner of Clark and Waveland. The service was free and security personnel watched the bikes.

What Happened

- Jim Murphy, owner of Murphy's Bleachers, died of liver cancer on January 28. Murphy purchased the former "Ray's Bleachers" in 1980 and turned the seedy little bar into a major business and tourist attraction. He also led the fight against Wrigley Field's bleacher expansion as president of the Wrigley Field Rooftop Owners Association and the Lake View Neighbors. Mr. Murphy was only fifty-four years old. On April 13, the city dedicated the portion of Waveland Avenue that runs past Wrigley Field, "Honorable Jim Murphy Way."[14]
- For $68 million over twenty years, the White Sox renamed Comiskey Park, "U.S. Cellular Field." Jerry Reinsdorf, White Sox chairman, said all naming rights money would go into park improvements, including eliminating the highest seats in the dizzying upper deck. Reinsdorf spent years defending his park from critics and fans who wouldn't sit in the nether reaches of his upper deck for free. Now he called his own bluff, spending tens of millions to dismantle a good portion of his twelve-year-old ballpark. It was a sad case of shortsighted-ness and a waste of public money.

Games of the Year

June 7—The Cubs and Yankees hadn't met since the 1938 World Series, so their three game series promised to be electric. Scalpers asked for and got $1,200 for the best seats to the most anticipated game of the series, pitting Roger Clemens, looking for his 300th career win against Cub ace Kerry Wood. In the fourth inning, first baseman Hee-Seop Choi collided with Wood going after a pop-up. Choi hit his head on the basepath, knocking himself unconscious. Wrigley Field grew silent when an ambulance entered the ballpark from the right field wagon gate and drove across the field to the stricken Cub. As it exited, with the first baseman inside, the fans chanted repeatedly, "Hee-Seop Choi!"

The Yankees led 1-0 in the seventh. After a single and a walk, Juan Acevedo replaced Clemens, who received a standing ovation from the crowd. The next batter, Choi's replacement, Eric Karros, hit the first pitch for a three-run homer. The Cubs bested the Yankees, 5-2, and it was Kerry Wood, with his 50th major league win and not Clemens, who achieved a milestone that afternoon.

New York Times writer Ira Berkow commented about the day: "This was a game that should have been bottled and put in a time capsule. If Rembrandt had painted a ballgame, this would have been it. It was all it had been touted to be and more, like a winning lottery ticket, maybe even your first kiss."[15]

September 27—The Cubs were a half-game ahead of the Astros with three to play. During the eighth inning of the first game of a Saturday doubleheader with the Pirates, the big scoreboard showed Milwaukee's 5-2 win over Houston. The message board below it flashed, "Magic Number: 2." A half hour later, after Mark Prior struck out 10 and the Cubs scrapped for runs, the 4-2 win lowered their magic number to just one. In the nightcap, Sammy Sosa's mammoth first inning homer into the upper center field bleachers set the tone. The Cubs put it away with five more runs in the second inning. Their 7-2 rout completed the sweep and earned a divisional title, their first since 1989. Wrigley Field exploded in pent-up excitement. The players walked the perimeter of the field, acknowledging the cheers while victorious Cubs sprayed the adoring bleacher fans with champagne. The love affair lasted an hour, until the lights were lowered and security cleared the park.

Before the postseason, the Cubs had one more piece of business. The last regular-season game was "Ron Santo Day" and the Cubs retired his uniform number. Former teammates Glenn Beckert and Randy Hundley hoisted his number "10" flag up the left field flagpole to join Ernie Banks's number 14 for sempiternity. Santo, now a lovable Cub radio color man, got a massive ovation in the pregame ceremonies. He waddled on two prosthetic legs, the result of diabetic amputations, to a microphone near home plate. Crushed after continually falling short in voting for Cooperstown, Santo said, "That flag is my Hall of Fame." Santo turned his attention to the team's imminent endeavor, saying, "We're going to go all the way. I know we are."[16] The old Cub received a heartfelt hug from each player, then circled the field in a golf cart, sharing the love with teary-eyed Cub fans. It would be an emotional send-off to the postseason.

Postseason

The Cubs split the first two playoff games against the Braves in Atlanta. Kerry Wood struck out 11 in a 4-2 victory, but the Braves won the second game, 5-3. Thousands of Cub fans filled Turner Field, a.k.a., "Wrigley Field South."

In Game 3 at Wrigley Field, Mark Prior tossed a two-hitter and Randall Simon drove in Kenny Lofton and Mark Grudzielanek with a first inning single, all the runs the Cubs needed for a 3-1 win. Prior's complete game win was the Cubs first in the postseason since Claude Passeau turned the trick in the 1945 World Series.

Cub fans came to Wrigley Field the next night, looking for the clincher. Instead, two Chipper Jones home runs overcame Eric Karros's two solo shots and the Braves bested Matt Clement, 6-4 to force a deciding fifth game the next night in Atlanta.

Kerry Wood, as he did in June against the Yankees, came up big again in a big game, pitching eight innings in a 5-1 win. Immediately after the last out, jubilant Cub fans came by the thousands to Clark and Addison to celebrate. These fans experienced something no other Cub fans have since 1908—a postseason series win, the first since their last World Series championship.

Oddsmakers called the Cubs slight favorites over Florida in the League Championship Series. The Cubs had home field advantage. They had Prior and Wood, two of baseball's hottest pitchers. They also snubbed history by winning their first playoff series in ninety-five years. Could they break their sorry tradition once more and reach a world series?

In the opener in Wrigley Field, the Cubs scored four times in the first inning. But 22-year-old Carlos Zambrano couldn't hold the lead as the Marlins scored five of their own two innings later. Florida's Mike Lowell hit a pinch-hit home run off Mark Guthrie in the eleventh inning for a 9-8 win. The two teams brought their bats, combining for six doubles, four triples, and seven home runs.

The Cubs continued to pound the ball in Game Two, driving 16 hits and feasting on the Marlins, 12-3. Kenny Lofton had four hits while Randall Simon chipped in three. Alex Gonzalez stroked two home runs and Sammy Sosa blasted a 495-foot shot off the camera shed in center field.

The *Chicago Tribune* reported on the frenzied atmosphere outside the ballpark: "The crowds grow with every game, a sea of fans that turns the streets around Wrigley Field into baseball's version of Carnival. No one has tickets, but all are intent on being as close to the action as they can get."[17]

Concerned that the huge crowds would cause a repeat of Tuesday night, when fans on the street mobbed a Sosa home run ball, police barricaded Waveland shortly after the game started, prohibiting fans from standing in the street. Police would give no official estimate of the crowd's size. One simply called it "too many."[18]

The North Siders and the Marlins headed to South Florida.

Doug Glanville's pinch-hit triple in the eleventh plated Kenny Lofton and the Cubs took Game Three, 5-4. Aramis Ramirez homered twice, including a grand slam and Matt Clement stopped the Marlins in Game Four, 8-3. The Cubs were one win away from their first pennant since 1945. Josh Beckett, however, pitched a most important victory, handling the Cubs on just two hits to win Game Five, 4-0. The series went back to Wrigley Field with the Cubs leading, three games to two.

Fans celebrating outside Wrigley Field (Associated Press/Steve Matteo)

The Cubs scored runs in the first and sixth innings of Game Six. Mark Prior, in total command, scattered only three meaningless singles through seven innings. Mark Grudzielanek's RBI single in the seventh inning seemed to seal it. With the fans roaring on every pitch, Prior got Mike Mordecai to fly to left to lead off the eighth. Juan Pierre then doubled down the left field line.

What happened next is achingly familiar to Cub fans. After fouling off two 3-2 count pitches, Luis Castillo popped one down the left field line. A Cub fan sitting in aisle 4, row 8, seat 113 deflected the ball just as Moises Alou was about to attempt a catch. Alou threw his hands down in disgust while Prior screamed for fan interference. Castillo eventually walked. Ivan Rodriquez singled, scoring Pierre, cutting the lead to 3-1. Miguel Cabrera grounded to shortstop, but Alex Gonzalez muffed the catch, eliminating at least a force at second and probably an inning-ending double play. (The fan-interference play was meaningless; this play turned the game.) Derrek Lee then doubled in two runners to tie the score. Kyle Farnsworth replaced Prior. After an intentional walk, a sacrifice fly gave the Marlins their first lead. After another intentional walk, Mordecai's double cleared the bases. Mike Remlinger replaced Farnsworth. A single scored the inning's final run.

Those twenty-seven minutes felt like a trip to hell to the Cub faithful. The game ended 8-3. Most fans, struggling to comprehend what just happened, left immediately after the final out.

A SABR researcher concluded that the Cubs, just five outs away from the clincher (and no Marlins on base) were 95.8 percent certain of winning the game.

The following night, Game Seven, the Marlins continued their onslaught, scoring three runs in the first inning. Kerry Wood tied it with a home run in the bottom of the second. But they'd be no miracles. The Marlins outscored the Cubs 6 to 3 from then on and took the deciding game, 9 to 6. But this time fans stuck around. Some shed tears. Others hoped they would wake from a bad dream. Most contemplated what might have been.

2004

The Season by the Numbers		
89-73	.549 3ʳᵈ 16 games out	3,170,154 (39,138 average)
45-37	.549 at home	128% of NL average

Home Opener

APRIL 12; CUBS (MADDUX) VS. PIRATES (BENSON); SUNNY, 41 DEGREES; 40,483 PAID

Pirates 13 Cubs 2—Four-time Cy Young Award winner Greg Maddux returned to Wrigley Field as a Cub for the first time since 1992. He didn't help today. Greg left in the fourth inning, giving up six runs, eight hits, and five walks. The Cubs' only runs came via three Pirate errors in the second inning.

Bill Murray threw out the first ball. He imitated Sammy Sosa's chest-thumping ritual then threw the ball twenty feet over the catcher's head.

Students from Lemoyne Elementary led the crowd in reciting the Pledge of Allegiance. Wayne Messmer sang the National Anthem. Before the game, the Cubs raised their 2003 National League Central Division championship flag up the left field flagpole.

What's New

- The team raised ticket prices again this year, an average of 17 percent. They also increased the number of "prime dates," those desirable games they charged more to attend. The price increases mattered little to fans who could not get enough of the Cubs and Wrigley Field. The team sold 572,000 tickets the first day of individual game sales, a major league record. By Opening Day, only obstructed-view seats remained for the rest of the season.
- The Cubs, thwarted on expansions plans since 2001, found success in negotiating changes individually instead of everything in a "package" deal.

The rooftop owners agreed to share 17 percent of their gross income with the Cubs for twenty years. The team agreed to promote the rooftops and assist with reconstruction of the rooftop clubs if their views were compromised by future bleacher expansions. The rooftops grossed over $17 million in 2004, more than twice their take in 2003. The Cubs took in an additional $3 million for "sharing" their product.

In January, the Chicago City Council's Landmarks Committee voted landmark status for Wrigley Field. The designation, however, granted limited status, including only the exterior, the marquee, the scoreboard, the ivy-covered walls, and the sweep of the grandstand and bleachers. The carefully worded document, hashed out between City Hall and the team, would open the way for future park expansions and renovations.

The city and the team also agreed on a plan to add up to twelve additional night games by 2006. To get them, the Cubs contributed $1 million to a neighborhood fund. The team also agreed to arbitration, not lawsuits, to settle future disputes with the Lake View community.

The Cubs added three rows of seats from dugout to dugout behind home plate. The 213 seats fetched upwards of $250 each per game, netting the Cubs $3.2 million a year. The new seats brought the backstop wall to less than fifty-two feet from home plate. The original bricks from the backstop wall were too damaged to reuse and were replaced with 8,000 new matching bricks.

(author's collection)

After gaining premium seats, extra night games, and peace with rooftop owners, the Cubs made another stab at a revised bleacher expansion. This third proposal in three years cut down the number of sidewalk posts to two per street. Lighting and cameras under the sidewalk overhang addressed the security issue. Between the ballpark and a proposed "Triangle Building" along Clark Street would be a pedestrian walkway lined with year-round shops. As an added nugget, the team planned to remove the 1960s precast concrete exterior and replace it all with brick and ivy. While these improvements brought the two sides closer, Alderman Tom Tunney said, "It's a starting point. They will have to negotiate."[19]

What Happened

- A recent poll revealed that of the 475 major leaguers who named their favorite ballpark, Wrigley Field topped the list. The top five:

Wrigley Field	66
Safeco Field (Seattle)	56
Yankee Stadium	54
SBC/Pac Bell Park (SF)	44
Fenway Park	36

- After a game on July 16, a six-inch long, three-inch thick piece of concrete fell from the underside of the third base upper deck, barely missing a five-year-old boy. Five days later, a worker found a fist-sized concrete piece in the stands. At the same time, it was revealed that on June 9, a brick-sized piece fell and narrowly missed an elderly woman. Wrigley Field, it seemed, was literally falling down.

The city immediately ordered a series of inspections to determine the worthiness of the cement underneath the upper deck, which was installed from 1968-71. If the condition was not preventable or repairable, there was talk of the Cubs canceling games, playing games at U.S. Cellular Field, Cinergy Field in Cincinnati, or playing games with no fans in attendance. Inspections showed the problem was not structural, so the Cubs played a home game on July 30 after workers wrapped nylon netting under a portion of the upper deck flooring.

Game of the Year

August 27—The Astros trumped a four-run first inning and a six-run ninth to thump the Cubs, 15-7. The Cubs frittered away a seven game wildcard lead, eventually losing out to the Astros by three games. But instead of taking personal responsibility for the collapse, players slammed broadcasters Chip Caray and Steve Stone for their perceived negativity. After the season, rather than work in this environment, Caray, who called Cub games for seven years, left for Atlanta and Stone, a twenty-year WGN veteran, retired.

The rancor helped take down Sammy Sosa, who also feuded with manager Baker and management and was suspected of using performance-enhancing drugs. The club unceremoniously traded Sosa, their recent superstar, for three players and cash before the 2005 season.

Quote of 2004

"If I die, I want it to be in Wrigley."[20]

A Cub fan in the Chicago Sun-Times—*July 31, 2004—on the prospects of being hit by falling concrete.*

2005

The Season by the Numbers

79-83	.488 4th 21 games out	3,099,992 (38,753 average)
38-43	.469 at home	121% of NL average

Home Opener

APRIL 8; CUBS (WOOD) VS. BREWERS (CAPUANO); SUNNY, 47 DEGREES; 39,892 PAID

Brewers 6 Cubs 3—The Cubs' Jason Dubois singled in two runs in the first inning. Jeremy Burnitz doubled in another in the sixth. But LaTroy Hawkins allowed the tying run to score in the ninth inning. The Brewers pushed across three in the twelfth inning off Jon Leicester.

Ryne Sandberg threw out the first pitch.

What's New

- Fans could now buy tickets to the eighty-two "complimentary" seats that were added six years ago beyond the first base dugout. The seats originally sat behind a fence; now they were behind a new brick wall.
- Wrigley Field received the major league's latest rotating signboard behind home plate. The 10-foot by 3-foot sign showed seventeen advertisements, one each half inning. Its $5 million annual income directly increased the team's payroll.
- The netting under the upper deck remained but was more unobtrusive, replaced by a tighter fitting version similar in color to the underside of the upper deck.

What Happened

- A ticket broker website claimed the Cubs trailed only the New York Yankees as the hottest entertainment tickets in the country. Following the Cubs were the Boston Red Sox, the Broadway musical *Wicked*, and the Los Angeles Angels.
- The *Chicago Tribune* and WGN conducted a public poll to determine the "Seven Wonders of Chicago." The results:
  - The Lakefront

- Wrigley Field
- The "L"
- The Sears Tower
- The Water Tower
- The University of Chicago
- The Museum of Science and Industry

- High expectations and disappointing results brought boo birds back to Wrigley Field. Cub second baseman Todd Walker, a former Boston Red Sox, likened the change in attitudes to those that had prevailed at Fenway Park. "They're not just happy coming to games. They expect you to win, they expect you to play well and if you don't, on any given pitch or any given at-bat, they'll boo."[21]
- Jimmy Buffett performed two concerts at Wrigley Field during the Labor Day weekend, singing twenty-six songs from a stage in center field. The Cubs gave up a lot before neighborhood groups sanctioned the deal: 3,000 tickets to area residents and a $150,000 donation to area schools. But they received a lot too: 100 percent of the net ticket profits and the requisite 17 percent of the rooftop income (though the rooftops needed special permission to open on a non-baseball night).

Game of the Year

August 28—In July, Ryne Sandberg was enshrined in the Baseball Hall of Fame in Cooperstown. Today, the Cubs retired his uniform number 23 in pregame ceremonies. Ex-Cubs Andre Dawson, Bob Denier, and Gary Matthews hoisted Ryne's number up the right field flagpole, joining Billy Williams's number 26. Derrek Lee hit two solo home runs and Jerry Hairston drove in four runs as the Cubs swamped the Marlins, 14-3.

Quote of 2005

"They can't win. Not like this. Not in this environment. Not with more stuff on the periphery than any other team. . . . Not with grills smoking from the rooftop. It's like trying to teach 3rd graders at an amusement park."[22]

Rick Morrissey in the Chicago Tribune—*July 17, 2005—on the Cubs' inability to win while playing in the circus-like atmosphere of Wrigley Field.*

2006

The Season by the Numbers

66-96	.407 6th 17.5 games out	3,123,215 (39,040 average)
36-45	.444 at home	126% of NL average

Home Opener

APRIL 7; CUBS (MADDUX) VS. CARDINALS (SUPPAN); CLOUDY, 40 DEGREES; 40,869 PAID

Cubs 5 Cardinals 1—The Cubs scored in each of the first four innings, including a first inning homer by Derrek Lee. Neifi Perez chipped in three hits and Ronny Cedeno drove in a run with a triple. Greg Maddux pitched into the seventh inning, winning his 319th major league game.

The fans observed a moment of silence for former DePaul University basketball coach Ray Meyer. Ray's son, Joey, threw out the first pitch.

What's New

- After nearly four years of bickering, grandstanding, and legal maneuvering, the Cubs and their neighbors agreed on the expansion of the Wrigley Field bleachers. It added 1,790 seats (over 600 less than the Cubs originally asked for) and preserved the view for the rooftops. The final compromise moved the exterior bleacher walls eight feet onto the sidewalk, eliminating the exterior pillars that caused so much consternation. The Cubs paid the city $900,000 for the added eight feet of sidewalk and $2.2 million for the parcel of land immediately west of the ballpark. The team also agreed to provide $250,000 toward a park adjacent to a nearby school. The Cubs, in return, would gross as much as $4.6 million in additional annual ticket sales.

  The $13.5 million bleacher expansion included:

  - 1,790 additional seats (5,213 total bleacher seats)
  - New bleacher entrance, complete with an elevator
  - Large aisle in back of bleachers to aid access
  - The Batter's Eye Lounge—like a skybox in the back portion of the center field hitting background, reserved on a game-by-game basis (the new lounge eliminated half of the juniper bush background)

- More restrooms, concessions, and a larger handicapped bleacher area
- A "knothole" screen door replaced a right field wagon gate, allowing a view of the field from Sheffield Avenue.
- In the right field corner—253 bleacher box seats

Capacity at the ballpark increased from 39,538 to 41,119. With the added seats, the bleachers appeared chunkier along its edges; gone was the sensual art deco sweep from its corners to the top of the scoreboard. But the whole project was in good taste. It looked like the additions had been there for years.

What Happened

- The Cubs broke their own one-day major league sales record. Fans bought over 600,000 tickets on February 24, the first day of single-game sales.

(author's collection)

- The Chicago White Sox won the 2005 World Series, and with it, bragging rights in the city. Last year's victory paid dividends for the South Siders. A poll conducted this year found that 53 percent of Chicagoans attended a Sox game, watched one on television, or listened to one on the radio. But the Cubs' 56 percent still led. And despite the Sox' championship, the 2006 Cubs led the Sox in tickets sold:

Cubs	3,123,215
White Sox	2,957,414

- The "Chicago Cubs Dixieland Band," led by seventy-one-year-old Ted Butterman, celebrated its twenty-fifth anniversary. The five-piece band played before and during games both inside and outside the park. The team believed the band was the only "roving" musicians at any major league ballpark.
- Purists derided the game on August 6; the first time fans ever completed a successful "wave" at Wrigley Field. Unofficially banned at the park since San Diego Padre fans performed it ad nauseam during the 1984 playoffs, old-timers blamed the episode on tourists or bored Cub fans grown tired of another lost season.

Game of the Year

July 2—The Cubs scored seven times in the first inning, got 20 hits, and waxed the White Sox, 15-11. Heroics came from unexpected sources; Neifi Perez hit a three-run home run and Angel Pagan hit his first two major league homers.

Quote of 2006

"Over the last few years, Cubs fans have become worldlier, nastier, more demanding. After 97 years of futility, you wonder what took them so long."[23]
   Rick Morrissey in the Chicago Tribune—*April 12, 2006*

2007

The Season by the Numbers

| 85-77 | .525 1ˢᵗ 2 games ahead | 3,252,462 (40,153 average) |
| 44-37 | .543 at home | 111% of NL average |

Home Opener

APRIL 9: CUBS (LILLY) VS. ASTROS (WILLIAMS); CLOUDY, 40 DEGREES; 41,388 PAID

Astros 5 Cubs 3—The Cubs' Jacque Jones and Michael Barrett each stroked two hits. But it wasn't enough; Adam Everett hit a two-run eighth inning home run to break a 3-3 tie. The loss spoiled manager Lou Piniella's home debut.

Chicago Bears return man Devin Hester threw out the first pitch.

What's New

- The Cubs raised ticket prices for the fifth time in seven years. Most tickets increased $2. Premium seats like dugout boxes and bleacher boxes increased $5. In the last twenty-five years, regular bleacher seats went from $2 up to $42. In fact, it cost nearly $100 more to purchase one dugout box seat this year ($255) than a bleacher seat for every home game in 1982 ($162).
- Under Armour, a sports clothing company, signed a multiyear deal to add their logo to two wagon gates in front of the bleachers. There was also an advertisement on the cover of the field tarp along the third base wall.
- Wrigley Field installed a new digital public address system. Phase one included the renovated bleachers in 2006. The next two phases included the lower and upper decks. Because of the park's new landmark status, the plans had to utilize the old horn speakers on the top of the scoreboard, which could not be removed.
- The team started a Wrigley Field tradition by rediscovering the old "Go Cubs Go" song. Written in 1984 by Steve Goodman, the buoyant song was popular during the team's remarkable run that year. Played infrequently since, it became a big hit again when the public address system blasted it and fans sang along after Cub wins.

What Happened

- The American Institute of Architects and Harris Interactive conducted a public poll of the favorite 150 pieces of American architecture. Wrigley Field finished 31st. (The top two were the Empire State Building and the White House.) The only other ballpark to make the top 100 was Yankee Stadium at 84th (Fenway Park finished 113th).
- The musical band, The Police, played Wrigley Field the nights of July 5 and 6. To ensure noise levels didn't offend residents, technicians stationed decibel meters throughout the neighborhood during preconcert sound checks.

  But the concerts ripped up the playing field in right and right center field. The Reds blamed the poor field on an injury to outfielder Ken Griffey Jr. Teammate Adam Dunn said: "It looks like they had a monster truck rally. It's terrible . . . It's unsafe."[24]

  Concerts at Wrigley Field became a regular occurrence. A representative list includes:

Jimmy Buffett	2005		Pearl Jam	2013
The Police	2007		Billy Joel	2014
Billy Joel/Elton John	2009		Blake Shelton	2014
Rascal Flatts	2009		Billy Joel	2015
Dave Matthews Band	2010		Zac Brown	2015
Paul McCartney	2011		AC/DC	2015
Bruce Springsteen	2012		Phish	2016
Brad Paisley	2012		James Taylor/Jackson Browne	2016
Roger Waters	2012		Pearl Jam	2016
Jason Aldean/Kelly Clarkson	2013			

- On July 19, Barry Bonds homered twice, leaving him two shy of Hank Aaron's 755 mark. Ball hawk Dave Davison captured the first shot on Sheffield Avenue. A thirteen-year-old boy plucked the second from the right filed basket.

  Pushing the bleachers higher and the back wall eight feet onto the sidewalk cut down on home runs reaching Waveland and Sheffield avenues. In fact, Barry Bonds's second inning shot was the first home run to land on Sheffield Avenue all season.
- On August 23, a violent storm collapsed the old car wash just west of the park, killing a pedestrian who sought shelter there during the deluge. The team had used the building to store bicycles of fans attending Wrigley Field. They razed the damaged building and by next year stored bicycles in an open-air, fenced-in area on the same site.

The bike storage area in 2008. Note a portion of the old Yum-Yum Donut Shop building visible above the woman's head (author's collection)

Games of the Year

June 2—The Cubs compiled a 22-29 record through May, having lost eight of their last ten games. Frustrated manager Lou Piniella came out to argue a call and had one of the greatest meltdowns in park history, going jaw-to-jaw with the third base umpire, kicking dirt on his shoes, and drop-kicking his own hat. The Wrigley Field crowd erupted. The Cubs still lost to the Braves, but following the outburst, they came to life, winning five of their next six.

June 29—The Brewers led the Cubs by seven and a half games and scored five runs in the first inning. But the Cubs scratched back and trailed 5-3 in the ninth inning. Singles by Alfonso Soriano and Mike Fontenot and a sacrifice fly by Derrek Lee brought Aramis Ramirez to the plate. Ramirez drove the first pitch into the left field bleachers for a season-defining, come-from-behind victory. Teammates mobbed Ramirez at the plate and the largest crowd of the regular season, 41,909, sang "Go Cubs Go" like never before. Optimism was back. The upstart Cubs went 17-9 in July. They caught and passed the Brewers on August 17. They clinched the division at Cincinnati on September 28.

Postseason

The Cubs faced the Diamondbacks in the divisional playoff series. Arizona easily took the first two games in Phoenix, 3-1 and 8-4. Game Three, in Wrigley Field, didn't go any better. The Diamondbacks scored two runs in the first inning off Rich Hill. That's all they needed in a 5-1 series-ending dismantling. In the three games the Cubs hit .194 and only .087 with runners in scoring position. Arizona outhomered the Cubs, six to one. Finally, quickly, the singing ended.

Quote of 2007

"Forgive me, but I must wax today about the numbing slice of baseball heaven at Clark and Addison. I'll also assume you have the pulse of a prehistoric mummy and business acumen of Homer Simpson if you can't grasp why the Cubs should remain there forevermore."[25]

Jay Mariotti in the Chicago Sun-Times—*April 10, 2007*

2008

The Season by the Numbers		
97-64	.602 1st 7.5 games ahead	3,300,200 (40,743 average)
55-26	.679 at home	121% of NL average

Opening Day

MARCH 31; CUBS (ZAMBRANO) VS. BREWERS (SHEETS); RAIN, 44 DEGREES; 41,089 PAID

Brewers 4 Cubs 3—Fans sat through two forty-minute rain delays by the third inning and no team scored until the ninth—the Brewers got three runs off reliever Kerry Wood and the Cubs newcomer Kosuke Fukudome hit a three-run home run. The Brewers scored the winning run in the tenth inning off Bob Howry.

Ernie Banks threw out the first pitch to Kerry Wood, the longest tenured Cub. Wayne Messmer sang the National Anthem.

- The team unveiled a statue of Ernie Banks on the Clark Street side of the park. The seventy-seven-year-old Banks was joined at the ceremony by Billy Williams, Fergie Jenkins, Ron Santo, and Hank Aaron.

What's New

- The Cubs raised ticket prices after holding the line last year. The average ticket price hit $34.30, the second highest in baseball.
- Seventy premium seats were added between the Cub dugout and the bullpen. The seats didn't have a designated price, but were sold to the highest bidder online.
- The digital signage along the upper deck facing tripled in size.
- A new state law put an end to smoking in restaurants, bars, and entertainment facilities, including Wrigley Field. Even the patio above the marquee, one of the park's last smoking bastions, was now smoke-free.
- The Cubs renovated the entire playing field; they were the last team to use an old-fashioned crowned field. That's why the right fielder was only visible above the waist from the dugout. And that's why the dugouts occasionally flooded during rainstorms.

    Workers trucked 15 million pounds of dirt to area landfills, dropping and leveling the field. Underneath went a state-of-the-art drainage system that sent excess water to the Chicago sewers, not to the dugouts.

What Happened

- In April 2007, Sam Zell purchased the troubled Tribune Company. To pay off debt, Zell planned to sell the Tribune's best assets: the Cubs and Wrigley Field. He hoped to sell the two in separate deals to maximize profits, upwards of $1 billion. But that move would confound future renovations of the park. It would be difficult enough renovating Wrigley Field with single ownership of the team and the park. With separate owners, major renovations seemed impossible and spelled trouble for its long-term viability.

    Before selling off the two, Zell said he'd consider selling naming rights to the ballpark. He said this about the longtime Wrigley name: "Perhaps the Wrigley Co. will decide that, after getting it for free for so long, that it's time to pay for it."[26]

    Fans and the media rebelled. A *Chicago Sun-Times* poll of 2,000 fans revealed that 53 percent would no longer attend Cub games if Zell renamed the ballpark. Rick Morrissey of the *Chicago Tribune* hit the mark, saying, "Buying naming rights to Wrigley is like buying naming rights to the sun."[27]

When the economy collapsed in the fall of 2008, cash became scarce. Suitors backed away from offering Zell top dollar. Selling both the club and the ballpark separately also made less economic sense. Zell would do well to sell both together at a "bargain" price.

- "Take Me Out to the Ballgame" turned 100 years old and 2008 marked the tenth anniversary of guest conductors at Wrigley Field. By year's end, over 500 different individuals or groups led the singing the past decade. The varied guest list included actress Bea Arthur, Barney the Dinosaur, and boxer Muhammad Ali. Through June, the most frequent guests over the last ten years were:

  - Ernie Banks, Ron Santo, Rick Sutcliffe (eleven times)
  - Pat Hughes, Ryne Sandberg, Digger Phelps (ten times)
  - Wayne Messmer, Wrigley Field grounds crew (eight times)
  - Tom Dressen, Bob Uecker (seven times)

Games of the Year

August 28-29—Aramis Ramirez hit a grand slam in the eighth inning to power the Cubs, 6-4 over the Phillies. The following day, a seven-year-old boy named Wrigley Fields threw out the first pitch. The Cubs came from behind again for a 3-2 win. Their 85-50 record and .630 winning percentage were high watermarks for the season. The lead over the Brewers swelled to six and a half games.

The Cubs ran away with the division and clinched on September 20, tripping the Cardinals 5-4 at Wrigley Field. After the game, the players performed their now traditional victory lap around the field, spraying the fans with champagne along the way. That day the team broke their single-season attendance record. Why not? Many called this the best Cub team since 1945. They seemingly had few weaknesses.

But the Cubs finished flatter than their new field for the second straight season. The Dodgers outscored the North Siders 17-5 in the two playoff games at Wrigley Field. Moreover, the Cubs committed four errors alone in Game 2. Two nights later in Los Angeles, the Dodgers completed the sweep, 3-1.

At the end, all that remained of this glorious season was a makeshift shrine of beer bottles, scrawled notes, and flowers at the corner of Waveland and Sheffield. One fan summed it up best, saying, "It feels like someone died."[28]

Quote of 2008

"The raw romance of Wrigley Field is being able to leave behind the troubles of 21st-century life, walk through ancient gates that spill off the street, and for three hours—or as long as it takes for the Cubs to lose—wrap yourself in green, unfettered timelessness."[29]

Jay Mariotti in the Chicago Sun-Times—*February 28, 2008*

2009

The Season by the Numbers		
83-78	.516 2nd 7.5 games out	3,168,859 (39,610 average)
46-34	.575 at home	120% of NL average

Home Opener

APRIL 13; CUBS (LILLY) VS. ROCKIES (JIMENEZ); RAIN, 36 DEGREES; 40,077 PAID

Cubs 4 Rockies 0—The first two Cub runs scored on a walk and a throwing error. Derrek Lee and Kosuke Fukudome drove in the other runs. Ted Lilly tossed a no-hitter into the seventh inning and ended up teaming with three relievers on a one-hitter.

To commemorate the twenty-fifth anniversary of the 1984 Eastern Division champions, Rick Sutcliffe threw the first pitch to catcher Jody Davis. The crowd observed a moment of silence for two recent deaths: Los Angeles Angels pitcher Nick Adenhart and Phillies broadcaster Harry Kalas. Wayne Messmer sang the National Anthem.

What's New

- Additional restrooms.
- A Gatorade dispenser replaced the old drinking fountain in the Cub dugout.
- Captain Morgan Pub replaced the Friendly Confines Restaurant along the first base concourse. The 500-seat eatery included both indoor and outdoor seating, taking over much of the outside area along Addison Street. It had a direct entrance gate to the park during the season and stayed open all year.
- In July, see-through gates replaced the two large doors down the far right field line. The change replicated the bleacher wall "knot hole" that allowed bleacher ticket holders and Shef-

field Avenue pedestrians to see the park from field level. The new gates gave a field view to fans on the first base concourse.

- In November, the Cubs razed the Yum-Yum Donuts building west of the ballpark. Since 2003, the team housed offices there. Long term, the Cubs planned to build the "Triangle Building" on the site. For the meantime, they joined the Chicago Park District and private sources to open a temporary outdoor ice rink. The rink returned seasonally through 2013.

What Happened

- In its long history, Wrigley Field hosted baseball, football, soccer, boxing, basketball, track, lacrosse, ski jumping, and rodeo. This year, it added hockey. On January 1, the Chicago Black Hawks and the Detroit Red Wings brought in the New Year with the second annual "Winter Classic" hockey game.

Winter Classic Hockey rink (Associated Press/M. Spencer Green)

The event mixed Wrigley Field tradition with a hockey twist. Ivy painted on plywood panels stood in front of the outfield walls. Grounds crew members changed the scoreboard by hand and fans watched the action from nearby rooftops. Blackhawks and Red Wings pennants flew from the park's roof and larger team flags flapped atop the foul poles. Blackhawks players replaced Cubs on the banners in the lower concourse.

The weather was perfect—temperatures in the mid-thirties. There was no snow, so manmade snow surrounded the rink, which sat on the infield between first and third base.

The Red Wings won, 6-4. The score hardly mattered. For the largest American television hockey audience in 34 years and the 40,818 who witnessed it live, the atmosphere was unique. Competing outdoors reminded the players of skating on frozen ponds of their youth. The Red Wings' Chris Chelios said he "never wanted it to end."[30] Wayne Drehs of ESPN.com added, "The Winter Classic left everyone with a mental scrapbook of memories that will never be erased."[31] Wrigley Field, it seemed, even scored in the dead of winter.

• In June 2008, a local landlord paid $8.35 million for the building at 3701 Kenmore Avenue, the one with the beer sign covering its roof. This year, a casino rented the space for $600,000, nearly twice what the brewer paid. In addition, the windowed alcove on the building's roof, constructed in 1929, was removed. Apparently, it was more important to provide a flat advertising roof than to provide an upstairs view of the ballpark.

Signs on the roof of 3701 Kenmore Ave. included:

1930s-1962—Ricketts Restaurant

Ricketts restaurant was located at 2727 N. Clark St., about a mile from the park. Also at some point during this period, Old Gold cigarettes advertised on the building's turret.

1963-1968—WGN

1969—Schlitz, WGN

At the end of the season, the WGN sign read THANK YOU CUBS FOR A FUN YEAR!

1970—Schlitz

1971-1987—WGN

The Tribune Company asked WGN to take down their longtime rooftop sign as they jockeyed to get lights at the ballpark. WGN advertised on the turret during a portion of 1988-89, but the large roof was empty for two years.

1990—Sapporo Beer

The Cub brass hated the garish Japanese beer sign and tried to remove it. More than the looks disturbed them—the Cubs wanted a roof advertiser branded to the club.

1991-2008—Budweiser

2009-2010—Horseshoe Casino

2011-2014—United Airlines

2015—Mosquito Squad (partial year)

- After two and a half years, Sam Zell finally sold the Cubs. The family of Joe Ricketts, the founder of TD Ameritrade, purchased 95 percent of the team, Wrigley Field, and a 25 percent stake in Comcast SportsNet for $845 million. New chairman Tom Ricketts called himself a fan; he lived part of his young adulthood in Wrigleyville and claimed to have met his wife in the Wrigley Field bleachers. Family ownership, as opposed to corporate ownership, was a good thing. No longer would team profits be weighed against short-term bottom lines or stockholder needs.

  At the initial press conference, Tom Ricketts said, "We're gonna win the World Series. We're gonna win the World Series by striving in every day and every way to be the best franchise in baseball."[32]

Game of the Year

May 3—Fergie Jenkins and Greg Maddux toiled 20 combined years for the Cubs and pitched the team's best baseball in the Wrigley Field era. And they both wore number 31. Today, the Cubs retired their numbers in a pregame ceremony. Jenkins's number 31 flag flew on the left field flagpole with his teammates: Ernie Banks's 14 and Ron Santo's 10. Maddux's flew on the right field pole under Billy Williams' 26 and Ryne Sandberg's 23.

Jenkins, by the way, wanted number 30 when he came to the Cubs in 1966 but it already belonged to Ken Holtzman. Maddux called the ceremony a "tremendous honor," adding, "I always considered it a privilege to wear the uniform."[33] The Cubs won the game that day, 6-4 over the Marlins, on a Derrek Lee grand slam.

Quote of 2009

"We love Wrigley Field and we're going to do everything we can to improve the Wrigley Field experience for the fans who are coming today and preserve the Wrigley Field experience for the future generations of fans to come."[34]

Tom Ricketts—October 30, 2009—at his inaugural press conference

2010

The Season by the Numbers
75-87   .463 5th 16 games out   3,062,973 (37,814 average)
35-46   .432 at home   118% of NL average

Home Opener

APRIL 12; CUBS (DEMPSTER) VS. BREWERS (DAVIS); 58 DEGREES; 41,306 PAID

Cubs 9 Brewers 5—The Ricketts Family era got off to a great start; Xavier Nady, Jeff Baker, and Aramis Ramirez homered and the Cubs led 8-1 by the fourth inning. The bullpen pitched 2 2/3 scoreless innings, holding the win for Ryan Dempster.

Bill Murray was scheduled to throw out the first pitch but canceled. Instead, the Ricketts randomly chose seven-year-old Wade Sluga. Students from nearby Blaine Elementary School recited the Pledge of Allegiance.

Wayne Messmer sang "God Bless America" and the National Anthem. The crowd observed a moment of silence for Polish President Lech Kaczynski, who died in an airplane crash two days earlier.

What's New

- The new ownership spent $10 million improving the ballpark. Changes included:

  - The back of the scoreboard received new sheet metal.
  - The brick wall down the left field line was replaced
  - Some precast concrete slabs outside the park along the right field corner were removed and replaced with fencing, giving that portion of the exterior a more historic look and the area inside the ballpark a more light and airy feel.
  - A 30 percent restroom capacity increase and those on the concourse behind home plate were renovated. For traditionalists, the men's urinal troughs remained.
  - A party area under the right field bleachers. Thanks to a one-way mirror, fans there could watch the Cubs in the batting cages under the stands.

- Six skyboxes along the left field line were remodeled. Corporations could buy a smaller number of season tickets ($24,300 each) for these instead of purchasing a whole suite. They held seventy-one fans.
- Increased the number of televisions around the park. Now all were flat-screened.
- The players received a new weight room and a lounge. The lounge for the players' families was renovated.
- A new umpires' quarters.

- The team hired a director of game day entertainment to oversee every aspect of a fan's day. They stationed uniformed team "ambassadors" around the ballpark.
- In addition:

Despite opposition from rooftop owners, the Chicago city council approved an illuminated, 40-foot-high Toyota sign above the back of the left field bleachers (although in negotiations the team agreed to not erect another sign for at least four years). The sign was intended to block the Horseshoe Casino ad on the roof of the 3701 N. Kenmore Avenue building.

More ads appeared at the ballpark: CITI Bank signs hung on the brick wall near the dugouts, Scott's lawn care signs were painted on the dugout roofs, and a series of Bud Light Bleachers logos emblazoned the fence on the front railing of the upper center field bleachers.

The bike valet moved from the area adjacent to the recently razed Yum-Yum Donut shop building to the corner of Clark Street and Sheffield Avenue.

What Happened

- The Cubs owned the most expensive tickets in the majors after a 10 percent price increase. The team's $52.56 average just edged out the Red Sox and the Yankees. In fact, the average cost of attending a Cub game nearly doubled in only four years.
- The Cubs moved the Harry Caray statue from its Addison and Sheffield location to a spot behind the bleachers at Sheffield and Waveland Avenues. The move cleared a space for a statue of Billy Williams that was unveiled on September 7. Ex-teammates Ernie Banks, Fergie Jenkins, Randy Hundley, Glenn Beckert, and Ron Santo honored Williams that day.
- The Cubs honored Ron Santo for his fifty years with the organization as a player (1960-74) and as a radio broadcaster (1990-date). Before a game on June 28, Santo tossed the first pitch. And as a tribute that night, every flag on the ballpark's roof read, "Santo 50."[35]
- Santo died on December 2 from complications of bladder cancer. That day, underneath the Wrigley Field marquee, which read "Ronald Edward Santo 1940-2010," fans constructed a makeshift shrine. After his funeral on December 10, the hearse drove Ron's remains on the streets around the ballpark. A few hundred Cub fans paid their solemn respect as the car drove by. Then they sang "Take Me Out to the Ballgame" and cheered as Ron's remains drove by one last time.
- To increase their season ticket base, the Northwestern University football team hosted Illinois on November 20. The game marked the first football contest at Wrigley Field since the Bears played there in 1970 and the first college football game since a DePaul-St. Louis game in 1938.

  The park turned festive for the occasion. Banners of great Northwestern football players hung in the concourse. Northwestern flags adorned the roof and the only results posted on the scoreboard were Northwestern-Illinois on the National League side and the other four Big Ten games that day on the American League side. Wildcat football photos hung around the main entrance and the topper—the famous marquee outside the park was painted purple.

  The grounds crew laid the field from the third base dugout to right field. But it was tight. So tight that the right field end zone ended only a foot from the outfield wall and workers affixed the goal post to the bleacher wall. Even though pads protected the players from the brick, a day before the game, Big Ten officials deemed it dangerous and ordered the teams to run all their offensive possessions in one direction, away from the right field wall. Historians and the 41,058 watching couldn't recall a college football ever played under these rules.

The strange rules didn't affect Mikel Leshoure and the Illini. The running back outdid Red Grange, gaining a school-record 330 yards rushing in Illinois' 48-27 win.

In February 2013, the Cubs and Northwestern University signed a five-year agreement that will allow Wildcat sports teams to utilize Wrigley Field. Baseball and women's lacrosse would come in 2013 and five football games beginning as early as 2014, or after the Cubs refigure the box seats and dugouts to allow "two-way" football on the gridiron.

Game of the Year

June 13—The Chicago Black Hawks brought their just won Stanley Cup to Wrigley Field. They shared the trophy with the Cubs, the White Sox, and over 40,000 exuberant fans in a pregame ceremony. The *Chicago Sun-Times* said this about the event: "The decibel level that fans said they haven't experienced inside the Friendly Confines since the 2003 National League Championship Series greeted the Blackhawks as they toured the field with the trophy."[36]

The Blackhawks' appearance would have been enough to sate any Chicago sports fan. But the game that followed was a gem. The White Sox's Gavin Floyd carried a no-hitter until two out in the seventh inning; Alfonso Soriano doubled and then scored on Chad Tracy's single. The Cubs' Ted Lilly did one better; he entered the ninth inning with a no-hitter of his own. But the first batter, Juan Pierre, hit a sharp single through the box. Lilly and Carlos Marmol settled for a one-hitter and 1-0 Cub win.

Quote of 2010

"With all the new, state-of-the-art ballparks, Wrigley's shortcomings have become more apparent. . . . Are they insurmountable hurdles? Obviously not. But in a competitive environment in which everyone seeks the tiniest edge, it is a disadvantage."[37]

Mike Dodd in the USA Today—*August 18, 2010—on Wrigley's lack of amenities for players*

NINTH INNING
2011-2016
SECURE FUTURE

By 2010, the Cubs, playing in ninety-six-year-old Wrigley Field, outdrew the eight franchises that only a decade earlier, with new stadiums, outdrew the Cubs. Wrigley Field's appeal was now unquestioned.

In November 2010, Cub Chairman Tom Ricketts unveiled plans to renovate Wrigley Field. The ambitious proposal called for structural repair and reinforcement of the grandstand. It would also increase the ballpark's "footprint," enabling the team to extract more revenue out of the park and its environs.

Ricketts sought to utilize a portion of the State of Illinois's ticket amusement tax to float bonds for about half of the renovations. The request seemed logical; in the past two decades the amusement tax financed among other things the Chicago White Sox's new Comiskey Park, the renovation of Soldier Field, and at least some of the construction of the United Center. But the state squelched the funding request. Illinois was deep in debt and the state couldn't assist a private enterprise with public money, even one that was its third-largest tourist attraction. The city of Chicago couldn't help either. A new mayor, although a Cub fan, dealt with few funds and more vital needs.

In 2013 the Cubs presented an updated renovation plan, and offered to pay the construction bills themselves. But they still butted heads with the local alderman and rooftop owners hell bent to protect their 2004 revenue-sharing agreement with the team. Even after getting city approval in July 2013 to renovate the ballpark, the Cubs delayed commencement through 2013 due to the threat of litigation from the rooftop owners. In May of 2014 the Cubs finally called the rooftops' bluff, won the day in court, and began their long-awaited project in October 2014.

The five-year renovation plan secures Wrigley Field's long-term survival, physically and financially. With it the ninth inning ends, the game is over, and the team, its fans, and all of baseball win.

2011

The Season by the Numbers		
71-91	.438 5th 25 games out	3,017,966 (37,258 average)
39-42	.481 at home	117% of NL Average

Opening Day

APRIL 1: CUBS (DEMPSTER) VS. PIRATES (CORREIA); RAIN, 41 DEGREES; 41,358 PAID

Pirates 6 Cubs 3—The Pirates scored all their runs on home runs: a fifth inning grand slam by Neil Walker and a two-run shot in the seventh by Andrew McCutchen. The Cubs scored on a throwing error, a force play, and an RBI single. At twenty-one years old, Starlin Castro became the youngest Cub to start a home opener since Ken Hubbs in 1962.

The biggest pregame ovation went to Kerry Wood, who returned to the team after two seasons in the American League. Actor Robert Redford threw out the first ball. Students from Blaine Elementary led the crowd in the Pledge of Allegiance and Wayne Messmer sang "God

Bless America" and the National Anthem. The crowd observed a moment of silence for Ron Santo and the survivors of the recent earthquake and tsunami in Japan.

What's New

- The team enlarged its training room, which now included x-ray equipment.
- The Sheffield Grill and Captain Morgan Pub were renovated. The Batter's Eye lounge in the center field bleachers traded fixed glass for open windows.
- Concessions offered gluten-free and lactose-free items for the first time. Chicago's famous Vienna Beef hot dogs returned to Wrigley Field for the first time since 1982. The Cubs switched hot dogs because 37 percent of Wrigley Field visitors were from out of state. To provide a real Chicago atmosphere, the team increased the number of local offerings.

What Happened

- A February blizzard dropped twenty inches of snow on Chicago and ripped off a portion of Wrigley Field's roofing near the press box. As a precaution, the city temporarily closed both Clark and Addison streets around the ballpark.
- On February 22, Chicago elected Rahm Emanuel, former White House chief of staff, as mayor. Emanuel, a Chicagoan and a former north side congressman, was a Cub fan. It was hoped that Emanuel's allegiance might make him more receptive than Mayor Daley to support Wrigley Field's expansion. But Emanuel was mayor first, a fan second when he said, "I'm going to represent the taxpayers of the city of Chicago and you [the Cubs] have to represent your interests."[1]
- The sluggish economy, ticket price escalation, and poor play dropped paid attendance and elevated no-shows at the park. For the first time in years, bleacher seats went unsold. In an unprecedented move, the team offered free shirts, discounted food, and cheap beer to bleacher fans.
- The Cubs unveiled Ron Santo's statue on August 10. The likeness of the Cub third baseman and WGN colorman marked the fourth statue outside the park, joining Harry Caray, Ernie Banks, and Billy Williams. Santo's family participated in the ceremony. Cub radioman Pat Hughes said, "This spot, Wrigley Field, was (his) favorite on earth."[2]
- With no postseason baseball at Wrigley Field again this year, on October 1, the Cubs and Groupon.com screened "Ferris Bueller's Day Off" at the ballpark. The twenty-fifth anniver-

Santo statue (author's collection)

sary celebration of the iconic movie, which includes a scene where Ferris catches a foul ball at Wrigley Field, attracted a sellout crowd of about 10,000.

The Cubs worked hard to endear themselves with Lake View residents, hoping to engender good will and make Wrigley Field an off-season destination. In addition to movie night, snowmobilers staged a jumping demonstration outside the park, and the ice skating rink opened for the third straight winter. The team also erected a Christmas tree near the main entrance and encouraged neighborhood children to decorate it.

Game of the Year

April 23—Starlin Castro and Darwin Barney were a combined 7-for-10 and drove in six runs as the Cubs came from behind to beat the Dodgers, 10-8. The win left the Cubs with a 10-10 record. More interestingly, they became the first team in major league history to reach .500 ten times through twenty games (1-1, 2-2, 3-3 . . .).

Quote of 2011

"To me, baseball is better with tradition, baseball is better with history, baseball is better with fans who care, baseball is better in ballparks like this, baseball is better during the day."[3]

—*Theo Epstein, the new president of baseball operations in the* Chicago Tribune—*October 25, 2011*

2012

The Season by the Numbers		
61-101	.377 5th 36 games out	2,882,756 (35,589 average)
38-43	.469 at home	111% of NL Average

Opening Day

APRIL 5: CUBS (DEMPSTER) VS. NATIONALS (STRASBURG); 41 DEGREES; 41,176 PAID

Nationals 2 Cubs 1—Washington scored their runs in the eighth and ninth innings on a walk and a single. Marlon Byrd drove in the only Cub run with a single in the fourth inning.

Bill Murray threw out the first pitch to Kerry Wood. Then Murray ran the bases and slid into home plate. Students from Blaine Elementary led the crowd in the Pledge of Allegiance. Wayne Messmer sang "God Bless America" and the "National Anthem."

It was the warmest March ever in Chicago. That's why the outfield vines were partially green; it's the first time in recent memory that they had sprouted by Opening Day.

What's New

- The team replaced the bleacher box seats in right field with the Budweiser Patio, a rooftop-type experience inside the ballpark. Below the patio, against the top of the right field wall, was a seventy-five-foot LED board that displayed player statistics and advertisements.
- A batting cage under the left field bleachers.
- The Cubs moved their offices from Wrigley Field to a building at Clark and Waveland. The old office space in the ballpark was left empty, reserved for upcoming renovations.
- New internal advertisements included signage on the small wagon gates on the left field wall (Tervis) and the right field wall (Target).

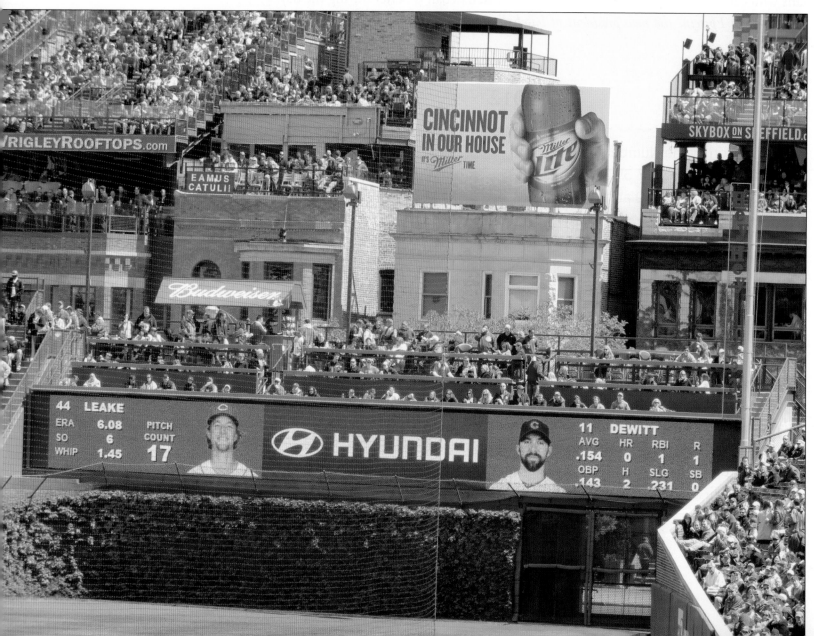

The new LED board and patio on April 21, 2012. Notice the early-season ivy and the missing numbers near the Eamus Catuli sign on the building across the street. (author's collection)

- The Ricketts family purchased the land across the street from the ballpark, the McDonald's property on Clark Street, for $20 million. For now, just south of the McDonald's, the team opened a store that sold memorabilia and game-used items. In January 2013, they announced plans to build a hotel on the spot.

What Happened

- The Cubs lost more than 100 games for only their third time in history. Subsequently, the team sold less than three million tickets for the first time in a decade. Still, their attendance number was a major league record for a team with that many losses.
- The building at 3633 N. Sheffield Avenue and its occupants, the Lakeview Baseball Club, were brought into bankruptcy court.

  The building sported two famous signs: the EAMUS CATULI (loosely translated to "Go Cubs" in Latin) and the list of numbers that indicated the years since the Cubs won a divisional title, a pennant, and a World Series. When the 2012 season began, the new owners kept the Latin phrase but removed the numbers that were a reminder of Cub futility. Before the 2013 season, however, the numbers returned, re-establishing the familiar twenty-year tradition beyond the right-field wall.

- Mayor Rahm Emanuel said he was nearing a deal between the city and the team to begin renovations and expansion of Wrigley Field. The mayor indicated that the team needed to finance the money to renovate the ballpark. He left open the option of the city assisting with the expansion around the ballpark. Emanuel wouldn't say whether the negotiations included the city forfeiting thirty-five years of amusement tax growth from the Cubs.

  Soon after, it was revealed that Joe Ricketts, the patriarch of the Ricketts family (but not a direct owner or director of the Cubs), was interested in bankrolling a $10 million advertising campaign against President Barack Obama. The miscue put the Ricketts family in direct odds with Emanuel, Obama's former chief of staff, and delayed renovation money from the city of Chicago.

Games of the Year

May 18—Cub reliever Kerry Wood battled injuries this season and sported an 8.64 ERA. Before the game, he announced he would retire after one more mound appearance. Wood was called into the game in the eighth inning. He faced one batter, striking out Dayan Viciedo of the White Sox on three pitches. When he left the mound, he received thunderous applause. His six-

year-old son met him near the dugout in a big embrace. He received handshakes and hugs from teammates in the dugout and then returned to the field to a standing ovation. One of the most beloved Cubs ended his career his way.

September 17—A three hour and forty minute rain held up the start of a Cubs-Pirates game until 10:42 P.M. It finally ended at 1:28 A.M. the following day, making it the latest-starting and latest-ending game in park history.

Quote of 2012

"It's been under-invested. We need to get it up to speed. We need a lot of money to re-do electrical, sewage, all the stuff that is 100 years old. We've got a lot on our plate, but we're going to get it done."[4]

Tom Ricketts—April 5, 2012—on Wrigley Field

2013

The Season by the Numbers

66-96	.407 5th 31 games out	2,642,682 (32,625 average)
31-50	.383 at home	101% of NL average

Home Opener

APRIL 8: CUBS (E. JACKSON) VS. BREWERS (ESTRADA); 61 DEGREES; 40,083 PAID

Brewers 7 Cubs 4—It was a tale of two games. Brewers' first baseman Martin Maldonado hit a bases-clearing, wind-blown, three-run double to right field in the first inning. In the ninth, with the wind now blowing in, Starlin Castro just missed winning the game with a bases-loaded drive that Norichika Aoki hauled in on the warning track. Welington Castillo hit a two-run shot for the Cubs in the 2nd inning.

The Brewers' Ryan Braun, recently accused of receiving banned substances, was roundly booed.

Wayne Messmer sang "God Bless America" and the "National Anthem." Students from Blaine Elementary led the crowd in the "Pledge of Allegiance." Fans observed a moment of silence for the victims of last December's Sandy Hook Massacre.

There were two first pitches: Fergie Jenkins to Jeff Samardzija and Billy Williams to James Russell.

What's New

- The scoreboard was repainted.
- The right field LED board, added last season, now displayed video in addition to still images.

What Happened

On January 19, the Cubs unveiled a $300 million Wrigley Field renovation plan. With no public funding forthcoming, the team offered to go it alone. Team Chairman Tom Ricketts summed up the new perspective on renovation finances, saying, "Let us go about doing our business, and then we'll take care of ourselves."[5] They asked the city for three things: allow the team to schedule 3:05 p.m. Friday games and more night games, allow the use Sheffield Avenue for pre-game activities, and allow more signage in the ballpark. The five-year project would begin in the fall of 2013 and run for five off-seasons. It would create 2,000 jobs and generate over $20 million in yearly revenues.

The plan included structural improvements to make the park viable for future generations and avenues to maximize income. The changes included:

- Structural steel, concrete, and seat replacement throughout
- New roof
- New electric, plumbing, and telecommunications
- New bi-level press box
- At least six elevators
- Renovated suites and lounges
- Additional clubs for season ticket holders
- New suite and club entrance on the west side of the park
- A 42% increase in restrooms
- A 100% increase in concessions
- Roof deck concessions
- Left field LED board and pavilion to complement those in right field
- In addition, the Ricketts family planned to build a $200 million hotel across Clark Street

The renovations would also provide more player comfort, something the team said it needed to attract and keep talent. These added a new clubhouse, training room, and batting tunnels.

The project would be wrapped in a Wrigley Field exterior mimicking that of the 1930s. Gone were the 1960 pre-cast concrete, replaced by stucco and decorative grillwork.

The team dropped the "Triangle Building." That often-discussed structure was to house, among other things, a parking garage. But since neighbors didn't want additional traffic at Clark and Addison, the Cubs envisioned the space supporting better community relations. They planned an office building and a pavilion there instead, the latter allowing for concerts and events like farmers markets and ice skating.

Less than a week after the Cubs' proposal, the rooftop owners floated a plan to ensure that signage wouldn't block their views of the field. They offered to erect seven 20'x7' digital signs on their rooftops, with the nearly $18 million in annual ad revenues going to support ballpark renovation. The Cubs quickly shot it down. They claimed the revenues would be much less than estimated since television views of the faraway rooftop signs would be infrequent.

In March, the suburb of Rosemont offered the Cubs 25 acres of free land near O'Hare airport to build a replica of Wrigley Field. The Rosemont plot had benefits, requiring no restrictions on signage, night games, or parking. But the Cubs didn't seriously consider the offer, or use it as leverage to get a better deal with the city. They kept their focus on Wrigleyville and renovating Wrigley Field.

The team set a self-imposed deadline of April 1 to get an agreement with the city. If nothing was settled by then, they surmised, they couldn't begin renovations at the end of the season. They continued to negotiate past that date and on April 14 the Cubs, the city, and Alderman Tunney hammered out a tentative deal. The most important elements for the Cubs included up to 40 night games a year, occasional street fairs on Sheffield Avenue, "bumping" out the park eight feet onto Waveland and Sheffield for more concession space. And signage—one 6,000 square foot video board beyond the left field bleachers and a smaller see-through sign in right field.

The rooftop owners were not part of the negotiations. When they got wind of the plan to allow signage behind the bleachers, they threatened to use "any and all means necessary" to block the Cubs.[6]

The Cubs and the city negotiated through the summer. On July 11, against the wishes of Alderman Tunney, the Commission on Chicago Landmarks approved a slightly smaller left field scoreboard and the see-through sign in right. Two weeks later, the Chicago City Council unanimously approved the deal for the ballpark renovations and the Ricketts' family hotel across Clark Street.

The approval allowed the Cubs to begin renovations after the season. But Tom Ricketts still kept one eye on the rooftops. He wanted to make sure they wouldn't sue the team and delay renovations by months or even years. He didn't want to start renovations, only to have then stopped by litigation. He needed to, in his words, make sure the rooftops wouldn't sue "before ordering steel and shovels."[7]

With that threat of a lawsuit, the Cubs did not begin renovations as planned following the 2013 season.

Game of the Year

May 27—The Cubs shutout the White Sox, 7-0. Cub fans who suffered through the last few seasons saw a hopeful glimpse of things to come. Twenty-eight year-old Jeff Samardzija pitched a complete-game two-hitter. Anthony Rizzo (23) doubled and tripled, driving in two runs. Starlin Castro (also 23) stroked two hits and stole a base.

Quote of 2013

"In exchange for a deal that includes no public subsidy, the Cubs should be allowed great leeway in how they renovate the ballpark. We say this confident that the Cubs' owners know better than anyone that transforming charming Wrigley Field—a better ticket seller than the players themselves—into Times Square would be a bad idea."[8]

Editorial in the Chicago Sun-Times—*July 12, 2013*

2014

The Season by the Numbers

73-89	.451 5th 17 games out	2,652,113 (32,742 average)
41-40	.506 at home	101% of NL average

Home Opener

APRIL 4: CUBS (T. WOOD) VS. PHILLIES (HERNANDEZ); 40 DEGREES; 38,283 PAID

Phillies 7 Cubs 2—The Phillies' John Mayberry Jr. and Chase Utley hit two-run homers. The Cubs mustered only three hits: a Welington Castillo solo home run and singles by Starlin Castro and Darwin Barney. Rick Renteria managed his first Cubs game at Wrigley Field, but lost to former Cub-Hall-of-Famer and Phillies' Manager, Ryne Sandberg. "This is home for me,"[9] Sandberg said of his return to Wrigley Field.

Wayne Messmer sang the "National Anthem" and "God Bless America" at his 30th consecutive home opener. The students from Blaine Elementary led the crowd in the Pledge of Allegiance.

Ernie Banks, Fergie Jenkins, Billy Williams, and Ryne Sandberg took part in the first pitch ceremonies. Williams threw a ball to Jeff Samardzija, Sandberg to Edwin Jackson.

What's New

- To celebration the 100th anniversary of Wrigley Field, the team added a huge sign above the main entrance that spelled out its centennial year slogan, "It's the Party of the Century," On the left of the marquee hung an over-sized "1914." On the right a "2014." Capturing the season's historical theme, murals of the Cubs past—photos of old-time players, the ballpark,

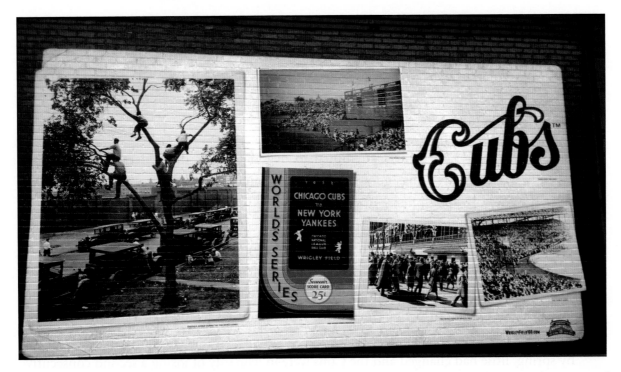

A 1932 World Series mural affixed to the ballpark's outside wall along Sheffield Avenue (Courtesy of Charles Bober)

and scorecards—were affixed to the walls along Waveland and Sheffield Avenues. A "Wrigley Field 100" emblem was painted on the grass behind home plate.

The team highlighted the centennial anniversary all year, with special scorecards, food and drink specials for the fans, and throwback uniforms.

- The season started with the ivy a few fell below the top of the left field wall. Workers replaced bricks and tuck pointed much of the wall over the winter, necessitating a painstaking process of first removing the ivy from the wall and bending it ninety degrees onto the outfield grass. When the grounds crew reaffixed the ivy vines to the wall before the season, it hung shorter than before. After the leaves sprouted, the ivy eventually grew back to its original height.

- The Cubs unveiled a mascot, Clark the Cub. Criticized unmercifully by the media for lacking pants and wearing a backwards baseball cap, the adults missed the point that the furry bear was aimed at children, who took to him immediately. In fact, the team constructed, "Clark's Clubhouse," a play area on the lower concourse.

- In an effort to decrease traffic congestion around the ballpark (and spread goodwill to the neighbors), the team established a free parking lot and shuttle service 2.5 miles from Wrigley Field. The 1,000 space lot, at 3900 N. Rockwell, replaced the DeVry lot that was in use for nearly 30 years. But fans utilized DeVry infrequently since the team charged $6 to park and shuttle to the ballpark. The new lot, used on nights and weekends, became popular for suburbanites driving to the game.

What Happened

The Cubs and the rooftop owners attempted to negotiate their differences throughout the fall and early winter. With things going nowhere and millions of dollars at stake, antagonism ran high. The rooftops took offense at comments made by Tom Ricketts at the annual Cubs Convention. They also filed a suit against a stadium financing consultant who called the impasse "One of the most ludicrous situations in the history of sports facility development....Protecting carpetbaggers stealing a product paid by others for their own profit, and, thereby stopping a $300 million investment."[10] The Cubs jabbed back, applying for a permit for the talked-about see-through sign in back of the right field bleachers, a sign that would block the views of some rooftops.

By spring, little had changed and the Cubs were in jeopardy of losing a second consecutive offseason of renovations. Finally, in May, Tom Ricketts released a revised renovation plan, this time with five additional view-stealing outfield signs, more seats, outfield lights, and expanded clubhouses and bullpens.

Ricketts had called the rooftops' hand; and the Cubs stopped playing nice. David Haugh of the *Chicago Tribune* wrote of the new proposal: "Those of us who have been urging Ricketts to proceed despite the threat of a lawsuit from rooftop owners would be hypocritical to criticize his unexpected bold move now. This needed to happen to spur action in a standoff the Cubs let drag on so much the most patient Ricketts sibling ran out of patience. It's about time"[11]

The rooftops and the city cried foul. The former counteroffered six weeks later, promising to not sue the team if they agreed to last year's proposal—the one with only two outfield signs. But the Cubs moved forward, not back, making only minor concessions to the city (trimming the square footage and placement of the new signs and limiting the adverse effect moving the bullpens under the bleachers would have on the historic ivy).

In July, the Cubs received another unanimous approval from the Commission on Chicago Landmarks. The following month, eight of the rooftop owners, the ones most affected by the proposed signs, finally filed suit in Cook County Court to force the Commission to reverse their decision and stop would-be renovation in the fall.

But the Cubs didn't hesitate this time. In early October, right after the season ended, they started preliminary work dismantling the bleachers. A few days later, on October 8, the outer

Clark and Addison Streets on the 100th anniversary of Wrigley Field, April 23, 2014 (Courtesy of Charles Bober)

bleacher walls along Waveland Avenue came down, and the long awaited Wrigley Field renovation, now called the 1060 Project, began in earnest (1060 is the ballpark address—1060 W. Addison St.).

By the end of October the left and the right field bleachers were gone. The only separation from the field to the street was the outfield wall, now barren of ivy leaves, but sure to spring anew again next season.

Game of the Year

The team celebrated the Wrigley Field centennial anniversary game on April 23, exactly 100 years to the day of the Weeghman Park curtain-raiser (a 9-1 Chi-Fed win over the Kansas City Packers). A 400 pound cake replica of Wrigley Field greeted fans at the Clark and Addison entrance. Famous Cubs (like Ernie Banks and Andre Dawson) and superstar Chicago Bears (like Dick Butkus and Gale Sayers) were introduced before the game. Charlie Weeghman's grandniece tossed the first ball. And fans sang "Happy Birthday" to the Friendly Confines. But the home team lost the first game of Wrigley Field's second century, a 7-5 defeat at the hands of the Arizona Diamondbacks (even though the Cubs sported Chi-Fed uniforms and the D-backs Packers' threads).

Former Cub pitcher Ryan Dempster had the perfect quote on this perfect day: "Everybody who ever puts on a major-league uniform should be so lucky to be able to put on a Chicago Cubs uniform and play at Wrigley Field. It's that special."[12]

Quote of 2014

"There's no manufactured quirkiness at Wrigley, as in the retro ballparks that replaced the multi-purpose stadiums starting in the early 1990s. The streets around Wrigley shaped its slightly asymmetrical contours. The retro parks can lift such signature Wrigley touches as the brick wall or the hand-operated scoreboard, but they can't match its intimacy or myriad layers of history."[13]

Blair Kamin in the Chicago Tribune—*April 23, 2014*

2015

The Season by the Numbers		
97-65	.599 3rd 3 games out	2,959,812 (36,540 average)
49-32	.605 at home	115% of NL average

Opening Day

APRIL 5: CUBS (LESTER) VS. CARDINALS (WAINWRIGHT); 44 DEGREES (NIGHT); 35,055 PAID

Cardinals 3 Cubs 0—Jason Heyward hit two doubles and Matt Holliday drove in two runs for the Cardinals. Cub relievers Phil Coke, Jason Motte, Neil Ramirez, Pedro Strop, and Hector Rondon threw 4¾ scoreless innings. The game marked the Cubs debut of Jon Lester and manager Joe Maddon.

The fans honored Ernie Banks, who died in January, with a moment of silence. This season Cub players wore Banks' number "14" on their right shoulders. The team also offered condolences for Cardinal outfielder Oscar Taveras, who was killed in an auto accident last fall.

Ernie Banks' sons, Jerry and Joey, threw out the first pitches.

Fans tonight saw the first results of the renovation project. In truth, Wrigley Field ran hot and cold. The big left field videoboard operated for the first time. It was the ballpark's most dynamic venture into the 21st century. What seemed almost unimaginable just a few years before, the board now filled the ballpark with a cacophony of new sights and sounds.

NINTH INNING 2011-2016 SECURE FUTURE

But the ballpark environs looked like a construction zone. Waveland and Sheffield Avenues were closed to traffic; their sidewalks even difficult to walk on. Clark Street wasn't much better. In January, management informed fans that the bleachers would not be completed by the opener. A persistent sewer issue outside the park and bad winter weather put the work schedule increasingly behind. The left field bleachers consisted of only steel girders and plywood floor framing. The right field section just the steel. To mask this inadequacy, management covered the bleacher area with tarps that displayed images honoring Ernie Banks.

The largest debacle this night came from an unexpected source—restrooms. Management knew the park would have fewer restrooms when the season began (three were inoperable for renovations until May or June). But when half the upper deck restrooms shut down too, many fans waited an hour for the chance to relieve themselves. Others couldn't wait. Some peed in cups, others in their pants. Many left the park to use the facilities at nearby bars. For the Cubs, it was a national embarrassment, leading some to ask why the team played this season in the unfinished ballpark. "Peegate" mostly resolved itself after the team scattered seventy porta-potties throughout the park. And over time the sketchy start to the season improved dramatically both on and off the field.

What's New

- The new left field video board measured nearly 4,000 square feet—42 feet high and 95 feet across. It provided sound and video to fans unfamiliar with advanced technologies at its ballpark (the main scoreboard was 77 years-old). The new board provided information on players, highlights of Cub history, public service announcements, and the most anticipated perk, instant replays. The team promised that they would limit its use for advertisements or trivial things like "kisscams."

  Only the most traditional fans didn't like the new board. Designers ensured that this electronic wizard complemented the 101 year-old ballpark; the unobtrusive green frame blended with its surroundings, and although much larger than the old scoreboard, it wasn't overwhelming. The video quality was stunning, and its information entertaining and useful. Sound from the board's 42 speakers, however, was uneven. Sitting in seats behind home plate gave fans noise-induced headaches. Yet on the peripheries it was sometimes difficult to hear. Neighbors complained about increased noise. The team frequently adjusted the level and direction of the sound to mollify the concerns.

  The right field board became operable on May 11. It measured about half as large as the left field board (only 2,000 square feet). It purpose was mainly informational, displaying the line-ups and a box score throughout the game.

The incomplete right field bleachers seen from Sheffield Avenue; April 8, 2015 (author's collection)

    Included in this technology blitz were ribbon boards on the facing of the far-reaches of the upper deck and an LED board in the left field corner in front of the bleachers, similar to the one built in right field in 2012.

- Over the winter, workers repaired and replaced portions of the right field bleacher wall, just like they did last winter in left field.

    The bleachers were a work in progress during much of the season. The left field bleacher section opened on May 11. It was spartan at first: just seats, restrooms, and a minimal number of concession stands. The center field bleachers, not new, finally opened too because fans had no access to them with both sides of the bleachers under construction.

    On July 3, the full bleachers opened. They seated nearly 5,000, about 500 more than in 2014. The whole bleacher area expanded, with a larger lower level and a wider upper level concourse that wrapped around the back of the seating area. The new bleachers offered expanded concession options, made possible by moving the park's outer walls over the

Waveland and Sheffield sidewalks and onto the streets. The bleacher's expanded lower level housed the "Waveland Grill" and the "Red Line Grill." The upper level housed "Three Fingers" (named after long-ago Cub pitcher, "Three Fingers" Brown) and the "Platform 14" (a nod to Ernie Banks). These four food concessions areas served everything from pulled pork sandwiches and a hoagie named after Joe Maddon to macaroni-and-cheese and mixed drinks. Bleacher fans finally had food selections far beyond the regular hot dogs and popcorn.

The bleachers also offered fans physical spaces reminiscent of the rooftops across the street. The "Left Field Porch" and the "Right Field Porch" stood under the left and right field boards. These areas accommodated up to 100 people and included both a patio area and some seating.

The "Left Field Well" allowed up to 50 fans seats and standing options directly behind the outfield wall near the left field corner. The vantage point was no better than that from a front row bleacher seat. But their separation from the rest of the bleacher seating and the option to stand provided an air of exclusivity that some fans appreciated.

The old Batter's Eye Lounge, in center field behind the juniper bushes, was renovated and became the Budweiser Bleacher Suite, accommodating up to 100 fans with food and drink packages.

What Happened

- As a group of rooftop owners awaited a ruling on their suit to stop Wrigley Field renovations, two of them faced foreclosure for failing to make mortgage payments, owing tens of millions of dollars. Beyond fighting to keep the team from blocking their views with the gigantic outfield boards, the rooftops had been hit hard by the Cubs' poor showings the last few seasons. It was difficult enough for the Cubs to get fans inside the ballpark to watch a non-competitive team. It was doubly trying to get them to drop $100 or more for a partial view from across the street.

  In February, a federal judge denied the rooftops' attempt to halt installation of the right field board. In early April, the same judge ruled that the Cubs had the right to block the rooftops' views. In the fall of 2015, she dismissed the rooftops' lawsuit. The 2004 agreement between the Cubs and the rooftops stated the Cubs could block the rooftops' view through an "expansion" of the park, but not an "addition" to the park. The judge ruled the right field sign was an expansion.

  In January 2015, the Ricketts' family began buying up rooftop businesses on Waveland and Sheffield Avenues. By January 2016, they had purchased nine of the sixteen buildings (and their cash-strapped rooftop businesses). Like the lights issue nearly thirty years ago, when the rooftop controversy finally exploded, it ended rather quickly.

- When Ernie Banks died of a heart attack on January 23, he left behind a legacy unmatched in Chicago sports. Banks got his baseball start in 1950 with the Kansas City Monarchs of the old Negro Leagues. On September 17, 1953 he became the first African-American to take the field for the Cubs. In 1955, he slammed 44 home runs, challenging the image of the slap-happy-hitting major league shortstop 30 years ahead of its time.

  Ernie Banks won back-to-back National League Most Valuable Player awards in 1958 and 1959, the first player to do so. He moved to first base in 1961 when his knees gave out, but still hit 512 home runs in a 19-year Cub career. Banks played in 14 all-star games and in 1977 entered to the Baseball Hall of Fame on the first ballot.

  While Ernie's on-field achievements remain legendary (his 277 home runs as a National League shortstop is still a record), his infectious personality and his love of baseball burned just as bright. He played during some of the most inept days in Cubs history, yet he never complained. He coined Wrigley Field's most affable moniker, "The Friendly Confines." During the dog days of summer he'd often exhort his teammates to, "Let's play two."

  Although limited to living on the South Side much of his career due to the racial intolerance of segregated housing covenants, Banks' appeal to Chicagoans was universal. It's remarkable that in the heat of the racial social struggles that marked 1960s Chicago, Banks became, with the possible exception of Mayor Richard J. Daley, the most popular man in the city.

  Ernie Banks star burnt bright to the end. He was the darling of Cubs Conventions 40 years after his playing days ended. Nearly everyone who met him remarked of feeling better about *themselves* afterwards. He was the Cubs' greatest player, and baseball will never see another one like him.

- When Theo Epstein took over director of baseball operations in October 2011, the team was rebuilding again after losing 87 and 91 games the previous two years. Epstein wanted to change the franchise's course by emphasizing player development and restocking the minor leagues to build a sustained wave of continued competitiveness. The team traded most players of value for draft picks and young players with untapped potential.

Cub players wearing Ernie Banks' 1958 throwback uniform; July 12, 2015 (AP / Andrew Nelles)

The 2015 season provided as much promise as any in recent memory. Many of these young players either came up to the big leagues late in 2014 (Javier Baez, Jorge Soler), or nearly ready as 2015 arrived (Kris Bryant, Addison Russell, and Kyle Schwarber). Add to this the signing of veteran manager Joe Maddon and pitcher Jon Lester, and Cub fans had reason to be cautiously optimistic.

Here's a chronological list of highlights from the 2015 season at Wrigley Field:

April 8—Following the opening loss, Jake Arrieta shut down the Cardinals, 3-0. It's the first of 22 regular season wins for the eventual Cy Young Award winner.

April 17—Kris Bryant called up from AAA Iowa. He'd win the Rookie of the Year Award.

April 21—Addison Russell called up from AAA Iowa.

May 11—The Cubs were 15-15 for the season. Kris Bryant and Anthony Rizzo homered in the first inning; Jon Lester held off the Mets, 4-3, the first of six straight wins.

May 26—Kris Bryant hit an estimated 477-foot homer that bounced off the left field video board; Addison Russell doubled in Jonathan Herrera in the 9th inning to beat the Nationals, 3-2.

June 16—Kyle Schwarber called up from AAA Iowa.

July 25—Cole Hamels of the Phillies no-hit the Cubs, 5-0; It's the first time the Cubs are no-hit since 1965 (a major league record for longevity) and only the third time at Wrigley Field.

July 27—Kris Bryant hit a two-run, game-winning home run against the Rockies; the Cubs' first come from behind, game-winning homer since 2007. Called the turning point of the season, the team won 22 of its next 27 games.

August 23—The Cubs hit five home runs (Bryant 2, Fowler, Schwarber, and Montero) to complete a four-game sweep of the Braves, 9-3.

September 28—Chris Denorfia broke a scoreless tie with an 11th inning game-winning home run. It's the first time in major league history a 0-0 game was decided by an extra-inning walk-off home run. The victory helped the Cubs to a second consecutive 19-9 month.

Postseason

The Cubs finished the last sixty games of the season with a 42-18 record. Their remarkable run earned them a one-game Wild Card game in Pittsburgh on October 7. The Cubs considered opening up Wrigley Field for a viewing party of the game, but logistics prevented it. It would have been something—Dexter Fowler and Kyle Schwarber hit home runs. Schwarber's landed in the Allegheny River. Jake Arrieta pitched a five-hit complete game for a 4-0 win.

The Cubs met the Cardinals in the National League Divisional Series. It was the first time the rivals ever played each other in postseason. The teams split the first two games in St. Louis.

Cub players celebrate after beating the Cardinals in Game 4 of the National League Division Series; October 13, 2015 (AP Photo/Nam Y. Huh)

The Cubs broke a postseason record hitting six home runs in Game 3: Fowler, Soler, Bryant, Rizzo, Castro, and Schwarber. Jorge Soler broke a record, getting on base his first nine appearances in the postseason. The Cubs clinched the series with a Game 4 victory. Rizzo, Baez, and Schwarber all homered. Schwarber's landed atop the right field information board, one of the most epic in Wrigley Field history.

The Cubs were four victories from their first World Series appearance since 1945. But the Mets' young pitching and clutch-hitting Daniel Murphy overwhelmed them. The New Yorkers outscored the Cubs 21-8, and swept the series. After the Mets celebrated on the field after Game 4, the Cubs came onto the field to salute the Wrigley Field crowd.

Chris Emma, writing for the local CBS station, said this about the team: "Nothing is guaranteed for the Cubs' future—insert any narrative if you must—but the team is built to last. That winning culture has been instilled. It was a rocky ending, but there's a bright future ahead. This 2015 campaign was a great success, and the best may be yet to come."[14]

The Cubs line up for the National Anthem before Game 3 of the National League Championship Series against the Mets. Note the left field video board; October 20, 2015 (AP Photo/Nam Y. Huh)

Quote of 2015

"It's a brand new day."[15]

Pearl Jam lead-singer Eddie Vedder in the Chicago Sun-Times, *October 14, 2015, on the young team making the postseason.*

POSTLUDE

When the Cubs set out to upgrade their team and their ballpark, the long-term plan had both improving on a similar plane and at a similar pace. And that's exactly what's happening. In the same month the first round of renovations finished (the bleacher renovation in July 2015), the team started playing like postseason contenders.

There's a parallel between the video board in left field—brash, exciting—and Kris Bryant, Kyle Schwarber, Addison Russell, Javier Baez, and Jorge Soler. They're all new and invigorating.

As the renovations unfold the next few years, with the new clubhouse, the plaza, new seats, and the added concessions, it will also be intoxicating to see these players mature, and more young players arrive to fill the gaps.

Other teams have noticed the Cubs' player personnel plan and already mimic it by stockpiling young talent, anticipating their own future "sustained wave of continued competitiveness." In the same vein, teams continue to watch Wrigley Field. For the past thirty years, other teams have built ballparks with Wrigley Field in mind—real grass, brick walls, urban settings. But since the Cubs erected their left field video board, their rivals, the Cardinals and the White Sox, announced plans for similar boards.

Just like Eddie Vedder said as the Cubs began their 2015 playoff run, it is a brand new day for the Cubs. Once thought of as the lovable losers, today they are thrilling and formidable. And it's a new day for the old ballpark too. Wrigley Field, whose future was uncertain less than a decade ago, is rebuilding for another century. Like this team, it will be around for a while, and it will be beautiful and secure.

CONCLUSION

*Eleven of the thirteen Classic ballparks, built between 1909 and 1915, were eventually abandoned. They survived an average of fifty-eight seasons. Eleven of the fourteen Modern stadiums built between 1960 and 1971 were eventually abandoned, too. They averaged only thirty-three baseball seasons and the Neoclassic Turner Field in Atlanta lasted just twenty. Wrigley Field, on the other hand, has thrived for over a century. Chicago's North Side ballpark survived the short-lived Federal League, world wars, the Depression, and the Classic, Modern, and Neoclassic ballpark eras.

If this book was about the Chicago Cubs baseball team, much of the blame for their lack of success would rest on the shoulders of P. K. Wrigley, the reluctant owner who knew everything about gum but seemingly cared less about baseball. But since this book celebrates the ballpark in which the Cubs have played in for a century, the light shines differently on Mr.

Wrigley. He heeded his father's bromides about ballpark cleanliness and fan comfort. Without P. K.'s constant doting—new cement here, wider seats there—Wrigley Field would have gone the way of Ebbets Field, Crosley Field, and the others; former decaying edifices that old men reminisce about and today's fans can only dream about. But they're gone, except for the recent attempts to build ersatz replicas—the Neoclassic ballparks: Citi Field and Great American Ballpark among them.

Wrigley Field has endured and has inspired in some way most Neoclassic ballparks built since 1992. Kevin Kaduk, in his book, *Wrigleyworld: A Season in Baseball's Best Neighborhood*, put it this way: "Baseball stadium architecture has always been about imagination and a desire to beat the Joneses across the league. It continues to be that way, and it's funny that a ballpark built in the middle of northern Chicago almost ninety years ago proves to be the standard that everyone still chases."[1]

Would Kaduk take Oriole Park at Camden Yards, the first and arguably best of the Neo-classic ballparks over Wrigley Field?

"No, but it's closer than you think. Wide aisles, quick trips to the bathrooms, and food that doesn't taste like mush all score points. But, for some reason, time-soaked tradition wins over comfort and convenience. No matter how well you construct a neighborhood around a new ballpark, you can't fake authenticity."[2]

Wrigley Field is old. But Wrigley Field is REAL. It and Fenway Park are the two remaining ballparks where you can watch a game in nearly the same environment as your grandfather did seventy years ago. Such a historical continuum builds tradition and loyalty that's burned into your bones.

Gary Smith, in a 2008 *Sports Illustrated* article mirrored that sentiment of Wrigley Field: "Something about this ballpark corrupted me—its intimacy, its age and its denizens, their rabidity and ribaldry."[3] It's this historical context, the dichotomy of grass and ivy in the urban city, the loyal fans, and the yesteryear neighborhood surrounding the ballpark that makes the Wrigley Field spectacle such a beautiful experience.

Longtime bleacher denizen Fred Speck, added this: "I've scuba-dived the Great Barrier Reef and motorcycled the Icefields Parkway in the Canadian Rockies, and, yes, they're both *beautiful*. But I realized when I first came here 45 years ago that this ballpark on a sunny day was one of the most beautiful things I'd ever seen, and that it *still* is today."[4]

It was my favorite place to spend a day as a ten year old. It's still the best place for me to be even after more than a half century on earth. And its current renovation project, with its structural improvements and revenue-enhancing additions—while keeping the beloved ivy, scoreboard, and classic neighborhood—will allow this one-time "outlaw" ballpark to seduce new generations of Cub fans until at least the next ballpark building frenzy, on or about 2040.

*Of the thirteen Classic era ballparks, only Wrigley Field and Fenway Park remain.

*Of the fourteen Modern era ballparks, only Dodger Stadium, Angel Stadium of Anaheim, and O.co Coliseum in Oakland remain in use for baseball.

APPENDIX

THE LONGEST HOME RUNS IN WRIGLEY FIELD HISTORY

Spotty documentation makes long home run "proof" allusive. First, video hardly exists before 1980. Next, newspaper accounts could be confusing. Does "off the building" mean it hit a Waveland or Sheffield Avenue building on a fly or on a bounce? In addition, some newspaper accounts made special mentions of long home runs while others, recounting the same home run, did not mention the distance.

The following are the longest known Wrigley Field home runs. They are divided into two lists—those before bleacher reconstruction in 1937 and those beginning in 1938.

The 1914-1937 list includes home runs that have been documented to have:

- hit on or near the field-level scoreboard, at least 440 feet from home plate
- were noteworthy mentions in newspaper accounts

The 1938 to date list includes home runs that have been documented to have:

- hit buildings across the street
- landed on Kenmore Avenue

- passed over the blocked-off center field bleachers onto the street
- landed in the center field bleachers to at least the aisle beyond the blocked out seats
- beginning in 2015, hit at least half way up the left field video board

Each listing is in chronological order. Newspaper quotes and other documentation are included. The acronym "nsm" means "no such mention," when papers didn't mention anything unusual about the length of the home run. The cited newspapers are:

AP	. . .	Associated Press
CA	. . .	Chicago American/Chicago's American
DT	. . .	Chicago Daily Times
CHA	. . .	Chicago Herald-American
CHE	. . .	Chicago Herald and Examiner
CinE	. . .	Cincinnati Enquirer
CinP	. . .	Cincinnati Post
DH	. . .	Daily Herald
DN	. . .	Chicago Daily News
LAT	. . .	Los Angeles Times
MS	. . .	Milwaukee Sentinel
MJ	. . .	Milwaukee Journal
MG	. . .	Montreal Gazette
PI	. . .	Philadelphia Inquirer
PP	. . .	Pittsburgh Press
PPG	. . .	Pittsburgh Post-Gazette
NYT	. . .	New York Times
RMN	. . .	Rocky Mountain News (Denver)
ST	. . .	Chicago Sun-Times
STPD	. . .	St. Louis Post-Dispatch
Tr	. . .	Chicago Tribune

DOCUMENTED LONG HOME RUNS 1914-1937

Hack Wilson . . . vs. Boston, May 23, 1926

"The longest home run ever knocked at the north side park . . . against the scoreboard" Tr

"Terrific home run over the deep-center field" CHE

"Cleared the screen in deep left-center" CHE

Hack Wilson . . . vs. Pittsburgh, June 24, 1928

"Into the farthest upper corner of the stand in left center. Four feet more toward center and it would have knocked numbers out of the score board" Tr

"It was a prodigious poke . . . next to the top row of the left center field bleachers" CHE

"Into the center field bleachers" DN

Hack Wilson . . . vs. Brooklyn, May 6, 1930

"Landed high up against the scoreboard" Tr

"Cleared the iron fence in deep center field" CHE

"Over the fence under the scoreboard" CHE

"Hit the centerfield fence under the scoreboard" CHE

"Wilson hit a home run over the center-field fence . . . one of the longest of his career" DN

"Into the center-field bleachers" DN

"Found its resting place under the shadow of the scoreboard" NYT

Kiki Cuyler . . . vs. New York, August 31, 1932

"Hit the scoreboard on the wing—a feat rarely accomplished in the history of Wrigley Field" Tr

"A prodigious home run drive into the deepest sector of the center field stands" CHE

"Cuyler lined a triple to the fence beneath the scoreboard" DN
(nsm NYT)

Babe Ruth . . . vs. New York Yankees, October 1, 1932

"A 440-foot ride to the center field flagpole, a liner without equal in the
history of Wrigley Field" DT
"You know that big flag pole just to the right of the scoreboard beyond
center field? Well, that's 436 feet from the home plate. Ruth's drive
went past that flag pole and hit the box office at Waveland and Sheffield Avenues" Tr
"The longest home run ever hit in the park." Tr
"Came down alongside the flag pole and disappeared behind the corner
formed by the scoreboard and the end of the right-field bleachers" NYT

Chuck Klein . . . vs. St. Louis, April 28, 1934

"Almost a park record breaker for distance . . . the ball dropping into
the far end of the right field bleacher just a few feet short of the
scoreboard. Only . . . Babe Ruth, Hack Wilson and Rogers Hornsby
have hit 'em farther at Wrigley Field" Tr
"In dead centerfield, out by the flag pole, practically as long as the one
Babe Ruth hit, to much the same spot" CHE
"Far out into the dead center-field bleachers, a tremendous wallop" DN
"A tremendous drive over the right field stand" NYT

DOCUMENTED LONG HOME RUNS
1938-DATE

Bill Nicholson . . . vs. St. Louis, April 24, 1948

"Whacked his homer into Sheffield" Tr
"Smashed his homer into Sheffield Avenue" ST
"The Pafko and Nicholson drives going into the streets beyond the ball-
park" CHA

"Walloped one over the right field fence" STPD
(nsm DN)

*This home run and the Clemente 1959 home run are frequently cited as
"just missing" the scoreboard. If it did, it did not make an enormous
impression on the newspapermen who saw it that day.*

Ralph Kiner . . . vs. Pittsburgh, September 3, 1949

"Far over left center field bleachers—485 ft." Jenkinson, p.101
"Into the street behind left center" Tr
"A tremendous one over the left-center bleachers, some 400 feet away"
PPG
"The ball sailed over the left-center wall and landed on a street beyond
Wrigley Field" PP
(nsm ST, CHA, DN)

Bill Serena . . . vs. New York, August 23, 1950

"Promenade deck of center field" Tr
"Far up into the center field bleacher" ST
(nsm CHA, DN, NYT)

Hank Sauer . . . vs. Philadelphia, August 28, 1950

"Against a house near the ball park" AP
"Tremendous homer of the day . . . against a house at 3701 Kenmore" ST
(nsm Tr, PI)

Hank Sauer . . . vs. Milwaukee, April 22, 1953

"Into Waveland av., over the base of the pyramid that forms the crown
of the center field bleachers" Tr
"Cleared the left-centerfield bleachers and landed on Waveland Av." ST
"Into Waveland av" CA
"Slammed one over the left centerfield bleachers" MS

Eddie Mathews . . . vs. Milwaukee, April 22, 1953

""This epic smash cleared the third 'step-up' atop the right center field
bleachers and flew 500 feet" Jenkinson, p. 39

"Into Sheffield av" Tr

"Into Sheffield av" CA

"At least a 450-foot smash which cleared the right centerfield bleachers
with plenty to spare" MS

"Local press greybeards could not recall a left handed hitter ever clubbing a ball as far." MS

"Traveled at least 500 feet. . . .Was the longest by a left handed batter
in Wrigley field history" MJ

(nsm ST)

Joe Adcock . . . vs. Milwaukee, August 15, 1953

"Across Waveland and up Kenmore" Tr

"Over Waveland . . . bouncing north on Kenmore" ST

"Tremendous drive . . . into Waveland av" CA

"Homer over the leftfield bleachers" MS

Roberto Clemente . . . vs. Pittsburgh, May 17, 1959

"An estimated 450 feet" Tr

"About 450 feet as it sailed over the fenced-in corner of the center field
seats and landed on Waveland av." CA

"Clemente hit the ball out of the park in center field" PPG

"Clemente's drive was truly one of tape measure distance and was estimated at close to 500 feet" PP

" . . . That cleared the left-center bleachers touched off some excitement . . . Players and fans said they never before had seen a ball go
over that section and it was close to a 500-foot sock" PP

"It passed out of view over the left-center bleachers and it must have
gone close to 500 feet . . . Even the Cubs admit it was the first one
they ever saw leave the park at that spot. Ernie Banks said later he

never hit one over that fence and never saw one hit as far as this one.
Even Rogers Hornsby acknowledged it was the longest he ever saw
hit at Wrigley Field."—Dick Groat PP

"Just to the left field side of the scoreboard. That's the longest one I've
ever seen hit there and we all agreed it must have traveled more than
500 feet"—Banks Tr 7/6/69

(nsm ST, DN)

*This home run and Nicholson's 1948 shot onto Sheffield Avenue have been
cited dozens of times as being home runs that "just missed" the scoreboard. If this home run did pass over the "fenced-in corner" of the left
field bleachers, it missed the scoreboard by nearly 100 feet. It was an
epic shot, but Mathews's 4/22/53 and Sosa's 4/28/95 and 5/8/00 home
runs were similar shots and were probably at least as close to the scoreboard as Clemente's.*

Sammy Taylor . . . vs. Philadelphia, May 19, 1959

"Tremendous homer into the second tier of the center field bleachers" Tr

"Tape-measure wallop" ST

"Into the center field bleachers" CA

(nsm DN)

Don Cardwell . . . vs. Cincinnati, June 29, 1961

"Landed in a yellow convertible parked in Kenmore avenue" Tr

"In open convertible parked on Westside of Kenmore 20 feet north of
Waveland" ST

"Plus 450-foot homer over the back of the outfield bleachers" CinE

(nsm CA, DN)

Orlando Cepeda . . . vs. San Francisco, July 4, 1961

"Plus-500 foot homer" Tr

"Landed in the second section of the center field bleachers, some six
rows up" CA

"Into the upper section of the centerfield bleachers, above the bleacher concession stand" DN

(nsm ST)

This may be the longest documented home run ever to stay inside the ballpark. It's probably the closest a home run ever came to hitting the 1937 scoreboard, falling about fifty feet short.

Joe Adcock . . . vs. Milwaukee, September 3, 1961

"A 500 foot homer" Tr

"Driving it an estimated 500 feet into the street" CA

"Sailed across Waveland Av . . . hit an apartment building two doors beyond." ST

"A tape-measure homer" MS

Willie Mays . . . vs. San Francisco, May 5, 1962

"500 foot blast over the left centerfield bleachers" CA

"Sailed out of the park over the vacant centerfield bleachers" CA

"Over the vacant centerfield bleachers" ST

(nsm Tr)

Ron Santo . . . vs. Los Angeles, August 8, 1963

"It bounded down the middle of Kenmore avenue" Tr

"Ruthian drive that sailed over . . . Waveland Av and when last seen was bouncing north on Kenmore Av. ST

"Over the left field bleachers" CA

(nsm DN, LAT)

Ron Santo . . . vs. Philadelphia, April 17, 1964

"Bounced far into Kenmore . . . 500-footer at worst" Tr

"Monstrous home run" DN

(nsm ST, CA)

Willie Stargell . . . vs. Pittsburgh, May 6, 1965

"Clearing Sheffield avenue and bouncing against a building" Tr

"A tremendous sock that almost broke a window" ST

"First of his two monumental home runs over the right field wall" PPG

(nsm PP)

Only one home run hit a Sheffield Avenue building on a fly (Dunn 2008) because of fewer left-handed hitters and more trees along the east side of Sheffield Avenue. Stargell's was the next closest.

Dick Simpson . . . vs. St. Louis, April 13, 1968

"Tremendous homer on the ramp atop the blocked-off center field seats" Tr

"Into the vacant center field seats" CA

(no article in ST, STPD)

Dave Kingman . . . vs. New York, April 14, 1976

"Struck the porch of the third house from Waveland Ave. corner on the fly" Tr

"Smacked into the upper story of the third house on Kenmore" NYT

"May have been as towering a blast as ever left Wrigley Field" DN

"It bounded high off Waveland Av about 420 feet away in left" ST

Mike Schmidt . . . vs. Philadelphia, April 17, 1976

"Carried into the second half of the centerfield bleachers, above the Astroturf" ST

"Into upper level of the center field bleachers—475 ft" Jenkinson, p. 33

(nsm Tr, DN)

Dave Kingman . . . vs. Atlanta, August 15, 1978

"Rattled birds' nests in a tree some 50' beyond Waveland . . . of 500-foot nature" Tr

"Long home run" ST

Dave Kingman . . . vs. Montreal, April 20, 1979

"Cross Waveland Avenue . . . northward bounce up Kenmore" Tr
"Was probably 450 feet or more . . . landed on Kenmore Ave" ST
"Kingman would lose a ball into the North Side of Chicago" MG
"Over Waveland Ave. in left field—475 ft." Jenkinson, p.104

Dave Kingman . . . vs. Philadelphia, May 17, 1979 (1ˢᵗ inning)

"Hit the building" at 1032 Waveland (ST photo)
    (nsm Tr)

Dave Kingman . . . vs. Philadelphia, May 17, 1979 (6ᵗʰ Inning)

Off the third house on the east side of Kenmore Ave. (WGN-TV)
    "A solo ICBM" PI
The ball hit the same house as Kingman's 4/14/76 blast. Today Kingman hit
    two of the longest home runs in Wrigley Field history in one afternoon."

Doug Frobel . . . vs. Pittsburgh, June 26, 1984

"Went about 450 feet in dead center" Tr
"Into the upper bleachers below the scoreboard" ST
"Came down about 20 rows up in the center field bleachers." PPG
"Traveled nearly 500 feet." PP

George Foster . . . vs. New York, June 27, 1985

"onto Waveland Ave." Tr
"Over the left field bleachers into the trees in the street beyond" NYT
"To building across street in left—480 ft." Jenkinson, p. 42
    (nsm ST)

Eric Davis . . .vs. Cincinnati, May 21, 1987

"Long three-run homer" Tr

"Was prodigious. It cleared the left-center mesh fence at its farthest
    point" ST
"470 ft shot . . . that landed onto Waveland Avenue" NYT
    (nsm CinE, CinP)

Barry Bonds . . . vs. Pittsburgh, April 17, 1988

"Hit one 475 Kingmanesque feet into the upper section of the bleachers
    in center field" Tr
"Landed in the second tier of bleachers in center" ST
"Into the fifth row of the upper level of the bleachers in center field" PPG
"Carried into the upper levels of the bleachers, easily 500 feet." PP

Ryan Klesko . . .vs. Atlanta, April 15, 1994

"landed near the WGN-Ch. 9 camera hut" Tr
    (nsm ST)

Andres Galarraga . . . vs. Montreal, July 5, 1994

"Hit the second floor of the two-story house on Waveland Avenue just
    opposite the left field flagpole" Tr
"On a small house between the Waveland Avenue apartment buildings"
    ST

Sammy Sosa . . . vs. Montreal, April 28, 1995

"One of the longest home runs in recent memory, over the tv camera
    shed in left-center field" Tr
"Over centerfield TV booth" ST

Doug Frobel . . . vs. Pittsburgh, June 26, 1984

"Went about 450 feet in dead center" Tr
"Into the upper bleachers below the scoreboard" ST
"Came down about 20 rows up in the center field bleachers." PPG
"Traveled nearly 500 feet." PP

Sammy Sosa . . . vs. New York, May 5, 1996

"Speeding toward the window of an apartment building some 450 feet away on Waveland" Tr

Hit the 2ⁿᵈ" floor of 1032 Waveland ST

"Sailed over Waveland Avenue and broke a second-story window." NYT

Sammy Sosa . . . vs. Milwaukee, September 13, 1998 (5ᵗʰ inning)

"A 480-foot, two-run homer onto Waveland" Tr

"It was one of two 480-footers [for Sosa] on this date" Jenkinson, p. 98

"480 feet to Waveland" ST

Sammy Sosa . . . vs. Milwaukee, September 13, 1998 (9ᵗʰ inning)

"Both balls landed on Waveland Avenue. The second one rolled up an alley" Tr

"Again reached Waveland" ST

"It was one of two 480-footers [for Sosa] on this date" Jenkinson, p. 98

Sosa hit numbers 61 and 62 for the season this day.

Sammy Sosa . . . vs. May 4, 1999 vs. Colorado

"485-foot shot . . . onto Kenmore Avenue" Tr
    (nsm ST)

Sammy Sosa . . . vs. New York, July 30, 1999

"465-foot blast into the centerfield bleachers" Tr

"The homer was one of Sosa's longest and nearly reached the scoreboard" ST

Mike Piazza . . . vs. New York, July 30, 1999

"High over bleachers in deep left center field—471 ft." Jenkinson, p. 46
    (nsm Tr, ST, LAT)

Sammy Sosa . . . vs. Colorado, August 20, 1999

"Launched a drive almost 500 feet" Tr

"Two mammoth home runs" ST

"500 foot rocket launch" DH
    (nsm RMN)

Glenallen Hill . . . vs. San Francisco, August 25, 1999

"495-foot, pinch-hit home run" Tr
    (nsm ST)

Sammy Sosa . . . vs. Milwaukee, September 19, 1999

"Estimated at 485 feet, though some thought it actually went more than 500" Tr

"Sailing beyond Waveland Avenue and bouncing down Kenmore" ST

Sammy Sosa . . . vs. Milwaukee, May 8, 2000

"Carried over the center-field camera nest in the bleachers' upper deck and blasted onto Waveland" ST
    (nsm Tr)

Glenallen Hill . . . vs. Milwaukee, May 11, 2000

"Landing on the rooftop of the three-story building at the corner of Waveland and Kenmore Avenues" Tr

This is the only home run to land on the roof of a building across the street—1032 Waveland.

Sammy Sosa . . . vs. Arizona, June 7, 2000

"Mammoth drive into the top section of the center field bleachers" Tr

"To the second tier of bleachers in center field, an estimated 520-feet from home plate" DH

"Estimated at 520 feet" ST

Adam Dunn . . . vs. Cincinnati, October 2, 2001

"A massive blast over the right center field bleachers that flew nearly 500 feet" Jenkinson, p. 139
(nsm Tr, ST)

Sammy Sosa . . . vs. Milwaukee, June 24, 2003

"Onto Kenmore Avenue . . . an estimated 520 feet" ST
Bill Jenkinson, in Baseball's Ultimate Power, *said the ball traveled 520 feet.* (Jenkinson p. 98*) But Moe Mullins claimed Sosa's shot beat Kingman's home runs by about six feet.* (Tr 6/26/03 4-3-4) *The website, ballhawk. com, said this: "Well, it's official - 536 feet, 2 inches, or at least as official as GPS gets. . . . Add to that, eyewitness accounts from Rich and Moe on the two Kingman blasts ('76 with the Mets and '79 with the Cubs), everyone seems to be in agreement that the Sosa home run is the longest one ever hit out of Wrigley. (http://www.ballhawk.com/wc.htm)*

Sammy Sosa . . . vs. Pittsburgh, September 27, 2003

"Landed in the first row of upper section of the center-field bleachers" Tr
"Carried over the shrubbery in straightaway center field" DH
"The 450-foot homer, which landed in the center field seats" PPG
(nsm ST)

Sammy Sosa . . . vs. Florida, October 8, 2003

495'—off camera hut—Game 2 of NLCS
"It traveled over the TV camera shack in center" ST

Moises Alou . . . vs. San Francisco, May 20, 2004

"Over left field wall" ST
"Onto Waveland Avenue" DH
"Cleared Waveland, went through the trees and landed near the front porch of the Budweiser house before bouncing into the next yard." www.ballhawk.com
(nsm Tr)

Adam Dunn . . . vs. Cincinnati, July 10, 2008

Just below 3rd floor of 3633 Sheffield (the "Eamus Catuli" building (WGN-TV))
"Hit one that might still be rolling down Sheffield Avenue. CinE
(nsm ST)
The longest right field home run in park history

Milton Bradley . . . vs. San Diego, May 12, 2009

to aisle of center field bleachers (WGN-TV)

Ryan Braun . . . vs. Milwaukee, August 30, 2012

"Monstrous home runs to Jonathan Lucroy and Ryan Braun" Tr
"The ball hit the facing of the camera building . . . where Sammy Sosa used to hit 'em." chicagocubsonline.com

Anthony Rizzo . . . vs. Texas, April 18, 2013

To right center field against the fence beyond the stairs leading up to the bleachers (WGN-TV)

Kris Bryant . . . vs. Washington, May 26, 2015

Hit high off the left side of the video board (CSN)
"According to Statcast™ Bryant's home run traveled 477 feet." ESPN.com

Kris Bryant . . . vs. Arizona, September 6, 2015

Hit top half of left side of left field video board (WGN)
"Calculated at 467 feet . . . according to ESPN Stats and Info." ESPN.com
"Was projected by Statcast™ to travel 495 feet" MLB.com

ENDNOTES

INTRODUCTION

1. Joe Mock, *Joe Mock's Ballpark Guide* (Round Rock, Texas: Grand-slam Enterprises, Inc., 2001), 35.

PROLOGUE

1. David Ibata, "Clubs Bat Around Town Since Opening in 1876," *Chicago Tribune*, April 13, 1986.

CHAPTER 1: FIRST INNING—1914-1926—YOUTHFUL EXUBERANCE

1. "Property Owners File Petition Against Fed Park," *Chicago Examiner*, February 22, 1914.

2. James Clarkson, "Feds Will Not Start Season," *Chicago Examiner*, January 11, 1914.

3. "Ban Johnson Declares War to Finish on Feds," *Chicago Examiner*, March 6, 1914.

4. Charles H. Weeghman, "Chifeds Spend $412,000—Weeghman Gives Facts," *Chicago Examiner*, April 5, 1916.

5. Sam Weller, Sam Wellerisms, Chicago Tribune, August 16, 1914.

6. Sam Weller, "Tinx Lose Two to Packers; Drop Fed Lead," *Chicago Tribune*, October 7, 1914.

7. Sam Weller, "Chicago Welcomes Feds, Who Triumph Over Packers, 9-1," *Chicago Tribune*, April 24, 1914.

8. Larry Woltz, "Sunshine and Thompson Help Baseball's Start," *Chicago Examiner*, April 11, 1915.

9. "Notes of the Whales," Chicago Tribune, June 2, 1915.

10. James Clarkson, "34,000 See Chicago Feds Win Pennant," *Chicago Examiner*, October 4, 1915.

11. I.E. Sanborn, "Peace Follows Baseball War as Year Ends," *Chicago Tribune*, December 26, 1915.

12. "Cub 'Faness' Objects to Club's Transfer," *Chicago Tribune*, December 21, 1915.

13. Bill Bailey, "Cubs Tie Up Opener at Home," *Chicago American*, April 21, 1916.

14. I.E. Sanborn, "Bombard Ump After Giants Beat Cubs, 6-4," *Chicago Tribune*, May 15, 1916.

15. G.W. Axelson, "United Chicago Today to Greet Tinker's Players," *Chicago Herald*, April 20, 1916.

16. Charles Dryden, "Cubs and Pirates Open on North Side To-Day with Plenty of Fuss," *Chicago Examiner*, April 11, 1917.

17. "No Game by Cubs Because of Cold," *Chicago Tribune*, June 8, 1917.

18. George C. Rice, "Cub Opening Rouses Fans," *Chicago Daily Journal*, April 11, 1917.

19. I.E. Sanborn, "Help Win War by Conserving Our Baseballs." *Chicago Tribune*, February 10, 1918.

20. "Aleck's Farewell," *Chicago Tribune*, April 27, 1918.

21. "Fans Glad Teams Will Go To Work," *Chicago Tribune*, September 12, 1918.

22. Walter Eckersall, "Wintery Looking Fans in Furs Warm Up As Soon As Play Begins," *Chicago Tribune*, April 25, 1919.

23. Charles Dryden, "Alexander is on the Job, the Mascot Reports, So the Cubs are All Set to Go," *Chicago Herald and Examiner*, April, 23, 1919.

24. Walter Eckersall, "More Football Than Ever With 'Pro' Elevens in Action," *Chicago Tribune*, September 25, 1919.

25. James Crusinberry, "Bleachers Not Expensive Enough for Big League Fans," *Chicago Tribune*, December 22, 1919.

26. Oscar C. Reichow, "Cubs Take Workout to Prepare for Reds," *Chicago Daily News*, April 21, 1920.

27. Harvey T. Woodruff, "Charles W. Murphy Again Stockholder in Chicago," *Chicago Tribune*, February 14, 1919.

28. James Crusinberry, "Alex Pitches Whale of a Game and Cubs Beat Pirates, 2-0," *Chicago Tribune*, September 6, 1920.

29. James Crusinberry, "Cubs Go 17 Innings To Beat Cards, 3-2; Aleck Mound Hero." *Chicago Tribune*, October 2, 1920.

30. George Phair, "Breakfast Food," *Chicago Herald and Examiner*, April 14, 1921.

31. James Crusinberry, "Card Wreckers Pound Out 8-3 Win Over Cubs." *Chicago Tribune*, July 4, 1921.

32. James Crusinberry, "Braves Scorch Cubs, 10-2, By Red Hot Hitting," *Chicago Tribune*, June 15, 1921.

33. Ed Sullivan, "Cubs Beat Reds, 3-1, Before 20,000," *Chicago Herald and Examiner*, April 21, 1922.

34. Frank Smith, "20,000 Fans See Cubs Beat Reds; in Second Place," *Chicago Tribune*, April 21, 1922.

35. Edward Moore, "Experiment Justified," *Chicago Tribune*, July 13, 1922.

36. Frank Smith, "Cut Rates For Boys at Bears' Football Games," *Chicago Tribune*, November 10, 1922.

37. "Giants Trim Cubs Before 27,000 Fans," *New York Times*, August 21, 1922.

38. Henry S. White, "World's Largest Single-deck Grandstand," *Popular Mechanics,* June 1923, 723-724.

39. Jess Altenberg, "A 'Main Street' Viewpoint of a Week in Baseball," *Sporting News*, December 20, 1923, 5.

40. Frank Schreiber, "Ruether Turns Cubs Back as Robins Win, 5-1," *Chicago Tribune*, August 7, 1923.

41. Lambert G. Sullivan, "Chicago's Greatest Ball Crowd at Game," *Chicago Herald and Examiner,* April 18, 1923.

42. Irving Vaughan, "Record Crowd Sees Reds Beat Our Cubs Twice," *Chicago Tribune,* May 31, 1924.

43. Elmer Douglass, "Say You! Meet Elmer, Radio Baseball Fan," *Chicago Tribune,* October 2, 1924.

44. "Memorial Day Sports," In the Wake of the News, *Chicago Tribune,* May 30, 1924.

45. Warren W. Brown, "Alex' Arm and Bat Too Mighty for Pirates," *Chicago Herald and Examiner,* April 15, 1925.

46. James S. Carolan, "Football," *New York Times,* November 23, 1925.

47. Notes of the Cubs and Sox, *Chicago Tribune,* May 12, 1926.

CHAPTER 2: SECOND INNING: 1927-1939—LEAGUE LEADER

1. Jimmy Corcoran, "Revamped Park Set for Cubs' Opening Tilt on April 12," *Chicago American,* April 7, 1927.

2. Gene Morgan, "Right in Morgan's Mitt," *Chicago Daily News,* April 12, 1927.

3. Irving Vaughan, "Cubs Drop Series Final to Giants, 7-5," *Chicago Tribune,* September 13, 1927.

4. Warren Brown, "Brown Jots Down Notes on Gala Opening," *Chicago Herald and Examiner,* April 19, 1928.

5. Irving Vaughan, "Cubs Whip Giants, 2-1, 5-4; In 2D Place," *Chicago Tribune,* July 22, 1928.

6. Harvey T. Woodruff, "Why Cubs are Popular," In the Wake of the News, *Chicago Tribune,* April 19, 1928.

7. It Might Interest You to Know That—, *Chicago Tribune,* September 3, 1929.

8. Arch Ward, "Another Defeat and 50,000 Fans Go Home 'Blue'," *Chicago Tribune,* October 10, 1929.

9. Harvey T. Woodruff, "Baseball," In the Wake of the News, *Chicago Tribune,* August 1, 1929.

10. Irving Vaughan, "Play First Night Baseball Game," *Chicago Tribune,* May 3, 1930.

11. Edward Burns, "Cubs Win, 10-9; Then Tie in 11 Innings, 3-3," *Chicago Tribune,* August 17, 1930.

12. James Crusinberry, "Blake Driven off Slab in Eighth Inning," *Chicago Daily News,* August 21, 1930.

13. "Left Field Sod Looked Good to This Big Crowd," *Chicago Daily Times,* April 14, 1931.

14. Cub Notes, *Chicago Tribune,* April 15, 1931.

15. "Cubs Apply for Writ to Prevent Ticket Scalpers," *Chicago Tribune,* August 30, 1931

16. Wayne K. Otto, "Cubs Win Twin Bill, 16-6, 7-6," *Chicago Herald Examiner,* September 21, 1931.

18. "Sports World Loses True Friend in Death of Wrigley," *Chicago Tribune,* January 27, 1932.

18. Howard Mann, "Keep Away From Mike and You'll Be All Right, Hack," *Chicago Daily News,* April 20, 1932.

19. "Babe Airs His Views of Cubs and 'Chiseling'," *Chicago Tribune,* September 30, 1932.

20. Herbert Simons, "Yankee Homers Beat Cubs, 7-5," *Chicago Daily Times,* October 2, 1932.

21. Peter Golenbock, Wrigleyville: A Magical History Tour of the Chicago Cubs (New York, NY: St. Martin's Press, 1996), 238-239.

22. Ed Sherman, "New Footage Refutes Ruth 'Called Shot'," *Chicago Tribune,* December 24, 1999.

23. Edgar Munzel, "Babe Begs for One Season in Wrigley Field," *Chicago Herald and Examiner,* October 2, 1932.

24. "Build Fountain in Memory of William Wrigley," *Chicago Tribune,* June 27, 1933.

25. Arch Ward, "Bidwell Buys Cardinal Pro Football Team," *Chicago Tribune,* September 6, 1933.

26. Jimmy Corcoran, "Beer, Hot Dogs, Band Ready for Cub Fans," *Chicago American,* April 11, 1933.

27. *"To Keep Chicago Fans Informed," Sporting News,* March 22, 1934, 4.

28. Harry Neily, "Visiting Major League Parks—Wrigley Field," *The Sporting News*, January 11, 1934, 5.

29. Wayne K. Otto, "Cubs Drill Here Today," *Chicago Herald and Examiner*, April 15, 1935.

30. "10,000 Camp Out All Night for Tickets," *Chicago Herald and Examiner*, October 1, 1935.

31. "Thousands Wait in Bleacher Line," *Chicago Daily Times*, October 4, 1935.

32. Edward Geiger, "'Scalping Evil Can be Stopped if Public Refuses to Pay Price'," *Chicago American*, October 2, 1935.

33. Arch Ward, Talking it Over, *Chicago Tribune*, June 3, 1936.

34. Ed Burns, "Wrigley Field, Chicago, 'Game's Most Beautiful Park'," *The Sporting News*, October 6, 1938, 2.

35. "Old Babe Ruth Landmark at Cub Park Destroyed," *Los Angeles Times*, August 10, 1937.

36. Edward Burns, "New Wrigley Field Blooms in Scenic Beauty—and Scoffers Rush to Apologize," *Chicago Tribune*, September 12, 1937.

37. Warren Brown, "Bleachers Hail Marty," *Chicago Herald and Examiner*, April 23, 1938.

38. Dick Farrington, Fanning with Farrington, *The Sporting News*, September 16, 1937, 4.

39. Edgar Munzel, "Terry Comments on Cub Bleachers," Sports Showup, *Chicago Herald and Examiner*, September 25, 1937.

40. Charles Bartlett, "Bleacher Fans Wait All Night to Buy Tickets," *Chicago Tribune*, October 5, 1938.

41. Ross Greenburg, (Executive Producer), *When it was a Game* (New York, NY: Black Canyon Productions, 1991), DVD.

42. John P. Carmichael, "Cubs Dandies Sport Raglan Sleeved Shirts," *Chicago Daily News*, April 16, 1938.

43. Bay View. In the Pressbox, *The Sporting News*, April 17, 1941, 2.

44. "Big Season Visioned by Bradley, Wrigley," *The Sporting News*, January 5, 1939, 10.

45. Hy Turkin, "Homers in Majors Vary from 257 to 505 Feet," *The Sporting News*, June 1, 1939, 2.

CHAPTER 3: THIRD INNING—1940-1949—STANDING STILL

1. "Wrigley Takes Active Command!" *Chicago Daily Times*, April 21, 1940.

2. J.G. Taylor Spink, 'Three and One' Looking Them Over with J.G. Taylor Spink, *The Sporting News*, August 1, 1940, 4.

3. "Organ Music to Soothe Cub Fans," *The Sporting News*, May 1, 1941, 4.

4. "N.Y. Writers Give Wrigley Bean Ball Tip," *Chicago Tribune*, June 26, 1941.

5. J.G. Taylor Spink, 'Three and One' Looking Them Over with J.G. Taylor Spink, *The Sporting News*, July 3, 1941, 4.

6. "Wrigley Says Cubs May Yet Install Lights," *Chicago Tribune*, March 21, 1942.

7. Fay Young, Through the Years, *Chicago Defender*, May 30, 1942.

8. "Wrigley Field Guests to Buy Defense Stamps," *Chicago Tribune*, April 12, 1942.

9. "On Your Day Off—Take the Strain Off Cub Slogan," *Chicago Cubs News*, June 22, 1943, vol 2 no. 8.

10. Irving Vaughan, "Indignant Cub Fans are Only Wasting Time," *Chicago Tribune*, May 20, 1943.

11. Edgar Munzel, "Cubs Nose Out Sox, 7-6," *Chicago Sun*, April 18, 1944.

12. "Chicago Joins U.S. in Honoring Radar Industry," *Chicago Tribune*, September 11, 1944.

13. "Pleasant Park Gets Assist on Cub Crowds," *The Sporting News*, June 29, 1944, 10.

14. Arch Ward, In the Wake of the News, *Chicago Tribune*, October 8, 1945.

15. Edward Prell, "7th Game Ticket Fans Besiege Cubs' Park," *Chicago Tribune*, October 9, 1945.

16. *"Getting Whose Goat?"* (photo), *Chicago Sun*, October 6, 1945.

17. "Efficient Andy Frain Gets Customer's Goat," *Chicago Sun*, October 7, 1945.

18. William Granger, "A City Landmark—Billy Goat," *Chicago Tribune*, December 26, 1967.

19. Tom Siler, "Cubs Opening Ceremony Over in 4 Minutes," *Chicago Sun*, April 21, 1946.

20. "Wrigley Spikes Story Cubs May Buy Riverview," *Chicago Tribune*, August 8, 1946.

21. Fay Young, Through the Years, *Chicago Defender*, April 19, 1947.

22. "Robinson Makes Chicago Debut; Fans are Orderly," *Chicago Defender*, May 24, 1947.

23. Edward Prell, "Hack Receives Gifts, Cheers from 27,523," *Chicago Tribune*, August 31, 1947.

24. "Cubs Reiterate Stand Against Night Baseball," *Chicago Tribune*, July 1, 1947.

25. Anton Remenih, Television News and Views, *Chicago Tribune*, July 28, 1953.

26. Edward Burns, "40, 280 Watch Dodgers Win Third in Row," *Chicago Tribune*, July 22, 1948.

27. On the Air Lanes, *The Sporting News*, March 2, 1949, 28.

28. Ed Burns, "Grimm Growling About Early Games Under Arcs," *The Sporting News*, May 4, 1949, 18.

CHAPTER 4: FOURTH INNING—1950-1959—MIDDLE AGE

1. John C. Hoffman, "Wight and Schmitz Choices for Openers," *Chicago Sun-Times*, April 17, 1950.

2. Edgar Munzel, "Cavvy-Paced Cubs Battle Koslo, Giants," *Chicago Sun-Times*, July 30, 1951.

3. Edgar Munzel, "Gate Drop Shakes Cubs Into Home Talent Hunt," *The Sporting News*, October 10, 1951

4. Anton Remenih, "Wilson Blows Hot For Cubs on Wind Waves," *Chicago Tribune*, August 4, 1951.

5. Bob Broeg, "Staley Remains Cards' Stopper; Victory Rides on Bilko's Homer," *St. Louis Post-Dispatch*, April 22, 1952.

6. 1952 Chicago Cubs Scorecard, 3.

7. "Detectives to Guard Spahn on Cub Visit," *Chicago Tribune*, July 15, 1952.

8. Edgar Munzel, "'Night Ball Like Drug,' Declares Holdout Wrigley," *The Sporting News*, February 20, 1952, 10.

9. "Wrigley Lists Terms—if He Peddles Cubs," *Chicago Tribune*, July 11, 1953.

10. Howard Barry, "Win Flag First, Then Sell Cubs, Wrigley Hopes," *Chicago Tribune*, July 23, 1953.

11. Edgar Munzel, "Extra Attraction at Wrigley Field on Easter Day—Usher Pops Fan," *The Sporting News*, April 28, 1954, 2.

12. Dan Daniel, "215 Night Games in American, 239 for the National," *The Sporting News*, February 10, 1954, 20.

13. Edgar Munzel, "'Daylight Play Answer to Gate Lag'—P.K.," *The Sporting News*, February 10, 1954, 2.

14. Edgar Munzel, "Ivy Walls Inspiring? Cubs Win Only Five of 17 on Home Stay," *The Sporting News*, June 23, 1954, 9.

15. Leo Fischer, "Fans Ask Cub Night Games, Better Parking," *Chicago American*, July 6, 1955.

16. David Condon, "An Analysis of Cubs by Phil Wrigley," *Chicago Tribune*, May 18, 1956.

17. "Robert C. Dorr," Obituary, *The Sporting News*, March 6, 1957, 32.

18. "Lone Ranger and Lassie Appear in 'Round-up'," *Chicago Tribune*, May 26, 1957.

19. "Scouting Reports—American and National Leagues," *Sports Illustrated*, April 15, 1957, 83.

20. Oliver E. Kuechle, "Wrigley Deserves What Cubs are Doing," Time Out for Talk, *Milwaukee Journal*, May 9, 1958, http://news.google.com/newspapers?nid=jvrRlaHg2sAC&dat=19580509&printsec=frontpage&hl=en

21. Howard Roberts, "Cubs Three Men Shy of Flag Run," *Chicago Daily News*, July 7, 1959.

CHAPTER 5: FIFTH INNING—1960-1972—FALLING BEHIND

1. Edward Prell, "Turn Away 10,000 Fans at Cub Game," *Chicago Tribune*, July 3, 1967.
2. Larry Casey, Sports Ledger, *Chicago Daily Defender*, September 12, 1968.
3. "Residents Work to Make Block Beautiful," *Chicago Tribune*, August 15, 1963.
4. "City Puts the Wraps on Ball Park Hot Dogs," *Chicago Daily News*, May 13, 1960.
5. Richard Dozer, "New Cub Pitches No-Hitter; Aided By 4 Fine Plays," *Chicago Tribune*, May 16, 1960.
6. "Wrigley Oks Lights for Cubs; But Not For Tilts at Night," *Chicago Daily News*, October 12, 1960.
7. David Condon, In the Wake of the News, *Chicago Tribune*, April 15, 1961.
8. Richard Dozer, "Cub Teen's Homers Announce Bright Future in 5-2 Victory," *Chicago Tribune*, September 28, 1961.
9. Bill Furlong, "Practical Wrigley has Amazing Ideas," *Chicago Daily News*, August 10, 1961.
10. Skip Myslenski and Linda Kay, "It was a Fix Fixed for History," Odds & INS, *Chicago Tribune*, April 27, 1987.
11. John P. Carmichael, "Fans Loyal Despite Cubs 'Soft Sell'," The Barber Shop, *Chicago Daily News*, May 9, 1962.
12. P.K. Prefers TV," *Chicago Daily News*, July 27, 1962.
13. "Parking No Worry for P.K., Shuns Land Deal Near Field," *Chicago Sun-Times*, May 17, 1966.
14. "Baseball Si; Politics, No, Cubans Find," *Chicago Tribune*, August 5, 1963.
15. Dick Hackenberg, "Stadium Not for Sox: Allyn," *Chicago Sun-Times*, May 15, 1963.
16. Edward Prell, "19,710 Cheer the Destruction of San Francisco, 9-5, 5-4." *Chicago Tribune*, June 6, 1963.
17. "Wrigley Tells Why He Prefers Matinees," *Milwaukee Journal*, January 10, 1964, http://news.google.com/newspapers?nid=jvrR laHg2sAC&dat=19640110&printsec=frontpage&hl=en
18. Warren Brown, "Today's Major Question: Will Wrigley Be on Hand?," *Chicago's American*, April 17, 1964.
19. "The Case Against Sports Stadium," *Chicago Sun-Times*, December 28, 1964.
20. Jerome Holtzman, "New Houston Stadium Makes Others Obsolete," *Chicago Sun-Times*, September 13, 1964.
21. Bill Gleason, "Cub Fans' Enthusiasm Amazes Banks, Santo," *Chicago Sun-Times*, July 23, 1967.
22. Harry Warren, "Bears Field Antiquated, Says Roselle," *Chicago Tribune*, November 2, 1965.
23. Joe King, Clouting 'Em . . . With Joe King, *Sporting News*, July 31, 1965, 9.
24. Rick Phalen, Our Chicago Cubs: *Inside the History and the Mystery of Baseball's Favorite Franchise* (South Bend, IN: Diamond Communications, Inc.), 1992, 251.
25. Richard Dozer, "Cards in New Home—Baseball in Round," *Chicago Tribune*, May 13, 1966.
26. "Please, Let's Not Disturb the Neighbors," *The Sporting News*, April 9, 1966, 16.
27. David Condon, In the Wake of the News, *Chicago Tribune*, May 31, 1967.
28. Steven Stern, *Chicago and the Cubs: A Lifelong Love Affair*, (New York, NY: Major League Baseball Productions, 1987), VHS.
29. George Langford, "Response of Cubs' Fans Raises the Goose Bumps," *Chicago Tribune*, July 2, 1967.
30. David Condon, In the Wake of the News, *Chicago Tribune*, July 1, 1967.
31. "New Sox Park By '72: Allyn," *Chicago Tribune*, September 6, 1967.
32. George Langford, "40,000 Keep Joyous Vigil," *Chicago Tribune*, August 21, 1975.

33. "Leo is No. 1 in Applause of Cub Fans," *Chicago Tribune*, April 14, 1968.

34. David Condon, In the Wake of the News, *Chicago Tribune*, April 6, 1968.

35. Jerome Holtzman, "Cubs Nip Phils 7-6 On Homer in 11th," *Chicago Sun-Times*, April 9, 1969.

36. Jack Griffin, "Magic of Cubs is Excitement," *Chicago Sun-Times*, April 10, 1969.

37. Jerome Holtzman, "Expos Deal Cubs First Defeat 7-3," *Chicago Sun-Times*, April 13, 1969.

38. George Langford, "Cubs Beat Expos," *Chicago Tribune*, April 14, 1969.

39. Rick Talley, "Cards May Never Burst Cubs Bubble," *Chicago Today*, May 14, 1969.

40. George Langford, "Cubs It: Astro Boss," *Chicago Tribune*, June 6, 1969.

41. Donna Gill, "Bedlam in the Bleachers, or Madness at Addison," *Chicago Tribune*, June 7, 1969.

42. Leonard Koppett, "Mets Closing in on Another Record," *New York Times*, June 24, 1969.

43. Robert Marcus, "Is Fun in Bleachers Getting Out of Hand?," *Chicago Tribune*, June 29, 1969.

44. "Bum Rap," *Chicago Daily News*, June 21, 1969.

45. George Langford, "'Cubs Kicked Hell Out of Us'," *Chicago Tribune*, June 30, 1969.

46. Robert Marcus, "Why All the Fuss? Cubs Can't Lose It," *Chicago Tribune*, July 12, 1969.

47. Kenneth Denlinger, "Good Guys Wear Yellow Hats," *Washington Post*, August 3, 1969.

48. Robert Dozer, "Cubs Lose, 3-1, Before Biggest Crowd," *Chicago Tribune*, August 22, 1969.

49. Jimmy Cannon, "Cannon: Cubs are Sick," *Chicago Daily News*, September 10, 1969.

50. Rick Talley, "Cubs Aren't Panicking: Durocher," *Chicago Today*, September, 12, 1969.

51. George Vass, "Hapless Cubs Near Point of No Return," *Chicago Daily News*, September 16, 1969.

52. George Langford, "Cubs Split With Cards, Gain on Mets," *Chicago Tribune*, September 20, 1969.

53. Richard Dozer, "Cubs Fumble Again, 4-1," *Chicago Tribune*, September 21, 1969.

54. Jim Enright, "Cubs Blow Chance to Gain, 'Hand' Cards 4-1 Triumph," *Chicago Today*, September 21, 1969.

55. Edward Prell, "Cubs and Fans Finish With a Bang(ks)," *Chicago Tribune*, October 3, 1969.

56. Bill Gleason, "Bleacherites End Season Like Bums!," *Chicago Sun-Times*, October 3, 1969.

57. "Leo Disappointed But Offers No Alibi," *Chicago Daily News*, September 25, 1969.

58. Jimmy Cannon, "Santo: We All Tried . . . Gave it Everything," *Chicago Daily News*, October 2, 1969.

59. George Vass, "Cubs Fell Short But Were Fun," *Chicago Daily News*, September 26, 1969.

60. John Husar, "'Typical' Crowd Back in 'Friendly Confines'," *Chicago Tribune*, April 16, 1970.

61. Jack Griffin, "Love Children, Bums, Execs, Blithe Spirits Welcome Cubs," *Chicago Sun-Times*, April 15, 1970.

62. "Change Comes at Wrigley Field," (photo caption), *Chicago Sun-Times*, May 5, 1970.

63. Bob Logan, "Cubs ½ Game Out! Mets Today," *Chicago Tribune*, September 4, 1970.

64. Robert Marcus, "Sick Society at Ball Park," *Chicago Tribune*, April 16, 1970.

65. John McHugh, "Brrrother! Did 'Bums' Enjoy Chilling Finish!," *Chicago Today*, April 7, 1971.

66. Paul Gapp, "Blight, High Rises Take Heavy Toll on Old Homes Here," *Chicago Tribune*, October 12, 1974.

67. George Strickler, "Grange, Bronko Now Only Memories," *Chicago Tribune*, September 19, 1971.

68. John Husar, "Fans Come; Spirit Gone," *Chicago Tribune*, April 16, 1972.

69. George Langford, "Cubs Bow," *Chicago Tribune*, October 5, 1972.

CHAPTER 6: SIXTH INNING—1973-1984—NEW APPRECIATION

1. Rick Talley, "Chicago Doesn't Need Super Stadium," *Chicago Tribune*, March 4, 1973.

2. Bob Logan, "Basket, Basket; Astros Find One with Home Run," *Chicago Tribune*, May 31, 1973.

3. Ray Sons, "Young Fans Jam Cub Stands," *Chicago Daily News*, April 9, 1974.

4. Cooper Rollow, "2d Major Pro Football League is Born," *Chicago Tribune*, October 3, 1973.

5. William E. Carsley, letter to the editor, *Chicago Tribune*, October 30, 1974.

6. Richard Dozer, "Oh, Brother! Cubs Blank Dodgers, 7-0," *Chicago Tribune*, August 22, 1974.

7. Rick Talley, "Cubs Team of Future? No Way!," *Chicago Tribune*, August 7, 1975.

8. Tom Fitzpatrick, "Cub Fans Have Wrigley—That's Enough," *Chicago Sun-Times*, April 4, 1976.

9. 1977 Chicago Cubs Scorecard, 3.

10. Jerome Holtzman, "Cubs Catch Some Pennant Fever," *Chicago Sun-Times*, May 29, 1977.

11. Rick Talley, "Inspired Cubs Cap Mayor's Day," *Chicago Tribune*, June 26, 1977.

12. Jack Hurst, "On the Mound Today Art Sagel Pitching Mounds of Clay," *Chicago Tribune Magazine*, June 26, 1977.

13. Michael Zielenzinger, "Homer Heroics: Cubs Serve Up Real Gem," *Chicago Sun-Times*, April 15, 1978.

14. John Husar, "Cubs' Fans Turn Opener into Very Messy Circus," *Chicago Tribune*, April 15, 1978.

15. Ibid

16. Bob Verdi, "Niekro's Diet of Knucklers Starves Cubs," *Chicago Tribune*, August 17, 1978.

17. David Israel, "22 Cub Runs One Too Few To Stop Phils," *Chicago Tribune*, May 18, 1979.

18. Bob Verdi, "Lee Beats Cubs with Timely Support," *Chicago Tribune*, July 5, 1979.

19. David Condon, "Cubs Aren't Up For Sale, Just Reappraisal: Wrigley," In the Wake of the News, *Chicago Tribune*, August 2, 1980.

20. Larry Casey, "Cubs", Notes, *Chicago Tribune*, April 30, 1981.

21. Bob Verdi, "Holy Clinker! Harry Doesn't Carry," *Chicago Tribune*, April 16, 1982.

22. Cubs Notes, *Chicago Sun-Times*, April 14, 1984.

23. "Out of Left Field," Notes, *Chicago Tribune*, February 24, 1982.

24. Bob Verdi, "Green Says Wrigley Field Lights an Eventuality," *Chicago Tribune*, March 11, 1982.

25. Daniel Egler, "Panel Takes Dim View About Wrigley Lights," *Chicago Tribune*, April 29, 1982.

26. "Cubs," Notes, *Chicago Tribune*, June 11, 1982.

27. (speakeasy.org/~bucky/elia_tirade.html)

28. "Cubs," Notes, *Chicago Tribune*, June 12, 1983.

29. Mike Kiley, "Finks Mulls Move Out of Wrigley," *Chicago Tribune*, December 4, 1983.

30. (http://speakeasy.org/~bucky/elia_tirade.html)

31. Fred Mitchell, "Twilight Zone Scares Cubs," *Chicago Tribune*, August 23, 1984.

32. Skip Myslenski, and Linda Kay. "Once More, With Feeling," Odds & INS, *Chicago Tribune*, July 9, 1984.

33. "There's [13-0] Joy in Cubville," *Chicago Tribune*, October 3, 1984.

34. "John McDonough Quotes," *Thinkexist.com*, thinkexist.com/quotes/john_mcdonough

CHAPTER 7: SEVENTH INNING—1985-1998—LOVE AFFAIR

1. Linda Kay, "Veeck Returns to his Old Sox Home," *Chicago Tribune*, July 19, 1985.

2. Rudolph Unger and James Strong, "No Lights, Judge Tells the Cubs," *Chicago Tribune*, March 26, 1985.

3. Jerome Holtzman, "Were Cubs Losers in Lights Case?," *Chicago Tribune*, March 26, 1985.

4. Linda Kay, "Green: No Move Planned," *Chicago Tribune*, June 28, 1985.

5. Bob Logan, "A Timeless City Beauty," *Chicago Tribune*, June 28, 1985.

6. Joe Goddard, and Dave Van Dyke. "Cubs Refuse Sox' Stadium Sharing Plan," *Chicago Sun-Times*, January 12, 1986.

7. Fred Mitchell, "A Photo Finish: Ballgirl Fired," *Chicago Tribune*, July 23, 1986.

8. Fred Mitchell, "Astros Launch Cubs Toward Record Low," *Chicago Tribune*, September 4, 1986.

9. Fred Mitchell, "Sutcliffe Weak After Illness Saps 14 Lbs.," Cub Notebook, *Chicago Tribune*, May 21, 1986.

10. "Consumer Guide," Baseball '87, *Chicago Sun-Times*, April 7, 1987.

11. "Cops Net Two in Cubs Caper," *Chicago Tribune*, January 6, 1987.

12. Ira Berkow, "All is Right at Wrigley Again," *New York Times*, May 20, 1987.

13. Wes Smith, and Paul Sullivan. "Thirsty Bleacher Fans Draw Walk," *Chicago Tribune*, April 16, 1988.

14. James Strong, "Alderman Angry Over Lights Editorial," *Chicago Tribune*, February 11, 1988.

15. James Strong, "Cubs' Pitch for Lights Passes Key Council Test," *Chicago Tribune*, February 24, 1988.

16. Ibid.

17. James Strong, "Council Vote Gives Cubs Lights, 1990 All-Star Game," *Chicago Tribune*, February 26, 1988.

18. Ibid.

19. Ibid.

20. Carolyn Walkup, "Cub Runs Mean Win for Feeders," *Nation's Restaurant News*, April 3, 1989, F8.

21. Jerome Holtzman, "Lights! Action! And then . . . ," *Chicago Tribune*, August 9, 1988.

22. Paul Goldberger, "Wrigley Field: A Baseball Park that Radiates Joy," *New York Times*, September 18, 1988.

23. Tom McNamee, and Frank Burgos. "Wild Thing! Oh, Wild Fling!," *Chicago Sun-Times*, September 27, 1989.

24. Jerome Holtzman, "Wrigley Field's Birthday a Party for Young and Old," *Chicago Tribune*, April 26, 1989.

25. Alan Solomon, "Sandberg's Power Lifts NL to Homer-Derby Win," *Chicago Tribune*, July 10, 1990.

26. Rick Kogan, "CBS Wanted a Knockout, But Got a Washout on its First All-Star Telecast," *Chicago Tribune*, July 11, 1990.

27. Mike Conklin, "And Finally," Odds & INS, *Chicago Tribune*, July 16, 1990.

28. Bob Verdi, "Well, the Ballpark was Beautiful," *Chicago Tribune*, April 19, 1991.

29. Ed Sherman, "At Least Comiskey II is a Winner," *Chicago Tribune*, April 19, 1991.

30. Bill Jauss, "For Workers at New Comiskey, a Labor of Pride," *Chicago Tribune*, April 15, 1991.

31. Jay Mariotti, "Cub Management Letting Down Loyal Fans," *Chicago Sun-Times*, August 19, 1996.

32. Dave van Dyck, "Dawson Boils Over in Victory at Wrigley," *Chicago Sun-Times*, July 24, 1991.

33. Barbara Brotman, "Lifelong Fan Dies at Home—Front Row of Bleachers," *Chicago Tribune*, October 11, 1991.

34. Mike Littwin, "Camden's Nice but no Fenway or Wrigley," *Chicago Sun-Times*, April 19, 1992.

35. Alan Solomon, "Cubs' Latest Loss Yet Another Team Effort," *Chicago Tribune*, June 21, 1993.

36. Maureen O'Donnell, "Old Friends Warm Up to New Season of Hope," *Chicago Sun-Times*, April 5, 1994.

37. Joseph A. Reaves, "Officials Won't Pop Bags on Heads if Others Can See," Cubs Notes, *Chicago Tribune*, May 4, 1994.

38. Marcia C. Smith, "Walkout Strikes Fear in Some Ticket Buyers," *Chicago Tribune*, August 8, 1994.

39. Joe Goddard, "So Far, Opener Far From a Sellout," *Chicago Sun-Times*, April 28, 1995.

40. Bernie Lincicome, "Nothing's Changed, Except (Perhaps) Fans' Interest," *Chicago Tribune*, April 3, 1995.

41. Toni Ginnetti, "Cubs Sneak Through Fog," *Chicago Sun-Times*, June 9, 1996.

42. Paul Sullivan, "The More Things Change, the Better Wrigley Looks," *Chicago Tribune*, November 29, 1996.

43. Carol Slezak, "Wrigleyville Hung Up Over Ban on Scalping," *Chicago Sun-Times*, February 12, 1997.

44. Mark Puls, "Tigers' New Stadium has Wrigley Feel," *Detroit News*, October 30, 1997.

45. Phuong Le, "Fans Create Own Shrine at Wrigley," *Chicago Tribune*, February 20, 1998.

46. Mike Kiley, "Caray's Tune Lives On," *Chicago Sun-Times*, March 24, 1998.

47. (photo), *Chicago Tribune*, September 21, 1998, 1-16-1.

48. Carol Slezak, "Wrigley Summer a Glorious Season," *Chicago Sun-Times*, June 24, 1998.

CHAPTER 8: EIGHTH INNING—1999-2010—GLORIOUS UNCERTAINTY

1. Richard Hoffer, "Our Favorite Venues," *Sports Illustrated*, June 7, 1999, 98.

2. Jay Mariotti, "Wrigley Should be Midsummer Night's Dream," *Chicago Sun-Times*, May 15, 1999.

3. Richard Roeper, "Angry Fans Always Part of our National Pastime," *Chicago Sun-Times*, June 6, 2000.

4. Rick Morrissey, "Series Title or Wrigley? Cub Faithful Split," In the Wake of the News, *Chicago Tribune*, May 22, 2001.

5. Ed Sherman, "WGN-TV Makes Finale a Tribute to Harris," *Chicago Tribune*, October 8, 2001.

6. Fran Spielman, "Wrigley Changes on Deck," *Chicago Sun-Times*, June 19, 2001.

7. Carol Slezak, "Cubs Try to be Neighborly," *Chicago Sun-Times*, July 12, 2001.

8. Mike Kiley, "Cubs Plan Patriotic Night to Remember," *Chicago Sun-Times*, September 26, 2001.

9. Mike Kiley, "'Do You Want Us to Win or Not?'," *Chicago Sun-Times*, September 11, 2001.

10. Fran Spielman, "Another Cubs Swing at Improving Wrigley," *Chicago Sun-Times*, February 26, 2002.

11. Ibid.

12. Teddy Greenstein, "MacPhail Wanted Vague Notice," *Chicago Tribune*, June 23, 2002.

13. Fran Spielman, "Another Cubs Swing at Improving Wrigley," *Chicago Sun-Times*, February 26, 2002.

14. Sean Parnell, "Murphy's Bleachers," *Chibarproject.com*, http://www.chibarproject.com/Reviews/Murphy%27s/Murphy%27s.htm

15. Ira Berkow, "A Masterpiece, Rendered on Canvas of Wrigley Field," *New York Times*, June 8, 2003.

16. Rick Morrissey, "Flag Day: Sun Shines on Santo," *Chicago Tribune*, September 29, 2003.

17. Brett McNeil and Jon Yates, "Where Magic, Madness Mingle," *Chicago Tribune*, October 9, 2003.

18. Ibid.

19. Fran Spielman, "Cubs Pitch New Expansion Plan," *Chicago Sun-Times*, June 19, 2004.

20. Stephanie Zimmerman, "City Building Officials OK Wrigley Field," *Chicago Sun-Times*, July 31, 2004.

21. Paul Sullivan, "Walker Applauds Cubs Fans' Passion," *Chicago Tribune*, June 11, 2005.

22. Rick Morrissey, "Book Speaks Volumes about Cubs' Problem," In the Wake of the News, *Chicago Tribune*, July 17, 2005.

23. Rick Morrissey, "Rusch-Hour Frenzy," In the Wake of the News, *Chicago Tribune*, April 12, 2006.

24. Gordon Wittenmyer, "Dunn is Down on Wrigley," Cubs in Brief, *Chicago Sun-Times*, September 20, 2007.

25. Jay Mariotti, "Still the Star of the Show," *Chicago Sun-Times*, April 10, 2007.

26. Fran Spielman, "Zell Says He Won't Hesitate to Sell Wrigley Field Naming Rights," *Chicago Sun-Times*, February 27, 2008.

27. Rick Morrissey, "Money for Nothing," In the Wake of the News, *Chicago Tribune*, February 29, 2008.

28. Maureen O'Donnell, "Cubs Fans Erect Shrine to Futility," *Chicago Sun-Times*, October 6, 2008.

29. Jay Mariotti, "Better Solution: Sell Zell," *Chicago Sun-Times*, February 28, 2008.

30. Wayne Drehs, "Wrigley Played Well in the Snow," Espn.go.com, January 1, 2009, http://sports.espn.go.com/espn/print?id=38044 20ttype=story?columnist=dreks_wayne&id=3804420

31. Ibid.

32. Sarah Spain, "New Chicago Cubs Owner Tom Ricketts: 'We are Here to Win'," *No Spain, No Gain*, (blog) October 30, 2009, http://sarahspainblog.wordpress.com/tag/tom-ricketts/

33. Dan McGrath, "An Honor They Earned," *Chicago Tribune*, May 4, 2009.

34. Sarah Spain, "New Chicago Cubs Owner Tom Ricketts: 'We are Here to Win'," *No Spain, No Gain*, (blog) October 30, 2009, http://sarahspainblog.wordpress.com/tag/tom-ricketts/

35. Toni Ginnetti, "Half-Century After His Debut, Cubs Celebrating Santo," *Chicago Sun-Times*, June 29, 2010.

36. Toni Ginnetti, "Close Encounters," *Chicago Sun-Times*, June 14, 2010.

37. Mike Dodd, "Why do Cubs Lose? Let us Count Ways," *USA Today*, August 18, 2010.

CHAPTER 9: NINTH INNING— 2011-2016—SECURE FUTURE

1. "Mayor to Meet Cubs About Wrigley," *Chicago Tribune*, October 13, 2011.

2. Dave van Dyck, "Cubs Unveil Statue, Power," *Chicago Tribune*, August 11, 2011.

3. David Haugh, "Epstein Offers Hope It's Not All Just Rhetoric," In the Wake of the News, *Chicago Tribune*, October, 26, 2011.

4. "Ricketts: Wrigley was 'Under-Invested'," *Chicago Cubs Report* (blog), *Espnchicago.com*, April 5, 2012, http://espn.go.com/blog/chicago/cubs/post/_/id/8978/ricketts-under-invested-wrigley-needs-work

5. Gordon Wittenmyer, "Cubs Say They'll Foot Bill," *Chicago Sun-Times*, January 20, 2013.

6. Fran Spielman, "Club Owners Hit the Roof," *Chicago Sun-Times*," April 6, 2013.

7. Fran Spielman, "Cubs Win! City Council Oks Wrigley Rehab," *Chicago Sun-Times*, July 25, 2013.

8. "Cubs Prevail in a Fair Deal for Wrigley Field," *Chicago Sun-Times*, July 12, 2013.

9. Toni Ginnetti, "All Feels Right for Returning Sandberg," *Chicago Sun-Times*, April 5, 2014.

10. Fran Spielman, "Playing Hardball," *Chicago Sun-Times*, January 23, 2014.

11. David Haugh, "Finally, Ricketts' Patience Runs Out," In the Wake of the News, *Chicago Tribune*, May 23, 2014.

12. Toni Ginnetti, "Wrigley Greats Still Marvel at Park," *Chicago Sun-Times*, April 24, 2014.

13. Blair Kamin, "Wrigley's Design Helped Fashion Lasting Passion," *Chicago Tribune*, April 23, 2014.

14. "Chris Emma, "Magical 2015 Season was Just the Beginning of Cubs' Contention,"http://chicago.cbslocal.com/2015/10/21/emma-magical-2015-should-be-beginning-of-something-special-for-cubs/

15. Rick Morrissey, "In the Face of History, Young Cubs Know Exactly What They're Doing," *Chicago Sun-Times*, October 14, 2015.

CONCLUSION

1. Kevin Kaduk, Wrigleyworld: *A Season in Baseball's Best Neighborhood* (New York, NY: New American Library, 2006), 219.

2. Ibid., 217.

3. Gary Smith, "Are You Ready for a Howling, Pagan, You Tube Oktoberfiesta?," *Sports Illlustrated,* September 29, 2008, 32.

4. Ibid., 37.

BIBLIOGRAPHY

Bleacher Banter

Chicago American

Chicago's American

Chicago Cubs News

Chicago Daily Journal

Chicago Daily News

Chicago Daily Times

Chicago Defender

Chicago Examiner

Chicago Herald

Chicago Herald-American

Chicago Herald and Examiner

Chicago Sun

Chicago Tribune

Chicago Today

Christian Science Monitor

Cincinnati Enquirer

Cincinnati Post

Daily Herald

Detroit News

Los Angeles Times

Milwaukee Journal

New York Times

Philadelphia Inquirer

Pittsburgh Post-Gazette

Pittsburgh Press

Rocky Mountain News

San Francisco Chronicle

St. Louis Post-Dispatch

The Sporting News

USA Today

Washington Post

1952 Chicago Cubs scorecard

1969 *Chicago Bears Media Guide*

1977 Chicago Cubs scorecard

"Addison (3600N/940W)." www.transitchicago.com. http://www.chicago-l.org/stations/addison-howard.html

"America's Favorite Architecture." AIA150.org. http://www.favoritearchitecture.org/afa150.php

Angle, Paul M. *Philip K. Wrigley: A Memoir of a Modest Man*. Chicago, IL: Rand McNally & Company, 1975.

Anonymous. "Chicago's Historic Wrigley Field Receives a Landmark Audio Makeover." *System Contractor News,* August 2007, 48.

"Ask Tom Why: What was Chicago's Hottest Summer?" Chicagotribune.com. February 25, 2012. http://articles.chicagotribune.com/2012-02-25/news/ct-wea-0225-asktom-20120225_1_hottest-summer-warm-nights-hot-weather

Buchanan, Andy and Audra Naylor. *Wise Guide Wrigley Field*. Chicago, IL: Wise Guides, Inc., 2006.

Carr, Jason and Katelyn Thrall. *2008 Chicago Cubs Media Guide*. Chicago, IL: Chicago National League Ball Club, 2008.

"Chicago 16, Cincinnati Reds 15." www.retrosheet.org /boxesetc/1977/B07280CHN1977.htm

Chicago Building Permit #50472, May 28, 1940

Chicago Building Permit #130088, April 12, 1942

Clark, Ally. "Wrigley Field Unveils Billy Williams Statue." Nbcchicago.com. September 7, 2010. http://www.nbcchicago.com/news/sports/Wrigley-Field-Unveils-Billy-Williams-Statue-102351784.html

"Complete April 29, 1983 Lee Elia Press Conference Tirade, The." http://speakeasy.org/~bucky/elia_tirade.html

"Cubs' Kerry Wood Retiring." Espnchicago.com. May 19, 2012. http://espn.go.com/chicago/mlb/story/_/id/7945053/chicago-cubs-kerry-wood-retiring

Deane, Bill. SABR-L mailing list. October 22, 2003. http://APPLE.EASE.LSOFT.COM/archives/SABR- L.html

"Defense: Sign-off for Conelrad." Time.com. July 12, 1963. http://www.time.com/time/magazine/article/0,9171,940303,00.html

Dermon, Dave III. "The Beatles on Tour 1963-1966." http://www.dermon.com/Beatles/details/tours.htm

Dodd, Mike. "For Cubs Fans, Renaming Wrigley is Dealbreaker." Usatoday.com. February 27, 2008. http://usatoday.com/sports/baseball/nl/cubs/2008-02-27-wrigley-naming-rights_N.htm

Drehs, Wayne. "Thank Caray, Chicago for Popularity of 'Take Me Out to the Ballgame'." Espn.go.com. July 8, 2008. http:// sports.espn.go.com/mlb/news/story?id=3476916

Drehs, Wayne. "Wrigley Played Well in the Snow." Espn.go.com. http://sports.espn.go.com/nhl/columns/story?columnist=drehs_wayne&id= 3804420

Emma, Chris. "Magical 2015 Season was Just the Beginning of Cubs' Contention." http://chicago.cbslocal.com/2015/10/21/emma-magical-2015-should-be-beginning-of-something-special-for-cubs/

Enright, James E. *A Century of Diamond Memories*. Chicago, IL: Chicago National League Ballclub Inc., 1976.

Finnell, Neil. "A Real Wild Walk-off Win—Cubs 12, Brewers 11." *Chicago Cubs Online* (blog). August 30, 2012. Chicagocubsonline.com/archives/2012/08 /cubsbrewers/30.php

"Frank Corr. Holy Sepulchre Catholic Cemetery." Graveyards.com. http://graveyards.com/IL/Cook/holysepulchre/corr.html

Fulk, David and Dan Riley. *The Cubs Reader*. Boston, MA: Houghton Mifflin Company, 1991.

Garagiola, Joe. *Baseball is a Funny Game*. Philadelphia, PA: Lippencott Company, 1960.

Gold, Eddie and Art Ahrens. *The Golden Era Cubs: 1876-1940*. Chicago, IL: Bonus Books, 1985.

Gold, Eddie and Art Ahrens. *The New Era Cubs: 1941-1985*. Chicago, IL: Bonus Books, 1985.

Golenbock, Peter. *Wrigleyville: A Magical History Tour of the Chicago Cubs*. New York, NY: St. Martin's Press, 1996.

Greenberg, Hank. *Hank Greenberg: The Story of My Life*. Chicago, IL: Triumph Books, 2001.

Greenburg, Ross (Executive Producer). *When it was a Game*. New York, NY: Black Canyon Productions, 1991. VHS.

"HA-LO to be only commercial advertising in Wrigley Field; Named official premium supplier of Chicago Cubs." *The Free Library*. (1996, March 19). http://www.thefreelibrary.com/HA-LO to be only commercial advertising in Wrigley Field; Named . . . -a018104292

Hartel, William. *A Day at the Park: In Celebration of Wrigley Field*. Champaign, IL: Sagamore Publishing, 1994.

Hayner, Don and Tom McNamee. *Streetwise Chicago: A History of Chicago Street Names*. Chicago, IL: Wild Onion Books, 1988.

"History of Illinois Boxing Legislation, Rules and Regulation." Boxrec.com http://boxrec.com/media/index.php/USA:_Illinois_Laws

Hoffer, Richard. "Our Favorite Venues." *Sports Illustrated*. June 7, 1999, 94-99.

Huang, Michael (Ed.). *Wrigley Field: The Official Tour Book*. Chicago, IL: The Chicago National League Ball Club LLC, 2009.

Ibach, Bob (Editor). "Wrigley Field, PLUS." *Chicago Cubs Program Magazine*, vol. 2 no. 2 (1983): 16.

Ibach, Bob (Editor). "Ticket Information." *Chicago Cubs Program Magazine Playoff Edition 1984*, 6.

Ibach, Bob (Editor). "Classic Corner." *Vineline*, April 1986, 30.

Ibach, Bob (1987). "Lucky Charlie's Baseball Palace." *Chicago Cubs Souvenir Program*, vol. 6 no. 2 (1987): 20-23.

Ibach, Bob (Editor). *Wrigley Field: Commemorating Wrigley Field's First Night Baseball Game*. Chicago, IL: Sherman Media Company, 1988.

Ibach, Bob and Ned Colletti. *Cub Fan Mania*. New York, NY: Leisure Press, 1983.

Ibach, Bob, Colletti, Ned and Sharon Pannozzo. *1985 Chicago Cubs Media Guide*. Chicago, IL: Chicago National League Ball Club, 1985.

Jenkinson, Bill. *Baseball's Ultimate Power*. Guilford, CT: Lyons Press, 2010.

"John McDonough Quotes." Thinkexist.com. http://thinkexist.com/quotes/john_mcdonough/

Kaduk, Kevin. *Wrigleyworld: A Season in Baseball's Best Neighborhood*. New York, NY: New American Library, 2006.

Kane, Basil G. *The Official Chicago Sting Book*. Chicago, IL: Contemporary Books, 1983.

Kaplan, David. "The Changes that are Coming to Wrigley Field and the Cubs." *Chicagonow.com* (blog). http://www.chicagonow.com/blogs/david-kaplan-chicago-sports/2010/02/the-changes-that-are-coming-to-wrigley-field-and-the-cubs.html defunct

Kaplan, Joel. "Foul Grounds." *Chicago*. September 1994, 45-46.

Kates, Maxwell. SABR-L mailing list. December 27, 2003. http://sabr.org/about/sabr-l-policy-statement

Ken. *The 2004 Waveland Chronicles* (blog). Ballhawk.com. May 20, 2004. www.ballhawk.com/wc2004.htm

Ken. *The Waveland Chronicles* (blog). Ballhawk.com. June 26, 2003. www.ballhawk.com/wc.htm

Kruse, Karen. *A Chicago Firehouse: Stories of Wrigleyville's Engine 78*. Mount Pleasant, SC: Arcadia Publishing, 2001.

Kyvig, David E. *Repealing National Prohibition*. Chicago, IL: The University of Chicago Press, 1979.

Levine, Bruce and Jessie Rogers. "Ricketts: Wrigley was 'Under-invested." *Chicago Cubs Report* (blog).Espnchicago.com. April 5, 2012. http://espn.go.com/blog/chicago/cubs/post/_/id/8978/ricketts-under-invested-wrigley-needs-work

Lowry, Philip J. *Green Cathedrals: The Ultimate Celebration of Major League and Negro League Ballparks*. New York, NY: Walker Publishing Company, Inc, 2006.

"Lucky Catch-22." Sportsillustrated.cnn.com. September 16, 1998. http://sportsillustrated.cnn.com/baseball/mlb/news/1998/09/16/ball_catcher

McNamara, Chris. "'How Many Do You Need?' Why You Can Always Get a Ticket at Wrigley Field."Chicagoreader.com. October 4, 2001. http://chicagoreader.com/chiago/how-many-do-you-need/content?oid=906655

Miner, Michael. "The Family Ricketts, Obama, and the Cubs." Chicagoreader.com. May 17, 2012. http://www.chicagoreader.com/Bleader/archives/2012/05/17/ricketts

Mock, Joe. *Joe Mock's Ballpark Guide*. Round Rock, Texas: Grandslam Enterprises, Inc., 2001.

Muret, Don. "Strike Forces Cubs, White Sox to Rethink Marketing Strategies." *Amusement Business*. December 5-11, 1994, 15.

"Murphy's Bleachers." Murphysbleachers.com. http://www.murphysbleachers.com/history.html

Muskat, Carrie. "Baird Puts Heart and Soul into Wrigley's Turf." The Official Website of the Chicago Cubs, MLB Advanced Media L.C. March 26, 2011. http://mlb.mlb.com/news/article.jsp?ymd=20110326&content_id=17134656&vkey=news_chc&c_id=chc&partnerId=rss_chc

Muskat, Carrie. "Council Approved Landmark Status." Wrigleyfieldnews.com. January 27, 2004. http://www.wrigleyfieldnews.com/art79.html

Muskat, Carrie. "Cubs Spread Holiday Cheer." *Muskat Ramblings* (blog). Mlblogsnetwork. December 24, 2011. http://muskat.mlblogs.com/2011/12/24/1224-cubs-spread-holiday-cheer

Muskat, Carrie. "Wrigley Lights Up the Night for 20 Years." The Official Website of the Chicago Cubs, MLB Advanced Media L.C. August 6, 2008. http://chicago.cubs.mlb.com/news/article.jsp?ymd=20080806&content_id=3267314&vkey=news_chc&fext=.jsp&c_id=chc

Newby, Samantha and B. R. Koehnemann. *2004 Chicago Cubs Information Guide*. Chicago, IL: Chicago National League Ball Club, Inc., 2004.

Okkonen, Marc. *Baseball Uniforms of the 20th Century: The Official Major League Baseball Guide*. New York, NY: Sterling Publishing Company, Inc., 1991.

Pacyga, Dominic A. and Ellen Skerrett. *Chicago: City of Neighborhoods, Histories and Tours*. Chicago, IL: Loyola Press, 1986.

Parnell, Sean. "Murphy's Pub." Chibarproject.com. http://www.chibarproject.com/Reviews/Murphy%27s/Murphy%27s.htm

Pastier, John. SABR-L mailing list. June 1, 2009. http://sabr.org/about/sabr-l-policy-statement

Phalen, Rick. *Our Chicago Cubs: Inside the History and the Mystery of Baseball's Favorite Franchise*. South Bend, IN: Diamond Communications, Inc., 1992.

"Players Directories." Thebaseballcube.com. http://www.thebaseballcube.com/salaries/1985.shtml

"Reconstruction of Grandstand at Chicago Ballpark." *Engineering News-Record*, August 2, 1923, 172-174.

Reidenbaugh, Lowell. *Take Me Out to the Ball Park*. St. Louis, Mo: The Sporting News Publishing Co., 1983.

"Ricketts: Wrigley was 'Under-Invested'." *Chicago Cubs Report* (blog). *Espnchicago.com*. April 5, 2012. http://espn.go.com/blog/chicago /cubs/post/_/id/8978/ricketts-under-invested-wrigley-needs-work

"Ridership Reports." Chicagotransit.com. http://www.transitchicago.com/news_initiatives/ridershipreports.aspx

Ross, Andrew and David Dyte. "Washington Park." http://www.covehurst.net/ddyte/brooklyn/washington_park.html

Rubenstein, Bruce A. *Chicago in the World Series, 1903-2005: The Cubs and White Sox in Championship Play*. Jefferson, NC: McFarland & Co. Publishers, 2006.

Schoenfield, David. "Kerry Wood and the Greatest Pitched Game." Espn.go.com. May 18, 2012. http://espn.go.com/blog/sweetspot/post/_/id/24585/kerry-wood-and-the-greatest-game-pitched

"Scouting Reports—American and National Leagues." *Sports Illustrated*. April 15, 1957, 45-83

"Security." The Official Website of the Chicago Cubs, MLB Advanced Media, L.C. http://chicago.cubs.mlb.com/chc/ballpark/information/index.jsp?content=security

Shea, Stuart. *Wrigley Field: The Unauthorized Biography*. Washington D.C.: Brassey's, Inc., 2004.

Silva, Drew. "Cubs Draw Thousands for 'Movie Night at Wrigley Field.'" NBCsports.com. October 2, 2011. http://hardballtalk.nbcsports.com/2011/10/02/cubs-draw-thousands-for-movie-night-at-wrigley-field/

Smith, Gary. "Are You Ready for a Howling, Pagan, Youtube Oktoberfiesta?" *Sports Illlustrated*. September 29, 2008, 28-39.

Solomon, Burt. *The Baseball Timeline: The Day-by-Day History of Baseball from Valley Forge to the Present Day*. New York, NY: Avon Books, 2007.

Spain, Sarah. "New Chicago Cubs Owner Tom Ricketts: 'We are Here to Win'." *No Spain, No Gain* (blog). October 30, 2009. http://sarahspainblog.wordpress.com/tag/tom-ricketts/

Spinner, Jenni. "Take Me Out to the Ballgame . . . and See the New Brick Wall: A Chicago Contractor Hits a Home Run at Historic Wrigley Field." *Masonry Construction.* July-August 2004, 46-47.

Stern, Steven. *Chicago and the Cubs: A Lifelong Love Affair.* New York, NY: Major League Baseball Productions, 1987. VHS.

Stout, Glenn and Richard A. Johnson. *The Cubs: The Complete Story of Chicago Cubs Baseball.* New York NY: Houghton Mifflin Harcourt, 2007. "Three Rivers Stadium." Ballparksof-baseball.com. http://www.ballparksofbaseball.com/past/Three%20Rivers%20Stadium.htm

Van Dyck, Dave. "Ron Santo's Statue Unveiled Outside Wrigley." Chicagotribune.com. August 10, 2011. http://articles.chicagotribune.com/2011-08-10/sports/chi-cubs-unveil-santo-statue

Veeck, Bill. *Veeck as in Wreck.* New York, NY: Putnam, 1962.

Vincent, David. SABR-L mailing list. August 12, 2004. http://APPLE.EASE.LSOFT.COM/archives/ SABR-L.html

Walkup, Carolyn. "Cub Runs Mean Win for Feeders." *Nation's Restaurant News*, April 3, 1989, F8.

Walkup, Carolyn. "Hot Southport Ave. Restaurants Sizzle in Chicago." *Nation's Restaurant News,* August 19, 1996, 78-79.

Wasserman, Shelly. *Jack Brickhouse Presents Great Moments in Cubs Baseball!* Chicago, IL: Major Official Productions, Inc., 1971. 33 1/3 rpm.

White, Henry S. "World's Largest Single-deck Grandstand." *Popular Mechanics.* June 1923, 723-724.

Whittingham, Richard. *The Chicago Bears: An Illustrated History.* Chicago, IL: Rand McNally & Company, 1982.

Wiggins, Robert Peyton. *The Federal League of Baseball Clubs: The History of an Outlaw League, 1914-1915.* Jefferson, NC: McFarland, 2008.

World Series of 1945, The. Directed by Lew Fonseca. Chicago, IL: Chicago Film Studios, 1945. VHS

Yellon, Al. "1:20 A.M. Baseball: Weird, But Awesome." Sbnation.com. September 18, 2012. http://mlb.sbnation.com/2012/9/18/3352282/cubs-pirates-recap-baseball-1-am-weird-awesome

Yellon, Al. "Cubs Name Single PA Announcer for 2009." *Bleed Cubbie Blue* (blog). March 7, 2009. http://www.bleedcubbieblue.com/2009/3/7/785367/cubs-name-single-pa-announ

Yellon, Al. "Before Ricketts was the Name of a Cubs Owner . . . (A Photo Essay)." *Bleed Cubbie Blue* (blog). November 15, 2009. http://www.bleedcubbieblue.com/

Yellon, Al. "The History of the Ownership of the Land Under Wrigley Field." *Bleed Cubbie Blue* (blog). July 9, 2010. http://www.bleedcubbieblue.com/

Yellon, Al. "A New Addition to Wrigley Field." *Bleed Cubbie Blue* (blog). July 27, 2009. http://www.bleedcubbieblue.com/2009/7/27/964117/a-new-addition-to-wrigley-field

Yellon, Al. "The Future of Wrigley Field." *Bleed Cubbie Blue* (blog). November 16, 2010. http://www.bleedcubbieblue.com/2010/11/16/1818194/the-future-of-wrigley-field

Yellon, Al. "Wrigleyville Classic: Illini Rout Northwestern in Classic Style." *Bleed Cubbie Blue* (blog). November 20, 2010. http://www.bleedcubbieblue.com/

Yellon, Al, Ignarski, Kasey and Matthew Silverman. *Cubs by the Numbers*. New York, NY: Skyhorse Publishing, Inc., 2009.

ABOUT THE AUTHOR

Sam Pathy was born and raised on Chicago's Northwest Side. When he was a boy, his mom took him to Ladies Day games at Wrigley Field. While he fell in love with the storied ballpark, his childhood adoration turned into an obsession. He's spent the last thirty years uncovering its history. Sam is a public librarian. He and his wife live in Worthington, Ohio.